Latin American Economic Outlook
2021

WORKING TOGETHER FOR A BETTER RECOVERY

This work is published under the responsibility of the Secretary-General of the OECD, the President of the Development Bank of Latin America (CAF) and the President of the European Commission. The opinions expressed and arguments employed herein do not necessarily reflect the official views of the Member countries of the OECD, the members of its Development Centre, those of the Development Bank of Latin America (CAF), or of the European Union, or the Member States of the United Nations.

This document, as well as any data and map included herein, are without prejudice to the status of or sovereignty over any territory, to the delimitation of international frontiers and boundaries and to the name of any territory, city or area.

The names of countries and territories and maps used in this joint publication follow the practice of the OECD.

Please cite this publication as:
OECD et al. (2021), *Latin American Economic Outlook 2021: Working Together for a Better Recovery*, OECD Publishing, Paris, *https://doi.org/10.1787/5fedabe5-en*.

ISBN 978-92-64-63983-6 (print)
ISBN 978-92-64-68231-3 (pdf)

Latin American Economic Outlook
ISSN 2072-5159 (print)
ISSN 2072-5140 (online)

CAF Reference Number: CAF-513i-2021

ECLAC Reference Number: LC/PUB.2021/12

European Union
ISBN 978-92-76-42389-8 (print)
ISBN 978-92-76-36201-2 (PDF)
Catalogue number: MN-03-21-331-EN-C (print); MN-03-21-331-EN-N (PDF)

Foreword

The *Latin American Economic Outlook* (LEO) analyses critical aspects related to sustainable and inclusive development in Latin America and the Caribbean (LAC). Since the first LEO launch in November 2007, the annual report has compared LAC's performance with that of other regions, analysed main development challenges and put forward policy recommendations, experiences and good practices.

The LEO benefits from the expertise and inputs of co-authors. Since 2011, the LEO has been published in conjunction with the United Nations Economic Commission for Latin America and the Caribbean. In 2013, the Development Bank of Latin America joined the team of authors and since the LEO 2018, the European Commission joined as a main partner.

This 14th LEO, *Working together for a better recovery*, aims to analyse and provide policy recommendations for a strong, inclusive and environmentally sustainable recovery in the region. The report explores policy actions to improve social protection mechanisms and increase social inclusion, foster regional integration and strengthen industrial strategies, and rethink the social contract to restore trust and empower citizens at all stages of the policy-making process. Moreover, it stresses the need to promote sustainable and adapted macro-economic frameworks to finance the recovery, and the importance of international co-operation to support these policy actions. Finally, the publication includes three crucial cross-cutting themes: climate change and the green recovery; the digital transformation and gender.

Acknowledgements

Partners of this report are the Economic Commission for Latin America and the Caribbean (ECLAC), the Development Bank of Latin America (CAF), the European Union (EU) and the Development Centre of the Organisation for Economic Co-operation and Development (OECD). This flagship publication is supported under Pillar 1 of the European Union Regional Facility for Development in Transition for Latin America and the Caribbean (LAC), a European Union-led initiative, jointly implemented with the OECD and its Development Centre and the ECLAC. Furthermore, it is a core activity of the OECD LAC Regional Programme.

The contribution of the OECD Development Centre to this report was led and managed by Sebastián Nieto-Parra, Head of the Latin America and the Caribbean Unit at the OECD Development Centre, with the support and co-ordination of Luis Cecchi, Policy Analyst at the Latin America and the Caribbean Unit of the OECD Development Centre, under the guidance of Ragnheidur Arnadottir, Director of the OECD Development Centre, Federico Bonaglia, Deputy Director of the OECD Development Centre and Mario Pezzini, former Director of the OECD Development Centre. The ECLAC's contribution was led by Sebastián Rovira, Economic Affairs Officer at the Innovation and New Technologies Unit, with the support of Andrés Boeninger and Nunzia Saporito, research assistants at the Innovation and New Technologies Unit, under the guidance of Mario Cimoli, Deputy Executive Secretary of the ECLAC. The contribution from CAF was led by Adriana Arreaza, Director of Macroeconomic Studies. The European Commission (EC) contribution was led by Sergio Martin Moreno, Programme Manager in the Latin America and the Caribbean Directorate at the Directorate-General for International Cooperation and Development of the European Commission (INTPA), and Pelayo Roces Fernandez, former LAC Programme Manager at INTPA, under the guidance of Jorge de la Caballería, their Head of Unit.

The report benefited from the research, drafting and fruitful collaboration among various authors across these organisations, including: Adriana Arreaza (CAF), Andrés Boeninger (ECLAC), Nathalie Basto-Aguirre (OECD), Adriana Caicedo (OECD), Cristina Cabutto (OECD), Luis Cecchi (OECD), Simone Cecchini (ECLAC), Mathilde Closset (ECLAC), Rita Da Costa (OECD), Laura Gutiérrez Cadena (OECD), Martina Lejtreger (OECD), Thomas Manfredi (OECD), Sergio Martin Moreno (EC), Alejandra Martinez (OECD), Nathalia Montoya González (OECD), Sofia Mora Restrepo (OECD), Sebastián Nieto Parra (OECD), René Orozco (OECD), Juan Ortegón Ocampo (OECD), Sara Piñero Mosquera (OECD), Sebastián Rovira (ECLAC), Nunzia Saporito (ECLAC), Daniel Titelman (ECLAC), Juan Vázquez Zamora (OECD) and Juan Nicolas Velandia (OECD). Agustina Vierheller (OECD), Julia Peppino (OECD), Olivia Cuq (OECD), and Isabel Sirven-Villaros (OECD) provided invaluable administrative support throughout the elaboration of the report.

A group of experts and colleagues have been particularly active and supportive during the production process, providing views, inputs or boxes, comments and strategic orientation to the report. We would like to highlight the support of Felipe Bosch (Le Grand Continent), Gabriela Casanova Rangel (Universidad del Rosario), Anthony Caubin (AFD), Angie Contreras Sanabria (DNP), Jason Gagnon (OECD), Juan Miguel Gallego (Universidad del Rosario), Daniel Gómez Gaviria (DNP), Lianne Guerra (Le Grand Continent), Bruno Leclerc (AFD), Marc Litvine (EC), Natali Maldonado Pineda (Universidad del Rosario), Natalia Moreno Rigollot (Telefónica), Lorenzo Pavone (OECD), Alexander Pick (OECD), Rafael Camilo Ramirez Correa (DNP), Laure Rogès (EC), Marta Salafranca (Telefónica), Juan Manuel Santomé Calleja (Eurosocial), Melanie Vilarasau Slade (OECD) and Felix Zimmermann (OECD).

The content of the report was enriched by constructive feedback received during the LEO 2021 online Brainstorming Session that took place on 28 January 2021; the informal consultation with the LAC countries and members of the OECD Development Centre Governing Board, on 5 February 2021; the virtual Experts Meetings on 29 and

30 March 2021, and the LEO 2021 virtual pre-launch event that took place on 15 July 2021 in the framework of the United Nations High-level Political Forum and as part of the "Development in Transition Dialogues to chart new paths for Latin America and the Caribbean". In addition to the LAC delegates to the Governing Board of the OECD Development Centre, we are particularly grateful to the experts, academics, private-sector representatives and other public servants who joined us during the Experts' meetings and the pre-launch event: Gloria Alonso (Colombia), Fernando Álvarez (CAF), Alberto Arenas De Mesa (ECLAC), Eric Beaume (EC), Mariano Berro (Uruguayan Agency for International Cooperation [AUCI]), Eduardo Bitrán (Chile), Romina Boarini (OECD), Adrián Bonilla (EU-LAC Foundation), Francisco Bustillo (Uruguay), Rodrigo A. Carazo (Costa Rica), Claire Charbit (OECD), Everly Paul Chet Greene (Antigua and Barbuda), Andrea Costafreda (OXFAM), Guillermo Cruces (CEDLAS), Silvia Da Rin Pagnetto (OECD), Luiz de Mello (OECD), Martha Delgado Peralta (Mexico), Koen Doens (EC), Karina Dzialowska (EC), Mayumi Endoh (OECD), Manuel Escudero (OECD/Spain), João Carlos Ferraz (Universidade Federal do Rio de Janeiro), Juan Flores (University of Geneva), Andrés García (Universidad del Rosario), Claudia Glintersdorfer (EEAS), Ana Güezmes (ECLAC), Sebastián Herreros (ECLAC), Galina Karamalakova (European External Action Service [EEAS]), Guillermo Larraín (University of Chile), Carlos Malamud (Elcano Royal Institute, Spain), Francisco Monge (Costa Rica), Juan Carlos Moreno-Brid (Universidad Nacional Autónoma, México), Ana Patricia Muñóz (Grupo FARO), Hugo Ñopo (GRADE Peru), José Antonio Ocampo (Columbia University), Juan Daniel Oviedo (DANE), Luciana Peres (Brazil), Wilson Peres (ECLAC), Ramón Pineda (ECLAC), Monika Queisser (OECD), Darío Rodriguez (Sorbonne University), Juan Ruiz (BBVA), José Antonio Sanahuja (Fundación Carolina, Spain) and Rubén Silié (Dominican Republic).

A group of colleagues from the OECD provided insightful inputs, comments and discussions that significantly improved the report: Aimee Aguilar Jaber, Jose Antonio Ardavín, Jens Arnold, Janos Bertok, Sofia Blamey Andrusco, Frederic Boehm, Monica Brezzi, Emanuele Ciani, Juan de Laiglesia, Charlotte Dubald, Mayumi Endoh, Manuela Fitzpatrick, Michael Förster, Mills Gary, Fabio Gehrke, Santiago Gonzalez, Felipe Gonzalez Zapata, Havard Halland, Jean-Jacques Hible, Michael Jelenic, Fatos Koc, Alexandre Kolev, Kamil Kouhen, Iris Mantovani, Claire Mc Evoy, Mauricio Mejia Galvan, Iris Mantovani, Alejandra Meneses, Martin Neil, Ana Novic, Masayuki Omote, Nestor Pelecha Aigues, Nicolas Penagos, Jan Rielaender, Jacob Arturo Rivera Perez, Camila Saffirio, Katherine Scrivens, Kimiaki Shinozaki, Ana Stringhini, Enes Sunel, Juan Yermo, Gabriela Villa Aguayo and Martin Wermelinger.

The country notes benefited from constructive inputs, scrutiny and verification by delegations to the OECD from Chile, Colombia, Costa Rica and Mexico, as well as the embassies in France of Argentina, Brazil, Dominican Republic, Ecuador, El Salvador, Guatemala, Panama, Paraguay, Peru and Uruguay.

The OECD Development Centre would also like to express its sincere gratitude to the Agence Française de Développement, Departamento Nacional de Planeación (DNP) of Colombia, the Spanish Ministry of Foreign Affairs, European Union and Cooperation, the Swiss Agency for Development and Cooperation, Telefónica and Universidad del Rosario (Colombia) for their support to the Latin American Economic Outlook.

Finally, many thanks go to the Publications and Communications Division of the OECD Development Centre, in particular, Aida Buendia, Mélodie Descours, Delphine Grandrieux, Elizabeth Nash, Irit Perry, Henri-Bernard Solignac-Lecomte and Anne Thomas, for their steadfast patience and expedient work on the production of this report and associated materials. The authors also sincerely appreciate the editing activities undertaken by Elizabeth Holbourne, from the OECD Development Centre, Jessica Hutchings and Jane Marshall, and the translation and Spanish editing services provided by Alejandro Barranco, Julia Gregory, Alexander Summerfield and Liliana Tafur.

Table of contents

Figures

Tables

Boxes

Acronyms and abbreviations

ACRF	ASEAN Comprehensive Recovery Framework
AEWG	Accelerated Education Working Group
AFD	French Development Agency
ASEAN	Association of South East Asian Nations
AU	African Union
Bancoldex	Banco de Desarrollo Empresarial de Colombia (Business Development Bank of Colombia)
BEPS	Base Erosion and Profit Shifting
BNDES	Brazilian Development Bank
CACM	Central American Common Market
CAF	Development Bank of Latin America
CARICOM	Caribbean Community
CARIFORUM	Subgroup of the Organisation of African, Caribbean and Pacific States
CCT	Conditional Cash Transfer
CIAT	Inter-American Center of Tax Administrations
CIS	Central American Council of Ministers for Social Integration
CIT	Corporate Income Tax
CoG	Centre of Government
COP	Colombian Peso
COVAX	COVID-19 Vaccines Global Access
COVID-19	Coronavirus
CRS	Common Reporting Standard
C-TAP	COVID-19 Technology Access Pool
CTCN	Climate Technology Center and Network
DAC	Development Assistance Committee
DiT	Development in Transition
DSSI	Debt Service Suspension Initiative
EC	European Commission
ECAF	Encuesta CAF (CAF Survey)
ECLAC	Economic Commission for Latin America and the Caribbean
EEAS	European External Action Service
EPTV	Estatuto de Protección Temporal para Venezolanos (Temporary Protected Statute for Venezuelan Migrants)
EU	European Union
FACE	Fund to Alleviate COVID-19 Economics
FAO	Food and Agriculture Organization
FDI	Foreign Direct Investment
FOGAPE	Fondo de Garantía para Pequeños Empresarios (Guarantee Fund for Small Entrepreneurs)
G20	Group of Twenty
GAD	MERCOSUR Group Digital Agenda
GDP	Gross Domestic Product
GHG	Green House Gases
GPI	Global Public Investment
GVCs	Global Value Chains
ICT	Information and Communications Technology

ICU	Intensive Care Units
IDB	Inter-American Development Bank
IFF	Illicit Financial Flows
IFI	International Financial Institution
IIF	Institute of International Finance
ILO	International Labour Organization
IMF	International Monetary Fund
IRENA	International Renewable Energy Agency
ITC	International Trade Centre
KAS	Konrad Adenauer Foundation
LAC	Latin America and the Caribbean
LAFTA	Latin America Free Trade Area
LAIA	Latin American Integration Association
LEO	Latin American Economic Outlook
MERCOSUR	Southern Common Market
MIC	Middle-income Country
MSMEs	Micro, Small and Medium-sized Enterprises
NAFTA	North American Free Trade Agreement
NDCs	Nationally Determined Contributions
NDP	National Development Plan
ODA	Official Development Assistance
OECD	Organisation for Economic Co-operation and Development
OGP	Open Government Partnership
OHCHR	Office of the United Nations High Commissioner for Human Rights
OLADE	Latin American Energy Organization
OOP	Out of Pocket
PACE	Platform for Accelerating the Circular Economy
PA	Pacific Alliance
PAHO	Pan American Health Organization
PAYG	Pay as You Go
PCD	Policy Coherence for Development
PEDN	Plan Estratégico de Desarrollo Nacional (National Development Strategic Plan)
PEP	Permiso Especial de Permanencia (Special Permit of Permanence)
PIT	Personal Income Tax
PRGT	Poverty Reduction and Growth Trust
R&D	Research and Development
RBC	Responsible Business Conduct
SDGs	Sustainable Development Goals
SDR	Special Drawing Rights
SEGIB	Secretaría General Iberoamericana (Iberoamerican General Secretary)
SEZ	Special Economic Zone
SICA	Central American Integration System
SISCA	Central American Social Integration Secretariat
SMEs	Small and Medium-sized Enterprises
TFA	Trade Facilitation Agreement
TRIPS	Agreement on Trade-Related Aspects of Intellectual Property Rights
UMSCA	Unites States-Mexico-Canada Agreement

UN HABITAT	United Nations Human Settlement Programme
UN Women	United Nations Entity for Gender Equality and the Empowerment of Women
UNEP	United Nations Environmental Programme
UNCTAD	United Nations Conference on Trade and Development
UNDESA	United Nations Department of Economic and Social Affairs
UNDP	United Nations Development Programme
UNIDO	United Nations Industrial Development Organization
USD	United States Dollar
VAT	Value Added Tax
WEF	World Economic Forum
WHO	World Health Organization

Editorial

Latin America and the Caribbean (LAC) has been the region worst affected by the pandemic and is only re-emerging from what is the deepest recession in the region's history. Although prompt and proactive policy responses since the beginning of the coronavirus (COVID-19) crisis averted more pessimistic scenarios, the pandemic has left profound scars, notably on the most vulnerable (in particular women and youth). Urgent and resolute action is still needed to overcome the pandemic, mitigate its long-term socio-economic consequences and lay the foundations for a better future.

The *Latin American Economic Outlook 2021* (LEO) conceives the recovery from the COVID-19 crisis as an opportunity to implement reforms to address structural challenges and discusses the kind of policies and international co-operation approaches that can help governments build forward better. The response to the crisis can provide the necessary impetus to design and implement a renewed strategy for development that promotes inclusiveness, resilience and sustainability, responds to citizens' expectations and accelerates progress towards the United Nations 2030 Agenda for Sustainable Development. The LEO 2021 takes forward the *Development in Transition* (DiT) approach as a general framing for domestic and international action, aimed in particular at fostering regional integration and reinforcing the social contract – two crucial goals for overcoming the vulnerabilities and development traps that hold back progress in the region.

The region is highly heterogeneous in terms of the impact of the pandemic and the ability to react to its challenges. However, LAC countries share an extraordinary common challenge. In the short term, implementing effective and equitable vaccination strategies as a key element for recovery. In the medium term, overcoming the pandemic impacts while transforming the region's development traps of low productivity, social vulnerability, institutional weakness and environmental unsustainability, into virtuous circles that set the region on a path towards greater well-being for all citizens.

We see the recovery also as an opportunity to continue reshaping the role and potential of regional and international co-operation, in line with the DiT narrative developed in the LEO 2019. Co-operation and policy dialogue will remain essential in bringing together the expertise of multiple actors to embark on a better trajectory to achieve the Sustainable Development Goals. Key ingredients for an enhanced policy dialogue within the LAC region and across regions include the strengthening of institutions, social cohesion, supporting a green transition and the digital transformation in a renewed production model. In this context, LEO 2021 places a particular focus on the potential of LAC to strengthen partnerships, including with the European Union and its Member States.

The COVID-19 crisis highlighted the global nature and interdependency of development challenges and reinforced the need to better co-ordinate recovery actions across national, regional and international levels.

At the national level, LAC governments should use fiscal, social and production transformation policies as part of building a new social contract. In particular, elements of inter- and intra-generational socio-economic mobility and equity should be duly considered, and the challenges associated to climate change and transitioning to a low-carbon development model.

The pandemic has shed light on the urgency to rethink and redefine national policies through greater consultation and consensus-building with citizens. Strengthening accountability and trust in institutions is key to embark on a virtuous cycle of pending national reforms needed for the recovery that can be packaged in the framework of a new social contract. Key objectives of the new social contract include greater social protection coverage, better and more accessible public services, a production transformation strategy, fairer fiscal frameworks and promoting citizen participation in the design and implementation of policies.

Greater financing for development will be key for the recovery and financing policies of a new social contract. Most LAC countries entered the crisis with limited fiscal space. While the situation reflects the anaemic growth over the past years, challenges in terms of economic structures and tax policy and administration cannot be downplayed. A strong, sustainable and inclusive recovery demands an urgent holistic fiscal response and should be implemented through a well-defined sequencing of reforms, backed by a broad consensus built through national dialogue and clear communication strategies. Better co-ordination in public debt management with all creditors and market actors will also be necessary. In this respect, the design of debt treatment will have to pay special attention to each country's characteristics, in particular the challenges that Small Island Developing States of the Caribbean and Central American countries face.

The COVID-19 crisis hit an already vulnerable social structure, resulting in a significant increase in poverty and inequalities. When the crisis hit the region, labour informality affected more than 50% of workers. LAC countries need to promote innovative options for formalisation and reduce social coverage gaps to protect the most vulnerable populations – in particular, women, youth, climate-vulnerable populations and migrants – while improving the quality and coverage of basic services, especially health care and education.

The main challenge LAC faces in achieving a strong and inclusive recovery is generating quality jobs. Ambitious policy actions from LAC countries to spur innovation and capacity development, diversify and upgrade the economic structure and attract quality investment are urgently needed.

At the regional level, an effective response to the health crisis could be the "big push" needed for LAC to move towards greater regional co-operation. National strategies should converge to promote a production transformation agenda and further regional and global integration.

LAC lags behind in terms of integration. Barely 14% of LAC exports stayed within the region in 2019, and the proportion has been declining steadily since 2014. Fostering intra-regional trade, creating regional value chains and improving the region's participation in global value chains, by better connecting firms, notably small ones, to markets remain key objectives in the post-COVID-19 context. Trade, industry and investment policies can play an important role in addressing the vulnerabilities in production structures that the pandemic has exposed. If properly designed, they can help deliver a triple dividend of greater competitiveness and job creation, better preparedness to withstand future crises and greater readiness to embark on the green and digital transitions. Some sectors that could specifically benefit from further regional integration and help reduce vulnerabilities are the automotive, pharmaceutical and renewable energy sectors, the circular economy, and sustainable agriculture.

Globally, international co-operation should be a facilitator for the emergence of a new development model and a new social contract in LAC. The impact of the pandemic has highlighted the importance of moving towards renewed and more effective multilateralism. With this in mind, it will be important for countries to consolidate the DiT narrative, relying on new approaches to national policy making and international co-operation that place sustainability, resilience and well-being at their core, and provide multi-dimensional policy responses including efforts to measure development beyond income. This implies further exploring mission-driven and equal-footing partnerships that are grounded on shared values and ensure greater policy coherence, co-ordination and synergies across national and international development efforts. Enhanced equal-footing policy dialogue, increased regional co-operation and renewed participatory mechanisms for citizens could be essential elements underpinning these reinforced partnerships and making full use of their potential. Last, a balanced combination of innovative sustainable finance, global rules and standards, technical co-operation and policy dialogue would be key to enhance the partnerships with LAC.

The LEO aims to stimulate the national and international debate on transitioning to better development models and partnerships. Three aspects give special relevance to its 2021 edition: *timeliness*, as the report's analysis and policy messages come at a crucial moment to address the transversal impact of the crisis in LAC; *readiness*, as each institution behind LEO is working to create new financial instruments and/or policy approaches to support the region; and *togetherness*, as, more than ever in these extraordinary times, there is a need to join forces to advance a strong, sustainable and inclusive recovery through the creation of participative dialogues that enable the emergence of a large consensus to underpin co-ordinated action at the national, regional and international levels.

Alicia Bárcena
Executive Secretary
ECLAC

Sergio Díaz-Granados
Executive Chairman
CAF – Development
Bank of Latin America

Mathias Cormann
Secretary-General
OECD

Jutta Urpilainen
European Commissioner
for International
Partnerships

Executive summary

The *Latin American Economic Outlook 2021* (LEO) sets out the key foundations for a strong, sustainable and inclusive recovery from the coronavirus (COVID-19) pandemic in Latin America and the Caribbean (LAC) and provides tailored policy messages to help stakeholders take action and build forward better.

The pandemic hit LAC at a time when the region already faced the deep development traps identified in the *Latin American Economic Outlook 2019*. It exacerbated existing socio-economic challenges inherent to the four traps: i) low productivity; ii) inequalities and social vulnerability; iii) institutional weaknesses; and iv) the threat to environmental sustainability. The post COVID-19 context should be seized as a unique opportunity to adopt a multi-dimensional strategy for development and to redefine national policies by building consensus among citizens and implementing the pending reforms needed to drive the recovery. Moreover, stronger regional integration and international co-operation that involves LAC countries on an equal footing, regardless of their development level, should play an important role in the region's recovery.

The socio-economic consequences of COVID-19 and the path to recovery

Despite rapid and well-targeted policy action to respond to the pandemic, LAC has been the most affected region in the world in socio-economic terms. Although positive growth is expected for 2021, gross domestic product per capita is not expected to return to pre-crisis levels before 2023-24. The impact of the crisis has been asymmetric, particularly affecting the most vulnerable groups. Poverty and extreme poverty levels have not been so high for the past 12 and 20 years, respectively. Demand policies, mainly through non-conditional cash transfers as well as other innovative measures, provided rapid support to public health systems, households and firms. Without this response, the losses in lives and increases in poverty and inequality would have been much steeper. Without government transfers to mitigate the loss of labour income, the Gini Index would have increased by 5.6% with respect to 2019, instead of the 2.9% recorded.

There is no unique approach or solution to ensure a strong, sustainable and inclusive recovery. The socio-economic characteristics of each country, coupled with the varying impacts of the crisis, call for a tailored approach. However, countries across the region share the need to implement well-defined sequencing of fiscal policy actions on expenditure, taxation and public debt management. Mobilising resources for the recovery will require efforts at the national level and better co-operation and co-ordination at the international level, notably regarding public debt.

Renewed social policies and quality public services for an inclusive recovery

The COVID-19 crisis revealed that current social protection mechanisms in the region are insufficient due to widespread labour informality, which affects more than 50% of workers. The prevalence of gender gaps in the labour market and the predominance of women in poorer households are also major structural challenges. The crisis dramatically exposed the need to improve access to and quality of basic public services, including health and education. LAC is the region with the highest average number of school days lost due to the pandemic worldwide (70% higher than in the OECD and 13% higher than the global average), posing a concrete threat to human capital development.

Social protection programmes in LAC need to move towards systems that ensure universal coverage. Improving social protection schemes, both pensions and healthcare coverage to support the elderly is key. Designing gender-sensitive policies for the recovery and ensuring a more equitable redistribution of household care work are essential measures to improve women's labour force participation and socio-economic conditions. Policy action, as part of the recovery, to tackle inequalities in education and skills acquisition at an early stage of people's lives is critical to increasing positive outcomes and opportunities.

Stronger regional integration should boost formal jobs and environmental resilience

The main challenge the region will face during the recovery will be to generate quality formal jobs while ensuring the long-term sustainability. The current productive structure hampers the development possibilities of the region.

LAC countries should take more ambitious policy action to enhance workers' skills, achieve productive transformation, upgrade the economic structure and attract sustainable investments. Productive policies should foster innovation, technological upgrading and the diversification of the productive structure in less resource-intensive sectors by promoting greener investments, a circular economy and the adoption of new technologies. Urgent policy objectives in the post-COVID-19 context include bolstering intra-regional trade, creating regional value chains and increasing the region's participation in global value chains and quality investment flows, and connecting micro, small and medium-sized enterprises with international trade. Further regional integration could strengthen competitiveness and job creation on sectors with high potential, including the automotive, pharmaceutical and renewable energy sectors, the circular economy and sustainable agriculture.

A new social contract for the post-pandemic world

Building consensus across citizens will be crucial to advance the ambitious reform agenda needed to drive the recovery. However, high levels of social discontent in LAC, demonstrated by the wave of protests across some countries of the region since 2019, present a significant challenge. The drivers of social dissatisfaction are multi-dimensional and in large part explained by unmet aspirations for better jobs, quality public services and greater political representation. These expressions of social discontent highlight the need for LAC countries to renew their social contract to improve people's well-being and ensure citizen engagement.

In practice, renewing the social contract entails striking pacts in specific policy domains (e.g. the fiscal pact) and building broad support among stakeholders (e.g. government, civil society, trade unions and the private sector). The building blocks of a post-pandemic social contract should revolve around two interconnected dimensions. First, it should be a transversal agreement across: i) socio-economic groups, through an intersectional approach mindful of income, gender, ethnic and racial differences, among others; ii) territories, taking into account different local needs and opportunities and bridging territorial divides; and iii) generations, ensuring that policy decisions strike a balance between the interests of current and future generations, providing opportunities to the youth and building on the notion of intergenerational solidarity. Second, it should aim to achieve: i) resilient and sustainable productive strategies that prioritise the creation of quality jobs and embrace the green and digital transformation; ii) broader and more effective social protection systems; and iii) a more sustainable financing for development model. The intersection of these two dimensions shows how the social contract in each country is underpinned by concrete and specific pacts in various policy domains.

An open and inclusive policy-making process that incorporates and empowers citizens and local authorities can promote greater accountability and more effective implementation of pending policy reforms, while involving all relevant actors in the discussion. Understanding the political economy of reform is crucial to reaching stable and long-lasting agreements or to revising them when necessary. An evaluation of the socio-political context, clear communication strategies and compensation schemes to make reforms fairer by mitigating their potential adverse distributional impacts will be key.

International co-operation for the recovery: Facilitating the new social contract in LAC

The global reach of the pandemic has shown that national responses to both the sanitary and socio-economic consequences of this crisis are not enough. Given rising social discontent and the increasing interconnection between national development dynamics and global megatrends, international co-operation has become critical to supporting LAC countries' recovery.

The Development in Transition approach proposes a new role for international co-operation as a facilitator to help LAC transform its structural challenges into development opportunities. Continued international and regional co-operation becomes essential to redefine the social contract in LAC.

Reinforcing partnerships that are grounded on shared values is necessary to support LAC countries in building new development models that place sustainability, resilience and well-being at their core. These new models should provide multi-dimensional policy responses, including efforts to measure development beyond income. To use full potential of international co-operation and multilateralism, they must continue to adapt and evolve, building on lessons learned and innovations during the crisis. Mission-driven partnerships, stronger regional co-operation and integration, as well as a balanced use of co-operation tools like sustainable financing, global rules and standards, technical co-operation and capacity building, could be catalysts to break existing vicious cycles between international and national development dynamics in LAC, therefore facilitating a new social contract in the region that comprehensively tackles its development traps.

Looking ahead, the multi-dimensionality and complexity of development call for these new partnerships to bring citizens into the international policy-making process, and to push for a comprehensive approach across international co-operation efforts, tools and actors, that promotes policy coherence to articulate sustainable and inclusive national, regional and global objectives for the post-COVID-19 world.

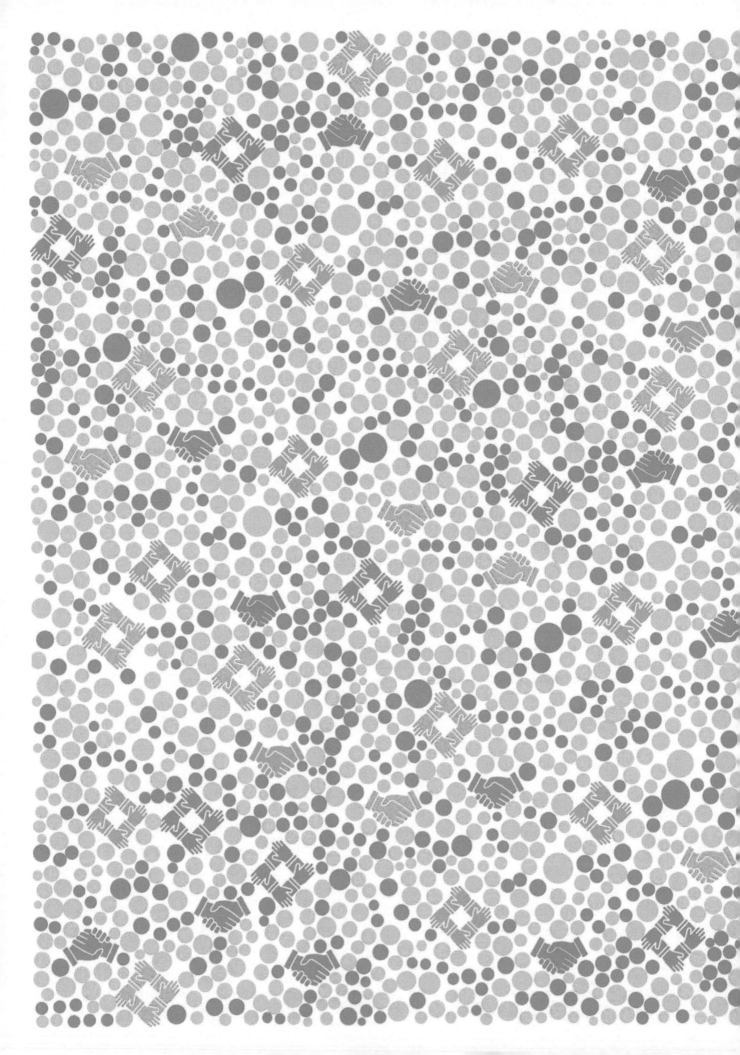

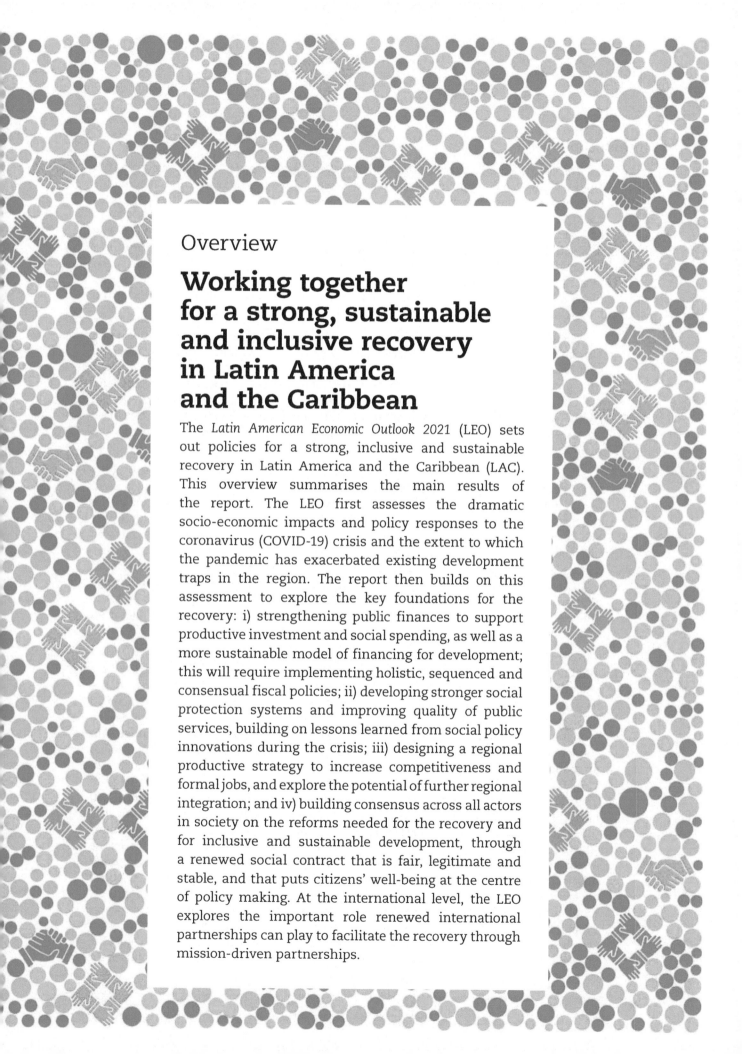

Overview

Working together for a strong, sustainable and inclusive recovery in Latin America and the Caribbean

The *Latin American Economic Outlook 2021* (LEO) sets out policies for a strong, inclusive and sustainable recovery in Latin America and the Caribbean (LAC). This overview summarises the main results of the report. The LEO first assesses the dramatic socio-economic impacts and policy responses to the coronavirus (COVID-19) crisis and the extent to which the pandemic has exacerbated existing development traps in the region. The report then builds on this assessment to explore the key foundations for the recovery: i) strengthening public finances to support productive investment and social spending, as well as a more sustainable model of financing for development; this will require implementing holistic, sequenced and consensual fiscal policies; ii) developing stronger social protection systems and improving quality of public services, building on lessons learned from social policy innovations during the crisis; iii) designing a regional productive strategy to increase competitiveness and formal jobs, and explore the potential of further regional integration; and iv) building consensus across all actors in society on the reforms needed for the recovery and for inclusive and sustainable development, through a renewed social contract that is fair, legitimate and stable, and that puts citizens' well-being at the centre of policy making. At the international level, the LEO explores the important role renewed international partnerships can play to facilitate the recovery through mission-driven partnerships.

Introduction

The *Latin American Economic Outlook 2021: Working together for a better recovery* (LEO) analyses and provides policy messages to design a strong, inclusive and sustainable recovery from the coronavirus (COVID-19) crisis in Latin America and the Caribbean (LAC). The crisis is radically transforming the region's economies and societies. COVID-19 has accentuated the long-standing, multi-dimensional development traps of low productivity, high inequality and informality, deficient public services and institutions, and environmental challenges in LAC. The pandemic hit the region at a time of high social discontent, expressed by the wave of protests across the region, confirming the need to reach a new, overarching consensus among citizens on a new development path for the region, and to rebuild society's trust in public institutions.

The COVID-19 recovery poses extraordinary challenges for LAC countries, but it can also be seen as a turning point to accelerate pending policy reforms in LAC. The crisis should be embraced as an opportunity to implement a renewed strategy for development that promotes inclusiveness, resilience and sustainability, increasing well-being and responding to citizens' expectations, while advancing the United Nations 2030 Agenda. Further regional integration and international co-operation involving LAC countries on an equal footing, regardless of their development level, would contribute to the region's recovery.

The specific socio-economic characteristics of each country, coupled with the varying impacts of the crisis, call for a tailored approach. Nonetheless, some shared aspects will be key for a successful recovery that leaves no one behind: i) paying attention to the political economy of policy reform; ii) establishing a well-defined sequencing of policies; and iii) addressing the socio-political context through clear communication strategies and compensation schemes to mitigate the adverse distributional impacts of reform, particularly those affecting the most vulnerable. The recovery should set in motion an open and inclusive policy-making process that ensures greater accountability and brings all relevant actors to the discussion to achieve consensus. This will require efforts at the national level – in particular, for the most disadvantaged groups – and better co-operation and co-ordination at the regional and international levels.

The LEO 2021 provides tailored policy messages to help stakeholders take action and build forward better. The report first examines the socio-economic impacts of and policy responses to the COVID-19 crisis. It also analyses the key macro-foundations for the recovery in the region. In particular, it insists on the need to implement holistic, sequenced fiscal policies backed by a strong consensus to achieve an inclusive and strong recovery (Chapter 1). Second, it highlights the need to learn from the pandemic and mainstream some of the social policy innovations adopted throughout the crisis to strengthen social protection systems and improve quality and accessibility of public services (Chapter 2). The LEO then highlights the importance of designing a regional productive strategy to increase productivity and boost formal job creation (Chapter 3). These policy efforts will need the backing of a strong consensus among all actors of society; in other words, the renewal of the social contract, one that is fair, legitimate and stable, and that puts citizens' concerns and well-being at the centre of policy making (Chapter 4). The LEO explores the important role of renewed international partnerships in facilitating the recovery through mission-driven partnerships that ensure equal-footing participation, greater policy coherence across levels of government, integrated approaches across policies, and tools to address the multi-dimensional nature of development, including efforts to measure development beyond income, both nationally and internationally (Chapter 5). The report emphasises that taking into account the political economy of reform and country-specific characteristics will be crucial to reach the stable and long-lasting agreements required for a recovery that works for all. The LEO includes three key cross-cutting themes: i) climate change and the green recovery; ii) the digital transformation; and iii) gender.

Holistic and consensual fiscal policies will determine the strength and inclusiveness of the recovery

In 2020, LAC experienced a historical economic downturn. Among the hardest hit by the pandemic, the region's gross domestic product (GDP) contracted by almost 7.0% and its per capita level is not expected to return to pre-crisis levels before 2023-24 (Figure 1). Moreover, growth and productivity growth are projected to decline, with an impact in terms of lower potential growth. The pace of recovery depends on the effective roll-out of vaccines, a favourable international context and the course of the political cycle in the region.

Figure 1. **Evolution of GDP per capita, constant prices**
Purchasing power parity; 2017 international USD

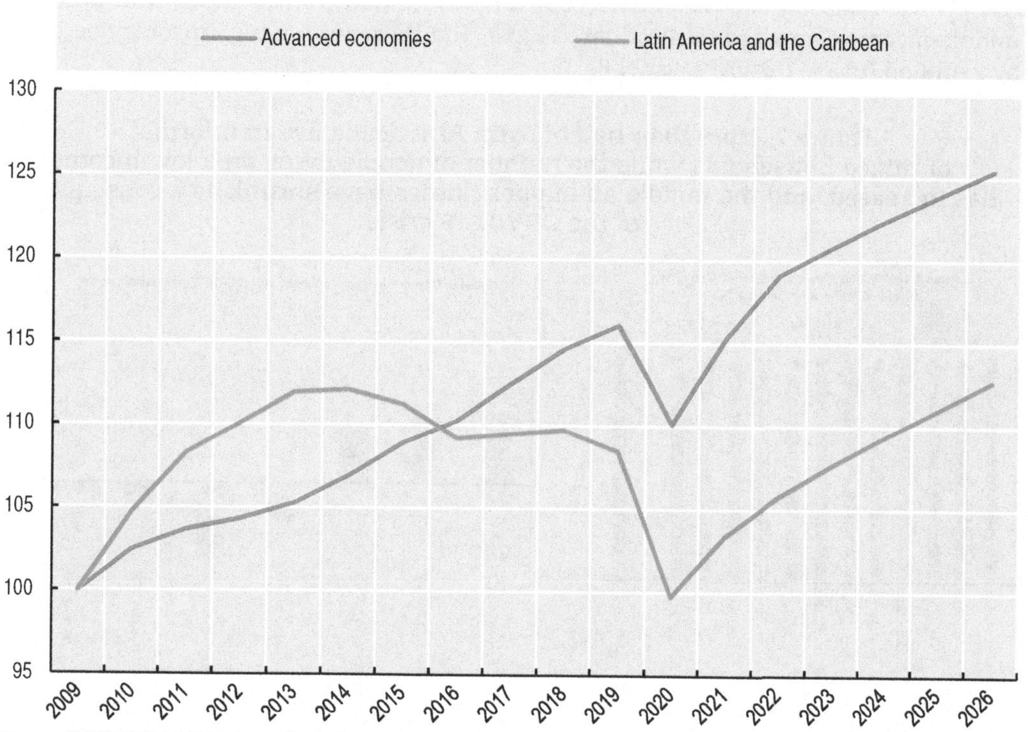

Source: OECD/ECLAC/CAF/EU calculations based on (IMF, 2021[1]), *World Economic Outlook, April 2021*, www.imf.org/en/Publications/WEO/Issues/2021/03/23/world-economic-outlook-april-2021.
StatLink ▨▨ https://doi.org/10.1787/888934286141

The impact of the COVID-19 crisis has been asymmetric, particularly affecting the most vulnerable groups and reversing some of the region's socio-economic gains of recent decades. As a result of the crisis, the extreme poverty rate is estimated to have increased by more than one percentage point in 2020, reaching 12.5% of the population. Moreover, the poverty rate is estimated to have increased by three percentage points, reaching 33.7%. Poverty levels have not been so high for the past 20 and 12 years, respectively. Inequality, measured by the GINI coefficient, is estimated to have increased by 2.9% in the most unequal region in the world, as those most affected by job losses were in the first income quintile.

Latin American labour markets are traditionally informal, fragile and exclusive. More than half of LAC workers have informal jobs (OECD, 2020[2]). Informal households – that depend on the informal economy for their income – are most affected by job loss brought about by the COVID-19 crisis. On average, 45% of the LAC population live in households that depend solely on informal employment, 22% live in mixed households with at least one member in an informal job, and 33% live in completely formal households (OECD, forthcoming[3]). Still, according to the Organisation for Economic Co-operation and Development (OECD) Development Centre's Key Indicators of Informality Based on Individuals and their Households, informality levels at the household level in LAC countries exhibit wide heterogeneity, from less than 20% in Chile and Uruguay, to more than 60% in Bolivia, Honduras and Nicaragua (Figure 2, Panel A).

The negative job and income dynamics exacerbated by the crisis have squeezed the middle class and threaten to deepen existing social and economic gaps. Some 32 million more people now earn a low income (vulnerable, poor and extremely poor) than before the crisis. By contrast, people earning a low middle-income decreased by 7 million, those with a mid middle-income decreased by 13 million (13.1%), those with an upper middle-income decreased by 4 million (14.2%), and those with a high income decreased by 2 million (10.5%) (Figure 2, Panel B).

Figure 2. More than half of Latin Americans live in informal or mixed households while the number of people living on a low-income has increased, and the middle and upper classes have shrunk as a consequence of the COVID-19 crisis

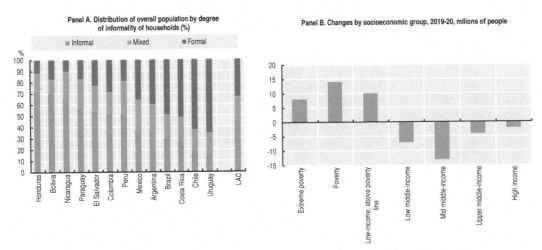

Notes: Panel A: using the classification by the OECD/ILO (2019[4]) and the ILO (2018[5]), individuals are assigned to one of three categories according to the degree of informality of their household. Formal households: all working members are formally employed. Informal households: all working members have informal employment. Mixed households: some working members have formal jobs and others have informal jobs. Panel B includes Argentina, Bolivia, Brazil, Chile, Colombia, Costa Rica, Dominican Republic, Ecuador, El Salvador, Guatemala, Honduras, Mexico, Nicaragua, Panama, Paraguay, Peru, Uruguay and Venezuela.

Source: OECD (forthcoming[3]), *Labour informality and households' vulnerabilities in Latin America*; ECLAC based on Banco de Datos de Encuestas de Hogares. Figures adjusted to United Nations population projections: UN (2019[6]), *World Population Prospects 2019*, https://population.un.org/wpp/.

StatLink ᵐˢᵖ https://doi.org/10.1787/888934286160

Monetary and fiscal policy have led the response to the crisis and will in large part determine how inclusive and strong the recovery will be. Fiscal policy, through a combination of tax relief measures, budget reallocations, additional expenditure and concessional lending, has been essential to mitigating the impact of the COVID-19 crisis on households and firms, particularly the most vulnerable, and to bolster public healthcare systems (ECLAC, 2021[7]).

Policy space is more limited in LAC countries that are highly indebted or where inflation is not under control. Expenditure, taxation and debt management approaches thus need to be tailored to each country's context. Some of these measures require further co-operation and co-ordination at the international level (Chapter 5).

First, a set of tax policy options could increase revenues without compromising the economic recovery or people's well-being; however, the sequencing of these policies, and the backing of a national consensus, will determine their success (Mora, Nieto-Parra and Orozco, 2021[8]). Options include measures to reduce tax evasion and avoidance, which in 2018 cost Latin America around 6.1% of GDP in lost personal income tax, corporate income tax and value added tax receipts, or eliminating inefficient tax expenditure (ECLAC, 2021[7]). Second, as long as the pandemic continues to put lives at risk, countercyclical public spending should continue to focus on protecting people, supporting the most vulnerable households and saving firms and jobs. Vaccination is key to exit the pandemic and reduce the uncertainty of stop-and-go confinement measures. Once the pandemic is under control, public spending should gradually start prioritising long-term capital expenditure aimed at achieving a productive transformation; one that generates formal employment, fully leverages the digital transformation and prioritises the environment. Third, along with strengthening citizens' trust in government, ensuring fiscal sustainability will be instrumental to the success of these efforts. Given the global implications of the pandemic, and as the financial resources needed to address its consequences increase, global co-ordination of public debt management should be a priority to address or avoid possible debt sustainability issues (OECD, 2020[2]).

Strengthening social protection and mainstreaming social policy innovations from the crisis for an inclusive and sustainable recovery

The crisis has revealed that current social protection mechanisms in the region are insufficient. LAC countries entered the crisis with close to 40% of workers without social protection coverage. This is largely due to the prevalence of labour informality in the region, affecting almost 60% of workers, although the situation is highly varied across countries.

Women, youth, the elderly, indigenous peoples, Afro-descendants and migrants have been disproportionately affected by this crisis. The ageing trend is already posing difficult challenges for societies. On average, before the crisis, around 75% of the population over age 65 received a pension, although the amount of transfers of contributory pensions was insufficient to replace a person's level of income during their productive life. Moreover, while almost one-third of pensions came from a non-contributory scheme, 42% of people over age 65 were covered by the public non-contributory healthcare system, limiting adequate coverage and access to quality care and adding financial pressure on social systems. Disparities in access to and quality of health care are associated with income, gender and urban/rural location. High out-of-pocket (OOP) expenditure and low ratios of human resources, such as specialised doctors, nurses and other physical resources, have constrained the response to the pandemic. People's discontent with healthcare services – already high compared to OECD countries – has increased during the COVID-19 crisis.

The pandemic and school closures amplified existing inequalities in access to and quality of education in Latin America. Many schools in LAC were forced to close to contain the spread of the virus (Figure 3). Since the start of the pandemic, schools were fully closed in LAC for an average of 26 weeks compared to 19 weeks globally, making it the region with the highest average number of school days lost (UNICEF, 2021[9]). On average, between March 2020 and May 2021, schools in LAC were closed 70% longer than in the OECD. Most LAC students do not have the resources to connect or use an electronic device, with a clear difference between advantaged and disadvantaged schools, resulting in further education inequalities among students from different socio-economic backgrounds. Prolonged education interruptions cause human capital loss and have caused women, who primarily bear childcare responsibilities, to lose their jobs, ultimately affecting the recovery.

Figure 3. **Longer school closures in LAC than in the OECD threaten to deepen education inequalities**

Number of weeks of full school closures due to COVID-19, March 2020 to May 2021

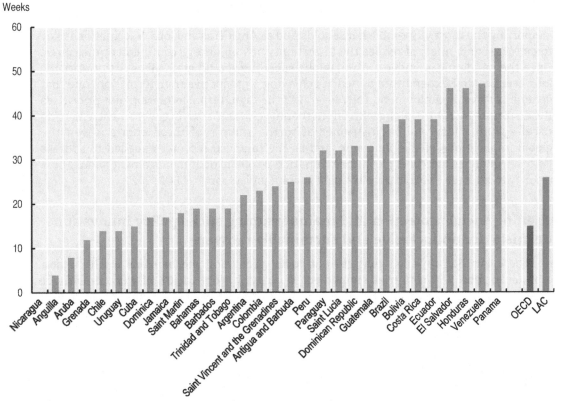

Note: OECD average includes the then 37 member countries. LAC average includes Brazil, Chile, Colombia, Costa Rica, Cuba, Dominican Republic, Ecuador, El Salvador, Guatemala, Haiti, Honduras, Mexico, Nicaragua, Panama, Peru, Uruguay and Venezuela. Updated until 1 May 2021.

Source: UNESCO (2020[10]), *Global monitoring of school closures caused by COVID-19*, https://en.unesco.org/covid19/educationres ponse#schoolclosures.

StatLink 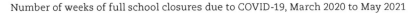 *https://doi.org/10.1787/888934286179*

The level of distrust in the social protection system is high, particularly among poorer groups and informal workers. Overall, more than one in three people in LAC doubt that they will ever receive a pension (Figure 4). The crisis presents an opportunity to reform social protection systems to make them more inclusive and more sustainable. Current protection mechanisms could be better adapted to the region's labour markets dynamics and workers' heterogeneous skills. Policy responses to the COVID-19 crisis present a basis to move towards universal, comprehensive and sustainable social protection systems.

Figure 4. **Proportion of workers who doubt that they will ever get a pension, by socio-demographic characteristics, selected LAC countries**

% of employed people

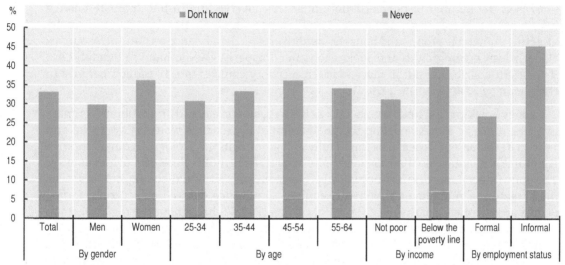

Notes: Data refer to an unweighted average of the following cities: Asunción, Buenos Aires, Bogotá, Ciudad de México, Ciudad de Panamá, El Alto, La Paz, Lima, Montevideo, Quito, Santiago and Sao Paulo. Because data refer to metropolitan areas (normally capital cities) and rural areas are excluded, some caution should be exercised in the analysis. However, the indicators are treated as representative of each LAC country.

Source: OECD estimates based on CAF (2020[11]); and ECAF (2019), *Percepciones de los Latinoamericanos sobre los Sistemas de Pensiones, Salud y Cuidados y el Avance Tecnológico en el Mercado Laboral*, http://scioteca.caf.com/handle/123456789/1646.

StatLink ᵐˢᵖ https://doi.org/10.1787/888934286198

Governments responded rapidly to the COVID-19 crisis by adopting innovative approaches to reach the most vulnerable population. This innovative response could set the basis for stronger social protection systems in the future. Social assistance during the pandemic targeted vulnerable populations not covered by existing social programmes or social protection mechanisms. As these populations are usually hard to identify, as many are unregistered, or to reach, as they do not always have a bank account, governments invested in improving registries, by crosschecking existing ones, and finding alternative ways of delivering money transfers, mainly through digital technologies and mobile phones (Basto-Aguirre, Nieto-Parra and Vazquez-Zamora, 2020[12]). Permanently targeting and providing vulnerable populations with social protection are key conditions of a functional and inclusive welfare state. Social protection in the LAC region needs stronger financing mechanisms, making social contributions more flexible with a mix of non-contributory, contributory and voluntary contributions. Improving social protection schemes to support the elderly, in terms of both pension and healthcare coverage, is key in ageing societies.

Policy action to tackle inequalities in education and skills acquisition at an early stage of people's lives, later translates into higher chances of getting quality jobs. This challenge has been exacerbated during the pandemic: the safe reopening of schools and the provision of training and extra-curricular support for the most disadvantaged students, are therefore priorities to facilitate an equal recovery in the region. Planning teacher supply and demand and improving training and access to the Internet and technologies for those who cannot return to school are intermediate steps that should be rapidly implemented to protect education access and quality. Likewise, the differentiated impact of the crisis for women has been particularly evident as a result of school closures. Designing gender-sensitive policies for the recovery and ensuring a more equitable redistribution of care work are key to improving women's socio-economic conditions.

The pandemic has amplified the urgency of addressing the challenges of inequality, climate change and environmental degradation together. While the pandemic has increased the number of people living under the poverty line in LAC, climate change is projected to result in an additional 5 million poor in the region by 2030, principally affecting vulnerable groups and households with greater dependence on natural resources. Nonetheless, green growth and socio-economic prosperity can go hand in hand in LAC. If the right policies are put in place, a green recovery could create 15 million net jobs in the region by 2030 (ILO/IDB, 2020[13]).

Policy making related to social welfare systems should incorporate climate considerations as a cross-cutting theme. Integrated approaches would allow social and human development issues to be taken fully into account in the ecological transition, with the aim of achieving global carbon neutrality and reducing multi-dimensional inequalities. The political economy of reforming social protection systems is challenging, but this crisis may create the enabling environment required to advance delayed structural reforms. People are well aware of the need for policy change. People throughout the region seem to be in favour of pension reform in general, but they seem to disagree on the policy options to implement it, especially if fiscal sustainability is taken into account. Well-informed citizens are more likely to support broad reforms but information alone is not sufficient, especially if trust in institutions is low. Managing the trade-offs and taking into account fiscal sustainability in reforming social protection and improving public services will be essential but not easy. Targeting interventions to support those most exposed to the current crisis may be a good starting point.

Increased regional integration and productive transformation to unlock development opportunities

The unprecedented disruptions in global trade and production systems caused by the COVID-19 pandemic exposed LAC's reliance on international production and its weak regional integration. The magnitude of the COVID-19 economic crisis and countries' capacity to react depend largely on the productive structure of their economies and companies' participation in regional and global value chains. In this context, developing stronger intra-regional industrial and productive policies is essential to allow the region to strengthen existing capacities and generate new ones in strategic sectors.

Regional integration must play a key role in the crisis-recovery strategies in the region. In a global context of increased production regionalisation, major industrial policy efforts will be required for LAC to develop stronger regional value chains and compete in highly diversified global supply chains. The convergence between existing integration mechanisms and institutions could provide an opportunity to boost investments in knowledge and technology, develop productive capacity and overcome regional market fragmentation.

Although regional integration remains weak in the region, it could be an engine for productive transformation. Most LAC integration initiatives have focused on trade and market integration, with little attention to productive integration. Despite its many intraregional trade agreements, LAC has one of the lowest levels of intraregional trade worldwide. Barely 13% of its exports stayed within the region in 2020, and that proportion has been declining steadily since 2014 (Figure 5). The scarce productive integration among LAC countries is evidenced by the less than 6% on average of intra-regional imported content in total exports. Similarly, LAC's integration into global value chains is low and has been mainly associated with the extraction and processing of raw materials.

Figure 5. **Latin America and the Caribbean: Intraregional exports, 1960-2020**

USD billions and percentages of total goods exports

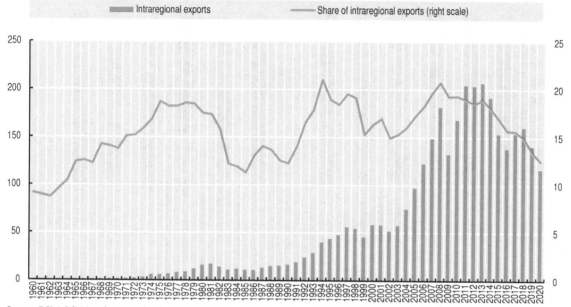

Source: ECLAC (2021[14]) *International Trade Outlook for Latin America and the Caribbean, 2020* (LC/PUB.2020/21-P).
StatLink ᐁᐧᒪ https://doi.org/10.1787/888934286217

LAC's productive structure, sectoral specialisation and business structure do not contribute to regional integration. LAC has not been able to achieve long-term productivity gains that allow it to sustain higher growth (Chapter 1). LAC has a poorly diversified productive structure, clustered in low added value sectors, and exports are concentrated in goods with low technological content. In the last two decades, 76% of the average GDP growth achieved in LAC was generated through the accumulation of employment and only 24% through increases in labour productivity. This pattern contrasts with countries like China, where the contribution of productivity is 96%, and India, where it is almost 80%.

The characteristics of the region's productive structure limit opportunities and incentives for technical change and diversification. The region's international integration is mainly limited to a small number of large companies in natural resource intensive sectors, offering few opportunities for participation in higher value-added activities. In parallel, there is an abundance of unproductive micro, small and medium-sized enterprises (MSMEs) that are disconnected from international markets. With limited incentives for those MSMEs to invest in productive or technological capacities, the region remains locked in a low productivity and low value-added trap.

The technological content of LAC exports is generally low. However, the proportion of the manufacturing content compared to primary products in intraregional trade in Latin America and the Caribbean, is higher than it is compared to exports to the rest of the world. On average, industrialised products accounted for 73% of intraregional flows in 2018-19, but only 63% in the case of extra-regional exports (Figure 6). These figures show the crucial role that intraregional trade could play in economic diversification, the development of manufacturing capacities and the internationalisation of small and medium-sized enterprises (SMEs).

Figure 6. Latin America and the Caribbean (main integration mechanisms): sectoral structure of goods exports, 2018-19

Percentages

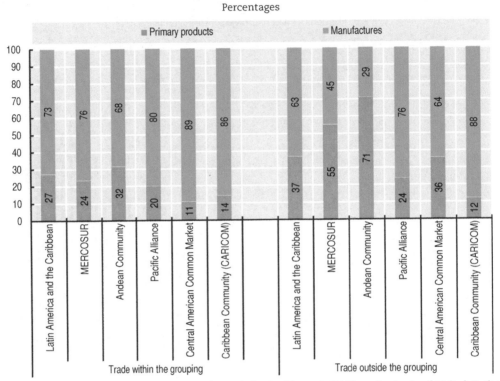

Source: Economic Commission for Latin America and the Caribbean (ECLAC) on the basis of United Nations Commodity Trade Statistics Database (COMTRADE).
StatLink ⎈ https://doi.org/10.1787/888934286236

A single market could be a way to foster technological development in LAC. The digital transformation is generating important changes for companies and market dynamics. While the digital transformation presents an opportunity to address the persistent challenge of low productivity, in a region where productivity disparities are considerable depending on the size of firm, there is also a risk of it reinforcing these differences (OECD et al., 2020[15]).

Regional integration and coordinated policy strategies will be key to ensure the creation of digital opportunities to increase productivity. Despite progress in terms of connectivity, the pace of the digital transformation has been moderate. On average in LAC, digital adoption in business was 4.5% between 2014 and 2016, well below highly dynamic countries in Southeast Asia (13.1%) or China (16.4%). An integrated market would be economically beneficial for the region. For example, since the creation of the digital single market strategy in the European Union, its degree of digitisation grew more than that of other OECD countries that are not part of this space.

Overall, the region needs a structural shift to overcome the limitations imposed by its current development model and increase productivity growth (ECLAC, 2020[16]).The production structure must shift towards more technology-intensive sectors with higher rates of demand and skilled employment. This should be achieved while preserving natural resources, biodiversity and the environment. Since markets cannot drive sustainable structural transformation alone, these changes call for a co-ordinated set of technological, industrial, fiscal, financial, environmental, social and regulatory policies to promote sustainability. Each country, given its productive structure and its societal priorities needs to determine the activities and policies to foster progressive structural change and the big-push for sustainability (ECLAC, 2020[16]).

Many COVID-19 recovery strategies in the region allocated resources to specific sectors to address national or regional development needs. The transformation of the productive structure and the combination of forward-looking investments to provide the basis for a big push for sustainability in the region could focus on sectors with high potential, including the automotive, pharmaceutical and renewable energy sectors, the circular economy and sustainable agriculture.

A renewed social contract will be key to support the reforms needed to boost the recovery and overcome structural weaknesses in the region

Social discontent, as demonstrated in the wave of protests shaking the region in recent years, mistrust of government and demands for greater democratic reforms are rising at a time in which the Covid-19 crisis is putting the resilience of LAC countries to the test.

In 2020, only 38% of the regional population trusted their government (Gallup, 2021[20]), more than half of LAC's citizens believed that their government was performing poorly in tackling corruption (Transparency International, 2019[18]), and most LAC countries exhibited medium and high impunity levels in the Global Impunity Index (CESIJ, 2020[19]). Confidence in government remained highly volatile as the COVID-19 pandemic evolved, and satisfaction with public services, including education and health, markedly decreased. In 2020, on average almost 50% of the population in LAC was dissatisfied with public education and 53% was dissatisfied with healthcare, in part due to the challenges to ensuring continuity of school curricula during lockdowns, the increased childcare burden during school closures and the lack of resources to respond to the health crisis (Figure 7).

Figure 7. **Dissatisfaction with public services has steadily increased in recent years, including during the COVID-19 crisis**

Share of people who are satisfied with the quality of health care and with the education system, LAC average, 2006-20

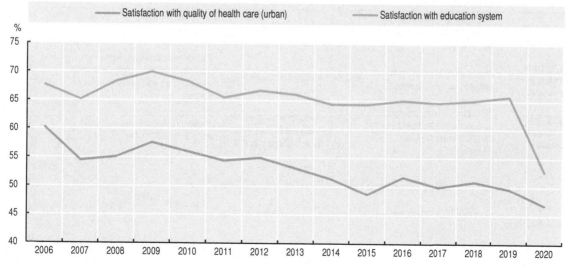

Notes: Unweighted LAC average including 16 LAC countries. 2020 data for satisfaction with health care are missing for Honduras and Panama. 2020 data for satisfaction with the education system are missing for Guatemala, Honduras and Panama.
Source: Gallup (2021[20]), *Gallup World Poll* (database), https://ga.gallup.com.
StatLink https://doi.org/10.1787/888934286255

Concentration of power has been another source of dissatisfaction, with 73% of Latin American citizens believing that their country is governed in the interests of a few powerful groups. Interpersonal trust has characterised the region historically, with a notable declining trend after 2011, reaching particularly low levels in 2020 (12%) (Latinobarometro, 2021[17]). Finally, identification with a political ideology has increased in recent years in LAC while trust in political parties has declined. Traditional mechanisms of representation have failed to channel growing and changing political demands, increasing popular frustration.

These dynamics suggest a profound erosion of the social contract in the region. The COVID-19 pandemic has accentuated these trends, while placing the region at a tipping point; without a strong consensus among all societal actors, the reforms needed to drive the recovery and overcome longstanding structural weaknesses will not come to fruition. This is why a new social contract is needed. LEO 2021 defines the social contract in broad terms as the comprehensive yet intangible and implicit agreement that binds society together and exists within a certain set of formal and informal rules and institutions.

The building blocks of a post-pandemic social contract should revolve around two interconnected dimensions. First, it should be a transversal agreement across: i) socio-economic groups; ii) territories; and iii) generations. Second, it should advance towards: i) broader and more effective social protection systems (Chapter 2); ii) resilient and sustainable productive strategies that prioritise the creation of quality and green jobs and embrace the digital transformation (Chapter 3); and iii) more sustainable financing for a low-carbon development model (Chapter 1). The intersection of these objectives shows that the social contract is underpinned by a set of social pacts across various policy domains that each country must adapt to its specific needs and goals (Table 1).

Table 1. The building blocks of a new social contract

	A PACT		
	Across socio-economic groups (including income, gender, ethnic and racial)	Across territories	Across generations
Reinvigorating regional productive strategies	Creating better-quality jobs for all and embracing the digital transformation	Adapting productive strategies to local potential	Fostering green growth
Expanding the reach of social protection and public services	Strengthening social protection systems and public services	Ensuring wide territorial coverage	Restructuring pension systems and supporting children, youth, the disabled and the elderly with stronger welfare systems
Underpinning sustainable finance for development	Developing fairer and stronger tax systems and improving the effectiveness of public expenditure	Ensuring sound systems of transfers across territories and strengthening capacity to raise local revenues	Managing public debt in a sustainable and responsible manner

Stronger and more inclusive governance

Note: Own elaboration.

Implementing a new social contract entails a profound rethinking of its foundational pillars (e.g. the current constitutional process in Chile) or more targeted attempts to reach an inclusive pact on critical areas of the recovery (e.g. fiscal, green and jobs). Whatever the nature of the endeavour, a key lesson learned from past experiences is that close attention to the process itself is of the utmost importance for building a consensus that is fair, legitimate and durable, especially in a context of high discontent and reduced fiscal space (Cabutto, Nieto-Parra and Vázquez-Zamora, 2021[21]).

Four main principles should contribute to guide the process of consensus building. They can be summarised by four Cs: conciliate, contextualise, compensate and communicate, not necessarily in that order (Cabutto, Nieto-Parra and Vázquez-Zamora, 2021[21]). First, the process must be inclusive. This means reconciling various interests and bringing all interested parties into the discussion from the very beginning. An inclusive policy-making process that leverages the ideas and resources of various players can result in greater accountability and trust, less concern over undue influence, greater policy commitment across time by all stakeholders, more sustainable reforms, and innovative solutions to complex issues. Second, context matters. Participatory processes can fail if not well designed. It is important to evaluate aspects of the socio-political context that may generate risks or opportunities for the strategy (Naser, Williner and Sandoval, 2021[22]). Third, compensating potential "losers" is crucial. Reforms can make things worse before they make them better and can leave certain vulnerable groups worse off. It is important to account for clear compensation mechanisms to mitigate the potential negative distributional impacts of a reform (Rodrik, 1996[23]; OECD, 2010[24]). Fourth, communication about the rationale and potential impact of reform is essential. In a context of polarised political discourses and rising misinformation, evidence-based analysis and effective communication are key to shed light on the benefits of reform. Independent *ex ante* and *ex post* evaluations are important to build the case (Worley, H. et al., 2018[25]).

The sequencing and speed of these steps are critical for successful reforms, although both dimensions are highly context specific. For instance, in the case of fiscal policy, the sequencing of policy action in terms of expenditure, taxation and public debt management is crucial to balance fiscal needs while financing policies to support the most vulnerable and ensuring wide support for the reforms (Mora, Nieto-Parra and Orozco, 2021[8]). Generally, successful reforms can help increase support for subsequent ones. Policy makers may prefer to bundle reforms into a comprehensive package so that losses from one reform are compensated by positive spillovers from others (Dayton-Johnson, Londoño and Nieto-Parra, 2011[26]), or if this is not possible, they may prefer to reach specific agreements in areas where there is potential for consensus.

Last, to reach and maintain a consensus, effective intermediary institutions are key to ensure the long-term sustainability of a renewed social contract. By acting as interlocutors between citizens and the state, intermediary institutions, such as political parties, trade unions and associations, make public institutions more accountable and give individuals the opportunity to voice grievances (OECD, 2021[27]). This two-way dialogue can promote social cohesion and provide useful feedback during the implementation and potential adjustment phase of reform. Strengthening the engagement of public institutions with these intermediary bodies stands out as a relevant area to underpin legitimacy and inclusive policy making (Cabutto, Nieto-Parra and Vázquez-Zamora, 2021[21]).

The role of international co-operation in facilitating a new social contract in LAC

The opportunity for a new social contract in LAC to overcome the crisis implies moving from today's fragmented status quo to a new equilibrium founded on equality of opportunities. Given rising social discontent and the increasing interconnection between national development and global megatrends, international co-operation becomes a critical policy sphere in supporting the region in this process by contributing to build new development models in the region. The current vicious cycle between global and national development dynamics in LAC calls for further consolidation of the Development in Transition (DiT) framework – proposed in the LEO 2019 – and for international co-operation to take on a facilitating role in supporting Latin American and Caribbean countries overcoming development traps – institutional, productivity, social and environmental – and setting the region's inclusive and sustainable development.

Figure 8. **A vicious cycle between global and national development dynamics in LAC**

Source: Own elaboration.

Although innovative practices in international co-operation emerged during the crisis, structural shortcomings in supporting the region prevailed. Despite efforts – official development assistance reached an all-time high in 2020 – current international financial mechanisms have proven to be insufficient, particularly for middle-income countries which make up the majority of LAC countries. Co-operation with and within the region provides innovative examples of technical, South-South, triangular and even South-North co-operation that took place in the region throughout the crisis. Concrete transformative proposals were made, advancing a DiT approach, for example the Fund to Alleviate COVID-19 Economics (FACE) proposed by Costa Rica and the new Team Europe scheme co-ordinated by the European Union.

Looking ahead, international co-operation that facilitates a new social contract in LAC and enables a virtuous cycle between national and international development dynamics, calls for: i) mission-driven partnerships that prioritise equal-footing co-operation, participatory approaches and policy coherence across objectives and actors; ii) regional co-operation that strengthens the voice of the region in the world; and iii) a balanced use of tools, such as sustainable financing, global rules and standards; and technical co-operation for capacity building; all of which must be sustained by stronger international political and policy dialogues.

Mission-driven international partnerships entail thinking beyond currently defined areas and institutions to encompass all relevant resources, tools and actors in issue-based coalitions. With a predetermined objective and time-bound, mission-driven partnerships could provide better incentives to achieve measurable development results. Mission-driven partnerships could also drive the experimentation of new ways of bringing citizens into the conceptualisation and implementation of international co-operation. The active participation of groups representing civil society, the private sector, subnational governments and academia in the agenda-setting process would positively politicise and increase the legitimacy of its mission, turning it into an opportunity to connect global governance more closely to citizens' daily concerns. Finally, mission-driven partnerships would put particular emphasis on addressing policy incoherence, whether among national and international objectives, or across policy objectives.

Regional co-operation and integration will be a key building block in this process. Regional initiatives have a big role to play to support national efforts towards new development models for the recovery, embrace megatrends like digital transformation as tools for recovery and create resilience in the face of future crises. The region is a unique space within which states facing similar challenges can share best practices and guidance on how to design policies, and compare results. Collaboration across the region can also help form a regional vision for action to face regional and global challenges. LAC could take stock of other regional initiatives, such as the European Union's long-term budget, the African Union's Agenda 2063 and the Association of Southeast Asian Nations' Comprehensive Recovery Framework, to amplify a common voice in the multilateral system and leverage more transformative policy actions across the region in the long term through shared development agendas. LAC has a lot to learn from its own regional experience, from the Central American Integration System to the most recent participatory experience, supported by the United Nations Economic Commission for Latin America and the Caribbean, that led to the signature of the Escazú Agreement.

Table 2. **Integrated approaches for international co-operation to enable a new social contract in LAC**

	Mainstreaming environmental sustainability	Expanding the reach of social protection and public services	Reinvigorating regional productive strategies
Sustainable financing	Mainstream environmental sustainability across financing instruments.	Ensure debt repayment schemes do not compromise expanding the reach of social protection and public services delivery.	Ensure sufficient public and private financing for strategic productive.
Global rules & standards	Adopt environmental regulations and standards, following the principle of common but differentiated responsibilities.	Adopt international regulations for the cross-border transfer of social security contributions and a global corporate tax rate. Agree on international standards for social protection, fair labour, taxation, international migration, etc.	Agree and implement rules conducive to LAC's productive diversification.
Technical co-operation for capacity building	Provide technical co-operation on sustainability practices, research and knowledge; promote policy dialogues with a focus on environmental sustainability.	Exchange policy experiences on social protection and public services delivery; foster capacity building in public institutions, including by enhancing understanding of the interconnections across national development strategies and global dynamics.	Transfer knowledge and technology to increase productivity; boost policy dialogues at regional and global levels to foster regional value chains.

Strengthen political and policy dialogues
with a balanced and integrated use of tools

Source: Own elaboration.

A balanced use of international co-operation tools, underpinned by strengthened international political and policy dialogues, is also crucial for LAC's recovery. First, a co-ordinated solution for managing the challenge of debt should be a priority, especially considering the investments to be made in the medium and long term to recover and attain the SDGs. Innovative financing mechanisms should also be a priority, including improving the participation of the private sector. Second, the cross-border nature of major development issues not only calls for the improvement of national capacities but equally, or even more importantly, it requires multilateral agreements on shared rules and standards that reduce global inequality and promote policy coherence. Finally, international co-operation efforts should place particular emphasis on transferring capacities and exchanging innovative policy options for reinvigorating regional productive strategies, expanding the reach of social protection or ensuring environmental sustainability.

Continued transformation of international co-operation is essential to achieve the full potential of a new social contract in the region, align it with global agreements and involve LAC in the governance of global trends through effective multilateral co-operation. LAC is a fertile ground to strengthen and experiment new forms of multilateralism by boosting policy dialogue within the region and beyond, through equal-footing international policy partnerships that put people and policy first. The pressing need to adapt international co-operation so that it contributes meaningfully to the recovery by building new development models in the region, should translate into an urgent global call to action.

References

Basto-Aguirre, Nieto-Parra and Vazquez-Zamora (2020), "Informality in Latin America in the post COVID-19 era: towards a more formal "new normal"?", http://vox.lacea.org/?q=blog/informality_latam_postcovid19. [12]

Cabutto, C., S. Nieto-Parra and J. Vázquez-Zamora (2021), "A post-pandemic social contract for Latin America: the why, the what, the how", *Vox Lacea (blog)*, http://vox.lacea.org/?q=blog/social_contract_latam. [21]

CAF (2020), *ECAF 2019. Percepciones de los Latinoamericanos sobre los Sistemas de Pensiones, Salud y Cuidados y el Avance Tecnológico en el Mercado Laboral*, https://scioteca.caf.com/handle/123456789/1646. [11]

CESIJ (2020), *Global Impunity Index 2020 (GII-2020)*, Center of Studies on Impunity and Justice, UDLAP Jenkins Graduate School, University of the Americas Puebla, Puebla, http://www.udlap.mx/cesij. [19]

Dayton-Johnson, J., J. Londoño and S. Nieto-Parra (2011), "The Process of Reform in Latin America: A Review Essay", *OECD Development Centre Working Papers* 304, pp. 1-60, https://dx.doi.org/10.1787/5kg3mkvfcjxv-en. [26]

ECLAC (2021), *Fiscal Panorama of Latin America and the Caribbean 2021: Fiscal policy challenges for transformative recovery post COVID-19*, United Nations publication, ECLAC, Santiago, https://www.cepal.org/en/publications/46809-fiscal-panorama-latin-america-and-caribbean-2021-fiscal-policy-challenges. [7]

ECLAC (2021), *International Trade Outlook for Latin America and the Caribbean 2020*, United Nations, ECLAC, Santiago, http://hdl.handle.net/11362/46614. [14]

ECLAC (2020), *Building a New Future: Transformative Recovery with Equality and Sustainability*, United Nations, ECLAC, Santiago, https://www.cepal.org/sites/default/files/publication/files/46226/S2000665_en.pdf. [16]

Gallup (2021), *Gallup World Poll (database)*, Gallup Inc. Washington D.C., https://ga.gallup.com. [20]

ILO (2018), *Women and men in the informal economy: A statistical picture*, International Labour Organization, Geneva, https://www.ilo.org/global/publications/books/WCMS_626831/lang--en/index.htm. [5]

ILO/IDB (2020), *Jobs in a net zero emissions future in Latin America and the Caribbean*, International Labour Organization, Geneva, Switzerland/Inter-American Development Bank, New York, http://www.ilo.org/americas/publicaciones/WCMS_752069/lang--en/index.htm. [13]

IMF (2021), *World Economic Outlook, April database*, International Monetary Fund, Washington D.C., https://www.imf.org/en/Publications/WEO/weo-database/2021/April. [1]

Latinobarometro (2021), *Latinobarómetro Survey 2020 (database)*, Latinobarómetro, Santiago, http://www.latinobarometro.org/latOnline.jsp. [17]

Mora, S., S. Nieto-Parra and R. Orozco (2021), *Fiscal policy to drive the recovery in Latin America: the "when" and "how" are key*, http://lacea.org/vox/?q=blog/fiscal_policy_latam. [8]

Naser, A., A. Williner and C. Sandoval (2021), *Participación ciudadana en los asuntos públicos: Un elemento estratégico para la Agenda 2030 y el gobierno abierto*, United Nations, ECLAC, Santiago, https://repositorio.cepal.org/bitstream/handle/11362/46645/1/S2000907_es.pdf. [22]

OECD (2021), *Perspectives on Global Development 2021: From Protest to Progress?*, OECD Publishing, Paris, https://doi.org/10.1787/405e4c32-en. [27]

OECD (2020), *COVID-19 in Latin America and the Caribbean: Regional Socio-Economic Implications and Policy Priorities*, OECD Publishing, Paris, https://www.oecd.org/coronavirus/policy-responses/covid-19-in-latin-america-and-the-caribbean-regional-socio-economic-implications-and-policy-priorities-93a64fde/. [2]

OECD (2010), *Making Reform Happen: Lessons from OECD Countries*, OECD Publishing, Paris, https://doi.org/10.1787/9789264086296-en. [24]

OECD (forthcoming), *Labour informality and households' vulnerabilities in Latin America (provisional title)*, OECD Publishing, Paris. [3]

OECD et al. (2020), *Latin American Economic Outlook 2020: Digital Transformation for Building Back Better*, OECD Publishing, Paris, https://dx.doi.org/10.1787/e6e864fb-en. [15]

OECD/ILO (2019), *Tackling Vulnerability in the Informal Economy*, Development Centre Studies, OECD Publishing, Paris, https://doi.org/10.1787/939b7bcd-en. [4]

Rodrik, D. (1996), "Understanding Economic Policy Reform", *Journal of Economic Literature*, Vol. 34/1, pp. 9-41, https://www.jstor.org/stable/2729408. [23]

Transparency International (2019), *Global Corruption Barometer Latin America and the Caribbean 2019: Citizen's views and experiences of corruption*, Transparency International, Berlin, https://images.transparencycdn.org/images/2019_GCB_LatinAmerica_Caribbean_Full_Report_200409_091428.pdf. [18]

UNESCO (2020), *Global monitoring of school closures caused by COVID-19*, UNESCO, Paris, https://en.unesco.org/covid19/educationresponse#schoolclosures. [10]

UNICEF (2021), *COVID-19 and school closures: One year of education disruption*, UNICEF, New York, https://data.unicef.org/wp-content/uploads/2021/03/COVID19-and-school-closures.pdf. [9]

United Nations (2019), *World Population Prospects 2019*, United Nations, New York, https://population.un.org/wpp/. [6]

Worley, H. et al. (2018), *Designing Communication Campaigns for Energy Subsidy Reform*, ESRAF Good Practice Note 10, ESMAP Paper, World Bank, Washington D.C., https://documents1.worldbank.org/curated/en/939551530880505644/pdf/ESRAF-note-10-Designing-Communication-Campaigns-for-Energy-Subsidy-Reform.pdf. [25]

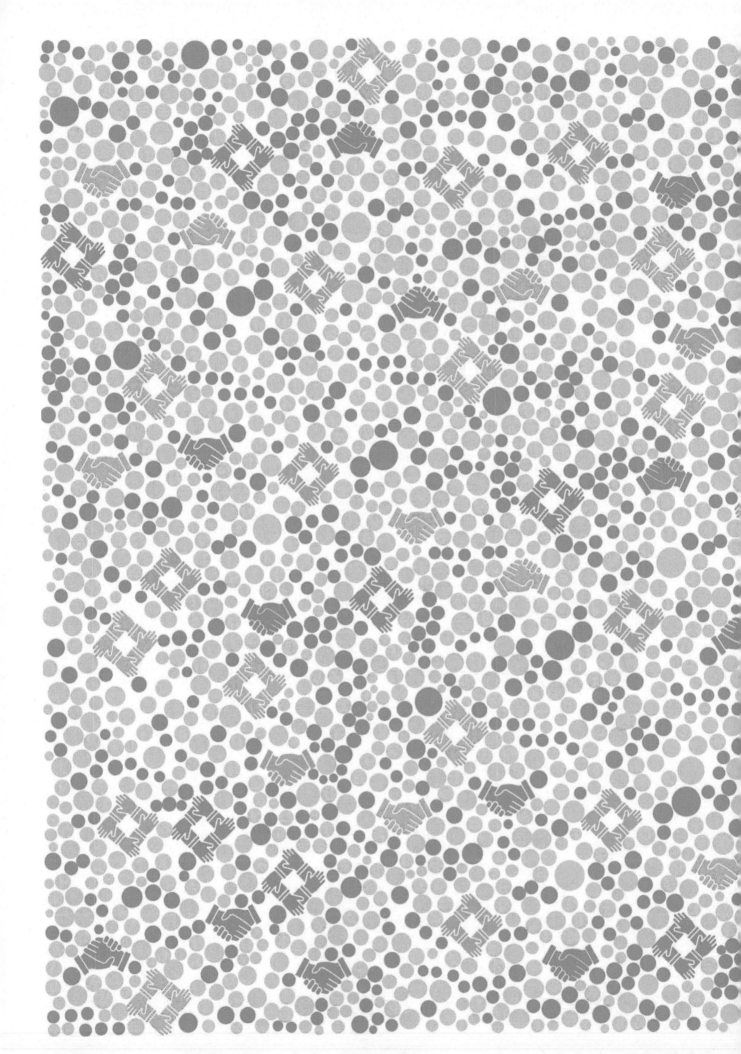

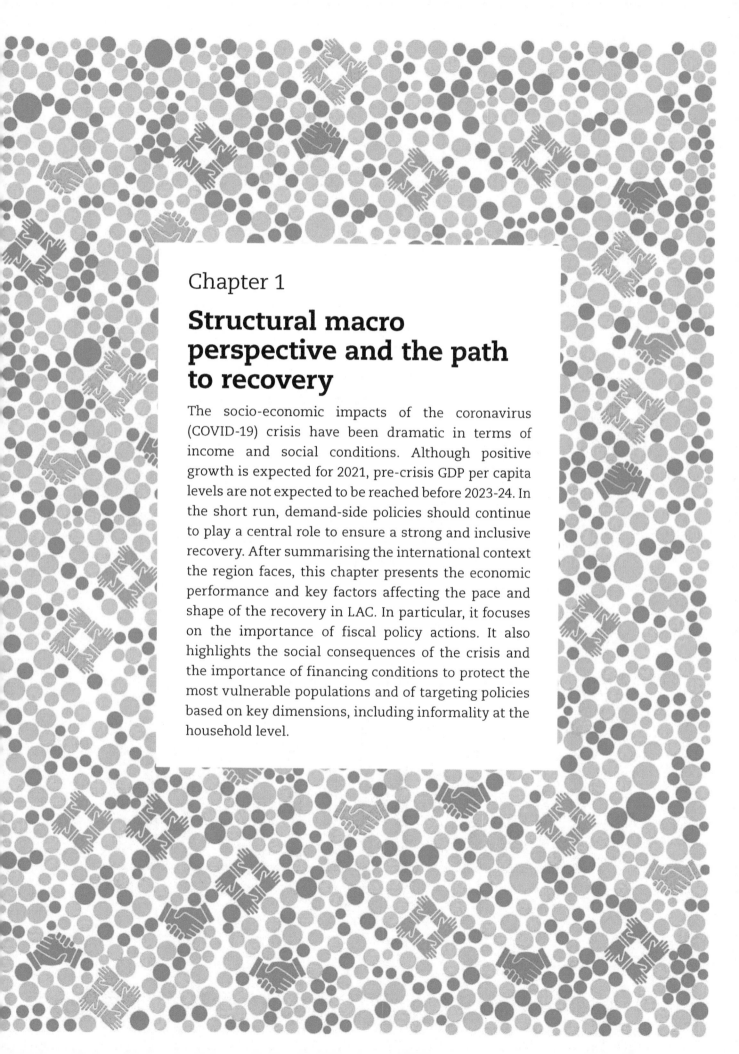

Chapter 1

Structural macro perspective and the path to recovery

The socio-economic impacts of the coronavirus (COVID-19) crisis have been dramatic in terms of income and social conditions. Although positive growth is expected for 2021, pre-crisis GDP per capita levels are not expected to be reached before 2023-24. In the short run, demand-side policies should continue to play a central role to ensure a strong and inclusive recovery. After summarising the international context the region faces, this chapter presents the economic performance and key factors affecting the pace and shape of the recovery in LAC. In particular, it focuses on the importance of fiscal policy actions. It also highlights the social consequences of the crisis and the importance of financing conditions to protect the most vulnerable populations and of targeting policies based on key dimensions, including informality at the household level.

TheeffectsoftheCovid-19crisis inLatinAmericaandtheCaribbean

IntheLACregion,2020 ended withthegreatesteconomicdownturn ofthepasttwocenturiesduetotheCovid-19crisis...

Theregionwillnot reachthepre-pandemic GDPpercapitalevels until2023-24

...putting annualisedGDP growthrates around -7.0%

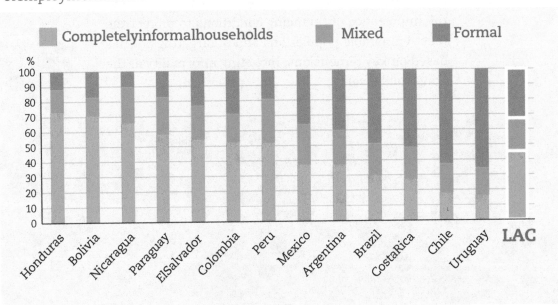

Thecrisishas damagedsome ofthelast decade'sprogress ineradicating povertyand inequality

The poverty rate in2020reached **33.7%**

and extreme poverty **12.5%**

Thisextreme poverty levelhas notbeenseen inthepast 20years

InformalhouseholdsarethemostaffectedbytheCOVID-19crisis,facingloss ofemploymentandlabourincome

Legend: **Completelyinformalhouseholds** **Mixed** **Formal**

Chart x-axis: Honduras, Bolivia, Nicaragua, Paraguay, ElSalvador, Colombia, Peru, Mexico, Argentina, Brazil, CostaRica, Chile, Uruguay, **LAC**

Chart y-axis (%): 0, 10, 20, 30, 40, 50, 60, 70, 80, 90, 100

Introduction

As a consequence of the coronavirus (COVID-19) pandemic, Latin America and the Caribbean (LAC) ended 2020 with the greatest economic downturn of the last two centuries, putting annualised gross domestic product (GDP) growth at rates around -7.0% (ECLAC, 2021[1]; CAF, 2021[2]), with immediate damages to the economic and social fabric and considerable risks of long-term scarring. Social costs are drastic in terms of inequalities and poverty, as the impact of the COVID-19 crisis has particularly affected the most vulnerable groups.

LAC economies should regain some ground in 2021, but uncertainty remains regarding the strength of the recovery. The recovery will likely be protracted, mainly explained by a statistical carry-over effect that will moderate in 2022, and with heterogeneity across and within countries.

The main threats to the recovery are increased contagions or a slow vaccine rollout that delays the normalisation of economic activity. Potential upsides include a larger than expected boost in global demand due to more robust recoveries in key partners for the region, including the European Union, the People's Republic of China (hereafter "China") or the United States. Similarly, the driving forces or tailwinds of growth will affect countries differently, but on average, pre-crisis per capita GDP levels are projected to be reached by 2023-24.

At the international level, the surge in some commodity prices and the recovery of global trade and industrial production should be favourable to LAC exports. Nonetheless, the region's external trade contraction during 2020 severely affected the economy, revealing existing trade fragmentations, especially regarding intraregional trade. In order to support a strong and more inclusive recovery while enhancing competitiveness and protecting against future exogenous shocks, it will be crucial to support stronger integration within and beyond LAC (Chapter 3) (ECLAC, 2021[3]). Development-oriented trade policies, coupled with competition and consumer policies, will also play an important part in the recovery and should contribute to achieving the United Nations 2030 Agenda for Sustainable Development, as well as to continued economic resilience (UNCTAD, 2020[4]).

While in 2020 LAC governments, in common with those of other emerging and developing economies, were capable of tapping capital markets with favourable financing conditions (OECD, 2021[5]), uncertainty remains regarding the international liquidity conditions for emerging markets. Moreover, some countries should remain without access to global capital markets, making them highly dependent on multilateral banks and public creditors to finance their recovery.

At the domestic level, policy makers in the region will face challenges in backing internal demand. Countries must overcome the health crisis in a race between new contagions and the vaccine rollout. The longer it takes to attain herd immunity through vaccination, the more likely uncertainty and stop-and-go policies will be, with increased likelihood of some permanent scarring to the economy.

Fiscal policy will have to continue to play a supportive role to ensure a strong and inclusive recovery but should be implemented in a holistic and sequenced manner. The use of tax and spending policies and the design of fiscal reforms, including actions such as strengthening the tax administration, should be co-ordinated and sequenced to offset the impact of the COVID-19 crisis on households and firms and to bolster public healthcare systems. Furthermore, there is a growing need for a holistic approach in terms of fiscal policy for the region that takes into account the political economy of fiscal reform, tax morale and the complex socio-economic conditions that resulted from the crisis. The proper use of fiscal resources could increase the level of satisfaction with public services, increase tax morale, strengthen trust and escape the "institutional trap" affecting many countries in the region (OECD et al., 2019[6]).

Governments must also manoeuvre between keeping fiscal stimulus going to cement the recovery and avoiding unsustainable fiscal positions. The premature withdrawal of the fiscal stimulus could derail the recovery and dent longer-term growth. Fiscal policy is therefore crucial to mitigate the immediate consequences of the crisis but also avoid the permanent scarring of the economy. It is key to design and finance well-targeted measures for the most vulnerable households and firms. Macroeconomic conditions are heterogeneous across the region, implying that the policy space is more limited for countries that are highly indebted or where anchoring inflation is becoming more difficult. This raises the need to adapt and tailor expenditure, taxation and debt management approaches to each country's context. Some of these actions require further co-operation and co-ordination at the international level (Chapter 5).

This chapter first examines the global context, with a focus on key partners of the region and the global financial and commodity markets. Then, it presents the economic performance in LAC, highlighting the region's heterogeneity, external accounts and the role of demand-side policies in sustaining the recovery. Third, it focuses on the key role of fiscal policy for the recovery and the need to build consensus and establish favourable sequencing of fiscal actions. Fourth, it highlights the social consequences of the crisis, the underlying conditions of informality at the household level and the need to finance the well-targeted social protection systems adopted during the pandemic. The chapter concludes with main policy messages.

Navigating a challenging international context

Global recovery gradual and uneven

The global economic recovery is underway but still depends on the vaccine rollout. Global activity contracted dramatically in 2020, with GDP falling by 3.4% (OECD, 2021[7]). By 2021, thanks to the gradual deployment of effective vaccines, additional fiscal support and successful measures in most countries to cope with the virus, economic prospects have improved markedly, and global GDP growth is projected to be 5.7% in 2021 and 4.5% in 2022. World output has now surpassed its pre-pandemic level, but output and employment gaps remain in many countries, particularly in economies where vaccination rates are low (OECD, 2021[7]).

The global recovery improved international trade, but trade will not reach pre-crisis levels for all goods and services in 2021. World trade is projected to strengthen in 2021, with an estimated 8.2% increase of trade volumes, after falling by 8.5% in 2020 (OECD, 2021[8]). For 2021, the gradual recovery of the global economy, combined with changes in consumption patterns (increased demand for medical items and technology for remote work, for example), has allowed merchandise trade to recover steadily; nevertheless, trade in services, notably tourism, will remain subdued as long as the pandemic requires sanitary restrictions and undermines travellers' confidence (OECD, 2021[8]) (Figure 1.1).

There are marked divergences across countries in terms of dealing with the health crisis and the recovery. The United States leads growth among advanced economies, boosted by the accelerated advance in the vaccination process and the Biden administration's sizeable stimulus package (OECD, 2021[7]). This will generate positive spillover in key trading partners, including LAC economies. In Europe, continued containment measures in the first half of 2021, a more limited fiscal support and the still-complicated epidemiological situation are delaying activity normalisation. Growth in the Euro Area will be in particular driven by private consumption (OECD, 2021[7]). Among emerging economies, China has caught up with its previous growth path and is set to stay on this trajectory in 2021 and 2022. Other emerging economies may continue to have large shortfalls in GDP relative to pre-pandemic expectations and are projected to grow at robust rates only once the impact of the virus fades (OECD, 2021[8]).

Figure 1.1. **Global merchandise trade (% change y-o-y, 3-month moving average)**

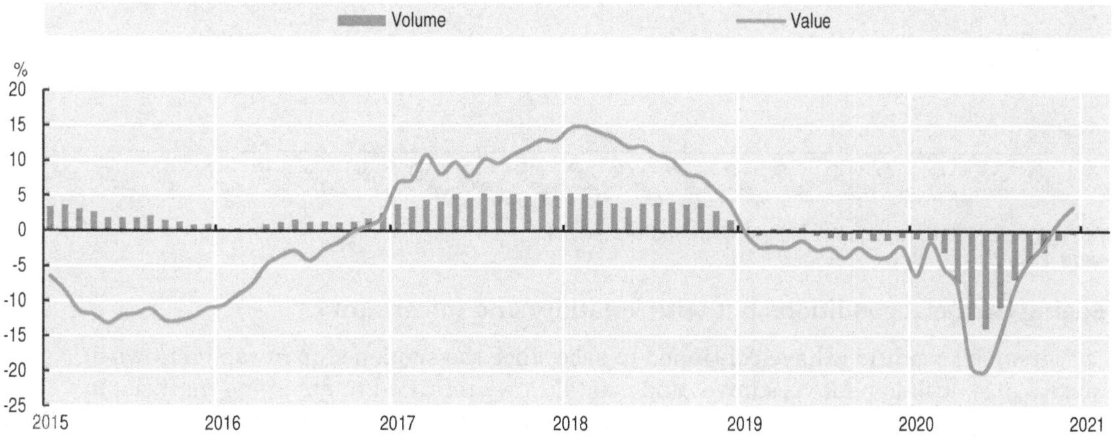

Source: OECD/ECLAC/CAF/EU based on CBP Netherlands Bureau of Economic Analysis; and WTO Short-Term Indicators.
StatLink ▨▨▨ https://doi.org/10.1787/888934286274

Commodity prices are on an upward trend

Most commodity prices have increased to above pre-pandemic levels (Figure 1.2). The COVID-19 crisis caused a sharp fall in commodity prices, but this trend has reversed as of May 2020. In 2021, the recovery in the global economy, production bottlenecks and changes in consumption patterns have continued to push commodity prices up. Energy prices, whose recovery lagged compared to other commodities, have risen rapidly since the end of 2020. These changes signal a recovery from last year's historical plunge but not necessarily the beginning of a new commodity supercycle. Commodity prices should stabilise once supply bottlenecks and the strong rebound in demand, particularly in China and to a lesser extent in the United States, ease and growth converges to potential. Moreover, looking forward, international action to tackle the climate emergency and the commitments to decarbonisation and reducing dependency on fossil fuels could cap oil prices while being positive for some metals. The shift to a more environmentally sustainable consumption model, mainly in developed countries, will increase the demand for some base metals necessary for components and batteries (e.g. copper and lithium), as seen with increases in electric vehicles.

Some of the drivers behind the last commodity supercycle – the rapid industrialisation of China and robust global trade – are less vigorous today. Moreover, globalisation was stalling even before the pandemic, which could increase the reshoring and fragmentation of some value chains, weakening the impulse of world trade. Therefore, as the world economy returns to previous growth trends, global trade, particularly commodity trade, will hardly play a substantial role in driving LAC economies' growth compared to before the 2008 financial crisis.

Figure 1.2. **Commodity prices (international commodity prices, January 2018 to May 2021; January 2018 = 100)**

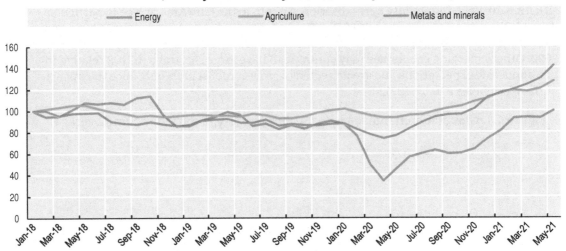

Source: OECD/ECLAC/CAF/EU based on World Bank Commodity Markets.
StatLink ᵍⁿᵈ *https://doi.org/10.1787/888934286293*

Easing financial conditions but with volatility and uncertainty

Financial conditions have continued to ease since the sudden stop in capital flows in March 2020. Risk appetite resumed, and capital flows returned to emerging markets. In contrast to previous international crises, the COVID-19 crisis was favourably accompanied with ample international liquidity thanks to the strong and co-ordinated monetary policy responses in major advanced economies. While interest rates will probably remain relatively low in advanced economies, the long end of the yield curve remains slightly subdued. In the case of the United States, and similar to the previous case of the "taper tantrum", rising US bond yields and a strong US recovery could trigger a reversal in capital flows and raise exchange-rate volatility (OECD, 2021[8]). The increase in yields since the beginning of 2021 indicates that markets expect a rise in medium-term inflation, in line with the economic recovery. However, financial conditions are not tight yet, since real interest rates remain near zero or negative.

Rising headline inflation should push central banks with inflation-targeting regimes to switch to a less expansionary policy stance. In many economies, headline inflation has been rising as energy and food prices are increasing, and currencies depreciate. These pressures are likely to trigger a sustained rise in wages and other costs, forcing central banks to switch to a less expansionary policy stance. Nonetheless, as long as output gaps remain negative, the overall slack in labour markets persists and expectations stay anchored, inflationary pressures should be transitory. In emerging economies where expectations are not so firmly anchored, central banks could take more neutral stances. However, exchange-rate depreciation pass-through, higher energy costs and increased food prices may lift inflation expectations and elicit interest rate hikes, particularly in countries where fiscal sustainability is on the line.

Access to external financing has not been a binding constraint for most LAC countries in the short term, although credit access remains differentiated. The appetite for debt securities in foreign currency has remained since the second half of 2020 and has been greater than for stocks (Figure 1.3, Panel A), allowing significant Eurobond issuance at relatively low rates by emerging markets. In Latin America, investment-grade issuers did not face significant obstacles issuing debt in the markets at low interest rates since April 2020 (e.g. Chile, Colombia,[1] Mexico, Panama, Paraguay, Peru, Uruguay). Other countries were in the process of debt restructuring without access to markets (Argentina and Ecuador), and for some others, credit has rapidly become more costly (e.g. Bolivia, Costa Rica, Trinidad and Tobago). Following debt restructuring in Argentina, the gap of sovereign bond spreads between non-investment and investment grade countries has remained high at close to 400 basis points (Figure 1.3, Panel B) (see section on debt management below). The recent increase in US yields prompted a rise in the cost of borrowing in local currency in domestic markets (IIF, 2021[9]; IMF, 2021[10]).

Figure 1.3. **Financial conditions in emerging markets and LAC**

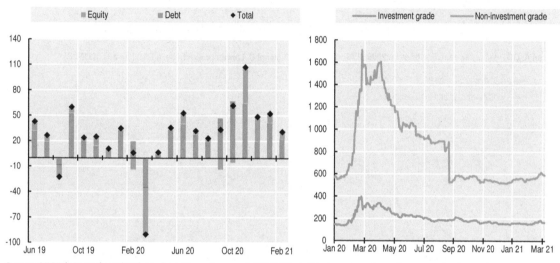

Panel A. Net non-resident portfolio flows to emerging markets (USD billion)

Panel B. Sovereign risk spreads in Latin America (JP Morgan EMBI+, EMBIG)

Source: OECD/ECLAC/CAF/EU based on Bloomberg and (IIF, 2021[9]); Weak economic performance in the region
StatLink https://doi.org/10.1787/888934286312

Insufficient growth for LAC in 2021, with high uncertainty

The LAC region was the hardest hit by the pandemic in the developing and developed world, registering one of the world's deepest contractions (Figure 1.4, Panel A). The recovery is likely to be more protracted than in other regions owing to the pandemic second wave's hefty toll and the slow return to normality.

Importantly, following the commodities bust in 2014, the COVID-19 shock represents the second shock to the LAC region in the last decade. Since 2014, the region has experienced little to no growth, which represents an additional threat, with some predictions that the region will not reach the pre-pandemic GDP per capita levels until 2023-24. Moving towards a recovery from the crisis, the danger of another lost decade must be kept in mind. Therefore, it is crucial to adopt a long-term view in terms of the structural reforms needed to achieve long-term and sustainable growth. For instance, productivity growth is the core engine of sustained economic progress, but in LAC aggregate labour productivity shows reduced and persistently low growth, with decreases since the 1960s relative to the OECD countries (Figure 1.4, Panel B).

Resuming steady growth will remain a daunting task for LAC economies until the health crisis has passed. In 2020, the pandemic induced economic crisis saw GDP on average fell by almost 7% (ECLAC, 2021[3]; CAF, 2021[2]). The effects of the pandemic continue to be felt in the first quarter of 2021, forcing further mobility restrictions that have weighed on activity. The impact of second-wave restrictions in LAC economies was not as severe as experienced in the second quarter of 2020. However, initially progress in vaccination has been slow except in few countries, in particular Chile and Uruguay.

Vaccination campaigns accelerated during the second semester in several countries, including Ecuador, Paraguay, Argentina, Colombia, Panama, the Dominican Republic and Brazil, as supply bottlenecks eased and vaccines availability increased. LAC faced obstacles to acquiring the vaccines – due to the unequal global distribution of vaccines across regions, bottlenecks in global production, little international co-ordination or financial restrictions in some cases. Beyond these challenges, most LAC countries face difficulties related to poor domestic logistics and limited local capacities to implement immunisation campaigns. Both aspects (vaccine accessibility and vaccination rollout strategies) could delay the normalisation of activities in most countries and thus hinder growth. The longer it takes to recover, the more pervasive the scarring and the more permanent the damage to the already low potential growth.

Figure 1.4. **GDP per capita and labour productivity in LAC**

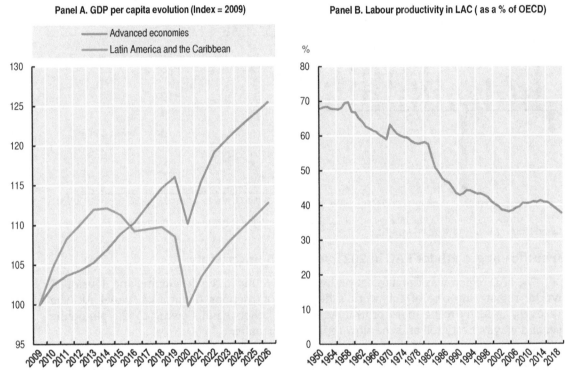

Source: OECD/ECLAC/CAF/EU based on (IMF, 2021[10]), *World Economic Outlook*, https://www.imf.org/en/Publications/WEO/Issues/2021/03/23/world-economic-outlook-april-2021.
StatLink ⬛ᵐᶻ▱ https://doi.org/10.1787/888934286141

Average growth around 6% is expected for 2021 in the region followed by a projected deceleration in 2022 (ECLAC, 2021[1]; CAF, 2021[2]; IMF, 2021[11]). Growth in 2021 is mainly attributed to the low basis of comparison – after the 2020 strong drop – along with the positive effects arising from external demand and the rise in the price of the commodities that the region exports, as well as to increases in aggregate demand (ECLAC, 2021[1]; ECLAC, 2021[3]). The scenario for the remainder of 2021 and for 2022 is subject to the evolution of the pandemic, and the surge of the Delta variant, the vaccine rollout and public discontent that has translated into social protests in some countries. The main driver of growth in the short term will be domestic demand, particularly consumption, as mobility restrictions are lifted, allowing services to resume. In addition, a packed political cycle in the region, with presidential and/or legislative elections between the second half of 2021 and end of 2022 in Argentina, Brazil, Chile, Colombia, Costa Rica, Ecuador,

El Salvador, Mexico and Peru, will weigh on expectations and could keep investment subdued. Finally, social unrest remains a key factor affecting economic stability. Recent social protests highlight the need to achieve a more inclusive growth model, improve citizens' well-being (see below and Chapter 2) and build consensus across citizens in a renewed social contract (Chapter 4).

The recovery will be uneven across the region. It will depend on countries' exposure to hard-hit service sectors, access to financing, carry-over effects and policy space to support demand. For instance, countries heavily exposed to tourism, as Caribbean economies, will exhibit weaker expansions, since tourism will probably lag in the recovery (Chapter 6). Panama and Peru, which experienced double-digit contractions in 2020, will be among the fastest-growing economies this year. In Chile and Peru (and, to a lesser extent, Colombia), public investment in infrastructure will underpin demand.

Back to the usual current account deficits in LAC

Current account balances in most LAC countries should come back to the usual deficits in 2021, mirroring structural challenges in the region. In contrast to previous years, the 2020 LAC average exhibited a narrow current account surplus as a result of considerable decreases in imports (ECLAC, 2021[1]). Current account balances should deteriorate further as domestic demand picks up. However, for 2021, deficits should not soar, as the increase in imports will not be large enough to override the improvement in exports. Foreign direct investment (FDI) continues to be key to finance these deficits. The implementation of a more interconnected market in LAC would provide substantial protection from future exogenous shocks while enhancing competitiveness (Chapter 3) (ECLAC, 2021[12]).

Net FDI fell by 35% in 2020, reaching 2.5% of GDP, the lowest value in the last decade (ECLAC, 2021[13]). The region needs to diversify the sources of FDI to promote further market competition and economic diversification, key dimensions to overcome the "productivity trap" described in (OECD et al., 2019[6]) (Chapter 3). Diversification also means attracting quality FDI, which can contribute to increase productivity and deliver a more job-rich and sustainable recovery (Box 1.1).

Box 1.1. **FDI and sustainable development**

Foreign direct investment (FDI) can make important contributions to sustainable development well beyond the capital invested by the affiliates of foreign multinationals. Foreign investors are often thought to have access to better technology and know-how than their domestic peers as a result of ties to their multinational parent firms. These technological advantages can be transferred to the host economy through supply chain linkages and market interactions with domestic firms. Consequently, FDI can enhance growth and innovation, create quality jobs, develop human capital and improve living standards and environmental sustainability. The OECD FDI Qualities Indicators seek to shed light on the extent to which FDI contributes to sustainable development, focusing on productivity and innovation, job quality and skills, gender equality and the low-carbon transition (OECD, 2019[14]). The forthcoming OECD FDI Qualities Policy Toolkit will further support governments in identifying policies and institutional arrangements to improve FDI impacts on sustainable development (OECD, 2021[15]).

In the case of Latin America, the OECD FDI Qualities Indicators show that, across most countries for which data are available, foreign investors are more productive and more likely to introduce product innovation or invest in research and development (R&D) than domestic firms (Figure 1.5, Panels A-C). This productivity and innovation gap suggests that there is potential for knowledge

Box 1.1. FDI and sustainable development (*cont.*)

and technology spillovers from foreign to domestic firms. Foreign firms also tend to offer higher average wages, suggesting that the productivity premium they enjoy is at least in part transferred to employees (Figure 1.5, Panel D). At the same time, in the majority of Latin American countries considered, compared to domestic peers, foreign firms tend to employ a higher proportion of unskilled workers and are significantly more likely to offer training opportunities (Figure 1.5, Panels E and F). This evidence suggests that foreign investors are an important source of employment for low-skilled workers in Latin America and can make a significant contribution to upgrading their skills and increasing their opportunities for future employment. In order to enhance FDI's contribution to inclusive and sustainable development further, investment promotion efforts in the region should be aligned with well-defined production strategies that promote economic diversification.

Figure 1.5. OECD FDI Qualities Indicators for selected Latin American countries

Foreign firms perform better than domestic firms if value > 0

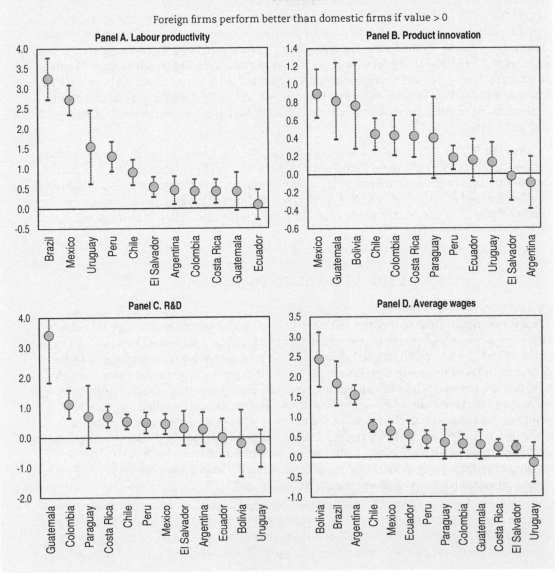

Box 1.1. **FDI and sustainable development** (*cont.*)

Figure 1.5. **OECD FDI Qualities Indicators for selected Latin American countries** (*cont.*)

Foreign firms perform better than domestic firms if value > 0

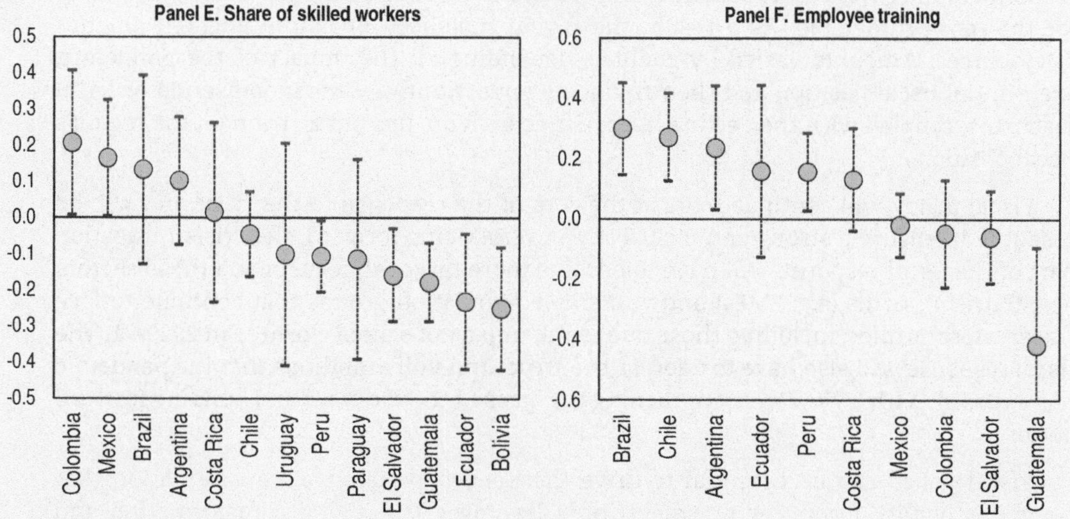

Note: Data circa 2017 except for Brazil, Mexico Chile and Costa Rica (circa 2010).
Source: Based on (OECD, 2019[14]), for methodological details, https://www.oecd.org/fr/investissement/fdi-qualities-indicators.htm.
StatLink https://doi.org/10.1787/888934286331

Limited capacity on the monetary front in most countries: Towards a hawkish policy

The space to stimulate activity during the transition to normality will depend on the policy space before the crisis and how much of that space countries have already used up. Monetary policy responses were uneven in LAC during 2020. Central banks in countries with credible monetary regimes (e.g. independent central banks with inflation targeting regimes) and well-anchored inflation expectations deployed countercyclical policies, cutting nominal interest rates to historical lows and even resorting to quantitative easing, for the first time in these countries' history. These measures were effective in avoiding disruptions in the payment systems and to prevent collapse in domestic credit. Admittedly, the slump in demand depressed prices in most countries, enabling such extraordinary measures while keeping inflation under control.

The recent pickup in inflation related to currency depreciation and energy prices should affect monetary policy but, overall, should not imply a strong change of its stimulative stance. Central banks with inflation-targeting regimes will closely monitor second-round effects that could drift expectations away from targets. Most central banks should be able to support the recovery by keeping interest rates low, as inflation remains under control and easy financial conditions persist. However, central banks will have less margin of manoeuvre because inflation expectations are already slightly above target and they have larger balance sheets (Cavallo and Powell, 2021[16]). In fact, several countries started to move towards a more neutral stance, including Brazil, Mexico, Chile and Peru.

Resource mobilisation to mitigate the crisis and ignite the recovery

Fiscal policy has been an essential instrument to mitigate the impact of the COVID-19 crisis on families and firms and to bolster public healthcare systems (ECLAC, 2021[3]; ECLAC, 2021[17]; ECLAC, 2021[18]). Across the region, a combination of tax relief measures, budget reallocations, additional expenditures and concessional lending have been adopted as a response to the health and socio-economic challenges posed by the pandemic, especially for the most vulnerable. As a result, the region mobilised an unprecedented amount of resources. Amounts varied by country, depending on the impact of the pandemic, their initial fiscal position and their financing opportunities. This mobilisation of fiscal resources, coupled with the decline in economic activity, has put a strain on the region's fiscal position.

Fiscal policy will continue to be at the core of the response to the crisis and will be essential to ensure a strong and inclusive recovery. Going forward, the crisis-mitigation part of the fiscal response will have to become more targeted, focusing on those sectors (e.g. tourism), firms (e.g. SMEs) and vulnerable population groups that continue to face the greatest hurdles, including those due to the impact of school closures in 2020-21. The fiscal response will also have to address the structural vulnerabilities that the pandemic has exposed, with a view to strengthening the basis of the recovery and building forward better.

Fiscal policy can be essential to drive the needed productive transformation that generates quality formal employment, fully leverages the digital transformation and prioritises the environment. This means increasing investment in human and physical capital (including infrastructure), targeting spending to the most vulnerable populations, improving the effectiveness of public spending and the quality of public services and coherently addressing the development and climate objectives. To finance these investments, there needs to be greater resource mobilisation at both the national and international levels in most LAC countries, which in turn implies greater progressivity of the taxation system and better tax administration and debt management. Similarly, further efforts are needed to eliminate the possibility of gender biases historically present in the current schemes. Current taxation systems place additional burdens on households' secondary earners (traditionally women) and discourage their participation in the labour market (ECLAC, 2021[17]). Ensuring fiscal sustainability will be instrumental to the success of these efforts, along with strengthening citizens' trust in government to overcome the institutional trap, which many countries were experiencing even before the COVID-19 crisis (OECD et al., 2019[6]).

Going forward, for fiscal policy to be effective, it must take into account the current complex context through well-defined sequencing of actions. It also needs to be backed by a broad consensus built through national dialogue and clear communication (Chapter 4). The political economy of fiscal policy is more important than ever. Additionally, there is no unique approach or solution to ensuring that fiscal policy translates into a robust, inclusive and sustainable recovery. The context-specific socio-economic characteristics of each country, coupled with the heterogeneous impacts of the crisis, call for a tailored approach. However, some overarching considerations can help LAC countries get their "policy menu" right and achieve a good balance between public spending, tax policy and public debt management.

Tax revenues in times of crisis

The region's tax revenues do little to reduce inequalities and in most LAC countries, they remain insufficient to finance the region's development agenda. Tax revenues remain low, as the average tax-to-GDP ratio in the LAC region was 22.9% in 2019, considerably below the OECD average of 33.8%, and fell on average by around 3% in 2020. There is strong heterogeneity among LAC countries in revenue collection as a percentage of GDP, ranging from Cuba (42.0%) and Barbados and Brazil (both 33.1%) to Paraguay (13.9%), Dominican Republic (13.5%) and Guatemala (13.1%). Furthermore, in contrast to most OECD economies, tax structures in LAC are more dependent on indirect than on direct taxes. Taxes on goods and services – mainly value added tax (VAT) and sales taxes – accounted for 49.8% of total tax revenues, compared to 32.7% in the OECD. In addition, while taxes on corporate income accounted for 15.5% of total tax revenues in LAC in 2018, the personal income tax (PIT) only represented 9.1%. In contrast to LAC, PIT accounts for a larger share of taxes in OECD economies (23.5% of total tax revenues), compared to corporate income taxes (CIT) (10.0% of total tax revenues) (OECD et al., 2021[19]).

The combination of tax reliefs to address the COVID-19 pandemic and severe contraction in economic activity caused a significant decline in public revenues in LAC. Value added tax (VAT) revenues, a principal source of tax revenues for LAC, fell especially strongly in many countries, with year-on-year declines in real terms of 40% in May 2020. This was higher in Antigua and Barbuda, Chile, Costa Rica, Ecuador, Grenada, Honduras and Jamaica. Income tax revenues also registered significant declines in the first half of 2020, principally owing to the extension of tax relief measures as the liquidation of 2019 tax liabilities was deferred and advance tax payments were suspended. In some cases, forgone revenues were more than 1% of GDP. In Chile, it is estimated that revenues fell by 1.4% of GDP (DIPRES, 2020[20]), similar to Peru (1.5% of GDP) (MEF, 2020[21]). The effectiveness of tax relief was hampered, however, by the region's outsized informal sector and the limited participation of individuals and small and medium-sized enterprises (SMEs) in the tax and social security systems (OECD et al., 2021[19]).

Tax measures were mainly aimed at strengthening health systems and supporting households, self-employed workers and firms. The region's underdeveloped health systems quickly became overwhelmed by the COVID-19 pandemic (OECD/The World Bank, 2020[22]), and governments enacted measures to support them, primarily by aiming to reduce the cost of importing crucial medical goods. Because of the region's dependence on external suppliers, many countries applied temporary exemptions or zero ratings to medical supplies to respond to equipment shortages (e.g. of alcohol, laboratory items, gloves, disinfectant, equipment and other health supplies). In some cases, these measures were accompanied by the exemption of medical goods from VAT, for instance in Colombia, or by temporary deductions for PIT to incentivise direct donations to health systems.

Governments implemented tax reliefs to compensate for the decrease in income of households and among the self-employed. The most common of these tax measures were deferrals, suspensions of advanced payments and the creation of favourable tax payment facilities of the VAT and PIT, such as instalment plans with no interest or penalties. Several countries, including Chile, Colombia, Peru and Trinidad and Tobago, also implemented accelerated PIT refunds to provide further support. In some countries, including Argentina, Colombia, Costa Rica, Dominica, Guyana, Honduras and Saint Vincent and the Grenadines, households were also supported by VAT exemptions on essential medical supplies, products from the basic basket of consumption goods, and services such as electricity. In Colombia, a VAT refund scheme targeting 1 million families living in poverty was implemented, extending five payments of COP 75 000 (Colombian peso) during the year (OECD et al., 2021[19]).

Similarly, tax relief for firms mainly consisted of temporary measures to bolster cash flow, especially in the early months of the crisis, through deferrals and suspension of advance payments of VAT and CIT. VAT relief in particular played an important role in the region, especially for micro, small and medium-sized companies (MSMEs). In several cases, tax relief was targeted at MSMEs or sectors particularly affected by the crisis, such as construction, tourism and personal services. Countries also extended relief to firms by modifications to social contribution schemes, such as the *Programa de Asistencia de Emergencia al Trabajo y la Producción* in Argentina, which introduced a reduction of up to 95% of employer contributions to the Integrated Social Security System. In Brazil, payments to the Unemployment Insurance Fund were suspended, and contributions to the *Sistema S* system, which finances technical and vocational education, were reduced by 50% (OECD et al., 2021[19]).

Looking forward, a set of tax policy options could increase revenues without compromising the economic recovery or well-being of citizens, but the sequencing of these policies, backed by a national consensus, will define its success (Mora, Nieto-Parra and Orozco, 2021[23]). These include measures to reduce tax evasion and avoidance which cost Latin America around 6.1% of GDP in revenue, mainly in PIT, CIT and VAT receipts (ECLAC, 2021[17]). Other options include policies to increase tax compliance, strengthen tax administration and eliminate tax expenditure that brings low benefits in terms of equity or job creation (overall tax expenditures averaged 3.7% of GDP in Latin America from 2015 to 2019) (OECD et al., 2021[19]). Coupled with international measures to avoid tax base erosion and profit shifting by multinational enterprises (e.g. through the implementation of the OECD/G20 Base Erosion and Profit Shifting project), these measures have an additional benefit: they improve fiscal morale and therefore the credibility of institutions. The digital economy, and tackling the challenges it brings, is another key international tax challenge for the region (OECD et al., 2020[24]; Mora, Nieto-Parra and Orozco, 2021[23]).

Countries may need to consider additional ways of raising revenues to address structural shortfalls (OECD et al., 2021[19]; Mora, Nieto-Parra and Orozco, 2021[23]). The timing, speed and shape of these policies should be adapted to each country and closely linked to citizen consensus. While in OECD economies taxes and transfers contribute to the reduction of the Gini coefficient by approximately 16 percentage points, the comparable reduction in LAC is below 3 percentage points, on average (OECD, 2020[25]; OECD et al., 2019[6]). However, in most countries, once the recovery is underway, actions to broaden the PIT base, and specific actions among top deciles should be considered. PIT is the principal factor behind the tax gap between LAC and the OECD, limiting not only potential revenues but also the redistributive power of the tax system (OECD et al., 2021[19]). Further action on specific taxes, including taxation of immovable property (Izquierdo and Pessino, 2021[26]) and of individuals' capital gains, should contribute to increasing revenues to finance the recovery and improve the progressivity of the taxation system. Other measures include wealth and inheritance taxes (OECD, 2021[27]), where their effective implementation requires improving the capacity of tax and statistics administrations (Mora, Nieto-Parra and Orozco, 2021[23]). The international tax reform, backed by 130 countries (23 LAC countries), will provide needed revenues. The reform will ensure a fairer distribution of profits and taxing rights among countries with respect to the largest multinational enterprises, including digital companies, and put a floor on competition over CIT through the introduction of a global minimum corporate tax rate, which countries can use to protect their tax bases (minimum rate of at least 15%) (OECD, 2021[28]).

As the recovery advances, there are tax policies the region has not fully explored. These include corrective taxes, such as environmental taxes. In LAC, on average, revenues from environment-related taxes amounted to 1.2% of GDP in 2019 (mainly energy taxes, most commonly from diesel and petrol), a lower level than the OECD average of 2.1% of GDP (OECD et al., 2021[19]). Public health-related taxes, such as on consumption of tobacco, alcohol, sugar and beverages, can play a key role in shaping incentives for economic actors to promote healthier diets, ultimately generating better health outcomes and reducing health-related costs. Measures to improve VAT efficiency by reducing the number and scope of exemptions and compensating the most vulnerable populations could be envisaged (OECD et al., 2021[19]). The COVID-19 crisis presents an opportunity to rethink traditional taxation policy in LAC, focusing on long-standing gender biases in taxation schemes. For instance, tax systems generally do not account for how women take on a larger share of unpaid work, making the tax burden disproportionate at the household level. Tax reliefs for male-dominated economic sectors is another example of gender bias in fiscal policy (ECLAC, 2021[17]).

Public spending should be countercyclical and with a long-term view enabled by capital expenditure

Public spending in the LAC region before the pandemic showed modest growth, with social spending and debt services on the rise. Public expenditure increased from 20.1% of GDP in 2010 to 21.5% of GDP in 2019. Overall, increases in public spending had been small, as many countries adopted fiscal consolidation policies to control a rise in public debt and there is low flexibility (OECD, 2020[29]). The main changes occurred in the composition of expenditure and were mainly driven by the increase in debt services that followed the rise of public debt and in current expenditure, which reflects the growth in social expenditure. To offset the increases in debt services and current spending, capital expenditure fell, increasing the investment gap between LAC and other economies (ECLAC, 2021[17]) and hampering productivity growth.

As a response to the COVID-19 pandemic, global current public spending increased significantly in 2020 to support public health systems, families and firms. In 2020, total central government spending in Latin America reached 24.7% of GDP, its highest level since the 1980s in the midst of the debt crisis. However, there remain significant differences across regions regarding the capacity to react to the crisis as the LAC region has, on average, adopted smaller-scale measures, compared to emerging Asia or advanced economies (IMF, 2020[30]). This can be in partly explained by weak automatic stabilisers and a large vulnerable populations with no safety nets or social protection systems to fall back on once the crisis hit. There is strong heterogeneity across LAC countries: while Argentina, Brazil, Dominican Republic and El Salvador saw their central government primary expenditure rise by more than 20% in the first nine months of 2020, Costa Rica, Ecuador, Honduras and Mexico continued their fiscal consolidation and reduced public spending. The heterogeneity of responses to the crisis encompasses countries' policy choices, impact of the COVID-19 pandemic, previous fiscal stance, capacity to tap domestic and global financial markets, multilateral lending institutions and capacity of central banks. The majority of the increases in public expenditure (70%) were focused on current transfers as relief measures and social benefits.

Expenditure measures were particularly important and focused on health systems, households and small enterprises. To support the health system, many countries reallocated or increased expenditure to buy medical supplies, hire additional personnel or expand infrastructure. Measures to support household income included the design of new programmes – or the strengthening of existing programmes – of transfers targeted to unemployed informal workers and vulnerable social groups (OECD, 2020[31]). Examples of newly created transfers include *Ingreso Familiar de Emergencia* in Argentina, *Auxílio Emergencial* in Brazil, *Ingreso Familiar de Emergencia* in Chile, *Ingreso Solidario* in Colombia, *Bono Proteger* in Costa Rica (OECD, 2020[29]), *Subsidio Pytyvõ* in Paraguay and *Bono Familiar Universal* and *Bono Independiente* in Peru (OECD, 2020[25]). Transfers were also directed to formal-sector workers, as with the *Programa de Asistencia de Emergencia al Trabajo y la Producción* in Argentina (Chapter 2). Countries also expanded or complemented social protection systems by expanding unemployment insurance (e.g. in Brazil, Chile, Ecuador, Mexico and Uruguay) and social security benefits, such as pensions (e.g. in Argentina, Colombia, Guatemala, Mexico and Paraguay). To support low-income households directly, in-kind support in the form of food packages and subsidies to cover the cost of basic household services (electricity, gas and water) were included.

In LAC, public spending was also directed to preserve productive capacity, with a special focus on MSMEs. The measures, subsidies and financing were mainly aimed to preserve employment and ensure that companies had sufficient liquidity, given the frequency of demand and supply shocks. Chile, Colombia, Peru and Uruguay adopted payroll subsidy programmes to protect employment. For example, Colombia established the *Programa de Apoyo al Empleo Formal* to provide a monthly subsidy, equivalent to 40% of the minimum wage, to assist with payroll costs for firms that could prove they suffered a 20% decline in revenues between February and March 2020. In Guatemala, Mexico and Panama, business subsidies were established to offset operation expenses related to the purchase of supplies needed in the agricultural sector. Some countries also used below-the-lines measures, such as the provision of special lines of credit and the capitalisation of state-owned financial institutions, to ensure that firms had access to necessary liquidity. For instance, Brazil expanded the Brazilian Development Bank's (the BNDES's) financing programmes. Chile made a large capital injection into the *Fondo de Garantía de Pequeños Empresarios*. In Colombia, Bancoldex launched new credit lines. The *Reactívate Ecuador* programme provided credit to MSMEs at a preferential rate. Peru established a new programme as part of the *Reactiva Perú*, where treasury-guaranteed credits were supported by a contribution by the central bank. Some countries, for instance Argentina and Peru, implemented productivity support programmes by financing R&D projects, promoting digitisation and entrepreneurship.

To avoid putting lives at risk and to ensure a strong and inclusive recovery, public expenditure must be implemented efficiently through a well-defined sequencing of actions (Mora, Nieto-Parra and Orozco, 2021[23]). As resources are scarce, the region must seek to reallocate expenditure from inefficient to efficient uses, for instance addressing leakages in social transfers or fraud, corruption and waste in government procurement (Cavallo and Powell, 2021[16]; OECD, 2020[32]) or increasing the share of government spending subject to public procurement (OECD, 2020[29]). In the short term, and as long as the pandemic continues to put lives at risk, the priority should continue to be to protect people, support the most vulnerable families and save firms and jobs. Vaccination is key to secure an exit from the pandemic and reduce the uncertainty of stop-and-go confinement measures. Additionally, countries should continue to support social assistance, aiming to design mechanisms that promote long-term economic effects. For instance, there is evidence that targeted cash transfers, especially conditional, can spur investment in child schooling (OECD, 2019[33]). Similarly, public spending should continue to support human and productive capacity development and protect viable MSMEs. It remains crucial to be aware of the gender-differentiated impacts of the crisis, as well as the lack of gender neutrality of traditional fiscal policy. Identifying and eliminating present biases that hamper non-discrimination and tackling the root causes of gender discrimination would support a more inclusive recovery (ECLAC, 2021[17]).

Once the pandemic begins to be under control, the focus of public spending should gradually shift. Public spending should gradually be reallocated from general to targeted support – with a focus on the sectors that need it the most – and from current to capital expenditure (Mora, Nieto-Parra and Orozco, 2021[23]). Traditionally, 80% of public spending in LAC is concentrated in current expenditure, and just 20% in capital expenditure (OECD et al., 2019[6]). As a result, the region lags behind other regions in terms of gross capital formation. Before entering the COVID-19 crisis, the gap was 4 percentage points of GDP vis-à-vis advanced economies and more than 21 percentage points of GDP against emerging and developing Asian countries (IMF, 2021[10]). More and better capital expenditure is fundamental to a robust recovery and to drive the infrastructure investments (including in digital and green technologies) needed to promote quality jobs and a production transformation that has the environment at its centre. Furthermore, especially concerning infrastructure, capital expenditure has a high multiplier effect (as high as two) in both economic activity and employment (Izquierdo and Pessino, 2021[26]). Last, LAC must gradually return to fiscal frameworks, including fiscal rules to safeguard investment; ensure clarity, efficiency and equity of expenditure; and add adequate escape clauses for exceptional events (Mora, Nieto-Parra and Orozco, 2021[23]).

Debt management and increasing available resources without compromising tomorrow: The role of international co-operation

The COVID-19 crisis has adversely affected the already vulnerable fiscal position of LAC countries. In 2020, the average overall deficit in Latin America reached almost -7% of GDP (ECLAC, 2021[17]). This is considerably higher than the 2019 average deficit of -4% of GDP or the 2009 average fiscal deficit of -3.6% of GDP that resulted from the global financial crisis. The historically high fiscal deficits in the region are mainly linked with the fall in tax revenues due to lower economic activity and the tax measures to confront the pandemic, combined with the implementation of expenditure packages, including current transfers to support families and firms. This fiscal strain arrived at a time when LAC economies were already undergoing fiscal adjustments, and growth was anaemic at best (OECD, 2020[25]; IMF, 2020[30]).

Deep fiscal deficits have resulted in a strong increase in public debt and debt service, accentuating an already existing trend. In 2020, central government gross public debt averaged 56.3% of GDP, an increase of 10.7 percentage points over 2019 (ECLAC, 2021[17]). The public debt-to-tax ratios, a proxy indicator of countries' financial capacity to pay for the public debt, also increased in most countries, leaving them in a weaker position to face the COVID-19 crisis than they were in 2007, before the 2008 financial crisis (Figure 1.6). The debt-to-tax ratio is expected to increase considerably in 2021, given the fall in tax revenues and the increase in public debt, leaving the region in an even weaker position to face future shocks (ECLAC, 2021[17]).

Figure 1.6. **Gross public debt-to-tax ratio in selected Latin American countries**

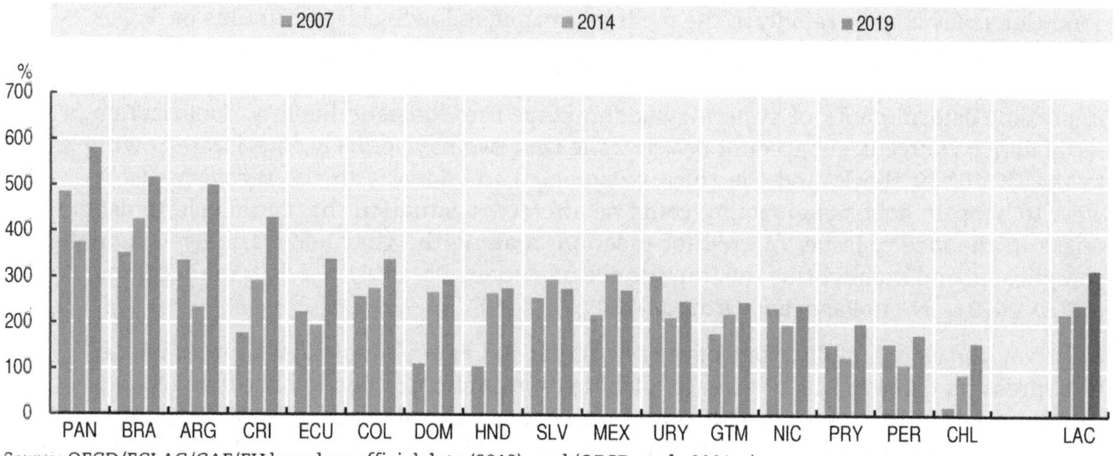

Source: OECD/ECLAC/CAF/EU based on official data (2019); and (OECD et al., 2021[19]).
StatLink ᵉᵐˢᴾ https://doi.org/10.1787/888934286350

Strong debt increases in 2020 illustrate how, despite the global crisis, financing opportunities have remained available for the region. Sovereign debt issuance in international markets rose by 45% in the first ten months of 2020, as some countries were able to tap international markets, often on favourable terms, to cover their increased financing needs and, in some cases, pre-finance their 2021 budgets. Most of the debt issuance came from the public sector (ECLAC, 2020[34]). This has been possible as emerging markets have benefited from the monetary policy responses and the subsequent liquidity expansion carried out by major central banks in developed countries. In particular, financing costs have substantially fallen in Colombia and Mexico, with yields on ten-year benchmark bonds dropping by 1.55 and 1.16 percentage points respectively, between December 2019 and December 2020. Those were larger decreases than those experienced in OECD countries (OECD, 2021[5]). In a context of ample liquidity and low global interest rates, LAC central banks have been able to lower their policy rates as an alternative response to fiscal policy to sustain aggregate demand. Additionally, thanks to the global liquidity expansion, financing costs remained low in many LAC countries. Emergency financing from international financial institutions (IFIs) was also significant, especially for countries with little to no access to international financial markets. IFIs extended USD 47.8 billion in new credit, while also redirecting existing credit lines (ECLAC, 2021[1]).

While the increase in debt issuance in 2020 is common to most LAC countries able to finance their expenditure through the issuance of bonds, differences persist in their relative capacity and conditions to secure financing. Interestingly, given the persistent liquidity in global financial markets and investors' increased appetite for risk, LAC countries have also been able to make greater use of their own currencies and markets to issue bonds. In particular, LAC countries that issue bonds mostly in domestic currency have been able to use local markets for their debt issuance (e.g. Brazil, Chile, Colombia, Costa Rica, Mexico and Uruguay). This greatly reduces the risk of debt sustainability crises and enables the possibility of raising more resources as the policy options to resolve domestic debt issues are more varied than those that deal with external debt (Kose et al., 2021[35]). Other countries issue debt mostly in foreign currency and in foreign markets (e.g. Panama, Paraguay and Peru) (Figure 1.7). These heterogeneities in debt issuance mechanisms will prove important in determining potential future risks, especially as countries' needs for resources to finance the recovery increase.

In the medium term, debt ratios in LAC should stabilise, but at higher levels than before the crisis. With abundant liquidity, international capital markets seem more willing to admit larger debt ratios at this point, and there is still access to capital flows. However, conditions may change rapidly in the medium term if, following large stimulus packages, monetary policy normalises in advanced economies. Additionally, in this uncertain context, risks of a sudden stop – an abrupt reduction of net capital inflows – remain. Important determinants of systemic sudden stops are domestic liability dollarisation, fiscal deficits and current account deficits. The first two have gravely deteriorated owing to the COVID-19 shock, and the third is expected to widen with the recovery. If this were to happen, debt sustainability could be affected, a situation that could lead to debt crises in the face of issuer or creditor inaction, making the global scenario even more complicated and highlighting the importance of globally co-ordinated debt management (OECD, 2020[25]; Nieto-Parra and Orozco, 2020[35]).

Given the global implications of the pandemic and as the financial resources needed to address its consequences increase, global co-ordination of public debt management should be a priority to avoid or address possible debt sustainability issues (OECD, 2020[25]). The compounded nature of the COVID-19 shock can raise the risk of public debt and currency crises, which threatens plans to respond to the crisis and to build back better. The recovery will depend on continued policy support; therefore, this might be the time for the international community to innovate regarding foreign debt instruments (Breuer and Cohen, 2020[36]), especially given the investments needed to pursue the Sustainable Development Goals (SDGs) and the 2030 Agenda (UNCTAD, 2020[37]).

Figure 1.7. **Annual government debt issuance in selected LAC countries by currency and by country of issue**

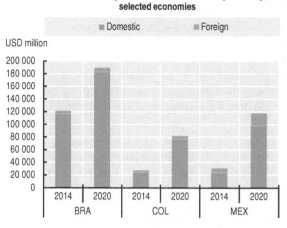

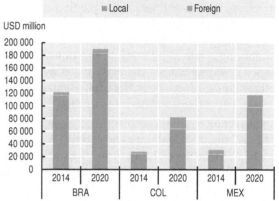

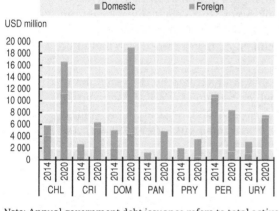

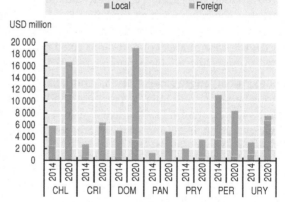

Note: Annual government debt issuance refers to total active government bond issuances including re-openings.
Source: OECD/ECLAC/CAF/EU based on Refinitiv.
StatLink 🔗 https://doi.org/10.1787/888934286369

There is no unique solution to ensure the necessary funds to fuel the recovery or to ensure against possible debt sustainability issues in LAC, but in many cases the economic recovery will require supportive international co-ordination, enabling debtor countries' continued ability to conduct countercyclical macroeconomic policies to respond to the crisis (UNCTAD, 2020[4]). Possible solutions to financing challenges will depend on countries' initial characteristics and their access to markets; however, these solutions must target restoring the region's capacity to service debt through investment, output and export growth rather than through expenditure, income and import contraction (UNCTAD, 2020[4]). Historical examples provide lessons for facing today's public finance challenges, for instance the outcome of the long 1980 debt crisis resolution process in the region (Box 1.2).

Box 1.2. **Waves of debt crises: A historical perspective**

The history of world economic crises confirms that economic recovery is never uniform. A historical case of unequal recovery from an economic downturn is the one observed during the 1980s. For Latin America, this decade exhibited sluggish economic growth, higher inequality and rising poverty (Székely and Montes, 2006[48]). It followed a period of upsurge in economic growth that had lasted at least a couple of decades. During the late 1970s, governments in poor countries had increased their level of public indebtedness. This debt stemmed mainly from loans granted by Western commercial banks, with interest rates that varied according to the interbank rates in the main creditor countries. In 1979, the Federal Reserve increased its interest rate to face mounting levels of inflation in the United States. A declining rate of economic growth in developed countries during the early 1980s was then accompanied by a fall in the prices of oil and other commodities, triggering a fall in export revenues in developing countries and a general rise in the cost of governments' debt service.

For some scholars, the severe economic and social costs that followed could have been averted if management of the crisis had been different (Diaz-Alejandro, Krugman and Sachs, 1984[49]). Several governments in developing countries restructured debts and adhered to adjustment programmes, while banks granted new loans through additional, albeit involuntary, lending to support the adjustment efforts (Devlin, 1989[50]). These short-term solutions, framed to face a liquidity rather than a solvency crisis, were followed by successive rounds of restructuring between 1984 and 1986 (Vasquez, 1996[51]). After 1985, as economic growth continued to struggle owing to deteriorating terms of trade and a decline in public expenditure, rescheduling and renewed financing began to be formally linked to economic growth in borrowing countries as part of what became known as the Baker Plan. Accordingly, access to a new loan package from banks and from multilateral and bilateral lenders was made contingent on the evolution of oil prices (in the case of Mexico) and a pre-fixed targeted economic growth rate, which had to be attained through liberalising economic reforms.

The outcome of lengthy negotiations and lack of debt relief is illustrated by the evolution of the ratios between total interest payments and exports, which remained relatively high during the first years of the crisis. The average for Latin America was 41% in 1982 and only slightly declined to 35% in 1985. A certain amount of debt relief was granted only after 1989 with the implementation of the Brady Plan.

The Brady Plan sought to reduce commercial bank debt while providing banks with the possibility of increasing or reducing their exposure to each debtor. This "menu" approach included the exchange of loans with newly issued bonds, with a change of face value, according to new capital provision and risk taking. One option included the conversion of loans to bonds securitised by US Treasury Bonds and financed by Mexico's own reserves and by loans from international financial organisations. Successive Brady deals differed in terms of debt reduction and new money provisions and were adopted by 18 countries. According to (Cline, 1995[52]), the typical deal led to 30% to 35% forgiveness of a country's debt.

There is strong disagreement among scholars regarding the benefits of the Brady Plan and whether the debt relief granted was sufficient to guarantee a healthy growth process and to raise the creditworthiness of each country. For (Rogoff, 1993[53]), plans such as the Brady Plan were more beneficial to the banks, as they raised the value of the remaining debt in their portfolios. While the Brady plan effectively reduced the indebtedness ratio for all countries, it increased thereafter. According to (Cline, 1995[52]), economic performance in the post-Brady years was better in terms of price stability, economic growth and lower interest rates. In fact, the plan allowed firms and governments to return to the market, most of the time under favourable terms (Buckley, 1998[54]).

For countries with little to no access to capital markets, it remains important that official support be directed towards them. So far, and to ease financial pressures, the G20 has supported low-income countries by suspending their debt service payments on bilateral government loans until December 2021. The International Monetary Fund (IMF) has also provided financial assistance and debt service relief for numerous countries thanks to, for instance, increases in rapid credit facilities, rapid financing instruments and flexible credit lines across income levels. These welcome measures have offered a temporary respite for more than 100 countries during the pandemic.

However, much-needed support for middle-income countries (MICs), many of which belong to the LAC region, remains largely missing in the international agenda. Even though MICs will benefit from the recent Special Drawing Rights (SDR) issuance agreement, that so a historic allocation equivalent to USD 650 billion (about SDR 456 billion), from which which SDR 193 billion (about USD 275 billion) will go to emerging markets and developing countries. Access to further multilateral financing is important for MICs, as the risk of decline in international private financing remains (Ocampo, 2021[38]). Among ideas proposed in this framework is to offer extraordinary liquidity to developing countries through the creation of liquidity funds. One example is the proposed Fund to Alleviate COVID-19 Economics, which would be capitalised with funds from developed countries channelled through multilateral institutions (ECLAC, 2021[17]).

For countries that might have access to capital markets but still face high debt costs due to potential downgrades in credit ratings or low future growth expectations, there are several policy options, including debt standstill/moratorium, debt relief, lengthening of maturities to limit short-term refinancing risk (OECD, 2021[5]), creation of a special vehicle to finance the crisis or pay the debt, and greater use of SDRs. In particular, either a new issue of SDRs or a reallocation of existing SDRs could be a vehicle to increase liquidity in an efficient manner, both in LAC and in developing economies, without increasing debt (ECLAC, 2021[17]). However, a long-term view – beyond the COVID-19 crisis – is important. SDRs remain underutilised as international community instruments, which calls for a discussion on their fundamental frameworks and traditional allocation (Ocampo, 2021[38]). The former require international co-operation, involving multilateral banks, developed countries or private creditors (OECD et al., 2020[24]; Nieto-Parra and Orozco, 2020[35]; Bolton et al., 2020[39]). So far, private creditors have remained uninvolved, and some countries have decided not to participate in international programmes to avoid possible downgrades in their credit ratings (OECD, 2021[8]).

Last, countries that already enjoyed ample fiscal sustainability must retain access to capital markets with low-risk premiums that allow them to raise funds needed to respond to the crisis. For countries in the region to reinforce their debt management capacities, accurate debt transparency, as well as technical assistance, should also be pursued at the international level (OECD, 2021[8]; Subacchi, 2020[40]).

Regarding debt restructuring mechanisms, strong co-ordination with bondholders and capital market stakeholders is crucial to minimise reputational risk (i.e. future access to capital markets). Recent debt restructuring experiences in Argentina and Ecuador show the importance of including Collective Action Clauses in sovereign bond contracts (OECD et al., 2020[24]). Even though the use of existing mechanisms is welcome, going forward, it is important to rethink international sovereign debt restructuring procedures to go beyond Collective Action Clauses (Ocampo, 2021[38]).

To facilitate a strong and inclusive recovery, LAC economies can use innovative policy options with social or environmental scope to meet their financing needs. For instance, debt-to-COVID, debt-to-SDG, debt for climate or debt for nature swaps could be implemented. Debtor governments and lenders, including private creditors, would benefit as debtor countries channel planned debt service payments into national COVID-19 mitigation measures, SDGs or climate- or nature-related investments (UN/DESA, 2020[41]; Steele and Patel, 2020[42]). Likewise, the implementation of social and environmental sustainability-linked "green" bonds would tie sustainable foreign financing with SDG commitments. This would allow countries to raise much-needed financial resources to deal with the COVID-19 crisis while also committing to the achievement of the SDGs (Caputo Silva and Stewart, 2021[43]). Mexico recently became the first country in LAC to issue a bond linked to the fulfilment of the SDGs: EUR 750 million at an interest rate of 1.35% (ECLAC, 2021[17]).

Countries vulnerable to climate change (as are most LAC countries) are associated with unfavourable credit ratings and are deemed by lenders to have a higher debt default probability than countries that are more resilient to climate change. In a time when the region must pursue a sustainable recovery from the COVID-19 crisis, LAC countries with limited fiscal space may benefit from alternative policy instruments that deploy resources to fight climate change while reducing debt burdens, debt costs and pressure on fiscal balances (Cevik and Tovar Jalles, 2021[44]). Last, future debt instruments that include "insurance-like" clauses while rearranging payouts to creditors conditioned on the debtor country's economic performance would provide some relief (Breuer and Cohen, 2020[36]; OECD, et al.[24]). Namely, in the Caribbean, where countries are highly exposed to natural disaster risks, hurricane clauses should become the norm in order to improve debt repayment capacity. In Grenada, the implementation of such clauses has reduced debt levels (ECLAC, 2021[17]).

In the case of economies such as those of the Caribbean, the recurrent exposure to natural hazards and their devastating social and economic effects can worsen the financial situation and lead to debt distress. Hurricane clauses enable the deferral of principal and interest payments or the possibility of fast-tracking debt restructuring operations in the event of a hurricane (or other insured natural disaster).

LAC economies must gradually return to their fiscal frameworks and undertake the necessary steps to ensure clarity and efficiency of expenditure. Fiscal rules, a key component of fiscal frameworks, are essential to reduce or reverse a LAC characteristic of procyclical behaviour of fiscal policy (Vegh and Vuletin, 2014[45]; Alberola et al., 2016[46]) and to protect public investment. As an exceptional measure, many countries in the region suspended their rules in order to undertake strong fiscal expansions. As the pandemic recedes and countries reduce public spending, and to avoid a long-term impact in future fiscal consolidations, returning to their fiscal frameworks or implementing fiscal rules can be a useful tool to protect public investment, boost investor confidence and thus add a growth-enhancing dimension (Ardanaz et al., 2021[47]). These fiscal rules must be clear and transparent and ensure escape clauses for exceptional measures.

Social effects of the COVID-19 crisis. Protecting businesses, jobs and livelihoods in LAC

Income losses translated into worsening living conditions, as well as substantial increases in unemployment, poverty and inequality (ECLAC, 2021[18]). The dramatic drop in income in the LAC region concentrates among the most vulnerable sectors. The informal economy, for example, is the primary source of job losses across all LAC economies. Households dependent on informal income or on sectors with lower labour income were unprotected from losses due to confinements, restrictions and other interventions.

The crisis triggered the closure of thousands of businesses, destroying millions of jobs, especially in the informal sector

Latin American labour markets have traditionally been informal, fragile and exclusive. More than half of LAC workers hold informal jobs (OECD, 2020[25]). "Informal households" – those depending on the informal economy for their earnings – are the most affected by the COVID-19 crisis, facing loss of employment and labour income. On average, almost half (45%) of the LAC population live in households that depend solely on informal employment, 22% live in mixed households and 33% live in completely formal households (OECD, forthcoming[56]). Still, according to the OECD Development Centre Key Indicators of Informality Based on Individuals and their Households (KIIBIH), informality levels in LAC countries exhibit wide heterogeneity, from less than 20% in Chile and Uruguay to more than 60% in Bolivia, Honduras and Nicaragua (Figure 1.8).

Figure 1.8. **More than half of Latin Americans live in completely informal or mixed households**

Distribution of overall population by degree of informality of households (%), 2018 or latest available year

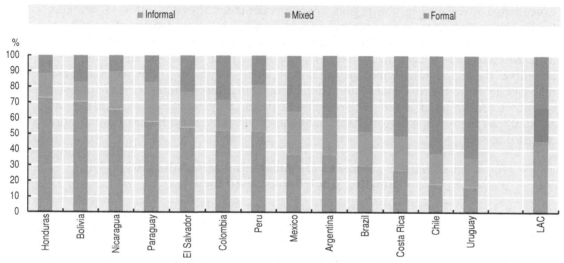

Note: Using the classification by the (OECD/ILO, 2019[56]) individuals are assigned to one of three categories according to the degree of informality of their household. Formal households: all working members are formally employed. Informal households: all working members have informal employment. Mixed households: some working members of the household have formal jobs and others have informal jobs.

Source: (OECD, forthcoming[56]), *Labour Informality and Households' Vulnerabilities in Latin America* (provisional title).

StatLink ▤▤ https://doi.org/10.1787/888934286388

Programmes targeted to those most affected need to consider the overall household dimension. The well-being of individuals living in households that are completely in the informal economy differs, sometimes significantly, from those in "mixed-status" or entirely in the formal economy. There is segmentation at the household level and it highlights the relevance of distinguishing "informal households that depend entirely on the informal sector" and "mixed" households with a mix of formal and informal revenues, when designing policy interventions. Both informal and mixed households represent an important share of the population.

A household perspective on informality is needed to capture the level of income poverty and income insecurity among informal workers, measure the capacity to pay for social protection, identify the possibility of accessing social protection through household members working in the formal economy, and assess the extent to which informal workers' vulnerability is passed on to their dependants (OECD, forthcoming[56]).

Owing to the lack of social protection or better labour conditions, informal workers are trapped in a vicious cycle, which keeps them vulnerable. In countries such as Bolivia, Ecuador, Paraguay and Peru, the differences between informal and formal workers living in poverty or vulnerability are significant. Informal workers not only have less or inadequate access to social protection, but their income instability prevents them from investing in human capital and moving into higher productivity jobs (OECD et al., 2019[6]).

The pandemic and its consequences led to significant setbacks in several labour indicators, including employment contraction (ECLAC, 2021[3]). The most affected were women and young people who, in addition to being highly affected by job losses, had to dedicate intensive time to unpaid care work given the limited functioning of education facilities and care services for dependent populations (Figure 1.9). In addition, the most vulnerable populations in the region, such as Afrodescendants, indigenous peoples, migrants and people with lower education levels, often work in the informal sector, which came to an almost complete halt during the confinements.

Pre-existing structural challenges, such as the digital divide and unequal access to finance, also affect informality levels and increase inequality. The digital divide has exacerbated inequality in the region, disproportionately affecting informal workers. Inequality arising from the pandemic is first and foremost evident in the ability to work from home, which is correlated with level of income. Lack of digital skills and infrastructure impede informal workers from working from home and from the overall benefits of the digital transformation (OECD et al., 2020[24]). Similarly, informal households may lack access to the financial system, impeding them from obtaining a loan to invest or to smooth consumption. In fact, lack of access to financial system services (loan, banking account) can hold back growth for informal enterprises and could hinder formalisation (OECD/ILO, 2019[56]).

Figure 1.9. **COVID-19 job losses are substantial across the LAC region, affecting women more than men**

Change in the employed population, by sex, Q2 2019-Q2 2020 (%)

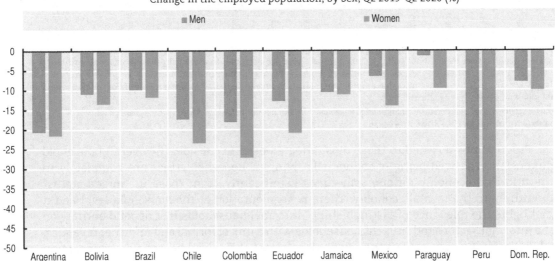

Note: Data for Argentina include only 31 urban agglomerations. Data for Bolivia include only urban areas. Data for Ecuador are for June 2019 to May/June 2020. Data for Jamaica are for July 2020. Data for Mexico are for May 2020.

Source: (ECLAC, 2021[18]), *Social Panorama of Latin America 2020*, www.cepal.org/es/publicaciones/46687-panorama-social-america-latina-2020.

StatLink https://doi.org/10.1787/888934286407

Millions of vulnerable Latin Americans have fallen into poverty and extreme poverty, while inequality gaps continue to widen in the region

The COVID-19 crisis has shattered some of the last decade's progress in eradicating poverty and inequality. Over the past few decades, governments in LAC have considerably reduced poverty, lifting around 42 million people out of poverty between 2004 and 2019. Before the crisis, around 30.5% of the total LAC population were living in poverty (187 million people), and 11.3% were living in extreme poverty (70 million people). As a result of the COVID-19 crisis, the extreme poverty rate in 2020 reached 12.5% and the poverty rate 33.7%. These poverty levels have not been seen for the past 12 years – 20 years in the case of extreme poverty (ECLAC, 2021[18]).

The crisis affected vulnerable groups, reducing jobs and income. The job and consequent income losses resulting from the COVID-19 pandemic have led to increases in poverty, a reduction of the middle class and an increase in inequality. Those most affected by job losses were in the first quintile, as the proportion of those workers who stopped earning labour income (based on 2019 incomes) increased by 5.7 percentage points, a value that decreases considerably in subsequent quintiles. In the richest quintile, the increase is 0.7 percentage points. Similarly, for those who retained their jobs, loss of income represents an estimated 15% contraction in the average labour income. For workers in the first quintile, for 2019, the estimated reduction is 42%, while for those in the fifth quintile, it is about 7% (ECLAC, 2021[18]).

Negative job and income dynamics have reduced the middle class and threaten to deepen existing social and economic gaps in an already highly unequal region. The number of people living on low incomes (vulnerable, poor and extremely poor) has grown dramatically, with 32 million more people than before the crisis. By contrast, people earning lower-middle income decreased by 7 million people, those with mid-middle income by 13 million (13.1%), those with upper-middle income by 4 million (14.2%), and those with high income by 2 million (10.5%) (Figure 1.10).

To sum up, informal households are the most affected by the COVID-19 crisis, facing employment losses and labour income drops. The pandemic effects led to significant setbacks in several labour indicators, including employment contraction. The most affected groups are women and the region's most vulnerable populations, such as Afrodescendants, indigenous peoples, migrants and people with lower education levels. Structural challenges, such as the digital divide and unequal access to the financial market also affect inclusion in the labour markets.

Figure 1.10. The COVID-19 crisis has increased the number of people living on low incomes and shrunk the middle and upper classes

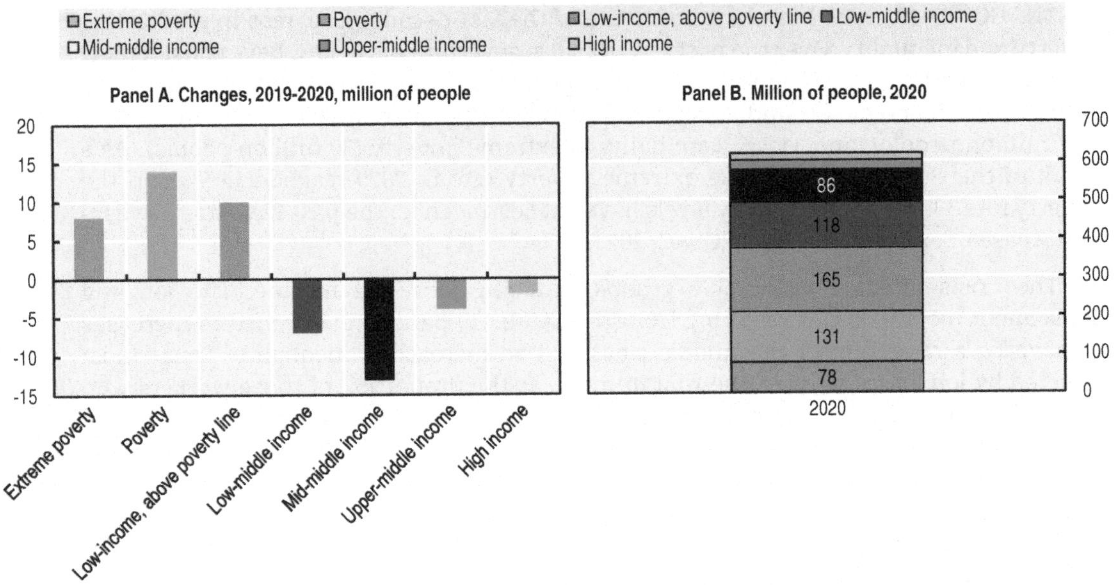

☐ Extreme poverty   ☐ Poverty   ☐ Low-income, above poverty line   ■ Low-middle income
☐ Mid-middle income   ☐ Upper-middle income   ☐ High income

Panel A. Changes, 2019-2020, million of people

Panel B. Million of people, 2020

Note: Includes Argentina, Bolivia, Brazil, Chile, Colombia, Costa Rica, Dominican Republic, Ecuador, El Salvador, Guatemala, Honduras, Mexico, Nicaragua, Panama, Paraguay, Peru, Uruguay and Venezuela. Data refer to the definition of income strata, as specified by the United Nations Economic Commission for Latin America and the Caribbean (ECLAC, 2021), Social Panorama of Latin America 2020 and (ECLAC, 2019), Social Panorama of Latin America 2019. The extreme poverty line represents the level of income that enables each household to meet the basic needs of all its members. The basic basket for measuring poverty is formed from a selection of food items, including the goods required to meet the nutritional needs, taking into account food prices in each country and geographical area. The amount required by households to satisfy basic non-food needs is then added to define the poverty line. Low-income non-poor are those households with per capita income of up to 1.8 times the poverty line; the low-middle stratum, the mid-middle stratum, the upper-middle stratum are defined as having, respectively, a per capita income of up to 3, 6 and 10 times the poverty line. The high-income stratum is defined as above 10 times the poverty line.

Source: Economic Commission for Latin America and the Caribbean based on *Banco de Datos de Encuestas de Hogares* (BADEHOG). Figures adjusted to United Nations population projections, *World Population Prospects 2019*, https://population. un.org/wpp/ and estimates of poverty trends for countries whose measurements are not available for the years indicated.

StatLink ▨▨ *https://doi.org/10.1787/888934286426*

Weak social protection mechanisms in the region failed to prevent the deep social crisis caused by the pandemic

Owing to the lack of robust social protection mechanisms in LAC, millions of families working in the informal economy experienced a dramatic drop in income during the confinements. Following the contagion-containment strategy worldwide, LAC countries shut down their economies (OECD, 2020[25]).However, while predominantly formal OECD countries provided unemployment insurance to their populations and supported enterprises to avoid job losses, LAC countries entered the pandemic with millions of families and businesses unprotected by social security mechanisms. On average, in the LAC region, more than 60% of economically vulnerable and informal workers do not benefit from labour-based social protection or a social assistance programme [such as conditional cash transfers (CCTs); Figure 1.11, Panel A].

The LAC region has a long history with social assistance programmes, starting with exemplary cases such as *Bolsa Família* in Brazil or Mexico's CCT programme (*Oportunidades* and, before being discontinued, *Prospera*). However, even though social assistance programmes are widespread and have been of great help to many families, around 50% of poor informal workers do not benefit from social assistance (Figure 1.11, Panel B).

Moreover, the heterogeneity of uncovered families across countries is substantial, ranging from 97% of poor workers in El Salvador to 26% in Argentina.

Social protection in LAC needs to move towards strengthening financing mechanisms, making social contributions more flexible with a mix of non-contributory, contributory and voluntary programmes. Social security contributions as a percentage of labour costs are relatively high in the region. LAC countries' averages are similar to those of OECD countries and exceptionally high for the lowest deciles (OECD/IDB/CIAT, 2016[57]). Reducing non-wage labour costs could encourage formal job creation, especially in the SME sector, thus supporting entrepreneurship. Similarly, shifting part of the tax burden from social security contributions to property taxes could also prove useful to reduce informality (OECD, 2020[29]). However, a clear productive strategy is key to support those policies (Chapter 3). It could also improve citizens' perception of state social protection, thus strengthening incentives for formalisation and tax payment (OECD et al., 2019[6]). Creating a social safety net decoupled from formal employment and financed through general taxation is one way to achieve this objective.

Figure 1.11. **Due to the lack of social protection, informal workers face a much higher risk of falling into poverty in the face of adverse shocks than their formal peers**

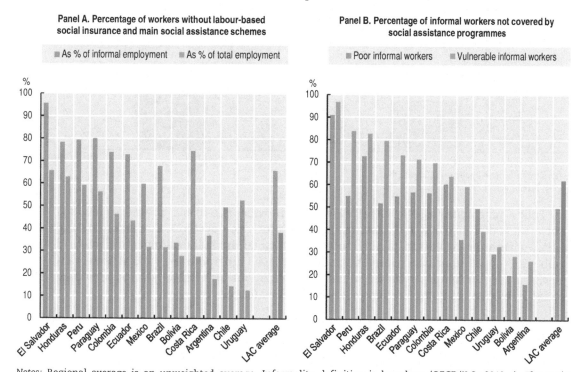

Panel A. Percentage of workers without labour-based social insurance and main social assistance schemes

■ As % of informal employment   ■ As % of total employment

Panel B. Percentage of informal workers not covered by social assistance programmes

■ Poor informal workers   ■ Vulnerable informal workers

Notes: Regional average is an unweighted average. Informality definition is based on (OECD/ILO, 2019[56]). The main social assistance programmes refer only to main CCT programmes and non-contributory social pensions, although the availability of data of beneficiaries in household surveys varies by country, which may result in non-comparable data that the harmonisation process cannot fully solve. In the case of Argentina and Brazil, these percentages are estimated based on social programme focalisation conditions. Owing to the systematic approach to produce internationally comparable data and the use of household surveys different from labour force surveys, informality estimates may differ from the estimates presented in other sources, including national statistics. These figures are subject to updates. Economic vulnerability refers to per capita income (PPP) USD 5.5-13 per day. Poverty refers to PPP lower than USD 5.5 per day.

Source: Authors' calculations based on household surveys: Argentina: EPH 2018. Bolivia: Encuesta de hogares 2018. Brazil: PNAD 2015. Chile: CASEN 2017. Colombia: ENCV 2017. Costa Rica: ENH 2018. El Salvador: EHPM 2017. Ecuador: ENEMDU 2018. Honduras: EPHPM 2014. Mexico: ENH 2018. Paraguay: EPH 2018. Peru: ENH 2018. Uruguay: ECH 2018.

StatLink ⟐ https://doi.org/10.1787/888934286445

Without rapid and efficient policy actions, it could have been worse

Policy actions to support workers, households and firms helped reduce the negative effects of the COVID-19 crisis on poverty and inequality. Latin American countries implemented rapid, effective and well-targeted policies for the most vulnerable groups (see fiscal policy section above and Chapter 2). For instance, cash transfers helped reduce the effects of poverty; without them, it is estimated that the number of people living in poverty would have been 21 million more (up to 230 million people) and 20 million more in extreme poverty (up to 98 million) (Figure 1.12). Similarly, without government transfers to mitigate the loss of labour income, the Gini Index would have increased by 5.6% – higher than the recorded in 2019; instead of 2.9%.

Figure 1.12. Selected social indicators with and without cash transfers to address the COVID-19 crisis in 2020

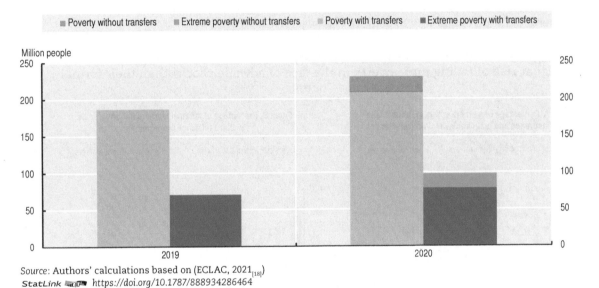

■ Poverty without transfers   ■ Extreme poverty without transfers   ■ Poverty with transfers   ■ Extreme poverty with transfers

Source: Authors' calculations based on (ECLAC, 2021[18])

StatLink ᐧᐧᐧᐧ *https://doi.org/10.1787/888934286464*

Policy responses to the COVID-19 crisis provide the basis to move towards universal comprehensive and sustainable social protection systems. To respond to the crisis, governments reacted rapidly by adopting social assistance support targeted to vulnerable populations not covered by traditional social programmes or social protection mechanisms. Continuing to target vulnerable populations after the crisis and providing social protection are key conditions of a welfare state (Chapter 2).

Conclusions

The COVID-19 pandemic has exacerbated what was an already complicated scenario in the LAC region. The region entered the pandemic with persistent structural challenges (i.e. low productivity growth, vulnerable middle class, labour informality, weak institutions) and limited space for expansionary policies both on the monetary and fiscal front. Nevertheless, and despite the complications and challenges brought on by the pandemic, the crisis and its recovery have provided momentum and opportunity that could be propitious for undertaking the structural changes that will ensure a sustainable and inclusive development path for the region.

The economic recession has translated into worsening living conditions and substantial increases in unemployment, poverty and inequality, with the most vulnerable paying a heavy toll. Informal workers have been the most affected, as lack of social protection or poorer labour conditions leave them more exposed. The crisis highlighted the need and opportunity to increase the coverage and quality of social protection systems.

So far, demand policies have been at the core of the response, supporting public health systems, households and firms, and fiscal policy will play a crucial role for the recovery. In some countries and despite prices increases, monetary policy should still continue to be supportive. However, its capacity remains limited and fiscal policy should play a larger role for a strong, inclusive and sustainable recovery.

To achieve this, co-ordinated actions on the fiscal front are essential. In particular, measures related to public spending, taxation and public debt management should be co-ordinated under a well-defined sequence of policies that can be adapted to the different stages of the recovery. Public spending should target most vulnerable populations and gradually be reallocated from current to capital expenditure, by taking into consideration the benefits of the digital transformation and by investing in the transition to a low-carbon economy. Mobilising the necessary resources will require a fiscal strategy that combines improvements in the structure of the taxation system, tax evasion and avoidance, and policies to increase tax compliance and to strengthen tax administration. In addition, new and innovative fiscal frameworks, including fiscal rules, should be implemented to ensure long-term fiscal sustainability. They should be clear, transparent and protect investment, with adequate escape clauses. Finally, national responses are not enough; the nature of this crisis and the interlinkages across countries require further co-ordination and co-operation at the international level. This is in particular evident in terms of public debt management.

Overall, there needs to be a consensus and national dialogue surrounding the timing and dimensions of required public actions. To achieve any structural changes, the political economy is more important than ever. Any structural reform must be done with the current context in mind and with a well-defined sequencing of actions. It also needs to be backed by a broad consensus built through national dialogue and clear communication (Chapter 4). However, some actions can be undertaken in the short term and can be highly effective, such as measures to reduce tax evasion and avoidance.

Box 1.3. **Key policy messages**

There is no unique approach or solution to ensuring that policies translate into a strong and inclusive recovery from the coronavirus (COVID-19) for Latin America and the Caribbean (LAC). The context-specific socio-economic characteristics of each country, coupled with the different impacts of the crisis, call for a tailored approach. However, some overarching considerations can help countries get their "policy menu" right and achieve a good balance between policies.

1. Implement effective and equitable vaccination strategies as a key element for recovery in the short term.

   - Ensure fast, effective and equitable vaccine rollout to enable the normalisation of economic activity at the national level.

   - Promote regional integration and international co-operation to foster research, development and production capabilities for vaccines and medicines in LAC.

2. Fiscal policy is at the core of the response to the ongoing crisis and will in large part determine how inclusive and strong the recovery will be. Despite highly varied national contexts, countries should consider some common factors and fiscal measures on the road to recovery.

Box 1.3. **Key policy messages** *(cont.)*

- A holistic fiscal response should make use of all fiscal policy tools. There are arguments for "bundling" reforms into a comprehensive package to build fiscal legitimacy in the region. Bundling reduces political constraints for fundamental reforms and addresses distributional issues.

- Fiscal measures should be co-ordinated under a well-defined sequence of policies that can be adapted to the various stages of the recovery.

- There needs to be a consensus and national dialogue surrounding the timing and dimensions of required public spending and taxes. A consensus can help renew the social contract.

- Well-focused actions in terms of both expenditure and income should promote further progressivity and sustainable formal job creation.

- New and innovative fiscal frameworks, including fiscal rules, should be implemented to ensure long-term fiscal sustainability. They should be clear and transparent and safeguard investment, with adequate escape clauses.

- National responses are not enough. The nature of this crisis and the linkages across countries require further co-ordination and co-operation at the international level.

3. If possible, continue with an accommodative stance for monetary policy to support the recovery.

- Continue with the stimulative stance for monetary policy. If inflation remains under control and easy financial conditions persist, most central banks should be able to support the recovery by keeping interest rates low, although with less space.

- Central banks with inflation-targeting regimes should closely monitor second-round effects that could drift expectations away from targets.

- Continue to support, monitor and supervise the financial system.

4. Attract quality foreign direct investment (FDI), as it can spur inclusive and sustainable growth.

- Quality FDI can make important contributions to sustainable development by increasing productivity and innovation, creating quality jobs, developing human capital and improving living standards. Better and higher FDI should be part of a broader productive strategy.

5. Protecting the most vulnerable populations, in particular informal households, requires well-designed policies.

- Programmes targeted to those most affected by the crisis need to consider the household dimension. Segmentation at the household level highlights the relevance of distinguishing between completely informal and mixed households when designing policy interventions.

- A household perspective on informality is needed to capture the level of income poverty and income insecurity among informal workers, measure the capacity to pay for social protection, identify the possibility of accessing social protection through household members working in the formal economy, and assess the extent to which informal workers' vulnerability is passed on to their dependants.

- Adopt policy actions that go beyond the social dimension to support formalisation. These include: i) promoting higher levels of financial inclusion, in particular of informal workers who do not have a bank account or cannot obtain a loan; ii) reducing the digital divide and increasing digital skills to make the most of new technologies;

Box 1.3. Key policy messages *(cont.)*

iii) improving government services; and iv) increasing the fiscal space to provide further targeted support to informal workers.

6. Finance social protection mechanisms while promoting job formalisation.

- Reduce non-wage labour costs to encourage formalisation, especially for low-income earners. Contributions to social security programmes are too costly relative to informal workers' incomes, especially for those at the lower end of the income distribution.

- Make use of the general taxation system to finance the expansion of social protection mechanisms.

Note

1. S&P reduced Chile's long-term issuance rating in March 2021 but maintained its investment-grade rating, and cut Colombia's sovereign rating to below the investment grade in May 2021 (OECD, 2021[8]).

References

Alberola, E. et al. (2016), "Fiscal policy and the cycle in Latin America: the role of financing conditions and fiscal rules", *BIS Working Papers*, Vol. No 543, https://www.bis.org/publ/work543.pdf. [47]

Ardanaz, M. et al. (2021), *Can the Design of Fiscal Rules Help to Protect Productive Public Investment from Budget Cuts?*, https://publications.iadb.org/en/research-insights-can-design-fiscal-rules-help-protect-productive-public-investment-budget-cuts. [48]

Bolton, P. et al. (2020), "Born Out of Necessity: A Debt Standstill for COVID-19", CEPR CEPR Policy Insight No 103, https://cepr.org/active/publications/policy_insights/viewpi.php?pino=103. [40]

Breuer, P. and C. Cohen (2020), *Time is Ripe for Innovation in the World of Sovereign Debt Restructuring*, International Monetary Fund, Blog, https://blogs.imf.org/2020/11/19/time-is-ripe-for-innovation-in-the-world-of-sovereign-debt-restructuring/. [37]

Buckley, R. (1998), *The facilitation of the Brady Plan emerging markets debt trading from 1989 to 1993 (Capital Markets and International Finance).* [55]

CAF (2021), *Economic Perspectives, Quarterly Report. Internal Manuscript*, CAF Group, https://www.caf.net/upload/accionista/1Q2021%20Results[1].pdf. [2]

Caputo Silva, A. and F. Stewart (2021), *My word is my bond: Linking sovereign debt with national sustainability commitments*, https://blogs.worldbank.org/climatechange/my-word-my-bond-linking-sovereign-debt-national-sustainability-commitments. [44]

Cavallo and Powell (2021), *Opportunities for Stronger and Sustainable Postpandemic Growth*, 2021 Latin America and the Caribbean Macroeconomic Report, https://publications.iadb.org/publications/english/document/2021-Latin-American-and-Caribbean-Macroeconomic-Report-Opportunities-for-Stronger-and-Sustainable-Postpandemic-Growth.pdf. [16]

Cevik, S. and J. Tovar Jalles (2021), *La vulnerabilidad al cambio climático perjudica las calificaciones crediticias de la deuda soberana*, International Monetary Fund, Blog, https://blog-dialogoafondo.imf.org/?p=15032. [45]

Cline, W. (1995), *International Debt Reexamined.* [53]

Devlin, R. (1989), *Debt and Crisis in Latin America : The Supply Side of the Story*, Princeton: Princeton University Press. [51]

Diaz-Alejandro, C., P. Krugman and J. Sachs (1984), *Latin American Debt: I Don't Think We are in Kansas Anymore*, Brookings Papers on Economic Activity, https://doi.org/10.2307/2534434. [50]

DIPRES (2020), *Informe de Ejecución del Gobierno Central Tercer Trimestre 2020*, https://www.dipres.gob.cl/597/articles-212454_doc_pdf_reporte_mensual.pdf. [20]

ECLAC (2021), *Fiscal Panorama of Latin America and the Caribbean 2021: Fiscal policy challenges for transformative recovery post COVID-19*, United Nations publication, ECLAC, https://www.cepal.org/en/publications/46809-fiscal-panorama-latin-america-and-caribbean-2021-fiscal-policy-challenges. [17]

ECLAC (2021), *Foreign Direct Investment in Latin America and the Caribbean 2021*, United Nations publication, ECLAC, https://repositorio.cepal.org/bitstream/handle/11362/47148.2/4/S2100318_en.pdf. [13]

ECLAC (2021), *International Trade Outlook for Latin America and the Caribbean 2020: Regional integration is the key to recovery after the crisis*, United Nations publication, ECLAC, https://www.cepal.org/en/publicaciones/pci. [12]

ECLAC (2021), *Economic Survey of Latin America and the Caribbean 2021: Labour Dynamics and Employment Policies for Sustainable and Inclusive Recovery Beyond the COVID-19 Crisis*, United Nations publication, ECLAC, https://www.cepal.org/en/publications/47193-economic-survey-latin-america-and-caribbean-2021-labour-dynamics-and-employment. [1]

ECLAC (2021), *Social Panorama of Latin America 2020*, United Nations publication, ECLAC, https://www.cepal.org/en/publications/46688-social-panorama-latin-america-2020. [18]

ECLAC (2021), *The recovery paradox in Latin America and the Caribbean Growth amid persisting structural problems: inequality, poverty and low investment and productivity*, United Nations publication, ECLAC, https://www.cepal.org/en/publications/47059-recovery-paradox-latin-america-and-caribbean-growth-amid-persisting-structural. [3]

ECLAC (2020), *Fiscal Panorama of Latin America and the Caribbean, 2020: Fiscal policy amid the crisis arising from the coronavirus disease (COVID-19) pandemic*, United Nations publication, ECLAC, https://www.cepal.org/en/publications/45731-fiscal-panorama-latin-america-and-caribbean-2020-fiscal-policy-amid-crisis. [34]

IIF (2021), *Institute of International Finance Database*, https://www.iif.com/Research/Data. [9]

Kose, M. A., et al. (2021), "The Aftermath of Debt Surges", *NBER Working Paper* 29266, DOI: 10.3386/w29266. [35]

IMF (2021), *World Economic Outlook: Managing Divergent Recoveries*, International Monetary Fund, https://www.imf.org/en/Publications/WEO/Issues/2021/03/23/world-economic-outlook-april-2021. [10]

IMF (2021), *Regional Economic Outlook, Western Hemisphere: A Long and Winding Road to Recovery*, International Monetary Fund, Publication Services, Washington DC. https://www.imf.org/-/media/Files/Publications/REO/WHD/2021/English/Text.ashx. [11]

IMF (2020), *Fiscal Policy at the Time of a Pandemic: How have Latin America and the Caribbean Fared?*, International Monetary Fund, https://www.imf.org/en/Publications/REO/WH/Issues/2020/10/13/regional-economic-outlook-western-hemisphere. [30]

Izquierdo, A. and C. Pessino (2021), *A Post COVID-19 Fiscal Strategy for Latin America and the Caribbean*, https://blogs.iadb.org/ideas-matter/en/a-post-covid-19-fiscal-strategy-for-latin-america-and-the-caribbean/. [26]

MEF (2020), *Reporte Fiscal Trimestral: Seguimiento de las Reglas Macrofiscales: Segundo Trimestre 2020*, https://www.mef.gob.pe/contenidos/pol_econ/Reporte_Fiscal/Informe_Trimestral_de_Reglas_Fiscales_II_Trim2020.pdf. [21]

Mora, S., S. Nieto-Parra and R. Orozco (2021), *Fiscal policy to drive the recovery in Latin America: the "when" and "how" are key*, http://lacea.org/vox/?q=blog/fiscal_policy_latam. [23]

Nieto-Parra, S. and R. Orozco (2020), *Public debt and COVID-19. Paying for the crisis in Latin America and the Caribbean*, https://legrandcontinent.eu/fr/2020/07/22/public-debt-and-covid-19-paying-for-the-crisis-in-latin-america-and-the-caribbean/. [36]

Ocampo, J. (2021), *Significant but insufficient progress in financial support for developing countries*, https://oecd-development-matters.org/2021/04/13/significant-but-insufficient-progress-in-financial-support-for-developing-countries/. [39]

OECD (2021), *130 countries and jurisdictions join bold new framework for international tax reform*, OECD Newsroom, Paris, https://www.oecd.org/newsroom/130-countries-and-jurisdictions-join-bold-new-framework-for-international-tax-reform.htm. [28]

OECD (2021), *OECD Economic Outlook, Interim Report September 2021: Keeping the Recovery on Track*, OECD Publishing, Paris, https://doi.org/10.1787/490d4832-en. [7]

OECD (2021), *OECD Economic Outlook, Volume 2021 Issue 1*, OECD Publishing, Paris, https://doi.org/10.1787/edfbca02-en. [8]

OECD (2021), *OECD Tax Policy Studies: Inheritance Taxation in OECD Countries*, OECD Publishing, Paris, https://doi.org/10.1787/e2879a7d-en. [27]

OECD (2021), *Policies for improving the sustainable development impacts of investment"*, Consultation Paper March 2021, OECD Publishing, Paris, https://www.oecd.org/daf/inv/investment-policy/FDI-Qualities-Policy-Toolkit-Consultation-Paper-2021.pdf. [15]

OECD (2021), *Sovereign Borrowing Outlook for OECD Countries 2021*, OECD Publishing, Paris, https://www.oecd.org/daf/fin/public-debt/Sovereign-Borrowing-Outlook-in-OECD-Countries-2021.pdf. [5]

OECD (2020), *COVID-19 in Latin America and the Caribbean: Regional Socio-Economic Implications and Policy Priorities*, OECD Publishing, Paris, https://www.oecd.org/coronavirus/policy-responses/covid-19-in-latin-america-and-the-caribbean-regional-socio-economic-implications-and-policy-priorities-93a64fde/. [25]

OECD (2020), *OECD Economic Surveys: Costa Rica 2020*, OECD Publishing, Paris, https://doi.org/10.1787/2e0fea6c-en. [29]

OECD (2020), *Government at a Glance: Latin America and the Caribbean 2020*, OECD Publishing, Paris, https://doi.org/10.1787/13130fbb-en. [32]

OECD (2020), *OECD's COVID-19 Country Policy Tracker*, https://www.oecd.org/coronavirus/country-policy-tracker/. [31]

OECD (2019), *Can Social Protection Be an Engine for Inclusive Growth?*, OECD Publishing, Paris, https://doi.org/10.1787/9d95b5d0-en. [33]

OECD (2019), *FDI Qualities Indicators: Measuring the sustainable development*, OECD Publishing, Paris, http://www.oecd.org/investment/FDI-Qualities-Indicators-Measuring-Sustainable-Development-Impacts.pdf. [14]

OECD (forthcoming), *Labour informality and households' vulnerabilities in Latin America (provisional title)*, OECD Publishing, Paris. [56]

OECD et al. (2021), *Revenue Statistics in Latin America and the Caribbean 2021*, OECD Publishing, Paris, https://doi.org/10.1787/96ce5287-en-es. [19]

OECD et al. (2020), *Latin American Economic Outlook 2020: Digital Transformation for Building Back Better*, OECD Publishing, Paris, https://doi.org/10.1787/e6e864fb-en. [24]

OECD et al. (2019), *Latin American Economic Outlook 2019: Development in Transition*, OECD Publishing, Paris, https://dx.doi.org/10.1787/g2g9ff18-en. [6]

OECD/IDB/CIAT (2016), *Taxing Wages in Latin America and the Caribbean 2016*, OECD Publishing, Paris, https://dx.doi.org/10.1787/9789264262607-en. [58]

OECD/ILO (2019), *Tackling Vulnerability in the Informal Economy*, Development Centre Studies, OECD Publishing, Paris, https://dx.doi.org/10.1787/939b7bcd-en. [57]

OECD/The World Bank (2020), *Health at a Glance: Latin America and the Caribbean 2020*, OECD Publishing, Paris, https://doi.org/10.1787/6089164f-en. [22]

Rogoff, K. (1993), *Third World Debt*. [54]

Steele, P. and S. Patel (2020), "Tackling the triple crisis. Using debt swaps to address debt, climate and nature loss post COVID-19", IIED Issue paper, 48 pages, https://pubs.iied.org/16674iied. [43]

Subacchi, P. (2020), *A Good but Incomplete Start to Debt Relief*, https://www.project-syndicate.org/commentary/g20-common-framework-debt-restructuring-by-paola-subacchi-2020-11?barrier=accesspaylog. [41]

Székely, M. and A. Montes (2006), *Poverty and Inequality*, The Cambridge Economic History of Latin America, Cambridge University Press, January, https://doi.org/10.1017/CHOL9780521812900.016. [49]

UN/DESA (2020), *COVID-19 and sovereign debt*, United Nations publication, UNDESA, https://www.un.org/development/desa/dpad/publication/un-desa-policy-brief-72-covid-19-and-sovereign-debt/. [42]

UNCTAD (2020), *From the Great Lockdown to the Great Meltdown: Developing Country Debt in the Time of Covid-19*, United Nations Publication, UNCTAD, https://unctad.org/fr/node/27494. [38]

UNCTAD (2020), *Impact of the COVID-19 pandemic on trade and development: transitioning to a new normal*, United Nations Publication, UNCTAD, https://unctad.org/system/files/official-document/osg2020d1_en.pdf. [4]

Vasquez, I. (1996), *The Brady Plan and Market-Based Solutions to Debt Crises*, Cato Journal 16 (2): 233-43. [52]

Vegh, C. and G. Vuletin (2014), "The Road to Redemption: Policy Response to Crises in Latin America", *NBER Working Paper*, Vol. 20675, https://www.nber.org/papers/w20675. [46]

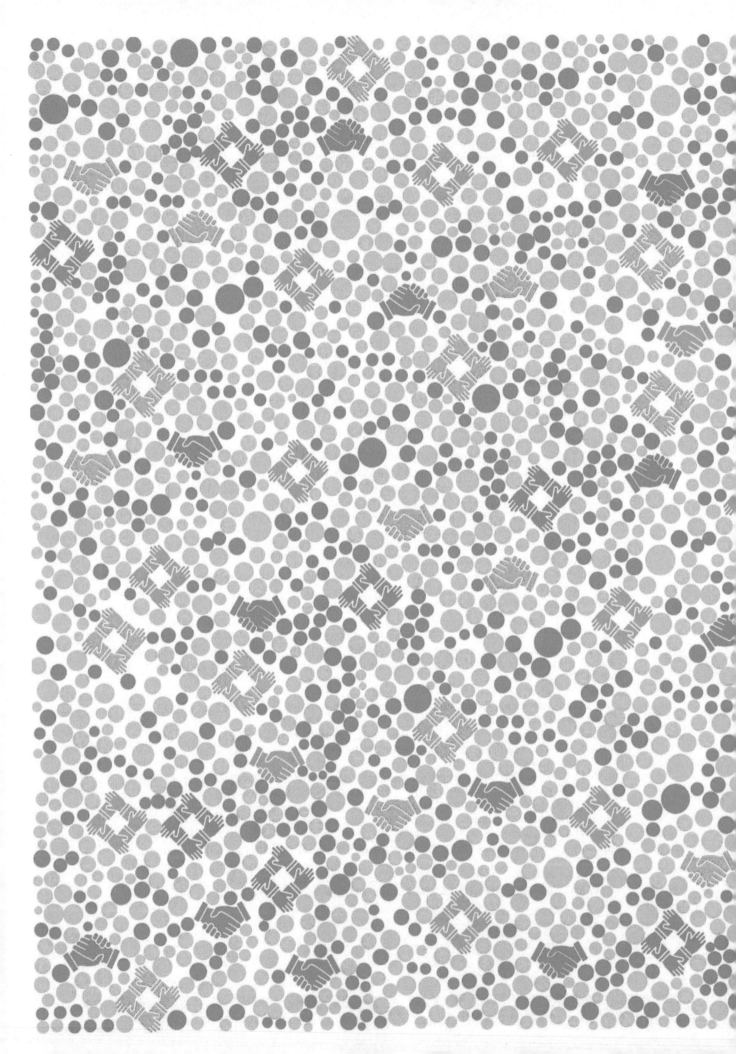

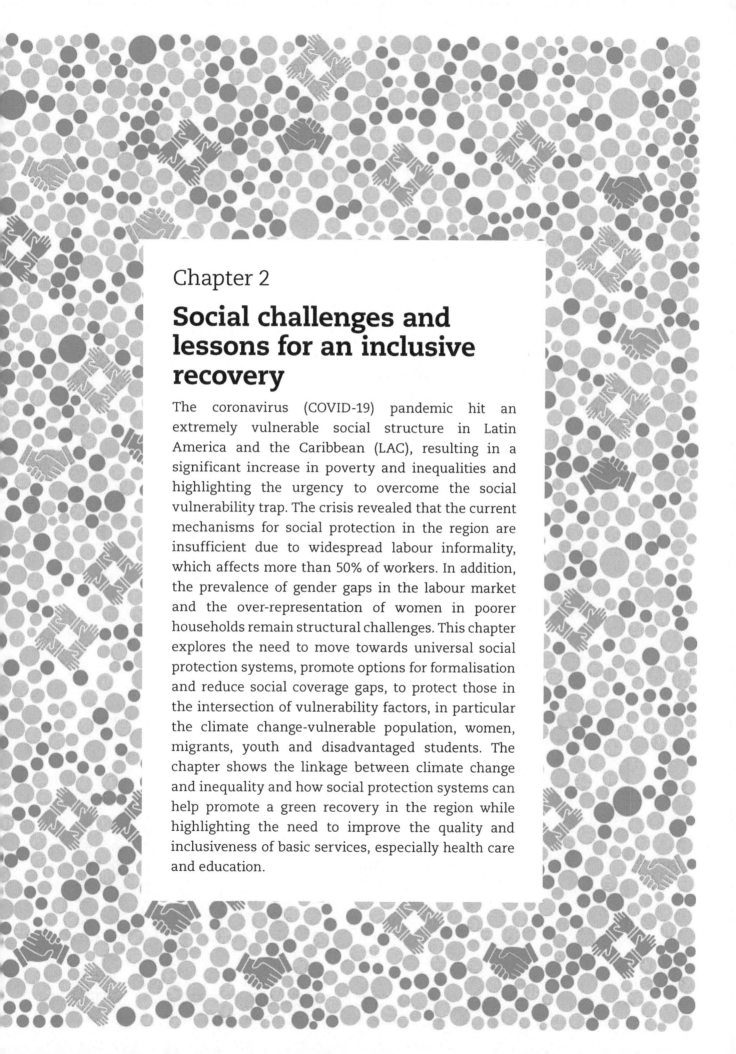

Chapter 2

Social challenges and lessons for an inclusive recovery

The coronavirus (COVID-19) pandemic hit an extremely vulnerable social structure in Latin America and the Caribbean (LAC), resulting in a significant increase in poverty and inequalities and highlighting the urgency to overcome the social vulnerability trap. The crisis revealed that the current mechanisms for social protection in the region are insufficient due to widespread labour informality, which affects more than 50% of workers. In addition, the prevalence of gender gaps in the labour market and the over-representation of women in poorer households remain structural challenges. This chapter explores the need to move towards universal social protection systems, promote options for formalisation and reduce social coverage gaps, to protect those in the intersection of vulnerability factors, in particular the climate change-vulnerable population, women, migrants, youth and disadvantaged students. The chapter shows the linkage between climate change and inequality and how social protection systems can help promote a green recovery in the region while highlighting the need to improve the quality and inclusiveness of basic services, especially health care and education.

Enhancingsocialprotectionandpublicservices iskeyforbuildingforwardbetter

Gender-focusedlabourmarketpolicies,bringingchildrenbacktoschool andpromotingagreentransitionshouldbeatthecentreoftherecovery

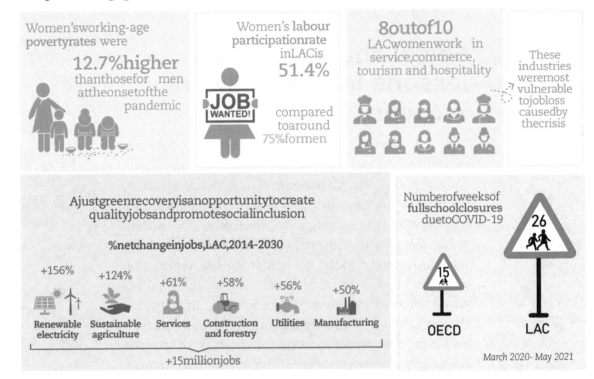

Women'sworking-age povertyrates were

12.7%higher
thanthosefor men attheonsetofthe pandemic

Women's **labour participation**rate inLACis
51.4%

JOB WANTED!

compared toaround 75%formen

8outof10
LACwomenwork in service,commerce, tourism and hospitality

These industries weremost vulnerable tojobloss causedby thecrisis

Ajustgreenrecoveryisanopportunitytocreate qualityjobsandpromotesocialinclusion

%netchangeinjobs,LAC,2014-2030

+156% +124% +61% +58% +56% +50%

Renewable electricity | Sustainable agriculture | Services | Construction and forestry | Utilities | Manufacturing

+15millionjobs

Numberofweeksof fullschoolclosures duetoCOVID-19

15 OECD

26 LAC

March 2020- May 2021

Socialprotectionsystemsmustbereformedtomeetpeople'sconcerns andaddressstructuralweaknesses

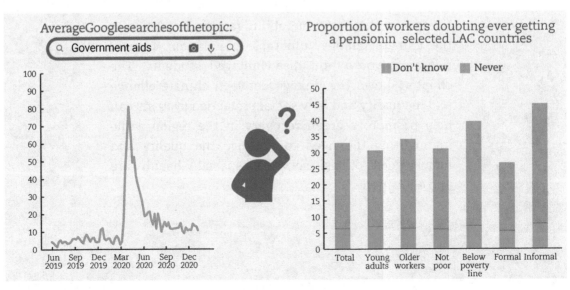

AverageGooglesearchesofthetopic:

Government aids

Proportion of workers doubting ever getting a pensionin selected LAC countries

Don't know **Never**

Total | Young adults | Older workers | Not poor | Below poverty line | Formal | Informal

Introduction

To confront the Coronavirus (COVID-19) crisis, governments in Latin America and the Caribbean (LAC) have reacted quickly, adopting policy actions to strengthen social protection measures and protect the most vulnerable populations. Social protection actions have been targeted to those most affected by the pandemic, including poor, informal and independent workers. In this sense, social protection programmes have evolved to cover a wider share of citizens.

Despite the rapid and effective response from many LAC countries, the COVID-19 crisis has pushed the region into its worst social and economic recession since the 20th century. Despite the global nature of the crisis, it has most profoundly affected LAC countries, given the high vulnerability of certain population groups to the consequences of the pandemic. COVID-19 is having a considerable impact on poverty and income inequality. Despite the exceptional social protection measures adopted during the pandemic, the number of people living in poverty increased in 2020 compared to 2019 by approximately three percentage points, and income inequality, measured by the Gini Index, increased by close to 2.9% in 2020 (Chapter 1) (ECLAC, 2021[1]).

The pandemic has exacerbated structural weaknesses in LAC. Social vulnerabilities have made it harder for governments to be resilient and respond rapidly to the adverse socio-economic effects caused by the COVID-19. Challenges to future development include: i) population ageing; ii) overcrowding in cities and lack of access to social services; iii) high informality; iv) weak social protection systems, including inadequate coverage and quality of healthcare systems and lack of integrated care systems; and v) high and persistent inequalities across various dimensions. In particular, the crisis trapped informal workers in a profoundly vulnerable condition due to a lack of quality stable jobs and limited social protection (OECD et al., 2020[2]; ECLAC, 2021[1]; ILO, 2021[3]). High informality limits the role social protection systems play in society, their effectiveness and their financial sustainability (Álvarez, 2020[4]). Informality also made it difficult to implement measures to contain the virus (such as confinements) and aggravated its impact on the population.

Beyond workers, individuals in the intersection of vulnerability factors have been disproportionately affected by the crisis. The groups most vulnerable to the harmful effects include the elderly, youth, women, migrants, indigenous peoples and Afrodescendants, all of which often face precarious conditions (ECLAC/UNICEF, 2020[5]). Uncertainty about the evolution and consequences of the pandemic in LAC persists, making the policy response to counteract its adverse effects and boost the recovery more complex.

In the short term, the governments of the region should focus on the immunisation of the population and continued support for the most vulnerable. In the absence of policy measures to reduce growing socio-economic gaps for these groups, the effects of the COVID-19 crisis will be long lasting and could undermine the socio-economic improvements achieved in the last decades (ILO, 2021[3]).

Returning to the pre-crisis social status quo should not be the goal of the recovery. The response to the crisis should be an opportunity to address structural challenges and inequalities while improving resilience. The pandemic requires co-ordinated action at various levels, together with increasing vaccination rates and boosting economic recovery and employment creation. Expanding social protection systems is crucial to protect livelihoods and lessen the negative shock to vulnerable groups' well-being while reducing long-lasting impacts. In the long term, social protection measures might contribute to consolidating the middle class. Social protection policies should soften the employment and income shock for affected individuals in the recovery process and beyond. Building a resilient system, where the economy, households and individuals are protected from macro and micro shocks, is crucial to address the region's challenges in the future and to prevent a substantial setback in development progress.

This crisis offers a unique opportunity to advance urgent and delayed reforms and redefine the region's social contract (Chapter 4). As part of this new social contract, key ingredients include new social models based on more robust and sustainable social protection systems and more inclusive and greener public services.

This chapter first explores the need to move towards universal social protection systems and takes into account several considerations for its implementation. Second, it insists on the need to support populations in a condition of vulnerability that are considerably affected by the pandemic, particularly the elderly, women, migrants, youth and disadvantaged students. Third, it explores the linkages between the transition to a low-carbon development model ("green transition" in short) and social inclusion. In particular, it highlights how the green transition relates to the objectives of creating quality jobs, reducing inequalities and redesigning social protection systems. Fourth, it presents citizens' perceptions in key socio-economic dimensions, including jobs, pensions and the quality of healthcare systems, and shows the importance of understanding and responding to citizens' preferences when designing and adopting reforms. The chapter concludes with key policy messages.

Broader social protection for more inclusive and resilient societies

Lack of social protection and household economic vulnerability are still important challenges in LAC (Chapter 1). Social protection is essential in every society. It provides security to individuals and households in the face of vulnerabilities and contingencies, guaranteeing access to care services, including health care and income safety, throughout people's life cycles. Weak social protection mechanisms leave households exposed to the direct effect of crises and external shocks. In LAC, high levels of informality in labour markets have been a determining factor in the low social security coverage. Before the pandemic, informal employment accounted for 56% of workers on average in the region (OECD, 2020[6]). In addition, the organisation of social care continues to be unfair and unbalanced, concentrated on households and especially women engaged in unpaid labour. Unequal division of care work is one of the main barriers to women's full participation in the labour market. Even before the pandemic, women's participation rate in the region was 51.4%, compared to around 75.0% for men (ECLAC, 2019[7]).

Despite significant efforts to escalate emergency programmes, the lack of robust social protection systems left vulnerable sectors unprotected from the shocks of the COVID-19 crisis. For instance, households that depended on income from informal work were unprotected from loss of income due to the confinements. The drop in external demand for certain export products also played a role in triggering a more profound crisis in LAC.

Many countries enacted bold crisis-response policy measures to protect the most vulnerable. Income assistance to targeted populations to stimulate consumption and investment efforts to promote productive activities will continue to be critical to overcome the crisis and promote sustainable development (Chapters 1 and 3). However, further action and more ambitious strategies, combined with much-needed policy reforms, will be necessary to consolidate the recovery and build resilience.

Universal social protection is essential to build inclusive growth and boost resilience in the aftermath of the crisis

The current crisis spotlights the need for social protection mechanisms to mitigate shocks and prevent households from falling into poverty. The crisis proved that implementing emergency measures is far less challenging in countries with robust social protection mechanisms, such as unemployment insurance, pensions and broader access to care and healthcare services. On the positive side, the crisis accelerated the scaling-up of social assistance programmes in the region.

A robust universal social protection system can bring together policies to reduce poverty, social exclusion and vulnerability throughout the life cycle. Social security systems generally offer many mechanisms that help secure people's income throughout their lives. It also secures access to healthcare services, seeking to protect the most vulnerable according to their age, gender and social class, among other dimensions (OECD, 2019[8]). Social protection systems also foster equality of opportunities through social assistance schemes.

Beyond protection for households, societies also benefit from having a social protection system through mechanisms at the aggregate level. At the society (macro) level, social protection can contribute to stimulating aggregate demand and thus increase employment. In addition, it can increase consumption and tax revenues. Stimulating aggregate demand through social protection is key during crisis periods as a countercyclical spending mechanism (OECD, 2019[8]). During crises, the aggregation of micro-level support can avoid a more profound economic recession and long-term scarring.

As a critical mechanism of social protection, well-targeted social assistance programmes can significantly contribute to levelling the positive effect of growth in two ways. First, it guarantees a minimum level of social and economic welfare. Social assistance insures against and mitigates the risks of falling into poverty among low-income households, and it fosters social mobility, contributing to closing inequality gaps. Second, social assistance enables more equal access to opportunities. In this way, it overcomes the constraints of low-income households in terms of savings and credit that hold back investments in human capital and perpetuate intergenerational poverty. If well designed, social assistance may also encourage labour market participation, innovation and entrepreneurship (OECD, 2019[8]).

Governments have made significant efforts to reach vulnerable individuals and households during the crisis by extending cash transfers programmes. They expanded social assistance measures by: i) broadening beneficiaries reached both by including additional individuals and households in traditional programmes and by creating new schemes to target unprotected portions of the population; and ii) increasing the amount and the frequency of benefits to replacing a greater share of income (OECD, forthcoming[9]). For instance, in Argentina, *Ingreso Familiar de Emergencia* is a new programme targeting unemployed individuals and households that depend entirely on informal and independent employment. The country has also increased the amount of transfers of *Asignación Universal* and non-contributory pensions, the most traditional social assistance programmes. The emergence of these new schemes, including *Auxílio emergencial* in Brazil, *Ingreso Familiar de Emergencia* in Chile, *Ingreso Solidario* in Colombia, *Subsidio Pytyvõ* in Paraguay and *Bono Familiar Universal, Independiente y Yo me quedo en casa* in Peru, offer new safety nets for vulnerable households and informal workers not covered before (OECD, forthcoming[9]).

These temporary measures can be the basis for rethinking social protection in the region and promoting a more universal and resilient social protection system that includes those traditionally excluded, making the economy and households more resistant to negative shocks.

The crisis offers an opportunity to build a broader and more inclusive universal social protection system in many countries. It has shown how vulnerable most LAC economies were due to their high informality levels and the importance of boosting formal employment as a central piece of the recovery process. Several elements should be considered when rethinking social policies in LAC, including the need for a more comprehensive social insurance system that covers vulnerable workers, the adaptability and robustness of unemployment insurance systems, a development strategy to boost employment and formal jobs, and the fiscal sustainability of these measures (ILO, 2021[10]). Social assistance registries can facilitate the identification of workers in vulnerable situations and their socio-economic conditions and improve the design and targeting of policy interventions. The extension of the coverage of these programmes to more people has not been straightforward. Public authorities encountered problems with identifying new beneficiaries, as many are not registered, and reaching them, as they do not always have a bank account. They resorted to cross-checking existing records and finding alternative ways of expanding databases and making money transfers, mainly using digital technologies and mobile phones. Co-ordination and co-operation with the private sector, in particular financial intermediaries, emerged as a priority to reach the uncovered population and those affected by the digital divide (in terms of access to technology or lack of skills). This public-private co-operation is key to develop more effective mechanisms, such as mobile banking and financial correspondents, targeted to such population groups.

An inclusive and sustainable recovery needs to protect and support social groups facing multiple vulnerabilities

Measures taken to support vulnerable groups not covered by traditional social assistance and insurance mechanisms can be the basis to reassess and promote more resilient social protection systems in the region. These measures have included introducing new social assistance programmes, extending the coverage of cash transfers or increasing the amount of benefits, and providing in-kind transfers, such as food and access to the Internet or digital devices (ECLAC, 2021[1]; OECD, 2020[6]).

Certain social groups have pre-existing characteristics that made them extremely exposed to shocks due to the crisis. These groups need to be at the centre of social policy strategies. Socio-economic pre-pandemic conditions that could determine individuals' and households' resilience to the crisis were unequally distributed. Beyond informal self-employed workers and poor households, other groups disproportionately affected by the crisis were women, youth, the elderly, indigenous peoples, Afrodescendants (ILO, 2021[3]; UNDP, 2020[11]) and migrants. Governments need to put in place policies that are sensitive to these groups' needs, designed with inclusive participation of representatives from these groups and targeted to protect their lives, livelihoods and well-being. Affected groups should be routinely consulted on relevant initiatives with transparent feedback programmes that respond to their particular needs and that do not entrench pre-existing discrimination and marginalisation. Public policies should apply an intersectional and gender approach to account for the multiple discrimination forms and structural barriers that various population groups face.

While efforts to increase social expenditure through non-contributory social protection evidenced a rapid response by governments, pre-crisis social protection capacity has determined countries' ability to contain the harmful effects of the crisis. The increase in additional resources to finance social protection programmes in Latin

America represented 1.25% of gross domestic product (GDP) in 2019. Traditional social assistance programmes have been vital to guarantee social protection for poor and vulnerable households. For instance, in Mexico, non-contributory pensions became universal in 2019 (ECLAC, 2021[1]), protecting the elderly who traditionally experience greater income and health vulnerabilities. In Paraguay, *Tarjeta Universal Social* covers around 12% of the population. In Uruguay, *Asignaciones Familiares* transfers cover around 11% of the population.

Focusing additional efforts to support individuals who experience multiple vulnerabilities is key to mitigate a loss in well-being and the potential effects on development trajectories. While the crisis affects the entire workforce, the disproportionately negative effects on informal workers, and especially on women and young people, indigenous people, Afrodescendants and migrants, result from the union of features and conditions of their socio-demographic characteristics that tend to accentuate vulnerabilities (UNDP, 2020[11]; ECLAC, 2020[12]). The next sections present challenges and policy recommendations to address the vulnerabilities of groups that face particular forms of discrimination in LAC.

Improving social protection systems to support the elderly population's needs is key to build resilience

LAC countries face a twin challenge: the coverage of social protection is unequal and expanding at an insufficient pace, while their dependency and working-age to old-age population ratios are worsening, due to ageing. While population ageing is the result of improvements in living conditions and health and development policies, it also presents challenges in terms of social protection and health care that need to be addressed by policy makers (Álvarez, 2020[4]). While Latin America is still a relatively young region, the demographic ageing process is advancing at an accelerated pace: the share of the population over age 65 is expected to reach 18% in 2050, more than double the current 9% (OECD/The World Bank, 2020[13]). Ageing rates vary significantly across countries, with Uruguay (15%), Chile (12%) and Argentina (11%) having the higher proportion of the population over age 65 (UNDESA, 2019[14]). Population ageing implies a decrease in the share of the working-age population. The ratio of the working-age population to the over age 65 population will evolve from 8.6 in 2015 to 3.4 in 2050, although the situation differs among countries. In particular, Chile, Costa Rica, Uruguay and Caribbean countries will see the most significant declines (UNDESA, 2019[14]). These demographic changes are likely to increase the financial pressure on healthcare systems, the sustainability risk of some pension regimes and the challenges for production processes and the economy as a whole. Families will also have to take care of older members for longer, in the absence of universal care systems. Women will be the most affected because they disproportionately bear the burden of care work. On average, women dedicate two-thirds of their time to unpaid work and one-third to paid work, while it is the inverse for men (ECLAC, 2021[15]).

In LAC, 42% of people over age 65 are covered by the public non-contributory healthcare system, representing limited adequate coverage and access to quality care and adding financial pressure on social systems. On average, only four out of ten elderly people have access to health care through the public system. LAC countries present high heterogeneity in the social security coverage of healthcare systems for the elderly, ranging from 94% in Argentina to 24% in Bolivia (Álvarez, 2020[4]). This status of healthcare social protection is linked to the high financial insecurity associated with private health expenditure. The current pandemic can be a starting point for strengthening care and healthcare systems since it has put pressure on governments to increase systems' preparedness for future sanitary crises and the challenge that population ageing poses.

The COVID-19 crisis put the spotlight on some inadequacies of health systems in Latin America. Among them are disparities in the effective access and quality associated with higher income and urban location. High out-of-pocket (OOP) healthcare expenditure, inequalities in immunisation rates and lower ratios of human resources, specialised doctors and nurses and other physical resources, such as beds and intensive care unit (ICU) places, have been limitations for LAC health systems in coping with the increased demand due to the pandemic. Strengthening healthcare provision is needed both in the short term and in the long term, as the share of elderly population will increase in LAC countries. Among the medium-term actions, governments in the region should increase financial coverage, reduce OOP expenditure and strengthen the long-term care workforce (Muir, 2017[16]).

Making pension systems sustainable and more robust is relevant to protecting the elderly population's well-being. High informality in Latin America – around 56% before the pandemic – implies that a high proportion of future elderly citizens will be less likely to receive a pension from a contributory scheme (OECD, forthcoming[9]). On average, before the crisis, around 75% of the population over age 65 received a pension in Latin America in 2017; however, a total of 28% of pension receivers are beneficiaries of non-contributory pensions (Arenas De Mesa, 2019[17]). Moreover, the amount of transfers of contributory pensions is insufficient to replace a person's level of income during their productive life. Only countries like Argentina and Ecuador exhibit a replacement rate of around 60%, while many others are below the standard level stated by the ILO (45%), including Chile, Mexico and Peru (Álvarez, 2020[4]). While solidarity pensions have improved access to pensions for the elderly in LAC, the capacity of these transfers to replace income is deficient in comparison with contributory pensions, especially for women. In many countries, such as Bolivia, Colombia, Ecuador and Peru, the amount of these transfers is below the poverty line, which makes it difficult for these programmes to reduce poverty rates and income inequality for people over age 65.

Social protection policies need to face population ageing by increasing coverage, the number of transfers and services they offer to guarantee a certain level of income and the quality of those services while promoting social protection systems' financial sustainability and inclusiveness. To achieve these goals, promoting job formalisation, finding alternative ways to fund social protection separately from labour status and designing social security incentive schemes that take into account heterogeneities in labour markets and economies across LAC countries are urgently required in line with the previous section.

Most countries will need to execute a set of reforms to improve social protection, including a profound transformation in contributory schemes, public systems and labour market regulations, and fiscal or expenditure reforms to meet citizen demands for welfare. Rethinking the social system to protect the elderly requires considering structural problems, such as informality, gender inequalities, low tax collection and a very limited fiscal space (Chapter 1). These problems intensified with the pandemic, and potential policy actions for the recovery will vary depending on country contexts. There is no unique solution, and each country needs to find a particular combination of policy options. For instance, in Chile, where the system is based primarily on individual mandatory capitalised accounts and contributions rates are low (10% of earnings), the net replacement rates of less than 40% (vs. the nearly 60% average for Organisation for Economic Co-operation and Development [OECD] countries) are relatively low (OECD, 2019[18]). In Colombia, the pension system remains complex. Its structure is unusual, as it comprises two parallel mandatory systems: a public pay-as-you-go (PAYG) defined-benefit scheme and a private defined-contribution scheme. Workers are allowed to switch between the two every five years up until ten years before retirement. Compared to the OECD average and only for formal workers, while the replacement rates are relatively high in the public PAYG system, they remain relatively low in the private system. Recent reforms have aimed to reduce old-age poverty risks for informal workers but remain insufficient. The old-age assistance scheme was strengthened in 2010 through the creation of *Colombia Mayor* (OECD, 2015[19]). In Costa Rica, in contrast to OECD countries, the government pays, along with employers and workers, a share of social security contributions of employees and the self-employed in both the private and public sectors. Such high government contributions explain, in part, the relatively low levels of informality among self-employed workers in Costa Rica – the lowest in Latin America (OECD, 2017[20]). However, minimum years of contribution (15 years for a reduced pension) discourage job formalisation among workers with fragmented working histories. In Mexico, where expected replacement rates are low (28.6% for men and 26.7% for women), the government was forced to introduce a new safety net for people aged 68 and over (*Programa Pensión para el Bienestar de Adultos Mayores*) to support retirees' incomes and avoid older workers, especially if informal, falling into poverty (OECD, 2020[21]). In Peru, publicly and privately funded pension components currently operate in parallel, competing with each other rather than ensuring complementarity. Strict eligibility requirements for the public system mean that individuals unable to achieve 20 years of contributions receive no public-system benefits. This floor discourages informal workers from entering the formal sector, and individuals switching to the private system will lose access to minimum pension benefits (OECD, 2019[22]). At the LAC regional level, in general, policy options include increasing the retirement age, allowing for part-time contributions, reducing requirements for contributions in the formal sector, funding social protection through general taxes, unifying social assistance programmes and increasing the amount of contributions. Last, the political economy involved in these reforms will have an enormous impact on the preparedness of Latin American economies to protect the elderly in the future.

Gender-focused labour market policies and redistribution of care work should be at the centre of the recovery

Material hardships associated with COVID-19 have disproportionately affected women (ILO, 2021[3]). Crisis-driven loss of income and micro shocks are more likely to affect women's socio-economic conditions (OECD et al., 2020[2]). The gender gap in asset holding, income generation, labour market participation and care work made women more vulnerable to the crisis. Women's incomes and wealth are, on average, lower than men's, and they are more likely to be poor. Before the pandemic, working-age women's poverty rates were 12.7% higher than those for men in the same age group (ECLAC, 2021[1]). Moreover, the hourly labour income was higher for men at PPP USD 6.0 (United States dollar) than the USD 5.7 for women (IMF, 2020[23]).

Women in LAC were particularly exposed to the effects of the virus since they represent most of the healthcare workforce. While women are under-represented among physicians and pharmacists, they are over-represented among nurses and midwives, who face direct contact with infected patients. Women in Latin America account for 46% of physicians and 86% of nurses.

Other variables associated with pre-pandemic conditions contributed to women vulnerabilities in facing the crisis. Women were over-represented in more affected industries, which made them more exposed to job loss (ILO, 2020[24]). In Latin America, eight out of ten women work in service, commerce, tourism and hospitality (Gutiérrez, 2021[25]). Moreover, 54% of women are in informal employment, compared to 52% of men. Labour market characteristics added additional vulnerabilities for women in LAC. On average, reduction in employment (18.1% vs 15.1% for men) and exit from the labour market (15.4% vs. 11.8% for men) were significantly higher for women (ECLAC, 2021[1]).

Youth, and in particular young women, lost their jobs and faced hardships during 2020. Some 34% of young men lost their jobs vs. 39% of young women, with heterogeneity in the gender gaps associated with job loss among LAC countries ranging from 20% in Colombia to 65% in Honduras (Gutiérrez, 2021[25]). The recovery process can be slower for women of childbearing age, for whom the burden of taking care of children and discrimination in the labour market can affect the labour trajectory (Tribin, Vargas and Ramírez, 2019[26]).

Confinement and closing of multiple services, including schools and other social services, imposed severe limitations on work for women and increased their unpaid workload, as they faced additional care responsibilities to support children's learning and provide care for family members who were sick or in need (OECD, 2020[27]; ECLAC, 2021[1]). Women had limited access to teleworking as a mechanism to continue working, given the female workforce's distribution in industries and sectors requiring personal interaction. Women may also find securing employment and income following lay-off more difficult because of greater caring obligations. In the region, men spend most of their time in paid work, while women spend most of it in unpaid work inside their households (ILO, 2019[28]). Before the crisis, 11.1% of women were employed as paid domestic workers, and only 24% of them were affiliated with or paying into social security systems (ECLAC, 2021[29]). Unequal distribution of domestic and care work, together with the ageing trends that will increase the demand for care, threaten economic and labour inclusion for women, in the absence of public and market provision of these services.

The confinement measures, together with the psychological implications of the pandemic and the economic hardship, might have increased violence against women (OECD, 2020[30]; ECLAC, 2020[31]), with an enormous negative impact on women's well-being. While there is not enough data for the pandemic period to quantify the increase in violence against women, during the first months of the crisis, violence reports showed an increase that raises awareness of the need for policy to offer services related to attention and support for victims in contexts of gender-based violence against women (ECLAC, 2020[31]). In Argentina, the number of inquiries concerning gender violence increased by 39%. In Brazil, a 50% increase in complaints was reported in Rio de Janeiro. In Colombia, complaints increased by 51% in the first days after the quarantine. In the Mexican state of Nuevo León, there was an increase of 30% in reports of cases of family violence (UN Women, 2020[32]; Gutiérrez, 2021[25]). Moreover, school closures and increased hardship at home resulted in a large number of girls permanently dropping out of school, notably from disadvantaged communities, and this led in turn to much higher risks of unwanted pregnancies and early marriages (Szabo and Edwards, 2020[33]). Urgent actions are required to protect girls and women's lives and well-being.

Digital transformation can offer opportunities for women to recover space in the labour market. New technologies and the acceleration of digitalisation during the pandemic can allow women to keep working from home, offer part-time work, balance family and work more effectively and reduce costs in transport time. However, the gender digital gap can impede the inclusion of women in the future of work, for instance resulting from differences in the age of first access to digital devices and in the perception of skills necessary to navigate the digital world (OECD et al., 2020[2]). Ensuring inclusive digital transformation that includes women's access to digital technologies and measures to provide the skills to use them and breaking down socio-economic barriers and thereby improving economic opportunities are necessary to promote women's autonomy in the post-pandemic context (ECLAC, 2021[29]). This will also facilitate remote learning, reduce unpaid work time and open the possibilities for women to join the labour market through new ways of work, such as through the platform economy.

LAC governments should promote greater labour participation and labour income for women, with a broad range of synergic policy interventions. First of all, redistributing care work by offering quality public and private care services may incentivise women to enter the labour market, or increase the working hours, in case they hold part-time informal jobs. Gender focused policy actions that allow women to balance family and work to increase labour productivity go in the same direction (ILO, 2019[28]). Subsidising early childhood education can provide alternatives to parent care (OECD, 2020[30]), allowing women to re-enter the labour market, after pregnancy. Comprehensive care systems for young students, the elderly and the sick that combine policies relating to the distribution of time, resources, benefits and services connected with health and education policies can prevent that women have an excessive burden of unpaid work (ECLAC, 2021[29]). These actions are particularly important in the context of the recovery, as there will be a need to catch up on learning for most students in the region, given the large number of days schools were closed compared to OECD countries (see the next section).

It is essential to expand social protection coverage to address the diversity of situations for women. LAC governments have widely used cash transfer programmes to mitigate the effects of the pandemic on households. However, suspending some conditionalities of these programmes might be necessary for women, youth and children to continue receiving benefits while returning to normal and avoiding extra unpaid work for women. Ensuring that women most affected by the crisis are targeted as beneficiaries, e.g. by making them the direct recipients of transfers among household members or prioritising female household heads, is key in the short term.

Transforming the social norms associated with an unequal distribution of care work might require considerable time. However, the pandemic offers an opportunity to raise awareness of the value of care and domestic work and increase effective communication and education on these issues to change the imbalance in unpaid work inside the household. In the medium term, men and boys need to be included in advancing essential goals for women's social and economic development, especially through redistribution of unpaid care work, challenging the idea that it is just women's responsibility. To achieve this, the inclusion of gender-equitable masculinities in a new social contract in the region can promote women's empowerment and provide support for gender equality. Gender-focused recovery policies should consider as a goal the promotion of this transformation of masculinities (OECD, 2021[34]).

Last, increasing women representatives' participation in the design process of gender-sensitive social protection programmes and taking the gender dimension into account in public policy must be a priority in the construction of a new social contract (Chapter 4).

Rapid actions to tackle inequalities in education and skills acquisition are key for the recovery

The COVID-19 pandemic amplified existing inequalities in the access to and quality of education in Latin America. LAC countries were not prepared to digitise education, affecting around 154 million students in the region (UNICEF, 2020[35]). Most students do not have the resources to connect to or use an electronic device, with a clear difference between students attending advantaged and disadvantaged schools. While 51% of 15-year-olds in advantaged schools have access to online learning platforms, only 21% in disadvantaged schools do (OECD, 2020[6]). The role of teachers can amplify gaps in students' learning during the pandemic. On average, across LAC countries, only 58% of 15-years-olds are enrolled in a school whose principal thinks that they can adapt their technical and pedagogical skills to integrate digital devices (OECD et al., 2020[2]).

Educational outcomes during the pandemic depend on the home environment and family background. About 73.6% of LAC's students in the poorest quintile of the income distribution have a study space (Jaramillo, 2020[36]). Parents' skills, social capital, time availability and capacity to help children to use technology for learning contribute to widening gaps (OECD, 2020[37]). Advantaged students are more likely to have parents with higher cognitive and digital skills who can support distance learning (OECD, 2020[38]). Most impoverished parents have not finished secondary school and rarely use information and communications technology (ICT) other than mobile phones. In LAC, the levels of parent involvement in school, measured as the percentage of parents who discussed their child's progress with a teacher on their own initiative, are below the OECD average (37% vs. 41%) (OECD, 2020[39]). Moreover, the index of parent involvement in home learning shows significant variation among socio-economic groups: between 10.4 and 22.6 times lower for the poorest quintile, compared to the highest (Jaramillo, 2020[36]).[1]

Many schools in LAC were forced to close to contain the spread of the virus. Globally, schools have been fully closed for, on average, 19 weeks at the time of writing. In LAC, the figure is 26 weeks of full school closures, on average, making it the region with the highest average number of lost school days (UNICEF, 2021[40]). On average, between March 2020 and May 2021, school closure status in LAC was more than 70% higher than in the OECD (Figure 2.1). Across LAC countries, there is considerable variation in school weeks lost; for instance, Chile and Uruguay have lost an average of 14 weeks due to COVID-19. Most of the time, schools in these countries remained open or partially open, while countries such as Brazil and Panama have lost 38 and 55 weeks, respectively.

Figure 2.1. School closures have been longer in LAC than in OECD countries, threatening to deepen education inequalities

Number of weeks of full school closures due to COVID-19

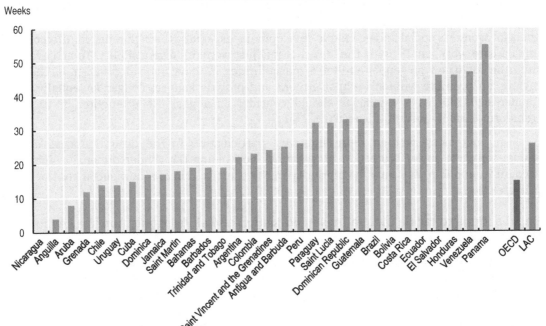

Note: OECD average includes the then 37 member countries. LAC average includes Brazil, Chile, Colombia, Costa Rica, Cuba, Dominican Republic, Ecuador, El Salvador, Guatemala, Haiti, Honduras, Mexico, Nicaragua, Panama, Peru, Uruguay and Venezuela. Updated until 1 May 2021.

Source: UNESCO (2020), Global Monitoring of School Closures caused by COVID-19 https://en.unesco.org/covid19/education response#schoolclosures.

StatLink ᠍᠍᠍ https://doi.org/10.1787/888934286179

The direct impact of closing schools is possible learning loss. Prolonged interruptions of studies (for example, due to vacations or strikes) are associated with a reduction in learning levels, especially among students in a state of vulnerability (Azevedo et al., 2020[41]; Busso, 2021[42]). Furthermore, this impact may differ among socio-economic groups and may increase inequality. Many LAC schools remain closed at the time of writing, and there is insufficient evidence to assess thoroughly the impact of the COVID-19 pandemic on student learning outcomes. However, preliminary data from the United States show that, between March and May 2020, students from high-income households using the Zearn mathematics platform temporarily learned less but soon went back to January baseline levels, while low-income students ended the school year almost 50% below baseline levels (Jaramillo, 2020[36]; Chetty, 2020[43]). The difference can be partially explained by the fact that high-income students – who already have developed digital cognitive skills, have access to ICT and have parents who can guide them through the use of online resources – can more readily benefit from digital technologies tools (Basto-Aguirre, Cerutti and Nieto-Parra, 2020[44]).

In addition to the most direct impacts, the prolonged closures of schools have also other indirect impacts. For instance, they are affecting the recovery from employment losses for women. The presence of school-age children is associated with a greater probability of unemployment during the pandemic due to increased household childcare needs, given that social norms encourage women to become the primary family caregivers (Cucagna and Romero, 2021[45]). The burden of unpaid domestic and care work among girls and adolescent girls could also increase. In addition, the pandemic could force children from poorer families into the labour market, increasing child labour rates to 7.3% of children aged 5 to 17 – some 10.5 million children (ILO/ECLAC, 2020[46]). The safe reopening of schools, and training and extra-curricular support for the most disadvantaged students, are therefore a priority to facilitate an equal recovery in the region.

Increasing evidence shows that in-person schooling is not a main driver of contagion, in case of stringent safety protocols including correct distancing, masks and case testing, and that pandemic's impact on children might be worse if they do not return to class (UNICEF, 2021[40]). Investing in improving the state of school infrastructure to ensure basic sanitation and the respect of hygiene conditions in the LAC region is urgently required to ensure a prompt and safe return to school since most countries opted to keep schools closed. Reopening should follow guidelines established by the World Health Organization and organisations such as UNICEF (WHO, 2020[47]; UNICEF, 2020[48]). Planning teacher supply and demand and improving training and access to the Internet and technologies for those who cannot return to school are intermediate steps that should be rapidly implemented to protect education access and quality in LAC.

The continuity of policy interventions that address the pandemic's crisis is essential, especially for those that can reduce inequalities in access to communications infrastructure, facilities, equipment and content (Basto-Aguirre, Cerutti and Nieto-Parra, 2020[44]). In LAC, around 100 education policy actions have been adopted since the beginning of the pandemic, but most related to the suspension of classes: 62 actions provided for remote learning tools (ECLAC, 2020[49]). Social protection programmes also constitute an important mechanism to reduce the pressure some households face due to coexistence or economic problems that might affect children's well-being (Jaramillo, 2020[36]). For example, in 2020 Colombia provided a special cash transfer incentive to the beneficiaries of the "Youth in Action Programme" (*Jóvenes en Acción*) with the only condition that they were enrolled in education since March 2021. The programme aims to guarantee access to quality education for youth experiencing economic disadvantages or in a vulnerable situation since 2012.

COVID-19 exacerbated education gaps and created new ones. It is essential to support schools by implementing initiatives that help students catch up on missed learning (OECD, 2020[50]). In Europe and North America, summer schools, accelerated education programmes and other relatable practices were designed to help disadvantaged students catch up. Summer schools have been implemented in Canada, Germany and the United Kingdom. Planning how to tackle arising inequalities will need to include implementing these types of initiatives to provide motivation and substantial learning gains in a short period for disadvantaged populations in LAC.

Countries can choose to implement accelerated programmes focused on core subjects, making them flexible and age-appropriate (OECD, 2020[50]). Norway is among countries implementing them, and organisations such as UNICEF and the Accelerated Education Working Groups (AEWG) advise using them to address the education gap. France financed 1.5 million additional teacher hours for after-school support of students. Designing and applying universal curricula, supporting non-formal learning activities at home and encouraging after-school tutoring constitute potential policy actions to close the widening education gaps. Last, it is important for the recovery to focus on the well-being and socio-emotional skills of students and teaching staff, as these skills allow them to approach traumatic situations calmly and with emotional stability (ECLAC/UNESCO, 2020[51]).

Policies should guarantee the basic rights of, and attention to, migrants, who experience multiple vulnerabilities in the region

Migration is on the rise in LAC, specifically driven by the Venezuelan crisis, among other important corridors. More than 11.6 million migrants resided in LAC countries in 2019 (UNDESA, 2019[52]). Increasing inequalities across the region have changed the shape and routes of migration. Migration figures have dramatically increased since 2015, with the humanitarian and economic crisis in Venezuela pushing around 4.7 million people to leave the country between 2015 and 2020, close to 4 million of whom have settled in LAC countries (OECD, 2020[6]). Colombia bore the largest part of this flow, but the migration crisis has since expanded to Chile, Ecuador and Peru. The situation has also been marked by increased emigration along a new migration route from Haiti to South America and the route that crosses Central America, Mexico and the United States (OECD/ILO, 2018[53]).

Migrants and their families are disproportionately affected by the crisis, warranting special attention by governments (OHCHR, 2020[54]). Previous economic crises have made it possible to ascertain the vulnerability of migrants in indicators such as health, employment, education and others (OECD, 2020[55]), which allows dimensioning the problems they face during the pandemic. Migrants in LAC are over-represented among the poorest segments of the population, and increased migration, coupled with the COVID-19 crisis, has shifted people's perceptions towards negative views of migrants.[2] Last, migrant families are more likely to be evicted owing to non-payment, given that many do not have a formal rental contract, and to live overcrowded in informal slums, with reduced access to essential public services and means to comply with sanitation recommendations (ECLAC, 2020[56]).

Migrant workers are concentrated in informal low-productivity sectors, which makes them more exposed to the virus and more likely to experience job loss. Lack of recognition of education and qualifications limits their access to the formal labour market and their capacity to recover in the post-pandemic period. Among migrants, women lay at the intersection of various deprivations and vulnerabilities. More than half of migrants are women (51.6%), and more than one-third of them are engaged in paid domestic work (35.3%) (ILO, 2016[57]). The significant impact of the crisis on the domestic service workforce has meant that many migrant women lost their source of income without the possibility of returning to their country of origin. Racism and xenophobia also represent important challenges to adequate protection and re-entry into the labour market after the crisis for migrants (ECLAC, 2020[56]). The legal status of migrants impacts as well on their integration in the labour market of the country of destination. Different legal requirements are often a barrier to employability. For instance, refugees may not be entitled to take up jobs in the formal sector, or have no rights to access public education, health or to benefit from public employment services and social assistance. The same may apply to irregular migrants. Rules are normally more flexible in the case of family reunifications, and migrants who join the families face higher chances of a smooth transition in the labour market of the host country (OECD/ILO, 2018[53]).

Facilitating migrants' access to social protection measures should be a priority. Replacing part of their income loss will help these families comply with social distancing measures. Allowing access to health care and immunisation will reduce the spread of the virus since most migrants hold jobs requiring in-person interactions. This externality is one of the main arguments in favour of prioritising groups most at risk in the context of a pandemic; universal social protection becomes a precondition for success in combating the spread of the disease (Lusting and Tommasi, 2020[58]). It is essential to guarantee migrants' access to health services (OHCHR, 2020[54]), especially in LAC countries that do not have a history of implementing these types of programmes. So far, Colombia has been one of the only countries to implement a policy to support migrants in the pandemic, mainly via detection and prevention (ECLAC, 2020[56]) (Box 2.1).

Extending coverage of support measures by modifying their access and duration to benefit the migrant population is part of the inclusive recovery policy actions that can accelerate socio-economic recovery in the region. Some OECD countries have changed their policies or regulations to extend coverage and support measures. Belgium and Spain reduced the minimum duration of work required to access unemployment benefits, which helps cover migrants through social protection responses (OECD, 2020[55]). In LAC, Brazil implemented an emergency fund to support informal or unemployed migrants (UNDP, 2020[59]), while Colombia and Peru introduced new cash transfer programmes (*Ingreso Solidario, Apoyo económico para migrantes venezolanos*). Similar policies have been set up in Chile (*Ingreso Familiar por Emergencia*), Panama (*Plan Solidario*) and Trinidad and Tobago (*Asistencia COVID-19*). At the global level, OECD donor countries have engaged in extending migrant and refugee access to public goods and services, such as public schools, formal labour market participation, entrepreneurship and skilled work in renewable energy (Gagnon and Rodrigues, 2020[60]).

Helping migrants who live or travel in inadequate conditions, with no access to water, sanitation or good hygiene, is key in the fight against the pandemic (OHCHR, 2020[54]). In LAC, countries including Colombia have helped Venezuelan migrants in border areas by building temporary shelters and distributing food (UNDP, 2020[59]). Actions to mitigate the problems that migrants experience should include: i) access to testing and health care to prevent COVID-19; ii) relocation of highly populated settlements; iii) a framework to suspend evictions; and iv) strategies to tackle gender violence.

Migrant workers are essential for many sectors of the economy, including those providing basic services during the pandemic (ICC, 2020[61]). This might raise awareness of the importance of extending their worker rights regularising migrants' labour situation so that they can access the same labour benefits as nationals. Colombia, for instance, extended the Special Permanence Permit (*Permiso Especial de Permanencia* [PEP]) to allow Venezuelan migrants to access the institutional provision in matters of health, nutrition services, education and work (UNDP, 2020[59]) (Box 2.1).

Box 2.1. **Colombia's national regularisation programme to respond to the Venezuelan crisis**

According to the United Nations Department of Economic and Social Affairs, over 5 million Venezuelans have left the country due to the political and economic crisis. Colombia has been the primary destination for Venezuelan migrants and refugees, hosting around 1.8 million Venezuelans as of December 2020, followed by Brazil, Chile, Ecuador and Peru. Some 56% of migrants in Colombia are in an irregular condition. According to the United Nations, Venezuelan migration has not shrunk during the pandemic. By the end of 2021, there could be 6.2 million Venezuelan migrants and refugees, of which a considerable proportion is expected to opt for Colombia as a new country of residence.

The Colombian government had implemented measures to protect its population from risks posed by COVID-19 and broadened them to include Venezuelan refugees and migrants among beneficiaries. Adopted measures included free access to emergency and COVID-19-related health services for irregular migrants. Even before the pandemic, the country granted full access to the national health system schemes for those with the Special Permanence Permit (Ministerio de Salud y Protección Social, 2018[62]), an identification document created in 2017 that allows registered migrants to access the same institutional services as nationals for two years.

Providing humanitarian attention in border corridors, offering access to some of the social protection programmes and promoting the co-ordination of action through international co-operation and with local governments have proven to be key elements in migrant support. Social assistance transfers through *Ingreso Solidario* and the in-kind school feeding transfers adopted in 2020 benefit vulnerable households without differentiation by nationality (Ministerio de Salud y Protección Social, 2020[63]). Promoting co-ordination and sharing information with local governments in high-impact areas and with international humanitarian actors has provided effective solutions to respond to migrants' needs.

In February 2021, Colombia extended integration measures for migrants by establishing the Temporary Protected Statute for Venezuelan Migrants (EPTV), making it a pioneer in the region in adopting universal measures to protect migrants. The EPTV consists of a complementary mechanism to the international protection regime for refugees, that allows closing existing gaps based on the migratory reality and the country's institutional, social and economic response capacity (Migración Ministerio de Relaciones Exteriores, 2021[64]). By providing ten-year residency visas for all Venezuelan migrants (regular and irregular) with the possibility of obtaining long-term residency, Colombia's new strategy protects the human rights of a part of the population currently in a condition of greater vulnerability. This new set of measures will provide legal status for over 1 million irregular migrants in Colombia.

The EPTV protects Venezuelans from exclusion from institutional services and involuntary returns. Moreover, it reduces the risk of exploitation in labour markets and safeguards Venezuelan households from the consequences of the pandemic. The new status increases migrants' access to public services and social protection and might improve their access to quality jobs and decent living conditions. Implementing such a large-scale initiative requires a significant investment of time, logistics and resources; however, the measure has received support from the international community and has reinforced the need for generous and bold actions to provide long-term solutions to migration challenges.

The potential of a green and inclusive recovery in LAC

Environmental and socio-economic risks are strongly interconnected. Post pandemic, risks that were previously seen as a distant threat appear to be a concrete opportunity to create the conditions for a more inclusive and sustainable development.

Advancing towards a low-carbon development model, or "green transition", is not only necessary to reduce the increase in temperatures and safeguard the planet, but can also be a way to reduce inequalities, create quality jobs and redesign social protection systems. At the same time, tackling inequalities and advancing towards more universal social protection systems, as suggested above, will have a key role in addressing the impacts of climate change that disproportionately affect the most vulnerable groups. It will also help workers in economic activities that are affected by the green transition to reduce the possible negative impacts and move into new employment opportunities.

Green growth and socio-economic prosperity can go hand in hand in LAC. Countries should seize the opportunity created by the pandemic to implement structural reforms to move towards a greener, more inclusive and more resilient development model. Stimulus packages should facilitate a "just transition", focus on direct benefits to people and address infrastructure gaps to meet the United Nations Sustainable Development Goals (SDG) of mobilising green investments and creating jobs.

The post-COVID world calls for an integrated vision of social and environmental development implemented at all levels of government. It is necessary to integrate social domains into the design of green transition policies, and it is key to mainstream climate mitigation and environmental considerations as cross-cutting issues across government areas, particularly regarding social protection systems. Failure to do so runs the risk of undermining societal acceptance of future ambitious policy proposals addressing the environment. Integrated approaches would allow social and human development issues to be taken fully into account in the ecological transition, to achieve carbon neutrality and drastically reducing multi-dimensional inequalities (AFD, 2019[65]). Moreover, adopting a well-being lens to address the green transition could help design climate strategies with the potential to accelerate climate change mitigation while improving wider well-being outcomes (OECD, 2019[66]).

Linking a green transition with the region's social challenges could enable a successful recovery from COVID-19 in at least three domains: i) reducing the unequal impact of climate change on vulnerable groups; ii) creating quality jobs; and iii) promoting social inclusion through broader social protection systems.

Tackling climate change to reduce inequality: Two intertwined challenges

The pandemic exposed the close interaction between human and animal health and the environment amplifying the necessity to address the challenges of inequality and environmental degradation together (OECD, 2021[67]). Climate change exacerbates existing inequalities and social tensions within and across countries, as the impacts of environmental degradation tend to be concentrated among vulnerable groups. There is a kind of "double punishment": those who suffer and will suffer the impacts of climate change the most are those who contribute the least to the problem (AFD, 2019[65]; AFD, 2018[68]). While the pandemic increased the number of people living below the poverty line in LAC (Chapter 1), climate change is projected to contribute an additional 5 million by 2030 (IDB, 2021[75]). Climate change threatens to reverse the global health gains of the past 50 years (The Lancet Commissions, 2015[69]).

Inequality represents a significant obstacle to the fight against climate change and ecological disruption. Indeed, the ambitious transition policies necessary to respond to climate and ecological challenges could affect the groups most at risk, through job restructuring, temporary job losses and loss of income (OECD, 2021[67]). These undesirable effects will likely be difficult to accept for fragile populations and social groups already under stress due to pronounced inequalities. Policies should consider this at the design and implementation phases (AFD, 2019[65]; AFD, 2018[68]).

In Latin American cities, groups living in precarious neighbourhoods are more susceptible to climate change effects and other phenomena, such as air pollution, due to high rates of residential segregation for socio-economic reasons. High urbanisation rates and the unregulated expansion of urban areas allowed those groups to locate in high-risk zones, such as floodplains and landslide-prone slopes, with deficient or non-existent infrastructure, elevating residents' health risks and vulnerability to extreme climate events due to their socio-economic status (CAF, 2014[70]). Cities have an enormous potential to contribute to both mitigation and adaptation efforts and achieving national climate targets. There is an increasing recognition of the urgency to develop effective territorial strategies and turn cities into better places to live, in harmony with nature, including through appropriate use of Nature-based Solutions and Ecosystem-based Approaches (OECD, 2019[71]).

Addressing the deficits in basic infrastructure and services in informal settlements and involving citizens in political decisions are ways to build climate resilience. Investing in "risk-reducing" infrastructure and services (e.g. quality and affordable water, electricity, sanitation, health centres and paved roads), as well as in climate change adaptation and mitigation, could improve well-being in informal settlements and making them more resilient to climate-related risks (OECD, 2021[67]). Incorporating citizens into the design and implementation of these policies is key (Chapter 4).

Air pollution also has unequal impacts across socio-economic groups. Air pollution is largely caused by the increase in private transport, which has notable effects in terms of mortality, morbidity, productivity and well-being (ECLAC, 2021[72]). It is estimated that the health effects of air pollution cost citizens 15% of their income (Hidalgo and Huizenga, 2013[73]). However, outdoor air pollution is not the only source of health and economic issues for people. Indoor pollution has also sizeable negative effects. Biomass burning for cooking and heating generates most of the emissions within households. Albeit declining, mortality rates in LAC from indoor air pollution were close to 15 per 100 000 in 2017 (OECD, 2019[71]).

In a region highly exposed to climate change and biodiversity loss, Caribbean countries will suffer the most (Chapter 6). Inequalities in potential climate change impacts vary across LAC countries. More than half of Caribbean nations face "extreme" exposure risks (CAF, 2014[70]). Key risks the Caribbean face include exposure to extreme weather events, such as hurricanes and severe storms, increased intensity and frequency of droughts, sea level rise and ocean acidification. Vulnerable groups will be the least prepared and the most affected by these events. Lack of information to identify the areas most susceptible to climate change and the absence of risk-mitigation tools to integrate climate change issues into policy making are the most important barriers to climate adaptation in the region (CAF, 2014[70]).

A just green recovery is an opportunity to create jobs and promote social inclusion

A green recovery for Latin America is expected to create 15 million net jobs by 2030 (ILO/IDB, 2020[74]) in the following sectors: renewable electricity (156% more jobs than in 2014), sustainable agriculture (124%), services (61%), construction and forestry (58%), utilities (56%) and manufacturing (50%) (ILO/IDB, 2020[74]). The number of jobs in agriculture will double by 2030 thanks to climate-resilient and low-emission agricultural approaches. By 2030, the low-carbon transition is expected to increase jobs in LAC by 4.0% compared to 2014. Brazil and Central America will particularly benefit, reaching a 5.5% increase (IDB, 2021[75]).

Decarbonisation in LAC is projected to create mostly medium-skilled and low-skilled jobs. This could promote social inclusion if combined with formalisation strategies. By 2030, of the projected 15 million jobs created by decarbonisation in the region, 60% will be medium skilled, 36% low skilled and 4% high skilled. This trend reflects the varying employment demand from sectors that win (e.g. plant-based agriculture and food manufacturing) or lose (e.g. fossil fuel-based electrical generation or energy distribution) in the transition (ILO/IDB, 2020[74]).

Sustainable adaptation infrastructure can generate significant economic, social and environmental benefits. Investment in adaptation infrastructure, such as weatherproof roads and climate-resilient housing, can have immediate positive effects on employment from construction-related jobs. The low-carbon and sustainable transition could add USD 535 billion to Brazil's GDP by 2030 (World Bank, 2020[76]).

Climate-proofing development gains are crucial for economic growth and the eradication of poverty. Investing in resilient infrastructure, sanitation, agriculture or simply protecting coastal ecosystems can yield USD 7.1 trillion in benefits by 2030 (Mena-Carrasco and Dufey, 2021[77]). Resilient infrastructure needs to be climate-proofed to make countries safer after the recovery. Doing so would cost approximately USD 13 billion per year by 2030 but would achieve a net benefit of USD 700 billion (World Bank, 2020[76]).

The circular economy approach complements and reinforces climate change mitigation actions. Current climate discussions focus on the transition to renewable energy and energy efficiency, which will help reduce 55% of total greenhouse gas emissions. The circular economy can eliminate the remaining 45% of emissions that are generated by the way goods are manufactured and used (Ellen MacArthur Foundation, 2019[78]).

Transition to a circular economy could create new jobs and help promote a just transition in the region. The circular economy approach has been gaining momentum in LAC since 2019, with more than 80 public policy initiatives implemented since then. The application of circular economy principles has the potential to generate 4.8 million net jobs by 2030 (ILO/IDB, 2019[79]). Job creation in steel, aluminium, wood and other metals reprocessing sectors is estimated to offset the losses associated with the extraction of minerals and other materials (ILO/IDB, 2019[79]). Chapter 3 focuses on how to develop a productive strategy for the region and provides more information about how the green transition and the circular economy, in particular, can contribute to socio-environmental and economic prosperity in the region.

Renewed social protection systems for a just transition

Social protection can help address the physical impacts of climate change (natural disasters) and the possible adverse effects of green policies and phasing out of fossil fuels on workers and communities in less sustainable industries and activities, helping achieve a just transition (ILO/AFD, 2019[80]).

Strengthened social protection systems could include providing unemployment protection, employment guarantee schemes and cash transfers that are flexible and rapidly scalable for workers who lose their jobs, have their working hours reduced or whose houses are destroyed by climate-related catastrophes. Several LAC countries have started implementing programmes that link social protection measures with environmental aspects through Payment for Environmental Services programmes mainly focused, for instance, on forest conservation in countries such as Brazil, Costa Rica and Ecuador and on hydrological services in Mexico (ILO, 2016[57]).

Social protection policies should be co-ordinated and coherent and should be enhanced not only by other socio-economic policies (e.g. employment, health, education, care and macroeconomic and fiscal policies) but also by incorporating environmental aspects responding to life cycle risks and facilitating a just transition to more environmentally sustainable economies and societies.

New narratives for a sustainable future in LAC?

The concepts of the "commons" and "climate justice" could provide new narratives to rethink the region's development model. Development policies have pushed forward their actions around different narratives. Such narratives are ways to bring together very diverse actors around converging views and interests, while they seek to legitimise the rules of the game and the player institutions (AFD, 2019[81]). New concepts and frameworks, such as the "just transition", the "commons" and "climate justice", could provide new ways to address the challenges exacerbated by the COVID-19 crisis in LAC regarding a fair transition for the future of work, producing innovative ways to protect strategic and finite natural resources and to reduce the inequalities enhanced by climate change.

Taking into account citizens priorities

During the COVID-19 pandemic, Latin Americans are concerned about losing their jobs, the effectiveness of social protection mechanisms and the health system's quality and affordability. Citizens' beliefs and concerns can be tracked from various sources, including 2019 *Encuesta CAF* (ECAF 2019) data, Gallup and Google Trends. Time-frequency, data collection and purposes vary considerably across these databases. For instance, the CAF Survey is a survey of individuals in households in 11 Latin American cities that CAF has carried out annually since 2008, whereas Google searches have the potential to reveal people's most pressing issues on a very timely basis and based on worldwide coverage.

This section provides citizens' perceptions on key social dimensions for the recovery, highlighting several concerns, including jobs prospects, pensions system reforms and the quality of health care. It helps guide debates around the topics to be covered in the social pacts needed in the region (Chapter 4 on rethinking the social contract).

Latin Americans are very concerned about the current jobs crisis

After the economic crisis that followed the COVID-19 pandemic, people's concerns about their labour market prospects rose and stayed high during 2020. Google searches on topics like "curriculum vitae" spiked just in the aftermath of the crisis, and after a sudden decline, constantly rose as expectations of a quick recovery vanished. The same is true for searches related to topics like "jobs searches" or "jobs boards". According to the most recent OECD estimates, based on Gallup data, in 2020, on average across the LAC region, 73.4% of people thought that local labour markets were experiencing a very bad situation, slightly higher than the OECD average (71.7%). The share of people concerned about the situation of the labour market in LAC increased by 8.4 percentage points compared to 2019, while the increase in the OECD was of 18.4 percentage points, indicating that the labour market situation was perceived as more precarious in LAC even before the COVID-19 crisis.

Concerns about the public policies regarding unemployment benefits or social assistance have followed a similar trend, with a clearer jump during the first period of the COVID-19 crisis (Figure 2.2). It is interesting to note how close the trends are for the selected LAC countries, a signal of how the economic crisis had a symmetrical impact on people's perceptions in the region overall.

Even before the COVID-19 pandemic, Latin American workers showed a high degree of concern about the changing features of the labour market. On a 1 to 10 scale, the risk of losing their job is perceived homogenously across socio-demographic groups, with the notable exception of poor workers, who are more concerned about losing their jobs (3.5, on average).

Figure 2.2. **Google searches of the topic "government aids",
selected LAC countries, 2018-20**

Hodrick-Prescott-filtered series, number of total searches

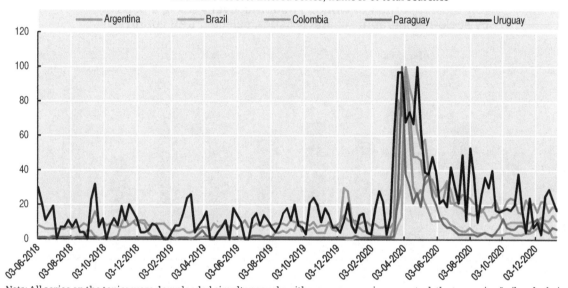

Note: All series on the topics were downloaded simultaneously with a common series as control: the term *migraña* (headache) (*enxaqueca* for Brazil) is relatively stable throughout the time range in LAC countries. The series were then filtered using the Hodrick-Prescott filter.
Source: OECD estimates based on Google Trends data.
StatLink ᕯᕤᕦ *https://doi.org/10.1787/888934286483*

Latin American workers are also worried about the possible changing tasks of their jobs. This is consistent with rapid technological change and automation (OECD, 2019[71]; OECD, 2020[82]). On average in LAC, the level of perceived technological risks is 5 on a 1 to 10 scale. It is exceptionally high in Bolivia (6.1), Ecuador (5.9), Mexico (5.4) and Peru (5.7). It is higher for males and younger workers (5.2), the most exposed to jobs requiring higher technological skills, and for workers living below the poverty line. No notable difference is found for informal workers, as their jobs usually entail fewer skills (OECD, 2019[71]). These findings suggest that policies should focus on retraining and other active labour market policies in case of jobs loss or should support workers in lifelong learning/training to help them face the changing nature of Latin American labour markets.

Many Latin American workers do not expect to retire

On average, over 40% of workers in LAC either do not know or do not think that they will retire (ECAF 2019). Expectations are even lower among women (48.5%) and older workers close to retirement (48.1%). In addition, workers living below the relative poverty line and informal workers have lower expectations of being covered by social security, compared to the overall population (59.6% and 53.8%, respectively) or do not expect to retire at all. People in Brazil, Bolivia, Panama and Paraguay, in particular, seem less optimistic.

One out of three workers in LAC think that they will never get a pension (Figure 2.3). Consistent with the previous evidence, the proportion of pessimistic views is higher among women (36.2%), middle-aged workers (36.2%), the poor (39.7%) and informal workers (45.2%). The indicator shows the inequalities embedded in the social protection system and the extent of citizens' lack of trust in it. Both aspects suggest the need for reforms to improve coverage for workers in the ageing context, informal workers and workers living below the poverty line, which will stretch the system further. The share of contributors or affiliates is close to 50% in LAC due to the high degree of informality (OECD/IDB/The World Bank, 2014[83]). This is particularly true for workers in the first income quintile, in which informal workers are over-represented.

Figure 2.3. **Proportion of workers doubting ever getting a pension, by socio-demographic characteristics, selected LAC countries**

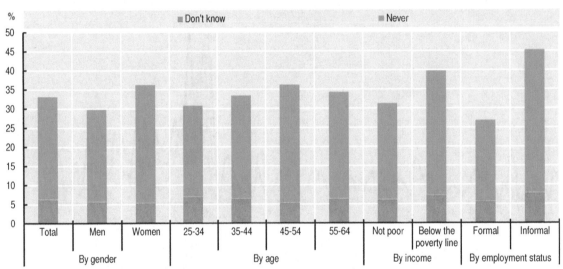

Note: Data refer to an unweighted average of the following cities: Asunción, Buenos Aires, Bogotá, Ciudad de México, Ciudad de Panamá, El Alto, La Paz, Lima, Montevideo, Quito, Santiago and Sao Paulo. Because data refer to metropolitan areas (normally capital cities), and rural areas are excluded, some caution should be exercised in the analysis. However, the indicators are treated as representative of each LAC country.

Source: OECD estimates based on CAF (2020[84]), *ECAF 2019. Percepciones de los Latinoamericanos sobre los Sistemas de Pensiones, Salud y Cuidados y el Avance Tecnológico en el Mercado Laboral,* http://scioteca.caf.com/handle/123456789/1646.

StatLink https://doi.org/10.1787/888934286198

Workers are not always in favour of broad pension reforms

Preferences for policies are connected and complementary to people's concerns. When asked about their policy preferences for pension reform, Latin American workers tend to favour postponing the current retirement age by one or two years, but the extent of agreement varies by socio-demographic characteristics. Figure 2.4 shows the results of an individual-level regression considering agreement with the reform as a dependent variable. The reference group consists of Argentinean males aged 25 to 34 in formal employment and not living below the relative poverty line. This group was chosen as it is the most likely to be more in favour of pension reform, and the public pension system has a high degree of coverage of this group (OECD, 2019[18]). Some 67.6% of these workers are in favour of a reform postponing the retirement age.

Agreement level does not significantly vary across gender or age groups. Informal workers are the only group showing a higher degree of preference for the reform (by more than five percentage points), probably because they have few years of contributions or have not contributed to the pension system at all (OECD/IDB/The World Bank, 2014[83]). Overall, in 4 out of the 11 Latin American countries covered (Brazil, Chile, Colombia and

Panama), there is no strong majority supporting an eventual pension reform, signalling the political difficulty of a policy change in those countries, especially if the expected postponement in the retirement age is more than two years.

Figure 2.4. **Effect in percentage points on the willingness to accept a reform postponing the retirement age by one or two years**

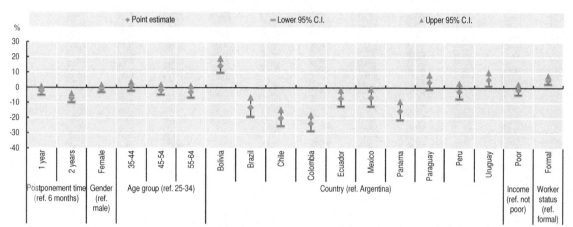

Note: Data refer to an unweighted average of the following cities: Asunción, Buenos Aires, Bogotá, Ciudad de México, Ciudad de Panamá, El Alto, La Paz, Lima, Montevideo, Quito, Santiago and Sao Paulo. Because data refer to metropolitan areas (normally capital cities), and rural areas are excluded, some caution should be exercised in the analysis. However, the indicators are treated as representative of each LAC country.
Source: OECD estimates based on CAF (2020[84]), ECAF 2019. *Percepciones de los Latinoamericanos sobre los Sistemas de Pensiones, Salud y Cuidados y el Avance Tecnológico en el Mercado Laboral,* http://scioteca.caf.com/handle/123456789/1646.
StatLink ⟪⟫ *https://doi.org/10.1787/888934286502*

People's preferences vary when more detailed information on the reform are added. Fiscal sustainability, particularly in LAC, is a serious constraint. High informality makes any workers postpone decisions to secure an income in old age. This translates into people using informal insurance mechanisms (Cecchini, 2019[85]; OECD, 2020[6]) or having no type of social insurance. Given the ageing and informality trends in LAC, many workers could reach retirement without any plan and face poverty and vulnerability (OECD/IDB/The World Bank, 2014[83]), resulting in a massive burden on the economy.

When asked about other possible policy options to reform pensions, taking into account fiscal sustainability, workers tend to prefer a balanced mix of policies consisting of postponement of the retirement age, a hike in social contributions and a cut in benefits (Figure 2.5). This is particularly true among younger workers: almost half of workers aged 25 to 34 tend to agree with these options, compared to less than 40% for both those close to the retirement age and those living below the poverty line.

Overall, workers tend to be much less likely, than the overall population, to support a cut in benefits and much more likely to support a well-mixed range of interventions. Workers close to retirement and those living below the poverty line still show significantly lower support, indicating the difficulty of getting agreement on a fiscally sustainable pension reform among those who would probably benefit less from it.

People are well aware of the need for policy changes. However, they do not always support broad social protection when asked about specific policy options. Managing trade-offs and taking into account the fiscal sustainability of potential reforms will be crucial but not easy. Targeting intervention to the most exposed to the current crisis may well be a good compromise. Reforms should focus on informal workers, those living below the poverty line and the vulnerable middle class, which can fall into poverty.

Figure 2.5. **Preferences for a pension reform aiming at fiscal sustainability, by socio-demographic characteristics**

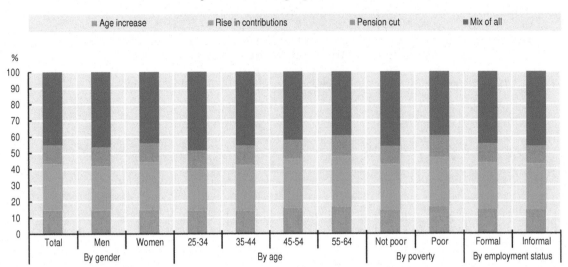

Note: Data refer to the question, "In order to maintain fiscal balance, among the following list of reforms, which one would you agree more with?" Data refer to an unweighted average of the following cities: Asunción, Buenos Aires, Bogotá, Ciudad de México, Ciudad de Panamá, El Alto, La Paz, Lima, Montevideo, Quito, Santiago and Sao Paulo. Because data refer to metropolitan areas (normally capital cities), and rural areas are excluded, some caution should be exercised in the analysis. However, the indicators are treated as representative of each LAC country.

Source: OECD estimates based on CAF (2020[84]), ECAF 2019. *Percepciones de los Latinoamericanos sobre los Sistemas de Pensiones, Salud y Cuidados y el Avance Tecnológico en el Mercado Laboral,* http://scioteca.caf.com/handle/123456789/1646.

StatLink ᵃᵐˢᵖ https://doi.org/10.1787/888934286521

However, promoting greater awareness of the actual situation in terms of ageing in their country does not seem to increase people's preference for a certain policy option. This is in line with previous evidence that illustrates the view that providing detailed information on some economic issues does not shift people's preferences for policy interventions in a significant way (Alesina, Stantcheva and Teso, 2018[86]; Kuziemko, Norton and Saez, 2015[87]), for instance on preferences for redistributive policies tackling rising income inequality.

People are very dissatisfied with the quality of health care in LAC

After the onset of the COVID-19 crisis, people's concerns about the quality of health services have increased, although unevenly across LAC countries (Figure 2.6). This may be linked to the severity of the health situation. Google searches for health care reveal a particular degree of concern in Peru, although as the pandemic hit hard in other countries, such as Argentina, Chile and Uruguay, people got more worried about the healthcare system situation.

The current health crisis exacerbated people's discontent with health care (Figure 2.7, Panel A; Chapter 4). The level of concern with the quality of access to health services varies across socio-demographic groups. Concerns are higher among middle-aged people and much higher among informal workers and people living below the poverty line, especially those not covered by any public or private health insurance (Figure 2.7, Panel B).

The concerns are well explained by the level of OOP healthcare expenditure that Latin American people face (OECD/The World Bank, 2020[13]). LAC households have high levels of OOP spending, and in most countries, there is no universal coverage. In 2018, the OOP expenditure in LAC was 30.1%, on average, vs. 13.7.% in the OECD (WHO, 2020[88]). On average, the proportion of households spending over 10% of income or consumption (depending on the proxy chosen) on OOP expenditure is almost 8%. The proportion is low (under 2%) in some countries, such as El Salvador, Guatemala and Mexico, but it is almost 17% in Barbados, followed by Chile and Nicaragua (around 15%).

Figure 2.6. **Google searches of the topic "health care", selected LAC countries, 2020-21**

Hodrick-Prescott-filtered series, number of total searches

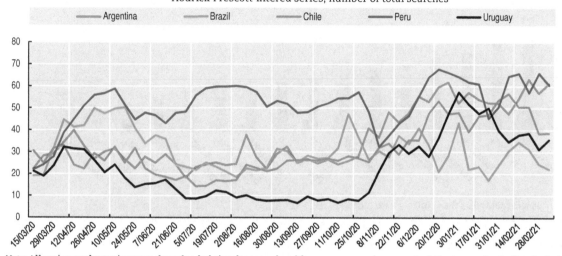

Note: All series on the topics were downloaded simultaneously with a common series as control: the term *migraña* (headache) (*enxaqueca* for Brazil) is relatively stable throughout the selected time range in LAC countries. The series were then filtered using the Hodrick-Prescott filter.
Source: OECD estimates based on Google Trends data.
StatLink ᵃᵐˢᵖ *https://doi.org/10.1787/888934286540*

Figure 2.7. **Perceptions of the quality of the healthcare system in LAC, 2019**

Mean on 1-10 scale

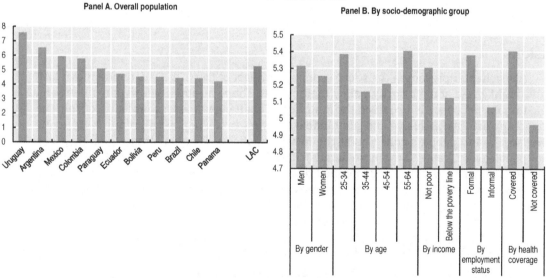

Note: Data are an average on a 1 to 10 scale, where 1 means totally unsatisfied and 10 means totally satisfied. Data refer to an unweighted average of the following cities: Asunción, Buenos Aires, Bogotá, Ciudad de México, Ciudad de Panamá, El Alto, La Paz, Lima, Montevideo, Quito, Santiago and Sao Paulo. Because data refer to metropolitan areas (normally capital cities), and rural areas are excluded, some caution should be exercised in the analysis. However, the indicators are treated as representative of each LAC country.
Source: OECD estimates based on CAF (2020[84]), ECAF 2019. *Percepciones de los Latinoamericanos sobre los Sistemas de Pensiones, Salud y Cuidados y el Avance Tecnológico en el Mercado Laboral,* http://scioteca.caf.com/handle/123456789/1646.
StatLink ᵃᵐˢᵖ *https://doi.org/10.1787/888934286559*

Figure 2.8. **Proportion of the population spending over 10% or 25% of income or household consumption in out-of-pocket healthcare expenditure**

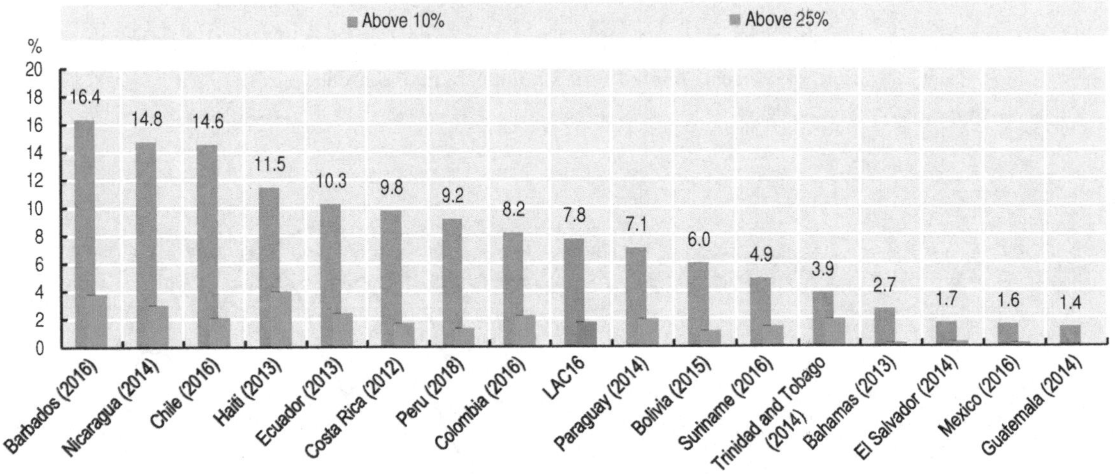

Note: Countries with data older than 2010 were excluded.

Source: OECD/The World Bank (2020[13]), *Health at a Glance: Latin America and the Caribbean 2020*, http://dx.doi.org/10.1787/6089164f-en.

StatLink https://doi.org/10.1787/888934286578

High OOP expenditure has a sizable effect on poverty. In 15 LAC countries, 1.7% of the population was pushed below the poverty line, compared with 1.2% in the OECD. To ensure adequate access and coverage for all groups, governments should introduce social protection policies that cushion the negative impacts of OOP expenditure. Common aspects of successful reforms include pooling or co-ordinating use of various revenue sources, progressively increasing the size of compulsory prepaid funds, and redistributing money from prepaid funds.

Conclusions

This chapter presented the socio-economic impact of the COVID-19 pandemic in LAC and highlighted some priority policy messages to shape a more inclusive, resilient and sustainable recovery. It discussed the main social challenges and lessons learned from the ongoing crisis. An inclusive and sustainable recovery in the region will require: i) putting well-being and people's concerns at the heart of policy making; ii) creating quality jobs for people (see Chapter 3 for more details); iii) advancing towards robust and sustainable social protection systems, underpinned by higher levels of formalisation; iv) protecting and supporting the most vulnerable groups, and facilitating their access to quality jobs; v) making the best of the green recovery potential to ensure a "just transition". Box 2.2 presents key policy messages to build back better in LAC.

Putting well-being at the heart of policy making

The pandemic changed the priorities and actions of governments in the LAC region. Before the crisis, governments focused on expanding the middle classes, which increasingly demanded public services and well-being policies. After the onset of the crisis, many Latin Americans will fall into poverty for the first time since 2010. Governments are therefore called upon to reduce poverty and protect the most vulnerable populations. To this end, productivity, employment and social protection will be essential and should be part of a renewed social contract (Chapter 4).

The crisis offers a unique opportunity to transform the focus of policy making to one centred on people's well-being and an understanding of the multi-dimensional nature of development. The pandemic has made the provision of quality healthcare and education services a priority and reinforced the need for more robust social protection systems.

Towards robust universal social protection systems

This juncture opens the possibility of moving towards universal social protection, e.g. including informal workers. Expansion of social protections systems goes hand-in-hand with a continued strong focus on employment generation and formalisation. Current protection mechanisms could be better adapted to the region's labour market dynamics. Increasing the adaptability of social protection contributions may help create a more inclusive formal sector by including part-time workers, those working in the digital platform economy, those earning below minimum wage and agricultural workers. Digital technologies offer great potential to develop innovative ways to contribute to the system and reach vulnerable populations (OECD et al., 2020[2]). Streamlining workers' switching between contributory and non-contributory social protection regimes could help extend coverage.

Policy responses to the COVID-19 crisis present a basis to move towards universal comprehensive and sustainable social protection systems. Governments responded rapidly to the crisis by adopting targeted social assistance support for vulnerable populations not covered by traditional social programmes or social protection mechanisms. Permanently targeting these populations and providing social protection are key conditions of a welfare state.

Social protection in the LAC region needs to move towards stronger financing mechanisms, making social contributions more flexible with a mix of non-contributory, contributory and voluntary contributions. Social security contributions as a percentage of labour costs are relatively high in LAC. LAC countries' averages are similar to those of OECD countries and exceptionally high for the lowest deciles (OECD/IDB/CIAT, 2016[89]). Reducing non-labour costs could encourage formal job creation, especially in the small- and medium-sized enterprise sector, thus supporting entrepreneurship. However, a clear productive strategy is key to support those policies (Chapter 3). It could also improve citizens' perception of the state's social protection system, thus strengthening incentives for formalisation and tax payment (OECD et al., 2019[90]). Creating a social safety net decoupled from formal employment and financed through general taxation is one way to achieve this objective.

Understanding citizens' demands to inform policy decisions

People, especially the more vulnerable, are very concerned about the current poor labour market prospects, lack of a sustainable pension system and lack of high-quality health care. The pandemic has increased people's concerns, which were already very high in many Latin American countries. Lack of adequate social protection is a multi-dimensional policy challenge, which if not addressed, may exacerbate the current economic crisis due to COVID-19.

People are well aware of the need for policy changes. However, they do not always support broad social protection and healthcare system reforms if asked about specific policy options. Managing the trade-offs and taking into account fiscal sustainability will be crucial but not easy. Targeting intervention to the most exposed to the current crisis may well be a good compromise. Reforms should focus on informal workers, those living below the poverty line and the vulnerable middle class, which can fall into poverty and show very high levels of concern and dissatisfaction with the current economic situation and the quality of social protection systems.

Increasing people's awareness of social policies and the constraints that any reform faces may be one way to boost inclusiveness in the process of redefining the social contract and to avoid social unrest or protests. Well-informed citizens are more likely to support broad reforms, but information alone will not solve the issue, especially if trust in institutions is limited. Evidence urges caution concerning the extent of a shift in people's preferences. Moreover, governments in LAC should include citizens and stakeholders, especially those generally excluded from policy discussions, in the prioritisation and design phases of the post-COVID-19 social policies (Chapter 4).

Box 2.2. **Key policy messages**

There are strong heterogeneities across countries in Latin America and the Caribbean (LAC). The impact of the coronavirus (COVID-19) pandemic and countries' ability to react to challenges and spur an inclusive recovery will vary, depending on their standing development position and individual characteristics. These particularities demand tailored policy actions in response to the COVID-19 crisis that take into account the country's characteristics and move towards overcoming structural challenges. The following key messages present a shared pool of policies to address common challenges in the region, which policy makers should adapt to their country's specific context.

1. LAC needs to consolidate robust and sustainable social protection systems to build resilience and recover from the social and economic devastation caused by the crisis.

- **Move towards universal and sustainable social protection systems** by targeting vulnerable populations not covered by traditional social assistance mechanisms and social protection systems.

- **Make social protection contributions more flexible.** Advance towards a system that allows workers to be formalised even if they earn below minimum wage, work via digital platforms or work part time, among other conditions of employment.

- **Move towards social protection systems in which coverage does not depend on employment status.** To avoid discouraging labour formalisation, general taxes instead of worker contributions could finance social protection systems.

- **Strengthen social protection information systems.** More efficient and integrated social protection information systems could allow, for example, expediting workers' shifting from contributory to non-contributory status. Countries have made significant progress during the pandemic, putting in place emergency programmes.

2. The asymmetrical impacts of the crisis across gender, income, age and ethnic group require governments to provide additional support for the most vulnerable.

- **Improve social protection schemes to support the elderly.** In terms of the healthcare system, increasing financial coverage, reducing out-of-pocket expenditure, and strengthening the long-term care workforce should be at the centre of policy actions.

- **Ensure social assistance measures respond to the needs of the elderly population that does not have access to contributory schemes in retirement.** Improving information to guarantee the coverage of these programmes for all in need, prioritising and simplifying transfers at the household level and increasing the amount of benefits, at least to the poverty line level, can improve social protection policies' effectiveness.

Box 2.2. **Key policy messages** (*cont.*)

- **Design gender-sensitive policies for the recovery, and include a more equitable redistribution of care work as key to improve women's socio-economic conditions.** Increase access to essential goods and services that help increase women's opportunities to participate in the labour market and boost human capital (e.g. access to information and communications technology [ICT]). In the short term, it is key to: i) prioritise vulnerable women as recipients of assistance programmes, reducing conditionalities; ii) reopen schools and support the most disadvantaged students; and iii) provide short-term and long-term resources and support for women experiencing domestic violence.

- **Promote the change of social norms that impose unequal care responsibility on women.** This requires offering quality government and private care services, increasing women's participation in the design of gender-sensitive social protection programmes, and raising awareness of the social and economic value of care and domestic work.

- **Implement critical policy actions to tackle inequalities in education and skills acquisition.** Improving the condition of schools to guarantee a safe and permanent reopening is urgently required. Targeting support for less advantaged students and providing digital resources, training and socio-emotional support for both teachers and students is key. Learning gaps exacerbated by school closures due to the crisis could be addressed through, among other practices, summer schools, accelerated education programmes and extra resources to help students catch up on missed learning, especially those from vulnerable backgrounds.

- **Promote the creation of quality jobs for youth.** Governments should give a high priority to tackling the elevated unemployment and underemployment affecting young people in the aftermath of the pandemic. Expanding existing social protection schemes (cash transfers among other support measures) and targeted policies (creating the conditions for young people to develop relevant capacities and skills) will be key to smooth youth transition from school to work and giving them access to quality jobs

- **Facilitate migrants' access to social protection measures in the short term and to social inclusion in the long term.** Providing access to income replacement programmes, healthcare systems and COVID-19 testing and immunisation has helped countries fight the spread of the virus in the short term. Guaranteeing fundamental human rights and promoting bilateral and multilateral co-ordination of actions to address migrants' specific needs might reduce adverse effects and boost migration's positive impacts.

3. LAC countries should conceive of the green recovery as an opportunity to reduce inequality and promote a just transition through broader social protection systems.

- **Incorporate climate considerations into social protection systems as a cross-cutting theme for policy making, following a whole-of-government approach.** Mainstreaming climate mitigation and environmental considerations as a cross-cutting issue across government areas, particularly regarding social protection systems, is key to develop a coherent and co-ordinated response to climate change. Integrated approaches would allow social and human development issues to be taken fully into account in the ecological transition, aiming to achieve global carbon neutrality and reducing multi-dimensional inequalities.

- **Promote quality green jobs in key sectors (e.g. sustainable agriculture, forestry, clean energy, and manufacturing and construction) for a just transition.** Providing unemployment protection, employment guarantee schemes and flexible and scalable cash transfers to workers who lose their jobs, have their working hours reduced or whose houses are destroyed by climate-related catastrophes are key measures to promote green jobs and foster a just transition. Early retirement schemes could be an option for workers of advanced age at risk of losing their jobs due to the phase out of carbon-intensive industries.

Box 2.2. **Key policy messages** *(cont.)*

Gender-sensitive measures should aim to increase women's participation in the growing sustainable sectors.

- **Develop programmes to provide new skills for both emerging jobs and existing jobs that are evolving throughout the transition.** Government and industry could create partnerships to finance reskilling and to ensure that training content meets the evolving needs of each sector. Social protection measures could be complemented with active labour market policies while investing in lifelong learning, vocational training and skills development, giving special attention to vulnerable groups.

- **Invest in sustainable infrastructure to reduce spatial inequalities and enhance resilience in vulnerable neighbourhoods.** Better aligning infrastructure plans with longer-term goals on climate, biodiversity, water and waste management, resource efficiency and land use transformation is fundamental to building or upgrading resilient infrastructure to reduce climate impacts on informal settlements.

- **Involve citizens and civil society in the green recovery.** Governments could co-create policies with a variety of stakeholders to gain support and upgrade settlements, enhancing resilience to climate change risks in vulnerable areas.

4. The state and policy makers must have the citizenry as an ally to rebuild the social contract; it is therefore necessary to understand citizens' demands and design more effective policies to improve their situations.

- **Take into account people's concerns, and raise awareness of the need for reforms.** Address workers' concerns over the current jobs crisis. When designing safety nets, in the context of the economic crisis, public servants should make sure to take into account the diversity of workers' needs. Redesigning labour market policies towards more resilient and inclusive policies will be crucial, especially for workers lacking the necessary skills.

- **Put people's views and needs at the centre, and incorporate an intersectionality approach when redesigning social protection systems.** Multiple and interconnected forms of discrimination based on race or ethnicity, age, gender, socio-economic status, place of residence or migration status need to be addressed. Progress should be made to prioritise those groups that lack adequate social safety nets.

- **Enhance pensions systems by matching people's preferences.** In some LAC countries, the majority of people are aware of the lack of robust retirement schemes in a context of population ageing and tend to be more in favour of reforming them. In other countries, there is a lack of support for reforms. Progress should be made in making people aware of the importance of fiscal sustainability and progressivity.

- **Reform healthcare systems.** Latin Americans were very concerned with the quality of health care even before the pandemic. Progress should be made to increase the coverage and quality of healthcare systems, alleviating the high burden of OOP expenditure on families' budgets.

Notes

1. This index contains the frequency with which parents perform the following activities with the child: discuss how the child has done in school, eat with the child at the table, take time to talk, help with science homework, ask how the child performed in science classes, obtain materials for science classes, discuss how science is used in everyday life, and discuss science-related career pathways. See details in Jaramillo (2020[36]).

2. Negative perceptions of migrants have been particularly high in specific cases, such as the 2021 protests in Colombia, where immigration issues linked to Venezuelan migrants merged with pandemic discontent, or the 2021 presidential election in Peru, when immigration issues were at the centre of political debates.

References

AFD (2019), *Commons: Towards a New Narrative on Development Policies and Practices?*, Agence française de développement, Paris, http://www.afd.fr/en/ressources/commons-towards-new-narrative-development-policies-and-practices. [81]

AFD (2019), *Territorial transition and ecological Strategy 2020-2024*, Agence française de développement, Paris, http://www.afd.fr/en/ressources/territorial-and-ecological-transition-2020-2024-strategy. [65]

AFD (2018), *Climate change impacts the fight against inequality*, Agence française de développement, Paris, https://ideas4development.org/en/climate-change-inequalities/. [68]

Alesina, A., S. Stantcheva and E. Teso (2018), "Intergenerational Mobility and Preferences for Redistribution", *American Economic Review* 108, pp. 521-554, http://dx.doi.org/10.1257/aer.20162015. [86]

Álvarez, F. (2020), *RED 2020: Los sistemas de pensiones y salud en América Latina. Los desafíos del envejecimiento, el cambio tecnológico y la informalidad*, Corporación Andina de Fomento, Caracas, http://scioteca.caf.com/handle/123456789/1652. [4]

Arenas De Mesa, A. (2019), *Los sistemas de pensiones en la encrucijada*, CEPAL, Santiago, http://www.cepal.org/sites/default/files/publication/files/44851/S1900521_es.pdf. [17]

Azevedo, J. et al. (2020), *Simulating the potential impact of COVID-19 school closures on schooling and learning outcomes: a set of global estimates. Conference edition*, World Bank, Washington, DC, https://pubdocs.worldbank.org/en/798061592482682799/covid-and-education-June17-r6.pdf. [41]

Basto-Aguirre, N., P. Cerutti and S. Nieto-Parra (2020), *COVID-19 can widen educational gaps in Latin America: Some lessons for urgent policy action*, VOXLACEA, Bogotá, https://vox.lacea.org/?q=blog/covid19_widen_educational_gaps. [44]

Busso, M. (2021), *Pandemic and Inequality: How Much Human Capital Is Lost When Schools Close?*, Inter-American Development Bank, New York, https://blogs.iadb.org/ideas-matter/en/pandemic-and-inequality-how-much-human-capital-is-lost-when-schools-close/. [42]

CAF (2020), *ECAF 2019. Percepciones de los Latinoamericanos sobre los Sistemas de Pensiones, Salud y Cuidados y el Avance Tecnológico en el Mercado Laboral*, https://scioteca.caf.com/handle/123456789/1646 [84]

CAF (2014), *Vulnerability Index to climate change in the Latin American and Caribbean Region*, Development Bank of Latin America, Caracas, https://scioteca.caf.com/bitstream/handle/123456789/509/caf-vulnerability-index-climate-change.pdf. [70]

Cecchini, S. (ed.) (2019), *Universal Social Protection in Latin America and the Caribbean: Selected texts 2006-2019*, United Nations Economic Commission for Latin America and the Caribbean, Santiago, https://repositorio.cepal.org/bitstream/handle/11362/45093/1/S1901140_en.pdf. [85]

Chetty, R. (2020), "The Economic Impacts of COVID-19: Evidence from a New Public Database Built Using Private Sector Data", *NBER Working Papers*, No. 27431, National Bureau of Economic Research, Inc., Cambridge, MA, https://opportunityinsights.org/wp-content/uploads/2020/05/tracker_paper.pdf. [43]

Cucagna, E. and J. Romero (2021), *The Gendered Impacts of COVID-19 on Labor Markets in Latin America and the Caribbean (English)*, World Bank, Washington, DC, https://documents.worldbank.org/en/publication/documents-reports/documentdetail/675641612934705667/the-gendered-impacts-of-covid-19-on-labor-markets-in-latin-america-and-the-caribbean. [45]

ECLAC (2021), *Building forward better: Action to strengthen the 2030 Agenda for Sustainable Development*, Economic Commission for Latin America and the Caribbean, Santiago, http://www.cepal.org/sites/default/files/publication/files/46696/S2100124_en.pdf. [72]

ECLAC (2021), *Panorama Social de América Latina 2020 [Social Outlook of Latin America 2020]*, Economic Commission for Latin America and the Caribbean, Santiago, http://www.cepal.org/es/publicaciones/46687-panorama-social-america-latina-2020. [1]

ECLAC (2021), "The economic autonomy of women in a sustainable recovery with equality", *Covid-19 Special Report*, No. 9, Economic Commission for Latin America and the Caribbean, Santiago, http://www.cepal.org/sites/default/files/publication/files/46634/S2000739_en.pdf. [29]

ECLAC (2021), *Time-use measurements in Latin America and the Caribbean*, Economic Commission for Latin America and the Caribbean, Santiago, https://oig.cepal.org/sites/default/files/c2100058_web.pdf. [15]

ECLAC (2020), *Addressing violence against women and girls during and after the COVID-19 pandemic: Financing, responses, prevention and data compilation*, Economic Commission for Latin America and the Caribbean, Santiago, https://oig.cepal.org/sites/default/files/c2000874_web.pdf. [31]

ECLAC (2020), *Medidas y acciones a nivel nacional*, Economic Commission for Latin America and the Caribbean, Santiago, http://www.cepal.org/es/temas/covid-19. [49]

ECLAC (2020), *The impact of COVID-19: An opportunity to reaffirm the central role of migrants' human rights in sustainable development*, Economic Commission for Latin America and the Caribbean, Santiago, http://www.cepal.org/en/publications/46354-impact-covid-19-opportunity-reaffirm-central-role-migrants-human-rights. [56]

ECLAC (2020), "The social challenge in times of COVID-19", *Covid-19 Special Report*, No. 3, Economic Commission for Latin America and the Caribbean, Santiago, http://www.cepal.org/sites/default/files/publication/files/45544/S2000324_en.pdf. [12]

ECLAC (2019), *CEPALSTAT (database)*, Economic Commission for Latin America and the Caribbean, Santiago, https://cepalstat-prod.cepal.org/cepalstat/tabulador/ConsultaIntegrada.asp?idIndicador=2470&idioma=e (accessed on 2 July 2021). [7]

ECLAC/UNESCO (2020), "Education in the time of COVID-19", *Covid-19 Report: August 2020*, Economic Commission for Latin America and the Caribbean/UNESCO, Santiago, http://www.cepal.org/sites/default/files/publication/files/45905/S2000509_en.pdf. [51]

ECLAC/UNICEF (2020), "Violence against children and adolescents in the time of COVID-19", *Covid-19 Report: November 2020*, Economic Commission for Latin America and the Caribbean/UNICEF, Santiago, http://www.cepal.org/sites/default/files/publication/files/46486/S2000610_en.pdf. [5]

Ellen MacArthur Foundation (2019), *Completing the picture: How the circular economy tackles climate change*, Ellen MacArthur Foundation, Cowes, UK, https://circulareconomy.europa.eu/platform/sites/default/files/emf_completing_the_picture.pdf. [78]

Gagnon, J. and M. Rodrigues (2020), "Towards more sustainable solutions to forced displacement: What measures are donor countries applying to forced displacement in developing countries?", No. 34, OECD Publishing, Paris, https://doi.org/10.1787/d1d44405-en [60]

Gutiérrez, D. (2021), *UNDP LAC C19 PDS No. 18. The Coronavirus and the challenges for women's work in Latin America*, United Nations Development Programme in Latin America and the Caribbean, New York, http://www.latinamerica.undp.org/content/rblac/en/home/library/crisis_prevention_and_recovery/el-coronavirus-y-los-retos-para-el-trabajo-de-las-mujeres-en-ame.html. [25]

Hidalgo, D. and C. Huizenga (2013), "Implementation of sustainable urban transport in Latin America", Vol. 40/1, pp. 66-77, http://dx.doi.org/10.1016/j.retrec.2012.06.034. [73]

ICC (2020), *ICC COVID-19 Response: Guidance on Protection for Migrant Workers during the COVID-19 Pandemic*, International Chamber of Commerce, Paris, http://www.iom.int/sites/default/files/defaul/2020_icc_guidance_for_migrant_workers_02.pdf?utm_source=IOM+External+Mailing+List&utm_campaign=68bcfa2ccc-EMAIL_CAMPAIGN_2020_08_10_11_24&utm_medium=email&utm_term=0_9968056566-68bcfa2ccc-43608941. [61]

IDB (2021), *10 key points on climate change impacts, opportunities and priorities for Latin America and the Caribbean*, Inter-American Development Bank, New York, https://blogs.worldbank.org/latinamerica/10-key-points-climate-change-impacts-opportunities-and-priorities-latin-america-and. [75]

ILO (2021), *Resolution concerning the second recurrent discussion on social protection (social security)*, International Labour Conference – 109th Session 2021, International Labour Organization, Geneva, Switzerland, http://www.ilo.org/wcmsp5/groups/public/---ed_norm/---relconf/documents/meetingdocument/wcms_806099.pdf. [10]

ILO (2021), *Employment and informality in Latin America and the Caribbean: an insufficient and unequal recovery*, International Labour Organization, Geneva, https://www.ilo.org/wcmsp5/groups/public/---americas/---ro-lima/---sro-port_of_spain/documents/genericdocument/wcms_819029.pdf. [3]

ILO (2020), *Observatorio de la OIT – tercera edición: El COVID-19 y el mundo*, International Labour Organization, Geneva, Switzerland, http://www.ilo.org/global/about-the-ilo/WCMS_743154/lang--es/index.htm. [24]

ILO (2019), *Panorama laboral temático No. 5. Mujeres en el mundo del trabajo: Retos pendientes hacia una efectiva equidad en América Latina y el Caribe*, International Labour Organization, Geneva, Switzerland, http://www.ilo.org/americas/publicaciones/WCMS_715183/lang--es/index.htm. [28]

ILO (2016), *Protecting people and the environment: Lessons learnt from Brazil's Bolsa Verde, China, Costa Rica, Ecuador, Mexico, South Africa and 56 other experiences*, International Labour Organization,

Geneva, Switzerland, http://www.ilo.org/global/topics/green-jobs/publications/WCMS_516936/lang--en/index.htm. [57]

ILO/AFD (2019), *Social Transition for a just transition*, International Labour Organization, Geneva, Switzerland/Agence française de développement, Paris, http://www.social-protection.org/gimi/RessourcePDF.action?ressource.ressourceId=55905. [80]

ILO/ECLAC (2020), *Technical Note No. 1. The COVID-19 pandemic could increase child labour in Latin America and the Caribbean*, International Labour Organization, Geneva, Switzerland/United Nations Economic Commission for Latin America and the Caribbean, Santiago, http://www.ilo.org/americas/publicaciones/WCMS_747662/lang--en/index.htm. [46]

ILO/IDB (2020), *Jobs in a net zero emissions future in Latin America and the Caribbean*, International Labour Organization, Geneva, Switzerland/Inter-American Development Bank, New York, http://www.ilo.org/americas/publicaciones/WCMS_752069/lang--en/index.htm. [74]

ILO/IDB (2019), *Jobs in a Net-Zero Emissions Future in Latin America and the Caribbean*, International Labour Organization, Geneva, Switzerland/Inter-American Development Bank, New York, http://www.ilo.org/wcmsp5/groups/public/---americas/---ro-lima/documents/publication/wcms_752069.pdf. [79]

IMF (2020), *World Economic Outlook Database April 2020: The Great Lockdown*, International Monetary Fund, Washington, DC, http://www.imf.org/en/Publications/SPROLLs/world-economic-outlook-databases. [23]

Jaramillo, S. (2020), *UNDP LAC C19 PDS No. 20. COVID-19 and primary and secondary education: The impact of the crisis and public policy implications for Latin America and the Caribbean*, United Nations Development Programme in Latin America and the Caribbean, New York, http://www.latinamerica.undp.org/content/dam/rblac/Policy%20Papers%20COVID%2019/undp-rblac-CD19-PDS-Number20-UNICEF-Educacion-EN.pdf. [36]

Kuziemko, I., M. Norton and E. Saez (2015), *American Economic Review*, Vol. 105/4, pp. 1478-1508, http://dx.doi.org/10.1257/aer.20130360. [87]

Lusting, N. and M. Tommasi (2020), *UNDP LAC C19 PDS No. 8. Covid-19 and social protection of poor and vulnerable groups in Latin America: A conceptual framework*, United Nations Development Programme in Latin America and the Caribbean, New York, http://www.latinamerica.undp.org/content/rblac/en/home/library/crisis_prevention_and_recovery/covid-19-and-social-protection-of-poor-and-vulnerable-groups-in-.html. [58]

Mena-Carrasco, M. and A. Dufey (2021), *A green and resilient recovery for Latin America*, Global Center on Adaptation, Rotterdam, the Netherlands/Government of Mexico, Mexico City/Community of Latin American and Caribbean States, Albany, NJ, https://reliefweb.int/sites/reliefweb.int/files/resources/A%20green%20and%20resilient%20recovery%20for%20Latin%20America.pdf. [77]

Migración Ministerio de Relaciones Exteriores (2021), *ABC Estatuto Temporal de Protección – Migrantes Venezolanos*, Ministerio de Relaciones Exteriores, Bogotá, https://www.migracioncolombia.gov.co/infografias/abc-estatuto-temporal-de-proteccion-migrantes-venezolanos. [64]

Ministerio de Salud y Protección Social (2020), *Lineamientos para la prevención, detección y manejo de casos de COVID-19 para población migrante en Colombia*, Ministerio de Salud y Protección Social, Bogotá, https://covid19-evidence.paho.org/handle/20.500.12663/1278?locale-attribute=es. [63]

Ministerio de Salud y Protección Social (2018), *Boletín Electrónico para los Actores del Sistema de Salud en Colombia*, Ministerio de Salud y Protección Social, Bogotá, http://www.minsalud.gov.co/sites/rid/Lists/BibliotecaDigital/RIDE/DE/COM/Enlace-MinSalud-97-Migrante-Venezolano.pdf. [62]

Muir, T. (2017), "Measuring social protection for long-term care", *OECD Health Working Papers*, No. 93, OECD Publishing, Paris, https://dx.doi.org/10.1787/a411500a-en. [16]

OECD (2021), *Man Enough? Measuring Masculine Norms to Promote Women's Empowerment*, Social Institutions and Gender Index, OECD Publishing, Paris, https://dx.doi.org/10.1787/6ffd1936-en. [34]

OECD (2021), "The inequalities-environment nexus: Towards a people-centred green transition", *OECD Green Growth Papers*, No. 2021/01, OECD Publishing, Paris, https://dx.doi.org/10.1787/ca9d8479-en. [67]

OECD (2020), *A helping hand: Education responding to the coronavirus pandemic*, OECD Publishing, Paris, https://oecdedutoday.com/education-responding-coronavirus-pandemic. [38]

OECD (2020), "Combatting COVID-19's effect on children", *OECD Policy Responses to Coronavirus (COVID-19)*, OECD Publishing, Paris, http://dx.doi.org/10.1787/2e1f3b2f-en. [37]

OECD (2020), *COVID-19 in Latin America and the Caribbean: Regional socio-economic implications and policy priorities*, OECD Publishing, Paris, http://dx.doi.org/10.1787/93a64fde-en. [6]

OECD (2020), *OECD Employment Outlook 2020: Worker Security and the COVID-19 Crisis*, OECD Publishing, Paris, https://dx.doi.org/10.1787/1686c758-en. [82]

OECD (2020), "Parental involvement in school activities", in *PISA 2018 Results (Volume III): What School Life Means for Students' Lives*, OECD Publishing, Paris, https://dx.doi.org/10.1787/29fed428-en. [39]

OECD (2020), *Pension Policy Notes: Mexico. May 2020*, OECD Publishing, Paris, http://www.oecd.org/els/public-pensions/OECD-Pension-Policy-Notes-Mexico.pdf. [21]

OECD (2020), *SIGI 2020 Regional Report for Latin America and the Caribbean*, Social Institutions and Gender Index, OECD Publishing, Paris, https://dx.doi.org/10.1787/cb7d45d1-en. [30]

OECD (2020), "The impact of COVID-19 on student equity and inclusion: Supporting vulnerable students during school closures and school re-openings", *OECD Policy Responses to Coronavirus (COVID-19)*, OECD Publishing, Paris, http://dx.doi.org/10.1787/d593b5c8-en. [50]

OECD (2020), "What is the impact of the COVID-19 pandemic on immigrants and their children?", *OECD Policy Responses to Coronavirus (COVID-19)*, OECD Publishing, Paris, http://dx.doi.org/10.1787/e7cbb7de-en. [55]

OECD (2020), "Women at the Core of the Fight Against COVID-19", *OECD Policy Responses to Coronavirus (COVID-19)*, OECD Publishing, Paris, http://dx.doi.org/10.1787/553a8269-en. [27]

OECD (2019), *Accelerating Climate Action: Refocusing Policies through a Well-being Lens*, OECD Publishing, Paris, https://doi.org/10.1787/2f4c8c9a-en [66]

OECD (2019), *Can Social Protection Be an Engine for Inclusive Growth?*, Development Centre Studies, OECD Publishing, Paris, https://dx.doi.org/10.1787/9d95b5d0-en. [8]

OECD (2019), *OECD Employment Outlook 2019: The Future of Work*, OECD Publishing, Paris, https://dx.doi.org/10.1787/9ee00155-en. [71]

OECD (2019), *OECD Reviews of Pension Systems: Peru*, OECD Reviews of Pension Systems, OECD Publishing, Paris, https://dx.doi.org/10.1787/e80b4071-en. [22]

OECD (2019), *Pensions at a Glance 2019: OECD and G20 Indicators*, OECD Publishing, Paris, https://dx.doi.org/10.1787/b6d3dcfc-en. [18]

OECD (2017), *OECD Reviews of Labour Market and Social Policies: Costa Rica*, OECD Reviews of Labour Market and Social Policies, OECD Publishing, Paris, https://dx.doi.org/10.1787/9789264282773-en. [20]

OECD (2015), *2015 Pension Policy Note: Colombia*, OECD Publishing, Paris, http://www.oecd.org/els/public-pensions/OECD-Pension-Policy-Notes-Colombia.pdf. [19]

OECD (forthcoming), *Labour informality and households' vulnerabilities in Latin America [provisional title]*, OECD Publishing, Paris. [9]

OECD et al. (2020), *Latin American Economic Outlook 2020: Digital Transformation for Building Back Better*, OECD Publishing, Paris, https://dx.doi.org/10.1787/e6e864fb-en. [2]

OECD et al. (2019), *Latin American Economic Outlook 2019: Development in Transition*, OECD Publishing, Paris, https://dx.doi.org/10.1787/g2g9ff18-en. [90]

OECD/IDB/CIAT (2016), *Taxing Wages in Latin America and the Caribbean 2016*, OECD Publishing, Paris, https://dx.doi.org/10.1787/9789264262607-en. [89]

OECD/IDB/The World Bank (2014), *Pensions at a Glance: Latin America and the Caribbean*, OECD Publishing, Paris, https://dx.doi.org/10.1787/pension_glance-2014-en. [83]

OECD/ILO (2018), *How Immigrants Contribute to Developing Countries' Economies*, OECD Publishing, Paris/International Labour Organization, Geneva, https://dx.doi.org/10.1787/9789264288737-en. [53]

OECD/The World Bank (2020), *Health at a Glance: Latin America and the Caribbean 2020*, OECD Publishing, Paris, https://dx.doi.org/10.1787/6089164f-en. [13]

OHCHR (2020), *Joint Guidance Note on the Impacts of the COVID-19 Pandemic on the Human Rights of Migrants*, Office of the United Nations High Commissioner for Human Rights, Geneva, Switzerland, http://www.ohchr.org/Documents/Issues/Migration/CMWSPMJointGuidanceNoteCOVID-19Migrants.pdf. [54]

Szabo, G. and J. Edwards (2020), *The Global Girlhood Report 2020: How COVID-19 is putting progress in peril*, Save the Children, St Vincent House, https://www.savethechildren.org/content/dam/usa/reports/ed-cp/global-girlhood-report-2020.pdf. [33]

The Lancet Commissions (2015), *Health and climate change: policy responses to protect public health*, Elsevier, Amsterdam, http://www.thelancet.com/action/showPdf?pii=S0140-6736%2815%2960854-6. [69]

Tribin, A., C. Vargas and N. Ramírez (2019), "Unintended consequences of maternity leave legislation: The case of Colombia", *World Development*, Vol. 122, pp. 218-232, http://dx.doi.org/10.1016/j.worlddev.2019.05.007. [26]

UN Women (2020), *Prevención de la violencia contra las mujeres a COVID-19 en América Latina y el Caribe*, United Nations Women, New York, https://lac.unwomen.org/en/digiteca/publicaciones/2020/05/respuesta-covid-19-transferencias-monetarias.   [32]

UNDESA (2019), *International Migrant Stock 2019 (database)*, United Nations Department of Economic and Social Affairs, New York, http://www.un.org/en/development/desa/population/migration/data/estimates2/estimates19.asp.   [52]

UNDESA (2019), *World Population Prospects 2019: Online edition Rev. 1 (database)*, United Nations Department of Economics and Social Affairs, New York, https://population.un.org/wpp/Download/Standard/Population/?.   [14]

UNDP (2020), *COVID-19 Policy Documents Series: Introduction*, United Nations Development Programme in Latin America and the Caribbean, New York, http://www.latinamerica.undp.org/content/rblac/en/home/library/covid-19--policy-papers.html.   [11]

UNDP (2020), *Early recovery responses to COVID-19 for migrants and host communities in Latin America and the Caribbean*, United Nations Development Programme in Latin America and the Caribbean, New York, http://www.latinamerica.undp.org/content/rblac/en/home/library/democratic governance/early-recovery-responses-for-migrants-and-host-communities-maxim.html.   [59]

UNICEF (2021), *COVID-19 and school closures: One year of education disruption*, UNICEF, New York, https://data.unicef.org/wp-content/uploads/2021/03/COVID19-and-school-closures.pdf.   [40]

UNICEF (2020), *COVID-19: More than 95 per cent of children are out of school in Latin America and the Caribbean*, UNICEF Latin America and the Caribbean, Panama City, http://www.unicef.org/press-releases/covid-19-more-95-cent-children-are-out-school-latin-america-and-caribbean.   [35]

UNICEF (2020), *Marco para la reapertura de las escuelas*, UNICEF, New York, http://www.unicef.org/es/documents/marco-para-la-reapertura-de-las-escuelas.   [48]

WHO (2020), *Checklist to support schools re-opening and preparation for COVID-19 resurgences or similar public health crises*, World Health Organization, Geneva, Switzerland, http://www.who.int/publications/i/item/9789240017467.   [47]

WHO (2020), *Global Health Expenditure Database*, World Health Organization, Geneva, Switzerland, http://apps.who.int/nha/database.   [88]

World Bank (2020), *A green recovery of Latin America and the Caribbean is possible and necessary*, World Bank, Washington, DC, http://blogs.worldbank.org/latinamerica/green-recovery-latin-america-and-caribbean-possible-and-necessary?deliveryName=DM80874.   [76]

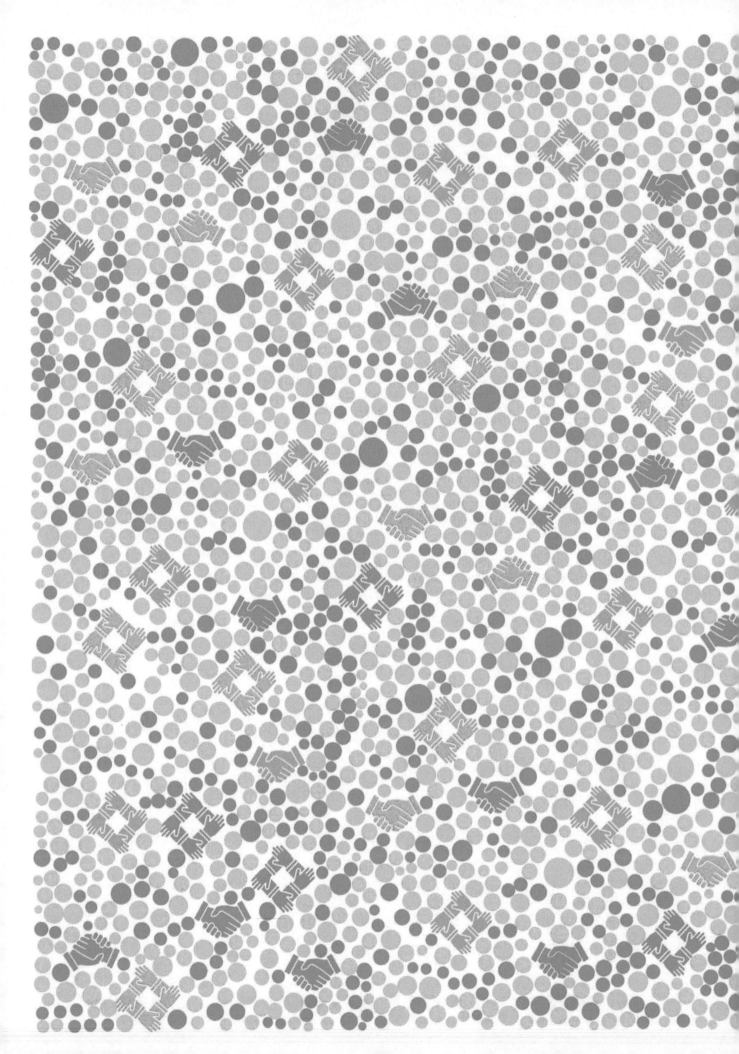

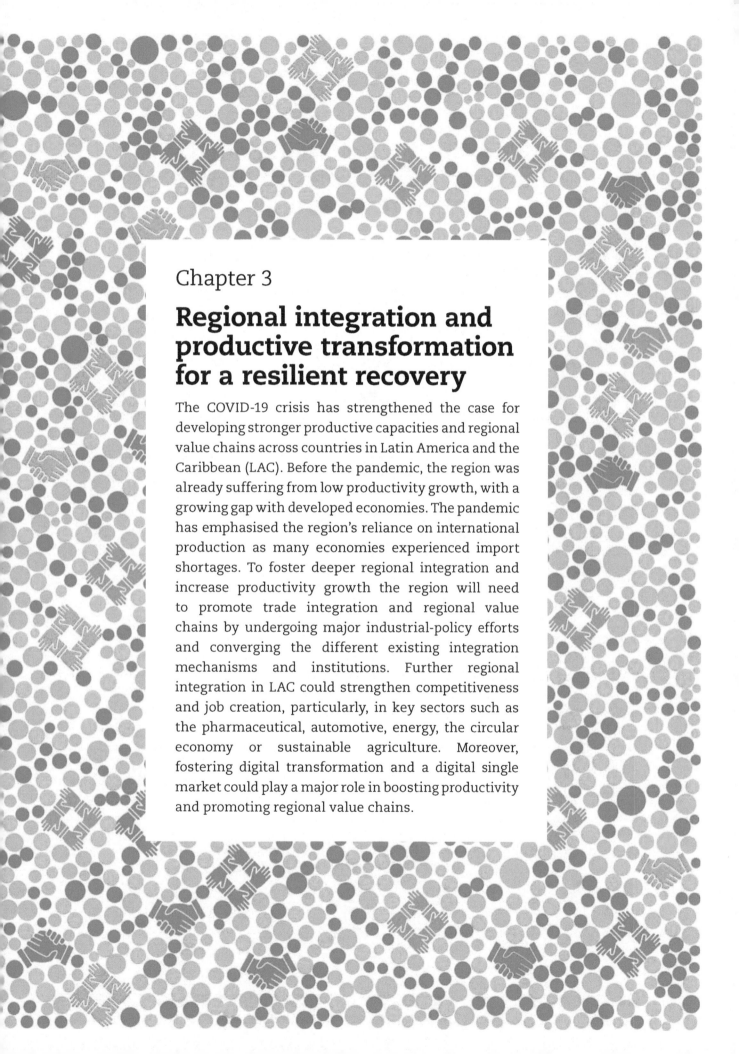

Chapter 3

Regional integration and productive transformation for a resilient recovery

The COVID-19 crisis has strengthened the case for developing stronger productive capacities and regional value chains across countries in Latin America and the Caribbean (LAC). Before the pandemic, the region was already suffering from low productivity growth, with a growing gap with developed economies. The pandemic has emphasised the region's reliance on international production as many economies experienced import shortages. To foster deeper regional integration and increase productivity growth the region will need to promote trade integration and regional value chains by undergoing major industrial-policy efforts and converging the different existing integration mechanisms and institutions. Further regional integration in LAC could strengthen competitiveness and job creation, particularly, in key sectors such as the pharmaceutical, automotive, energy, the circular economy or sustainable agriculture. Moreover, fostering digital transformation and a digital single market could play a major role in boosting productivity and promoting regional value chains.

Regionalintegrationandproductive transformationtoovercomeLAC's structuralweaknesses

Regionalintegrationcouldbetheenginetoproductivetransformation

LAC'ssharein **worldexports** ofgoods hasnotexceeded sincethe1960s
6%

LAChasoneofthe lowest levelsofintraregional tradeworldwide

13% ofitsexports staywithin theregion

LAC'sintegrationinto globalvaluechains islow

andhasbeenmainlyassociated withthe extractionand processingofrawmaterials

Intraregional tradehas ahigher manufacturing contentthan theexports totherest oftheworld

Onaverage,industrialisedproducts accountedfor

 73% ofintraregional flows

 63% ofextra regional exports

Digitaltransformation hasbeenmoderate

Averagedigitaladoption inbusiness,2014-16

4.5% — LAC
13% — Southeast Asia
16% — China

LAC'sproductivestructure,sectoralspecialisationandbusinessstructure donotcontributetoregionalintegration

LACaverageGDPgrowthinthepast20years wasgenerated

76% throughthe accumulation ofemployment

24% throughincrease inlabour productivity

Incomparison,thedecomposition ofgrowthofChina'sGDPwas

4% throughthe accumulation ofemployment

96% through increase inlabour productivity

Keysectorsforproductiveintegrationandsustainabletransformation intheaftermathofCOVID-19inLAC

Pharmaceutical sector

Automotive sector

Sustainable agriculture

Energy

Circular economy

Promoting regional value chains and increasing LAC's participation in international trade as a means for recovery

Latin America and the Caribbean in Global Value Chains. A historical perspective

Since the 1990s, the increasing complexity of global production has transformed the nature and pattern of international trade leading to today's complex global value chains (GVCs). Driven by rising labour costs and the search for efficiency, regional and national export specialisation patterns have changed. This was the result of technological advances and geopolitical and economic changes that allowed the fragmentation and relocation of production, the reduction of trade-related costs and the co-ordination of complex cross-border supply networks (ECLAC, 2020[1]). In some developed economies, such as the United States and Japan, the share of medium- and high-technology manufactures in exports declined as a result of the relocation of some manufacturing activities to emerging economies. In parallel, the share of medium- and high-technology exports has increased in some developing countries, such as China, which has rapidly moved from low-technology to medium- and high-technology manufacturing exports (ECLAC, 2020[1]).

In the last decades, LAC's exports patterns have also changed. South America's specialisation in primary commodities and natural-resource-based manufacturing deepened, with these two categories accounting for nearly 75% of total exports (Figure 3.1): minerals in Bolivia, Chile and Peru; hydrocarbons in Colombia, Ecuador and Venezuela; and agricultural products in Argentina, Paraguay and Uruguay constituted the main export categories. While Brazil is also a major exporter of primary goods, its export basket is more diversified and includes manufactured products of varying technological intensity.

Figure 3.1. Exports of goods, by selected regions and countries and type of product, 1995-2018

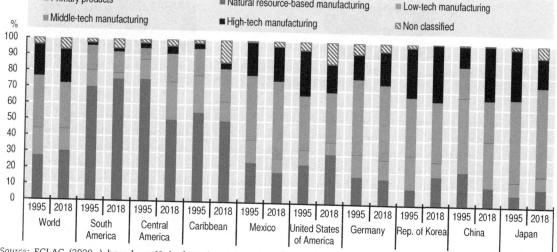

Source: ECLAC (2020[2]) based on United Nations Commodity Trade Statistics Database (COMTRADE) (online), https://comtrade.un.org/.

StatLink ⟡ https://doi.org/10.1787/888934286597

Central America's exports of manufactured goods (mainly low-technology products, such as clothing) increased, while the relative importance of primary commodities declined thanks to proximity to the United States and low relative wages (Figure 3.1). With the signing of the North American Free Trade Agreement (NAFTA), Mexico became a very important link in the regional value chains of North America and progressively increased the technological intensity of its exports, mainly to the United States.

Central America, particularly Mexico and the Caribbean have a close economic relationship with the United States that goes beyond trade including foreign direct investment (FDI), migration, tourism and remittances (ECLAC, 2014[3]).

Global value chains in a new economic context

As a consequence of the COVID-19 outbreak, internationalisation of production has experienced a slowdown in LAC since 2010. The COVID-19 outbreak has deepened this trend although it has not yet triggered a major reconfiguration of global value chains (Figure 3.2). Advances in technology as well as geopolitical and other economic changes, such as increased protectionism, are some factors that explain this slowdown.

Figure 3.2. **Immediate consequences of COVID-19 for trade and production, and opportunities to strengthen regional integration in Latin America and the Caribbean**

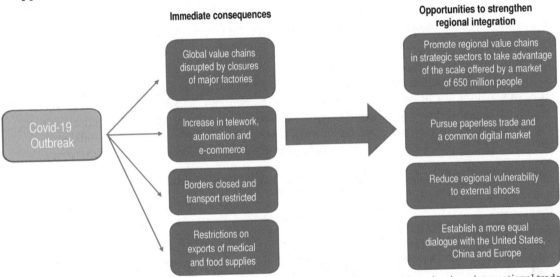

Source: ECLAC (2020[5]) Own calculation. "The effects of the coronavirus disease (COVID-19) pandemic on international trade and logistics", https://repositorio.cepal.org/bitstream/handle/11362/45878/1/S2000496_en.pdf.

Technological transformations, especially in communications and transportation, have enabled the increasing complexity of global value chains since the 1990s. Today, digital transformation is changing production possibilities across the world. However, its consequences for global value chains are still unclear. For example, lowering the costs of technologies that reduce the need for labour – such as digitisation, automation and additive manufacturing (3D printing) – tends to cancel out the disadvantage in labour costs found in the more industrialised countries, theoretically allowing reshoring – returning production and manufacturing back to a company's original country – or nearshoring, which brings them closer. The COVID-19 pandemic and the impact of new technologies on the labour market are consistent with the growing concerns among LAC workers about job losses or changes in jobs (Chapter 2).

Moreover, the pandemic has highlighted the vulnerability of global value chains, which were the main transmission channel for the economic effects of the COVID-19 crisis on world trade. The restrictions applied by China in January 2020 (the temporary lockdown of Hubei province and the closure of the country's borders) resulted in the suspension of exports of inputs for industries such as automotive, electronics, pharmaceuticals and medical supplies. Since China is the world's leading exporter of parts and components with 15% of global shipments in 2018 (ECLAC, 2020[1]), the suspension of exports triggered the shutdown of factories for several weeks in North America, Europe and Asia. In LAC, the trade in goods fell 17% between January and May 2020 and inter-regional trade fell even more, by 24%, in the same period. The contraction of intraregional trade was particularly hard for manufacturing. The automotive sector was the hardest hit with a fall of close to 55% of the value of exchanges between January and May 2020. Moreover, the contraction of intraregional trade affected all the main economic integration blocks with a year-on-year decrease of between 20% and 31% in the same period. The only exception was the trade level between the members of the Central American Common Market (CACM), which showed a higher resilience falling only by 5.6% (ECLAC, 2021[4]).

The pandemic will likely reinforce two inter-related trends that were already emerging before the crisis. The first is a trend towards a lower level of productive, commercial and technological interdependence among the main world economies, in particular between the United States and Europe, on the one hand, and China, on the other. The second is a trend towards world trade with a lower level of openness, more permeated by geopolitical and national security considerations, more prone to conflicts and weakened multilateral governance. The net result would not be a reversal of globalisation, but a more regionalised world economy organised around three major productive hubs: North America, Europe and East and Southeast Asia.

For LAC, the ongoing transformations will bring important challenges but also unprecedented opportunities. In a context of geopolitical, technological and post COVID-19 changes, the region will be influenced by forces acting in opposite directions: one towards the reshoring of companies in countries of origin, and the other towards regionalisation. Indeed, supply chain integration is expected to grow at a regional level in response to the impact of COVID19. Regional integration must be expected to play a key role in the crisis-recovery strategies in Latin America and the Caribbean.

Latin America and the Caribbean's participation in GVCs has been uneven. Most of the countries participate in global production networks as suppliers of raw materials and basic manufacturing products and only a few countries have diversified their productive structure and become critical actors within global production networks.

As never before, the model of insertion into the international economy, based on specialisation in raw materials, assembly manufactures and tourism, is open to discussion. The disruption of various global value chains due to the pandemic has highlighted the risks posed by excessive regional dependence on imported manufactures. At the same time, the pandemic has laid bare the vulnerability of the region's productive structure. It is estimated that more than 2.7 million firms are at risk of shutting down because of the economic crisis, adding more than 8 million people to the ranks of the unemployed (ECLAC, 2020[6]). The magnitude of the impact and the capacity of countries to react depend largely on the productive structure of LAC economies, the participation of companies in value chains, and the existing productive capacities (Box 3.1). In this context, industrial and productive policies are essential to allow the region to strengthen existing capacities and generate new ones in strategic sectors.

Regional integration and regional value chains should play a key role in the future development strategy of the region. An integrated market of 650 million inhabitants would constitute an important insurance against supply or demand shocks generated outside the region, and supports reaching the scale required to make new industries viable, promoting shared production and research networks. Regionalisation and regional production networks offer the opportunity to foster productivity growth, higher wages and inclusive labour markets while redefining the connection and integration of the region to international production and innovation hubs.

Box 3.1. **The role of the external sector to boost economic activity and employment: the case of Costa Rica**

The external sector has the potential to collaborate in a strong recovery. During the Covid-19 pandemic, three groups of products and services were identified: pro-cyclical, those that have suffered significant contractions in their export flows; countercyclical, which increased their exports; and neutral, which have remained stable.

In Costa Rica, exports of medical, surgical and veterinary instruments and apparatus (accounting for 10.7% of total goods exports in the period March-August 2020), unroasted and non-decaffeinated coffee (4.5% of total goods exports in the same period) and business services (64.4% of total services exports in the second quarter of 2020) showed a countercyclical behaviour. In contrast, exports of syringes, needles, catheters, cannula and similar instruments (12% of total goods exports in the period March-August 2020) showed a pro-cyclical behaviour.

In the context of post-pandemic, an array of policy actions are available to Costa Rica to strengthen the economic recovery through diversification and export-induced domestic value-added, as well as through employment.

a) Strengthening and deepening linkages with national production. For instance, to explore increases in local production chains of the medical and dental instruments and supplies. This sector not only contributes in terms of gross exports dynamics, given its volume of trade and growth but also generates significant amounts of national added-value and employment.

b) Continue deepening the diversification of agricultural exports. Data reveal that agricultural activities such as vegetables, chayote, cassava and watermelon, among others, show great potential in the generation of domestic value-added and employment.

c) Promote the increase of exports in activities that, despite having lower employment generation, generate high domestic value-added. These activities include computer services or financial management, human resources and other sophisticated business services.

d) Develop new skills and training to encourage the reallocation of the labour force to more dynamic activities, such as the services sector. Given the large indirect impact of export activity in the generation of value-added and employment in the services sector, the design and implementation of training programmes should facilitate the integration of people who have lost their jobs in primary and secondary activities into services activities. In this sense, it is advisable to facilitate the transition of highly qualified employment, linked to sophisticated services, as well as less qualified employment, which can be absorbed by activities such as tourism, with a special impact on non-urban areas.

Source: Based on COMEX and ECLAC (2021[7]), Valor agregado y empleo inducido por el sector exportador de Costa Rica, Nota de política, https://www.cepal.org/es/publicaciones/46922-valor-agregado-empleo-inducido-sector-exportador-costa-rica-nota-politica.

Regional integration: An opportunity for LAC?

Regional integration has always featured in Latin America and the Caribbean's development agenda, although integration experiences have tended to prioritise trade and market integration over productive integration. A common market is an opportunity to develop: "[…] a more rational organisation of the productive system by means of which industry will attain more economic dimensions and will thereby be able to reduce its costs and utilise natural resources more effectively […]. The putting into operation of the common market as speedily as possible will help to expand and diversify trade and to accelerate the economic development of each and all of the Latin American countries, with the consequent rise in the standard of living of its people" (ECLAC, 1959[8]). In the COVID-19 crisis context, this view presents a strategy for recovery.

Five decades of regional trade and market integration in LAC

The first formal experience of regional integration came in 1960 with the Central American Common Market (CACM), and the Latin America Free Trade Area (LAFTA), which in 1980 evolved into the Latin American Integration Association (LAIA, or ALADI in Spanish). These initiatives were followed by the creation of the Andean Community (CAN) in 1969 and the Caribbean Community (CARICOM) in 1973.

The quest for trade integration gained renewed political and economic impetus in the aftermath of the debt crisis of the 1980s, leading to the creation of the Southern Common Market (MERCOSUR) in 1991. New trade initiatives have emerged since then, such as the Pacific Alliance (PA) in 2011.

Most LAC integration initiatives since 1960 have been focused on trade and market integration, with little focus on productive integration. This regional integration strategy has not injected energy into the regional economy, nor spurred integration into world trade: the region's share in world exports of goods has not exceeded 6% since the mid-1960s. Despite its many intraregional trade agreements, LAC has one of the lowest levels of intraregional trade in the world. Barely 13% of its exports stayed within the region in 2020, and that proportion has been declining steadily since 2014 (Figure 3.3). In comparison, trade among European Union (EU) countries as a share of total trade in goods ranged from 34% to 80% in 2020 (Eurostat, 2021[9]).

Figure 3.3. **Latin America and the Caribbean: Intra-regional exports, 1960-2020**

USD billions and percentage of total goods exports

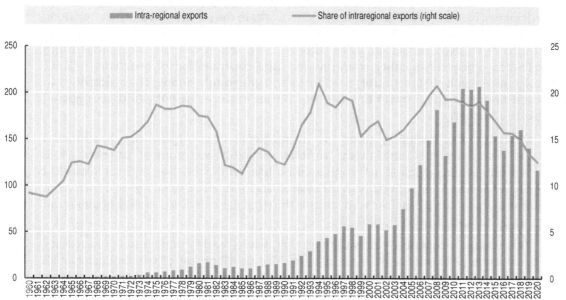

Source: ECLAC (2020[2]), based on United Nations Commodity Trade Statistics Database (COMTRADE) (online) https://comtrade.un.org/, and Latin America and the Caribbean in the World Economy, Santiago, various years. The figures for 2020 are projections.
StatLink ▒▒▒ https://doi.org/10.1787/888934286217

Low productive integration among LAC countries is evidenced by the share of intra-regional imported content in total exports that reaches less than an average of 6.0%. The content imported from the rest of the region is particularly low in the exports of its two largest economies: Brazil (3.0%) and Mexico (2.0%) (Figure 3.4).

Figure 3.4. **LAC: Structure of imported content in total exports by origin, 2017, selected countries (%)**

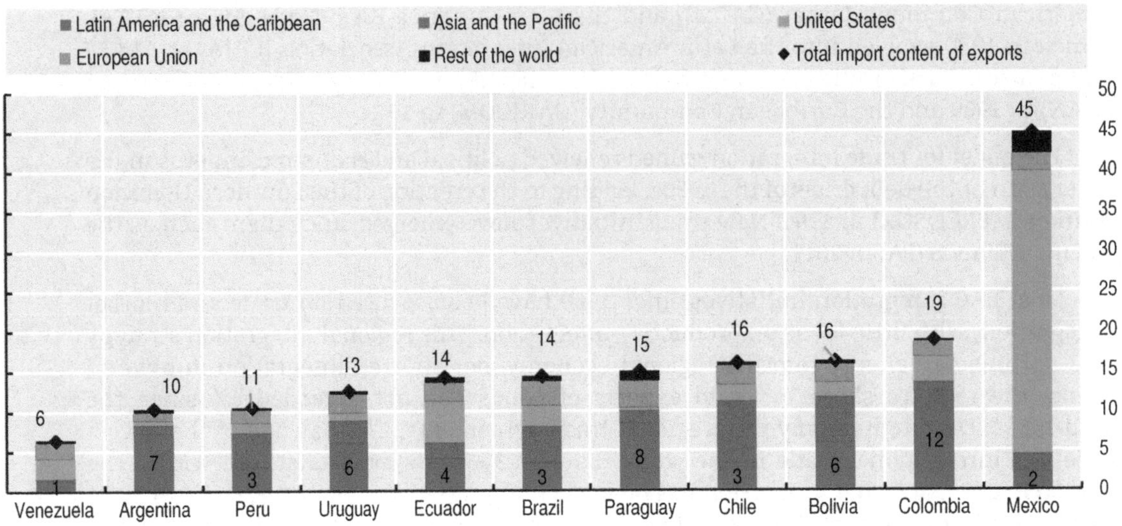

Source: ECLAC (2017[10]), *Global Input-Output Tables: Tools for the analysis of the integration of Latin America with the world*, https://www.cepal.org/en/events/global-input-output-tables-tools-analysis-integration-latin-america-world.

StatLink https://doi.org/10.1787/888934286616

LAC's integration into global value chains has been mainly associated with the extraction and processing of raw materials. Mexico's export manufacturing industry participation in North American production networks in the electronics and metalworking (especially automotive) sectors is the exception. Mining is the most integrated sector, in terms of forward participation, i.e. exports from this sector are incorporated into production processes in other countries for final consumption or re-export (ECLAC, 2020[1]). As a result, LAC countries are mostly integrated into simple chain activities in natural resources and forward linkages which thus exclude the possibility for regional backward linkages.

Moreover, the declining trend of intraregional trade has been accentuated by the emergence of China as the region's second-largest trading partner. While China's burgeoning demand for commodities has reinforced the region's historical primary export pattern, especially in the case of South America, the large-scale arrival of Chinese manufactures has displaced trade within the region in a wide range of industrial sectors (ECLAC, 2021[4]; OECD, 2007[11]).

This regional scenario reflects the fact that, while market integration is necessary to boost trade performance, it is not enough. The development of regional productive capacities and regional value chains is key to boosting international productive linkages, fostering economic development and increasing the wellbeing of societies.

Linking integration processes and structural changes in LAC

The main rationale for regional economic integration is overcoming the limits imposed by the size of national markets, to take advantage of economies of scale and achieve sustained increases in productivity. Technological change and productive diversification acquire a fundamental role by altering the optimal market size. The challenge of integration far transcends the trade agenda, covering a wide range of development policies. In particular, during the pandemic there has been in the region growing recognition of the crucial role to be played by integration in reducing regional dependence on international trade and increasing resilience to external shocks. The persistence of a poorly sophisticated productive structure, mostly characterised by natural resources driven sectors, has opened a debate about how integration policies must be grounded on structural change policies, unleashing processes that dynamise regional comparative advantages in more sophisticated sectors.

Historically, the manufacturing industry was the productive nucleus that benefited the most from market expansion because of its capacity to generate and take advantage of economies of scale. Manufacturing is an engine for the integration of new markets, first in national economies and then in large regional or global spaces. In that sense, regional integration could foster industrialisation in the region based on production complementarity, which would expand the intraregional trade of manufactured products. An additional benefit would be to reduce dependency on commodity exports, thus helping to overcome the external constraint that has long hindered regional development (ECLAC, 2021[4]).

The limits that Latin American integration has faced are largely the limits of its industrialisation process. The brake on industrial expansion in the late 1970s meant the loss of a crucial engine for integration. For example, one of the most successful integration processes in the region took place in Central America; however, the productive integration of Central America with the world economy takes place mostly through manufacturing activities carried out in special economic zones (SEZ). Compared to the subregion of Central America and Mexico, South America registers lower levels of intraregional trade and productive integration. This is the result of various factors: its large territorial extension, complex geography, deficient transport infrastructure, the institutional fragmentation of its market, and it's export specialisation in natural resources.

The relationship between manufacturing and integration is essential to understanding the advances and limitations of economic integration processes. In Western Europe and East Asia processes with a strong industrial component have been successful even with very different models of political articulation. With or without centralised formal institutions, successful examples of integration have been based on industrial production chains, among which: electronics, metalworking and textiles, and clothing.

The technological content of LAC exports is generally low. However, inter-regional trade in Latin America and the Caribbean has a higher manufacturing content than the region's exports to the rest of the world. On average, industrial products accounted for 73% of intraregional flows in 2018-19, but only 63% in the case of extra-regional exports (Figure 3.5). This same pattern applies to all the integration mechanisms, with a larger share of manufactures in exports within each grouping – especially among the Central American countries, where the figure rises to nearly 90%. These figures show the crucial role that intraregional trade plays in economic diversification and the internationalisation of small and medium-sized enterprises (SMEs).

Today, productive integration opportunities are not limited to manufacturing, sectors associated with natural resources also show a great scope for innovation and adding value. Technological content and knowledge intensity, whether in the manufacturing or other sector, are central elements in the proposal for integration and structural change advocated in the region in the last few years. There is no space for regional integration without productive diversification. Fostering regional integration entails encouraging the transition toward new activities characterised by higher levels of knowledge intensity and productivity. This requires targeted industrial policies to strengthen existing comparative advantages (incorporating technologies in existing sectors) or to create new competitive advantages (investing in new sectors).

Figure 3.5. **Latin America and the Caribbean (main integration mechanisms):
Sectoral structure of goods exports, 2018-19**

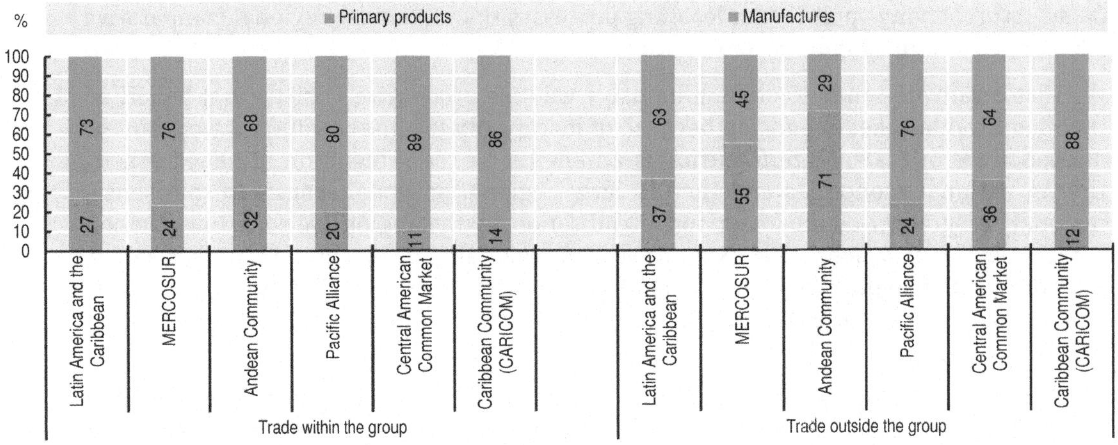

Source: ECLAC (2021[4]), *International Trade Outlook for Latin America and the Caribbean, 2020* (LC/PUB.2020/21-P), Santiago, 2021, https://www.cepal.org/sites/default/files/publication/files/46614/S2000804_en.pdf.
StatLink 🖳 https://doi.org/10.1787/888934286236

The weakness of LAC integration is linked to its productive structure, sectoral specialisation, and its business structure

Latin America and the Caribbean, as a region, has not been able to achieve long-term productivity gains that allow it to sustain higher growth (Chapter 1). A decomposition of GDP growth in the contributions of employment and labour productivity for a group of countries in the region and other countries and regions during the period 2000-19 shows that in LAC 76% of the average growth achieved in the last two decades was generated through the accumulation of employment and 24% through increases in labour productivity. This pattern contrasts with the decomposition of growth in economies such as China, India, Japan and the Republic of Korea. In the case of China, the contribution of productivity was 96% and that of labour, 4%; in India the ratio is almost 80% and 20%, respectively.

The productivity gap is explained by LAC countries' productive structure and structural heterogeneity – defined as a wide variation in labour productivity between and within sectors – (Pinto, 1970[12]). The region has a poorly diversified productive structure, concentrated in sectors with low added value and exports are concentrated in goods with low technological content (ECLAC, 2020[13]). Moreover, there is a close relationship between the productive structure and the structural heterogeneity of LAC countries. The impacts of the productive structure on average labour productivity at the country level are rooted in structural heterogeneity (Porcile and Cimoli, 2013[14]; Cimoli, Mario, et al., 2005[15]). This means that the sector in which a firm operates impacts the productivity level of the firm but also the productivity gap between companies of different sizes (Closset and Leiva, 2021[16]). In Mexico for example some sectors have an average productivity 100 times higher than others, and, within these sectors, a high productive heterogeneity is also observed. For example, the average productivity of large mining companies is up to 200 times higher than microenterprises in the sector (Closset and Leiva, 2021[16]). Structural heterogeneity is observed between and within the sectors in all LAC countries. The literature on the region shows that behind the stagnation of productivity there is a contrast between important dynamism in large and technology-intensive firms, with stagnant or declining productivity for the vast majority of small firms, which is often related to the lag in the adoption of new technologies. The size of the firm is a crucial determinant of investment decisions in information technology across all economic sectors. Returns on innovation investment are linked to the presence of complementary inputs, such as skills and financial resources that are typically found in large companies.

The largest LAC companies are concentrated in the production and export of agricultural and mining products or low-tradeable services. Companies that participate in advanced manufacturing activities (for example, EMBRAER or Tenaris) operate with a world market perspective beyond regional integration, which, in any case, would be insufficient for their purposes.

The productive structure prevents the region from growing at a sufficient rate to absorb population growth. The low levels of dynamism and poor diversification of the economy due to the predominance of low technological intensity sectors limit formal employment and generate lower-quality jobs, often in the informal sector. This negatively affects wages and aggregate demand, which keeps the region in a vicious cycle of volatile growth and low productivity.

Likewise, the characteristics of the region's productive structure limit opportunities and incentives for technical change and diversification. The region's international insertion, which is characterised by a small number of large companies in sectors that are intensive in natural resources, offers few opportunities for broad participation in higher value-added activities. With little international competition and few incentives to invest in productive or technological capacities, the productivity of companies stagnates, and the region remains in the trap of low productivity and low value-added integration.

Increasing productivity while promoting the creation of intraregional productive linkages, requires industrial policies responsive to the global context characterised by the increasing centrality of digital technologies and environmental sustainability. These emerging trends make policy action at the national level relevant but insufficient. If the aim is to promote the development of productive capabilities, while shifting toward more sustainable and sophisticated sectors, industrial policies have to include multinational components, i.e. objectives and instruments shared by several countries. Opportunities and policies will depend on the specificities of each sector and the number of countries involved but could include the development of common technical standards, quality certification programmes, training programs, traceability, development of environmental and sustainability standards, etc. At the same time, the promotion of multinational development actions should be promoted, including trade and investment facilitation agreements, joint sectoral mechanisms to attract investments, joint financing of regional infrastructure, trade agreements to promote regional interlinkages and skills development.

A concrete example offered by regional or subregional co-operation for policy implementation concerns the creation of a single market to foster the adoption and development of digital technologies in Latin America and the Caribbean. Moving up regional value chains and SMEs competitiveness requires a deliberate and systematic effort to incorporate technology into agricultural, mining, forestry, energy and services.

A single market to foster technological development in Latin America and the Caribbean

Productivity growth is the central engine of sustained economic growth. Since the first industrial revolution, the introduction of new technologies has contributed to better productivity (Dossi, 1984[17]). The development and incorporation of new technologies in production processes are essential for development. Digital technologies overall – the Internet of Things, big data analysis, cloud computing, augmented reality and platform usage – are changing the microeconomics of production and can play a key role in productivity growth. However, those technologies are at different stages of development and penetration in the business environment. On one hand, they benefit firms in developing countries by reducing transaction costs and facilitating market access and integration into global value chains; on the other, they highlight and deepen the technology gap with industrialised countries and accentuate the market power of large digital platforms, stimulating economic concentration phenomena that penalise less-developed countries. Although in developing countries the impact of digital technologies on productivity is conditioned by the productive structure and structural characteristics of firms, the digital transformation is generating important changes in the organisation of companies and the functioning of market dynamics.

During the last decade, LAC experienced important advances in terms of digital transformation. Digital technologies can play an important role in the region's recovery by addressing the persistent challenge of low productivity. In a region where productivity disparities are considerable according to the size of the firm, the digital transformation brings opportunities, but also the risk of reinforcing these differences (OECD et al., 2020[18]).

Despite progress in connectivity, the rate of digital transformation in the region has been moderate. The digitisation of production processes is strongly lagging behind other regions in LAC. The average growth of digital adoption for productive transformation in the region has been relatively moderate compared to the advances made in other emerging economies, particularly China and in Southeast Asia. In LAC, on average digital adoption in business was 4.5% between 2014 and 2016, well below highly dynamic countries in Southeast Asia (13.1%) or China (16.4%). Similarly, digital adoption has been heterogenous among firms of different sizes. Larger companies have managed to have higher connection speeds, which also conditions the type of services they can access and offer and can create productivity gaps.

Even though the incorporation of digital technologies in productive processes is still lagging behind in the region, the COVID-19 pandemic has accelerated the process in business activities. The pandemic and subsequent containment measures have shown the increasing importance of new technologies for consumers and firms. The online interest for delivery services has increased since the beginning of the confinement measures in Latin American countries, showing a potential consumption habit shift towards e-commerce after the crisis (OECD et al., 2020[18]). This greater use was also reflected by the increase observed in the number of firms with an online presence and by the sophistication of the online services offered by firms, represented by the transition from informative to transactional websites (ECLAC, 2020[19])

Comparing the pre-pandemic period, February-August 2019, with the same period in 2020, shows a strong increase in business websites. In Brazil, Chile, Colombia and Mexico, a significant increase was recorded in April 2020, followed by a decrease in May, but with a steady increase during the following months (ECLAC, 2020[19]).

E-commerce platforms have also seen an increase in participation by firms, especially SMEs. During the pandemic, data captured from Mercado Libre.com, evidenced an explosion in terms of newly registered sellers. In countries with the most developed marketplaces, new sellers multiplied by 4, while in countries with less platform development, the growth was 6 times (Figure 3.6).

Likewise, analysing the product catalogues of SMEs that use Shopify as an electronic commerce platform shows that half of the products offered on line by SMEs in Brazil, Chile, Colombia and Mexico, as of October 2020, were published for sale shortly after the beginning of the pandemic.

Figure 3.6. **Number of sellers in e-commerce in LAC 2019-20, selected countries**

Panel A. Countries with greater marketplace development

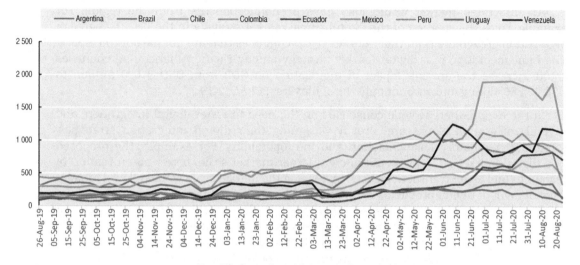

Panel B. Countries with less marketplace development

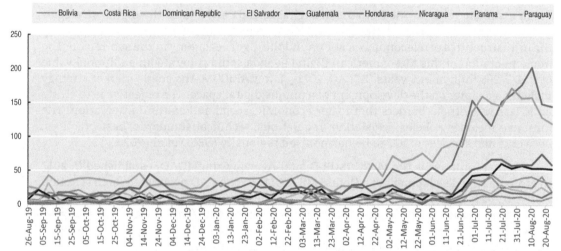

Source: ECLAC (2021[20]), *Post Pandemic COVID-19 Economy Recovery: Enabling Latin America and the Caribbean to Better Harness E-Commerce and Digital Trade,* Own calculations, https://www.cepal.org/sites/default/files/publication/files/46858/S2100269_en.pdf.
StatLink ▄▆■ https://doi.org/10.1787/888934286635

This accelerated digitisation occurred mainly in links of the production chain mostly related to the sale, commercialisation and relationship with suppliers and not in the incorporation of digital technologies in the production process itself. Furthermore, this digitisation is mostly linked to the use of mature technologies such as broadband and not to the use of advanced technologies such as big data, artificial intelligence, machine learning or the internet of things (ECLAC, 2021[21]).

Regional integration and co-ordinated policy strategies will be key to ensuring the creation of digital opportunities. Fragmentation in different markets for the development of telecommunications infrastructures and the incorporation of advanced technologies can be a barrier to taking advantage of economies of scale and integrated digital markets (Cullen International, 2016[22]). Harmonisation, co-ordination, and interoperability at the regional level are essential to facilitate the development of a digital single market, particularly in areas such as the protection of the consumer, personal data protection, digital identity, digital payments, digital values, transport and logistics standards, and tax regimes (ECLAC and Internet & Jurisdiction, 2020[23]).

An integrated market would also have economic benefits from the region. For example, since the creation of the digital single market strategy in the EU, its degree of digitisation grew more than that of other OECD countries that are not part of that space. The implementation of a digital market strategy among Pacific Alliance (PA) countries could increase the annual impact of digitisation on GDP from USD 9 620 million to USD 13 886, taking into account only the spillovers (ECLAC, 2021[24]).

In the region, there is wide consensus on the need to foster digital integration, and several integration blocks are already designing their digital integration strategies, to support regulatory harmonisation and interoperability. For example, the proposed PA's digital market strategy would allow a larger market scale, better co-ordination of resources and fewer transaction costs. Increasing the market scale would allow a broader development of digital products and services, and would facilitate the creation of digital productive capabilities to compete in the content industry and platform development on a global scale. The digital market strategy could be an important instrument for co-ordinating resources from research and technological development and innovation to reduce the transaction costs for firms that could then operate in a harmonised regulatory framework.

In a similar vein, the Mesoamerican Digital Agenda articulates the digital strategies of the member countries of the Mesoamerica Project. One of its goals is to develop the infrastructures of telecommunications and the digital economy in the sub-region. The implementation of this Mesoamerican digital agenda could generate an additional value of USD 3 305 million in 5 years (ECLAC, 2021[24]). In CARICOM, the single market strategy includes a chapter on the development of a unique digital space. The objective is to create an ICT space without borders that foster economic, social and cultural integration. The initiative includes policies, legislation, regulations, technical standards, best practices, networks and services of ICT to be harmonised regionally (OECD et al., 2020[18]).

Another initiative is the MERCOSUR Digital Agenda Group (GAD) established in 2017 to promote "the development of a Digital MERCOSUR". The GAD negotiated its first Action Plan (2018-20) in 2018, with commitments to digital infrastructure and connectivity; security and trust in the digital environment; digital economy; digital skills; digital government, open government and public innovation; technical and regulatory aspects, and co-ordination in international forums (MERCOSUR, 2020[25]).

Recovery strategies to foster sustainable structural changes

The COVID-19 pandemic is having historic negative effects in the productive and social spheres, with lasting consequences on development and growth opportunities for the region. Regional productive capabilities are at risk, with productive chains facing constraints to reach the before-pandemic levels of activity, and external pressure on natural resources and commodity prices. There is a growing risk of regressive structural change, with market incentives pushing toward "reprimarisation". In this scenario, active industrial policies will be needed to resume and support growth and productive activities and to promote an agenda for structural transformation.

Recovery strategies represent an opportunity the region cannot afford to miss. Co-ordinated policies at the regional level are needed to develop regional capabilities, promote structural transformation, and facilitate the integration of the region in global productive networks. To be competitive in the international context, the region needs to be able to anticipate structural changes in the global productive organisation.

The COVID-19 crisis has demonstrated that the current development path has reached a point that has put the survival of the ecological system that supports it at risk. Markets cannot stop these processes, as rates of return do not take into account the destruction of nature or many of its effects on health and well-being. Climate change caused by human activity is the clearest and best-known expression of the economic model's inability to incorporate environmental variables. Ecosystems and biodiversity are being reduced at alarming rates: more than 1 million species are in the process of extinction (IPBES, 2019[26]). Global efforts towards curbing climate change and biodiversity loss will shape economies going forward. In the framework of the Paris Agreement, countries are expected to update Nationally Determined Contributions (NDCs) to combat climate change and are invited to formulate and communicate long-term development strategies aimed at lowering greenhouse gas (GHG) emissions and fostering resilient development.

In this context, a common feature of COVID-19 recovery strategies is the specific sectoral orientations with an emphasis on sustainability, green transition, a prominent role for industrial policy, and a big push towards greater national or regional self-reliance. These strategies aim to allocate resources to specific sectors to address national or regional development needs, taking advantage of positive trends accelerated by the pandemic, and adapting to the current geopolitical environment.

In July 2021, the European Commission revealed its ambitious plan to make the European Green Deal a reality. The plan for 2021-27 acknowledges the need to transform the economy to carbon neutrality by 2050 and proposed 13 policies, which, if adopted by the European Parliament, will not only reshape the European economy but will also have an impact on the EU's commercial partners. The plan includes the implementation of a carbon border adjustment mechanism. The plan will also ban *de facto* the sale of diesel and petrol cars by 2035 which will consequently influence the transformation of the global automotive industry.

China's plan for 2021-25, ratified in March 2021, aims to increase self-reliance and boost the domestic market. At the same time, the country's "dual circulation" strategy involves improving national productive capacities through industrial policies with a focus on sectors prioritised by the 2015 "Made in China 2025" policy and maintaining access to international markets. The plan also includes a strategy for reducing CO_2 emissions by 2030 and controlling non-CO_2 greenhouse gases.

In the United States, based on the USD 4.2 trillion in budget resources allocated to support households, protect businesses, and strengthen the healthcare system since the outbreak of the pandemic, the proposed American Jobs Plan would allocate nearly USD 2 trillion of spending on transportation infrastructure, utilities and digitalisation, as well as on manufacturing and innovation, with a strong orientation towards mitigating climate change and facilitating the energy transition. In G20 countries clean energy commitments have risen to USD 245 billion, 79% of which has been allocated as conditional support (Energy Policy Tracker, 2021[27]).

In the context of reshaping the global economy, some current engines of growth for Latin America may suffer, but this transition also brings emerging opportunities. A significant challenge is to transform the carbon-neutrality goal from a challenge to an economic opportunity for the region. For example, oil and coal exports could suffer strongly in the long term; especially since international demand plays an important role in this sector (45% of the oil and 58% of the coal produced in the region is exported). If global demand for fossil fuels falls to levels consistent with the 1.5°C target, imports of them will decline dramatically (it is estimated that between 50% and 70% of oil reserves will be unused by 2035). Such a shift will depress global oil prices, have strong implications for labour in the fossil-fuel sector, and will significantly affect fiscal revenues in oil-exporting countries (Solano-Rodriguez et al., 2019[28]).

At the same time, countries in Latin America and the Caribbean face similar environmental challenges that are linked to their productive structure and the characteristics of their development model. Economic growth has mostly been based on a production structure with static competitive advantages based on natural resources. Despite the progress in the last years and the commitment of the region in pursuing the global agenda, natural resources have often been used in a way that has been detrimental to both the environment and the society: irreversible expansion of the agricultural land, pressure on woodland, coastal areas and biodiverse ecosystems, air and water pollution.

A change of development model will not be brought at the national level. Systemic change is required to develop competitive advantages that generate productive incentives toward more sustainable sectors.

The region is facing the challenge of the transition to sustainability inside its own boundaries and for its own needs, while simultaneously facing the challenge of having to reshape its economy to align it with the global challenge of addressing climate change and the economic transformation already happening elsewhere in the world. At the same time, the region needs a structural shift to overcome the limitations imposed by its development model (ECLAC, 2020[13]). The production structure must shift towards more technology-intensive sectors with higher rates of demand and more skilled employment. The structural transformation must be achieved while preserving natural resources, biodiversity, and the environment. Since markets cannot drive sustainable structural transformation alone, these changes call for a co-ordinated set of policies, summarised by the Economic Commission for Latin America and the Caribbean (ECLAC) as a big push for sustainability.

The big push for sustainability consists of a set of co-ordinated technological and industrial, fiscal, financial, environmental, social and regulatory policies. It aims to establish a new structure of incentives for investment, the creation of higher productivity and higher-waged jobs within the development of local and regional production chains. It involves technological upgrades and environmental and climate efficiency (ECLAC, 2020[13])

The transformation of the productive structure and the development of local and regional production capabilities are at the essence of the big push for sustainability. Each country, given its productive structure and its societal priorities, needs to determine the activities and policies needed to foster progressive structural change and the big push for sustainability (ECLAC, 2020[13]).

Seven sectoral systems can provide the basis for a big push for sustainability in the region: non-conventional renewable energy; electromobility; digitisation; the healthcare manufacturing industry; the bioeconomy; the circular economy; and tourism. Co-ordinating investments and industrial policies around these sectors provides ample scope to generate better quality jobs, pursue innovation, incorporate technological progress, diversify exports, adapt to and mitigate the effects of climate change and undertake regional integration efforts.

Building upon the analysis undertaken by ECLAC in *Building a New Future Transformative Recovery with Equality and Sustainability*, the next section analyses opportunities in regional capacity development and integration in five sectors: (i) pharmaceutical, (ii) automotive, (iii) renewable energy, (iv) sustainable agriculture, and (v) the circular economy.

This selection of sectors is meant as a guide to a sustainable transformation based on the development of regional capabilities. A combination of forward-looking investments, together with industrial, fiscal, social and skill-development policies can spur the growth of new sectors as well as foster conversion and new branch development in existing sectors. Moreover, investment to promote climate efficiency and circularity within existing sectors can also offer new opportunities to diversify the economy while achieving low-carbon development. Productive integration around strategic value chains and sectors will speed up the transition and decrease its cost while increasing its efficiency.

From domestic to regional: Sectoral experiences as an opportunity for productive integration and sustainable transformation

There is no recipe for sustainable structural transformation and regional productive integration. The characteristics of each sector shape how countries integrate and strengthen their productive capabilities. Industrial structure, firms' size, trade agreements, and resource endowments are some of these characteristics. Hence, productive integration policy making requires an integrated approach, which is largely sector-specific. That makes it useful to focus on sectoral experiences in the region to draw lessons and identify future opportunities to develop regional capabilities while generating incentives for more sustainable and sophisticated productive models. This chapter analyses five sectors that could play a key role in transformative recovery strategies in LAC: pharmaceuticals, the automotive sector, renewable energy, sustainable agriculture and the circular economy.

The pharmaceutical sector: strengthening regional capabilities

In the last 18 months, all countries in Latin America have faced a singular challenge in sourcing the medical products required to launch systematic public responses to the COVID-19 emergency. Access to medicines in the context of the pandemic has highlighted health inequities globally. High dependence on imports of medicines in general, and COVID-19 critical-care products specifically, have constrained the ability of governments to guarantee essential protection for medical workers, enable access to tests, provide respirators and oxygen when required, and rally the arsenal of pharmacological agents used to combat the effects of COVID-19 (Delgado et al., 2020[29]). In short, the global pandemic has exposed LAC's supply-chain vulnerability. Designing policies aimed at strengthening local pharmaceutical industries and investing in the development of local production capabilities will, at the same time, strengthen the reaction capacity of the region and foster knowledge and industrial development.

The pharmaceutical industry is comprised of public and private entities whose activities include research and development, manufacturing, packaging and marketing of medicinal products aimed at prevention and treatment of medical conditions. In Europe and the United States, these industries are significant drivers of economic and technological development. They fit tightly into a web of complex economic activities that include food processors, cosmetics, chemicals and paint, engineering and other interlocking technological activities.[1]

Across LAC, pharmaceutical production is highly concentrated in the final phases of the industry's value chain – namely, importation of active pharmaceutical ingredients, their combination, packaging, distribution and marketing. This reality shapes import and export patterns and the value of the pharmaceutical industry in terms of a percentage of national GDP.[2] Latin America and the Caribbean is not a leading region in pharmaceutical production; the share of the pharmaceutical industry as a percentage of GDP was 0.37% in 2017.

By contrast, in OECD countries, pharmaceutical industries represent more value in the overall economy, accounting for 0.83% of GDP. In LAC, there are no countries with high aggregated value in the pharmaceutical industry. Argentina (0.7%) has the highest regional level, followed by Brazil (0.54%), Mexico (0.46%) and Chile (0.27%). Latin America's pharmaceutical market as a percentage of GDP contrasts markedly with small European countries such as Ireland (7.6%), Denmark (3.2%) and Slovenia (2.9%) where pharmaceutical industries deliver high value-added goods and create spillover effects for other technology-based economic activities (Feinberg and Majumdar, 2001[30]; Grupp and Mogee, 2004[31]; Grupp, 1996[32]).

Latin America's total pharmaceutical market value is dramatically weighted towards three countries that represent 80% of the regional market: Brazil (USD 24.6 billion), Mexico (USD 7 billion) and Argentina (USD 4.6 billion) (Figure 3.7). Market sizes in the region are a factor in determining the concentration of country-level pharmaceutical production and innovation systems. Still, Argentina, Brazil and Mexico that represent nearly 80% of the entire regional pharmaceutical market's value, are not significantly more export-competitive than their smaller-market neighbours. While the value of Central American countries' combined market value represents less than 5% of the regional market, there are notable cases of individual countries that have developed niche-driven export platforms especially in the case of Mexico's medical device industry (Valverde, 2014[33]). Figure 3.7 illustrates the high concentration of value in the region's market, with these three countries accounting for nearly eight out of every ten dollars in annual market share.

Figure 3.7. **Pharmaceutical industry market value, selected LAC countries, 2019**

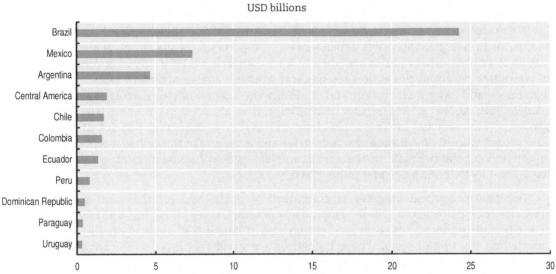

USD billions

Source: Statista (2020[34]), *Revenue of the worldwide pharmaceutical market from 2001 to 2020*, https://www.statista.com/statistics/263102/pharmaceutical-market-worldwide-revenue-since-2001.

StatLink 🔗📊 *https://doi.org/10.1787/888934286654*

The region does have pockets of high-value pharmacological production, most notably in the large-scale generics production in Brazil and in a recent strengthening of biotechnology in Argentina. On the whole, however, since the 1980 and 1990s the region has pursued a model of importation of pharmaceutical products and medical devices, relying primarily on foreign producers (Sweet, 2017[35]; Sweet, 2013[36]). The region's dependence on the supply of active ingredients and finished products from external sources is evidenced by the fact that a large part of the countries of the region have import ratios over sectoral added value greater than one. For 2014, this indicator takes the values of 1.2 in Brazil, 1.1 in Argentina, and 1.4 in Chile and Colombia. By contrast, the export ratios over sectoral added value in OECD countries (excluding Latin American members) range between 25% and 45%.

Lack of harmonised regulatory frameworks at the regional level and insufficient human resources have resulted in a production model focused on national markets and mostly concentrated in the development of conventional, "small molecule" drugs. These productive activities are buttressed by training centres throughout the region. Governments must capitalise on the need for persistent investment in both the quality and the number of researchers in this area. Robust innovation systems require varied and deep human-resources capacities. Specific researchers in both narrow fields and broad networks are essential to creating ecosystems in this space. There are indications of growing segments in health care professions working on scientific research more generally however, this has "not been accompanied by a similar rate of patents applied for and obtained, nor of new products on the market" (ECLAC, 2020[13]).

Latin America currently does not have a regional platform for researchers to co-operate with administrative or institutional ease. Prioritising university-level exchanges, so that researchers can build on the respective advantages of their national contexts, would strengthen innovative activities in the medical technology sector. This requires simplifying and streamlining co-operative systems for researchers, similar to the EU's ERASMUS programme, that would facilitate the mobility of academics in health and promote co-operation between universities and research centres in the region. Additional advantages to promoting programmes that facilitate research collaboration and exchange would be the formation of work teams from different countries in the region.

In recent decades, there has been sustained interest at the regional level in promoting policies that would harmonise safety and efficacy standards to reap the scale advantage of a larger Latin American market. This would enable more accessibility for people in the region to new products while ensuring their quality and safety. Since as early as 2006, the aim of integration of these systems has been promoted by the World Health Organization (WHO) and the Pan American Health Organization (PAHO) to strengthen regulatory agencies through "the sharing of information, convergence and reliance of regulatory processes, not in the absolute harmonisation of norms and standards" (PAHO, 2010[37]). In other words, the aim of the PAHO and other international agencies thus far has not been the ambitious, politically driven project of creating one system of standards, but co-ordinating and opening dialogue between those systems.

Import systems in the region also create barriers to the entry of new products. The costs and complexity of these systems in and of themselves represent an issue. In the case of Argentina, the previous system of DJAI – an acronym representing a "Sworn Advanced Affidavit of Imports" system – has been replaced by a new *Sistema Integral de Monitoreo de Importaciones*" which will allow for automatic licensing of products (SIMI, 2021[38]). In the five years since this regulation was created, it has allowed for the automatic authorisation of 18 000 of 19 000 products registered in the imports system.[3] Brazil's regulatory agency, ANVISA could be improved, as certifications and related fees can double the cost of products. Similarly, entry barriers in Colombia's pharmaceutical market include increased stringency in the new "National Development Plan" as well as "price controls, counterfeiting, patentability criteria, weak patent enforcement and issuance of a declaration of public interest to force a price discount" (US Commercial Service, 2019[39]).

The automotive sector: Integration and sustainability

The automotive industry is one of the most important in LAC. Characterised by extensive upstream and downstream linkages to many diverse industries and sectors it plays a central role in the development of industrial capabilities in the region. The pandemic has seriously affected the sector and is driving a profound transformation in its organisation and geographic location around the world. Many car parts supplier companies have closed or have failed to maintain pre-pandemic production levels, strongly affecting vehicle manufacturing worldwide. In 2020, global vehicle production decreased by 15.8% to 77.6 million units, a figure similar to that recorded in 2010 (Figure 3.8). Among the regions with the greatest drops were the EU (23.5%), North America (20.5%) and South America (30.4%). In this scenario, the automotive industry is likely to be going through the worst crisis in its history.

All the ongoing changes in the automotive sector could represent an opportunity to strengthen manufacturing capabilities and create quality jobs in the region. The automotive industry is concentrated around three macro-regions: North America, the EU and Asia, while a small group of countries (the United States, Germany, Japan, the Republic of Korea and China) maintain strong hegemony in terms of production, vehicle manufacturers, suppliers and technological development. Despite the high degree of concentration in production, the value chain of the automotive sector is highly fragmented, both geographically and by task. This characteristic of the sector provides scope for regional integration to foster capacities all along the value chain, research and development, design, testing, and assembly and production.

Figure 3.8. **Vehicle production, selected regions and countries, 1950-2020**

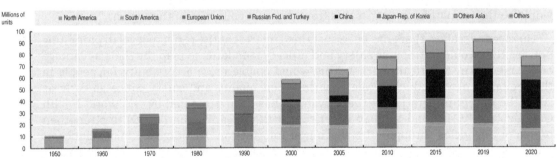

Source: Own elaboration based on data from the International Organization of Motor Vehicle Manufacturers (*Organisation Internationale des Constructeurs d'Automobiles* –OICA-) (2021[40]) 1950-2020 Car production statistics, https://www.oica.net/category/production-statistics/.
StatLink ᐧᐧᐧ https://doi.org/10.1787/888934286673

The automotive industry is undergoing one of the greatest revolutions in its history, as its borders are expanding, and new players, products and business models are appearing. The convergence of traditional manufacturing with electronics and software is modifying the structure of the production chain and the leadership it sustains. Although there are many expectations for new forms of mobility and the role that the automotive industry will play, there are also many questions about the future of the industry.

Latin America has not been immune to the changes in the automotive industry at the global level. In the 1990s, most countries abandoned protectionist schemes and with it, the automotive industry in Latin America practically disappeared, except in the largest economies. Vehicle manufacturers, within the region, through the deployment of strategies that combined efficiency, complementarity, and specialisation, grouped automotive activities around three hubs. The modern production platform in Mexico was strongly integrated with the North American market. Production plants supported by integration schemes for the domestic markets of South America focused on the Mercosur, mainly Argentina and Brazil (Figure 3.9). Finally, the hub of the Andean Community catered for the markets of Colombia, Ecuador and Venezuela.[4]

In recent years, particularly after the global financial crisis of 2008, the Mexican automotive industry has accelerated its transformation process, going from a low-cost export platform for the assembly of mass consumption vehicles to a better-integrated production chain with more diversification in products and greater technological sophistication. In 2017, the Mexican industry reached its all-time high with almost 4 million units produced. This growth has allowed for specialisation and higher technological content, which strengthens Mexico's position in an industry subject to strong pressures from new trends with strong economic impact.

Figure 3.9. **Argentina, Brazil and Mexico: Automobile production, 2000-20**

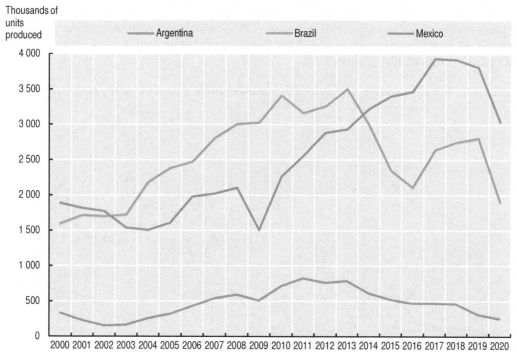

Source: Own elaboration, based on information from the *Asociación de Fábricas de Automotores* (ADEFA), http://www.adefa.org.ar/es/estadisticas-anuarios, *Asociación Nacional dos Fabricantes de Vehículos Automotores* (ANFAVEA), https://anfavea.com.br/estatisticas, and *Asociación Mexicana de La Industria Automotriz* (AMIA), http://amia.com.mx/.
StatLink ᵫ₃┗ https://doi.org/10.1787/888934286692

The harsh impact of the financial crisis on the automotive industry in the United States prompted dozens of companies to modify their expansion and localisation strategies. This led to a huge increase in foreign direct investment (FDI), both from manufacturers and suppliers and in trade with Mexico. Between 2009 and 2020, the Mexican automotive industry received more than USD 56.8 billion in FDI, 51% of which went to the auto parts sub-sector.

With deepening integration between Canada, the United States and Mexico, the supplier base became much broader and more diverse. Automotive production in North America is highly interconnected: vehicle manufacturers and suppliers purchase parts and components throughout the sub-region, which can cross the borders of member countries up to eight times before final installation in a vehicle in an assembly plant in one of the three countries (Wilson, 2017[41]). There is greater US content in an average vehicle manufactured in Mexico or Canada than in a vehicle assembled in any other country in the world, largely owing to the strict origin regimes of NAFTA and especially of the Unites States-Mexico-Canada Agreement (UMSCA) (ECLAC, 2018[42]).

The productive integration scheme in the Mercosur context and the size of local markets led the largest companies in the automotive industry to make large investments in Brazil, and to a lesser extent in Argentina. Production has been aimed at supplying domestic markets and is guided by a clear policy of specialisation: compact cars in Brazil and larger displacement vehicles, particularly work trucks, in Argentina. In Brazil, the concentration of production in compact cars offers companies greater production scale and, therefore, lower costs and greater competitiveness.

With the formation of Mercosur, a division of labour between Argentina and Brazil has increasingly developed, laying the foundations for the creation of a regional automotive value chain. Between 2000 and 2020, Brazil was responsible for 84.5% of the bloc's car production. In 2013, Brazil reached an all-time high of around 3.5 million units produced, then experienced a significant drop to 1.9 million vehicles in 2020; Argentina suffered a similar dynamic, with a record of 830 000 vehicles manufactured in 2011, and then a fall to 260 000 units in 2020 (Figure 3.10).

Figure 3.10. **Brazil: exports and imports of automotive products with Argentina, 1990-2020**

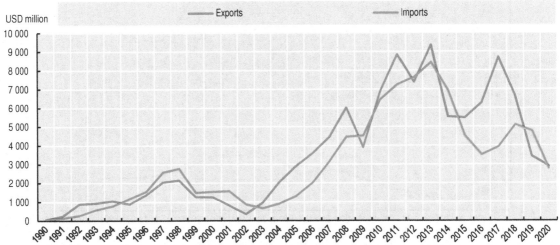

Source: ECLAC (2020[2]) based on United Nations Commodity Trade Statistics Database (COMTRADE) https://comtrade.un.org/.

StatLink ᵃ⁵ᵖ https://doi.org/10.1787/888934286711

Argentina and Brazil have developed complementarity in the trade of intermediate and final goods for the automotive industry. Since the creation of MERCOSUR, bilateral automotive trade grew strongly until the mid-2010s (Figure 3.10). With the growth of the industry, Argentina has tended to specialise in the export of final goods and Brazil in the export of intermediate goods, with which the former accumulated a significant trade deficit (Amar and García Díaz, 2018[43]).

The future concept of mobility is changing rapidly, which will affect Latin American countries. Public policies, and global commitments, are driving vehicle manufacturers towards low-carbon options and greater energy efficiency. The next 20 years will bring significant changes: electrification, shared mobility, connectivity and digitisation, and eventually autonomous vehicles. In this scenario, several countries are competing to build new high-value industrial clusters for mobility products.

Against this background, the region faces multiple challenges, starting with the restructuring of the productive base of the Latin American automotive industry to adapt it to the needs of the new reality. Hence, public policies are needed to strengthen the capacities of the productive and innovation ecosystem, as well as those that favour a greater and more efficient articulation between the main agents of the production chain to take advantage of the opportunities that are beginning to emerge from these changes. This is how niches can be identified where competitive advantages could be developed in the face of the new demands that will arise in the coming years. For the countries of the region that have a presence in advanced manufacturing sectors, such as the automotive industry, with an environment marked by products with shorter life cycles, a growing level of technological sophistication and greater demands for research, development and innovation, the systems production companies should strengthen their capacities in both traditional and disruptive technologies.

The new complex production systems require a large variety of capacities and cannot depend on a single agent, so it is increasingly important to develop mechanisms to promote associations and synergies. Shortened innovation cycles and the need for large amounts of investment have made partnerships and alliances increasingly attractive. Unlike global companies and leading countries in advanced manufacturing, Argentina, Brazil and Mexico have shown difficulties in advancing in this direction, with weak intermediate enterprises and little participation of local companies, particularly those of smaller size, in production. To take advantage of existing capacities in the automotive industry, the region presents favourable conditions for the production of electric mobility components. The need to proceed with the renovation of public transport systems offers a great opportunity to begin to develop new mobility capacities, particularly electromobility (ECLAC, 2020[13]).

The energy sector: Renewable energy sources and regional integration

The energy sector is undergoing the greatest technological change in a century. The transition towards renewable and sustainable sources of energy is a global challenge for public policy. On a global scale, fossil fuels will continue to play a relevant role in primary energy demand by 2040, even though power derived from renewable sources will grow faster (EIA, 2018[44]).

In Latin America, the share of renewables in overall energy production has reached 29%, which exceeds the world average. Hydropower and biomass (mainly firewood and charcoal) are largely responsible, although Brazil stands out as a country where biomass is transformed. The energy transition should be identified as a means of creating economic opportunities in the region.

Although the region has traditionally had higher participation of renewables in its mix, the percentage of renewable energy supply in the Total Primary Energy Supply grew only marginally between 2000 and 2018 (less than 1%), while its renewable energy index has varied very little, increasing by 1.7% in the same period (Figure 3.11). On a sub-regional level, the Andean Zone, Mexico and the Caribbean have substantially decreased their renewability indices, while Central America, Brazil and South America have increased theirs.

Latin America and the Caribbean is a region endowed with vast resources for renewable energy (Paredes, 2017[45]). While wind and solar generation capacity is growing rapidly, representing 57% of additional capacity in 2017, it represents only 6.5% of installed capacity (IRENA, 2018[46]). Latin America and the Caribbean could generate up to 80% of the region's electricity from renewable sources in an affordable way, making use of the abundant wind and solar potential as the cost continues to decrease. The enormous potential for renewables in the region is reflected in the increasing amount of foreign direct investment flowing into the sector within the last decade. During the COVID-19 crisis, the only sector in which investment forecasts increased was in renewable energy (Figure 3.12).

Figure 3.11. **Renewable energy index**

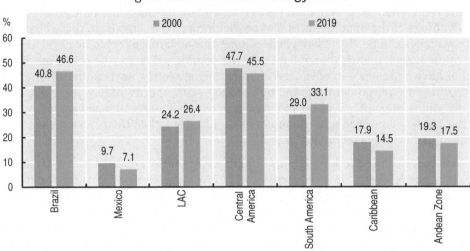

Source: Own calculations, based on Latin American Energy Organization (OLADE) online data, http://www.olade.org/.
StatLink ᎍ᎑ https://doi.org/10.1787/888934286730

Figure 3.12. **Announced investment in renewables projects in LAC**

USD million, Percentage of LAC total

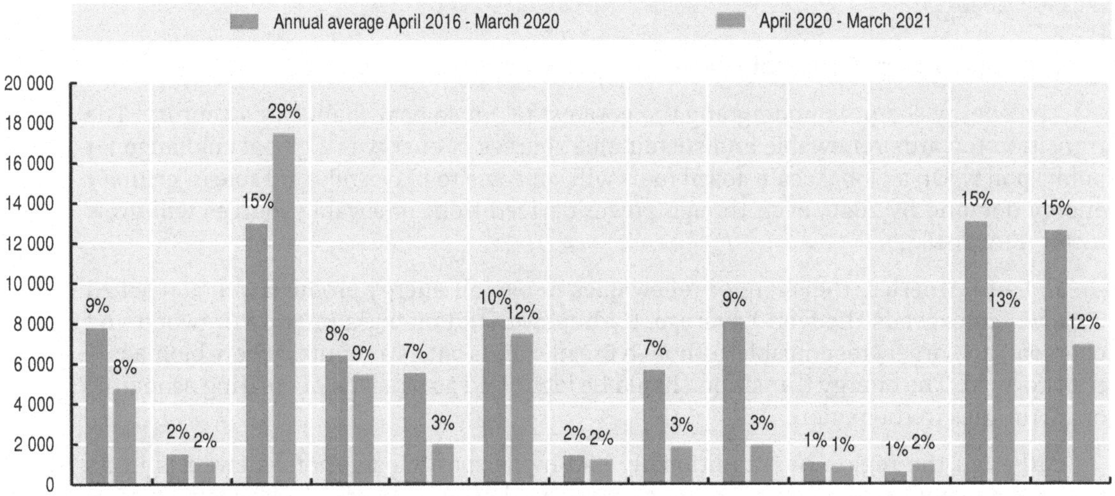

Source: Own elaboration based on the Financial Times, fDiMarket (online database), https://www.fdimarkets.com/.
StatLink ᎍ᎑ https://doi.org/10.1787/888934286749

Significant penetration of renewable energy and high integration of regional transmission will require the incorporation of a greater share of renewables in the electricity grid with higher dispatchable base load generation and deeper regional integration. Therefore, for the next ten years, it will be necessary to increase electricity generation mainly through hydropower, where the role of regional integration of countries with serious hydraulic potential, such as Paraguay, could play a fundamental role. The heterogeneity of the distribution of energy resources present in the region currently implies a costly and complex transition for many countries as they cope with the challenges of meeting the increase in electricity demand in the coming decades, including those linked to the electrification of the transport sector and increased industrial use of energy.

More use of renewable energy sources and greater regional integration should lower electricity-generation costs (fuel, transmission, operation and maintenance) and the costs of investment in new generation capacity (solar, wind, geothermal technology and others). Several countries in the region could access generation surpluses from third countries, so it may not be necessary to build new electricity generation plants; however, it would require political will and sophisticated energy planning (Box 3.2).

Box 3.2. How to meet growing energy demand with clean and sustainable electricity

ECLAC, in partnership with the Latin American Energy Organization (OLADE), the International Renewable Energy Agency (IRENA) and the Inter-American Development Bank (IDB), analysed the complementarity of regional electrical systems and the penetration of renewable energies. As part of this initiative, three scenarios of the electricity sector by 2032 were designed using the PLEXOS methodology.

1. The baseline scenario (BASE) is constructed considering data from the OLADE and the long-term expansion plans of countries. In this scenario, the penetration of renewable energies is based on national energy plans and there is little integration of transmission between countries.

2. The second scenario (RE) incorporates a high proportion of renewable energy (80%, including large-scale hydropower) but maintains the same regional interconnections as in the baseline scenario.

3. The third scenario (RE+INT) incorporates both a high penetration of renewables and a high level of interconnection.

The results are clear efficient decarbonisation of the electricity sector implies the transition towards renewable energies and the promotion of integration initiatives in the regional electricity network. The main results are:

1. BASE scenario: energy planning by countries in the region (2018–32), with no increases in renewable energy (solar, geothermal, mini-hydro, biomass and ocean) and not including large-scale hydropower suppose an increase in their total share of electricity generation from 12.7% to 24.6%.

2. RE scenario: renewable energy (excluding hydropower) increases from 12.7% to 41.1%, with a total cost of 1.35% of annual GDP between 2020 and 2032 and a 30.1% reduction in CO_2 emissions.

3. RE+INT scenario: renewable energy (excluding hydropower) increases from 12.7% to 39.5%, with a total cost of 1.33% of annual GDP between 2020 and 2032 and a 31.5% reduction in CO_2 emissions.

Although the costs of renewable energies are trending downwards (e.g. the average price of photovoltaic modules fell by almost 61% between 2011 and 2017), the current costs of large-scale storage, which range from USD 1 000 to USD 5 000 per megawatt-hour, limit their use on a massive scale. However, in the long term, lower storage costs might be an incentive for greater direct penetration of renewable energy sources. The challenges created by rising electricity demand over the coming decades look even greater when the need to electrify transport and industry is considered. In this context, fostering regional integration could be a way to reduce the cost and increase the environmental efficiency of electricity generation.

Scenarios	Share of no-hydraulic renewable energies in installed capacity	Total cost (% of annual GDP 2020-2032)	CO_2 emissions (gigatons 2020-2032)
Base scenario	12.7%	-	6 (2010-2020)
Energy planning by countries	24.6%	1.40%	4.8
Renewable energy with no integration	41.1%	1.35%	-30.1%
Renewable energy with integration	**39.5%**	**1.33%**	-31.5%

Source: ECLAC (2020[13]) Building a New Future: Transformative Recovery with Equality and Sustainability. Summary (LC/SES.38/4), Santiago, 2020.

The high penetration of renewable energy and significant regional integration would very likely result in greater efficiency, resulting in lower losses and a decrease in emissions. In addition, the investments necessary to achieve energy integration implies the development of sustainable electrical infrastructure, and the opportunity to create approximately 7 million new jobs by 2032. Likewise, if the renewable-energy industry were to be located in LAC manufacturing solar panels and wind turbines would represent almost 1 million more jobs for the region (ECLAC, 2020[13]).

Sustainable agriculture

Modern trends in food consciousness have placed societal and market pressures on agriculture to develop differentiated products. The production of agro-specialities, based on the demands of consumers, is more intensive in knowledge and technology and generates more value for the producers. Firms producing agro-specialities tend to be price makers (Shapiro, 1987[47]).

Many factors explain this process of differentiation, including structural changes (e.g. globalisation), market integration and the expansion of retail, and cultural changes (environmental and food consciousness). This process has been accelerated by rapid digitisation, which has facilitated the monitoring of production chains and by the numerous food crises since the 1990s. The result is an increasingly conscious and demanding consumer looking for higher nutritious quality, fair trade products, agroecological sound origins, indigenous community rights, local labels of origin, reduced environmental footprints, and reduced climate impacts, among others. Products that have a higher nutritional density (proteins, vitamins, others) and that improve health, such as fresh products, as well as those that take care of the environment or that connect with other global causes, acquire more and more importance. COVID-19 may further accentuate this process.

The trend, therefore, is towards agri-food industries with more spending on services and sustainability (certifications, logistics and marketing), than on agricultural raw materials. Progressively, agri-food products are transformed into "products-services", which serve to find a "solution" to a given problem: quality, health, environment, culture, community rights and social inclusion.

Another complementary trend during the last three decades has been generated by the development of biotechnology and the emergence of the bioeconomy. This phenomenon, when complemented with materials sciences and technologies (especially nanotechnology) and information sciences (ICT) has allowed previously unthinkable advances in the productivity of agricultural resources and much more sustainable production models in the bioeconomy that have the potential to generate systemic changes (Fraunhofer, 2018[48]). There are already many countries implementing National Bioeconomy Strategies, such as the United States, Germany, the Netherlands, Sweden, Finland, Norway and Denmark. These strategies are also promoted in the European Union, China and India. In the LAC region, Argentina and Costa Rica for some years have been deploying initiatives for their development (Rodríguez, Mondaini and Hitschfeld, 2017[49]).

Sustainable agriculture can also contribute to a transformative green transition based on quality jobs and socio-economic development. In the next few years, all sectors, including agriculture, will be under pressure to comply with environmental standards and firms will be increasingly challenged to comply with high safety and sustainability standards to compete in the global market. In this scenario, organic agriculture could represent a valid alternative for the diversification of production through innovation and standards development. Organic agriculture involves the application of agronomic, biological and mechanical methods of production in place of the use of synthetic chemical inputs. The development of harmonised standards and certifications is essential to the commercialisation and export of organic products. Recent literature shows that producers who do not obtain certifications do not obtain premium prices for their products. Many small farmers in LAC do not use chemical inputs in their production processes, developing standards and regulations for specific products could help SMEs integrate into regional and international markets, especially the European.

For example, to reduce the contribution of agriculture to global deforestation and forest degradation, the European Commission is working on a legislative proposal to avoid or minimise the placing of products associated with deforestation or forest degradation on the EU market. Regional agriculture policies should anticipate these trends, promoting compliance with higher environmental standards. Targeted investments in the sector and initiatives to help comply and adapt to standards, regulation, and improve transparency should accompany the process. If supported by the correct policy mix, sustainable and speciality-based agriculture could have the triple advantage of improving environmental sustainability, fostering knowledge incorporation, and supporting MSMEs in accessing global markets.

In Latin America and the Caribbean, the agri-food sector accounts for 25% of regional exports and 5% of regional GDP. Commodities occupy between 70% and 80% of the cultivated area of the region, with a significant economic, ecological and social impact. There is, however, much potential for expanding the production of specialities. Shifting towards specialities and sustainable agriculture could generate quality jobs and contribute to building a regional agribusiness that incorporates knowledge and that generates complementary industries such as bioplastics, protein concentrates or waste treatment.

Figure 3.13. **Harvested area by crop in LAC, 2018**

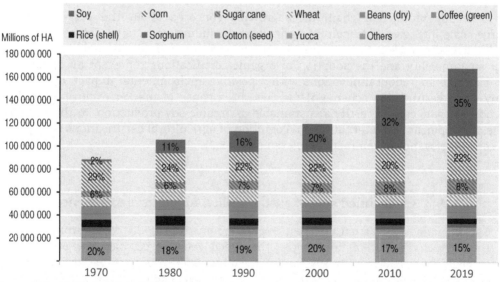

Source: FAO and ECLAC (2020[50]), *Food systems and COVID-19 in Latin America and the Caribbean: Impact and risks in the labour market.* Bulletin 5. Santiago, http://www.fao.org/3/ca9237en/ca9237en.pdf); and FAO (2021[51]) FAOSTAT [online] http://www.fao.org/faostat/en/#home.

StatLink ⧉ https://doi.org/10.1787/888934286768

Soy production is the most important crop in the regional food system, occupying a third of the planted area and generating exports worth approximately USD 65 billion (17% of the total exported by the five producing countries in the region) (Figure 3.13, Table 3.1). The soy value chain plays a strategic role in global food and geopolitical balances, especially owing to its relationship as a privileged supplier of grains for consumption in Asia, mainly China. It is notable for its industrial possibilities, as a supplier of intermediate products that are required in large volumes by companies producing food, biofuels and other industrial products. The production pattern of soy in the region is as a purely primary commodity (both as a grain and its derivatives). However, there is an increasing incentive to incorporate more knowledge and technology value-added, with the growth in demand for differentiated products to allow identification of the origin of the product, traceability and environmental footprint.

Table 3.1. **Soybean producing countries of the Americas: Harvested area, production, yield and number of producers, 2019**

Country	Harvested area		Production		Yield	Farms	Average Farm Size
	Ha	%	Ton	%	Ton/ha	N°	Ha
United States	30 352 150	25.2	96 793 180	29.0	3.2	302 963	100.2
Canada	2 270 500	1.9	6 045 100	1.8	2.7	31 52	72.0
Brazil	35 881 447	29.8	114 269 392	34.2	3.2	236 245	151.9
Argentina	16 575 887	13.8	55 263 891	16.6	3.3	58 443	283.6
Paraguay	3 565 000	3.0	8 520 350	2.6	2.4	27 735	128.5
Bolivia	1 387 973	1.2	2 990 845	0.9	2.2	14	99.1
Uruguay	966	0.8	2 828 000	0.8	2.9	2 229	433.4
Others (producing countries)	62 125 321	51.6	149 799 214	44.9	2.4	yes	yes
World	120 501 628	100.0	333 671 692	100.0	2.8	yes	yes

Source: Own calculation with data from FAOSTAT 2021 for the harvested area, production and yield. For the number of holdings: United States, Agriculture Census 2017, mentioned in ERS-USDA, 2021; Canada, Agriculture Census 2016, mentioned in Soy Canada, 2021 2016; Brazil, Agricultural Census 2017, IBGE, 2019; Argentina, National Agricultural Census 2018, INDEC, 2019; Paraguay, Agricultural Census, 2008 DCEA-MAG, 2009; Bolivia, Agricultural Census2013, INE, 2015; Uruguay, General Agricultural Census, 2011 MGAP, 2011

The soy production chain faces growing concerns about the sustainability of large-scale intensive monoculture agriculture, including impacts on deforestation, loss of biodiversity and soil degradation. The growing concern of international soy consumers for sustainability and the adoption of organic certifications represent an opportunity to generate and adopt innovations with a positive environmental impact, but, as with any trade certification scheme, it can also be a cause of market exclusion for those producers who cannot certify a sustainable or organic soy production. In this scenario, the development and international recognition of agricultural certifications is acquiring a central relevance in commercial relations (Box 3.3).

Box 3.3. **Certified soy for sustainability, Argentina's experience**

The Argentine Association of Direct Sowing Producers (AAPRESID) has worked with the soybeans producers to monetise the added value of certified soy production through the development of soy credits. Producers who certify greater sustainability, transparency and traceability throughout the soy value chain can have access to the Sustainable Agriculture Certification (ASC, by its Spanish Acronym). The Argentinean ASC certification was already recognised by the European Federation of Animal Feed Manufacturers (FEFAC) for producing standards that are compatible with the European market. Since March 2021, the European buyers paid a price premium in form of credits per ton of soybeans producers to certified sellers. In this first instance, the benefit will only cover soybeans, although work is being done to add other crops such as corn, wheat and cotton.

Box 3.3. **Certified soy for sustainability, Argentina's experience** (*cont.*)

On the other hand, Argentina is also promoting the RTRS certification. The "Round Table on Responsible Soy Association" (RTRS) is a global non-profit organisation founded in 2006 in Zurich, Switzerland, which promotes the production, trade and use of responsible soy through the co-operation with relevant actors in the soy value chain, from production to consumption. It guarantees zero deforestation and zero conversions in soy production.

The ASC and RTRS certification standards have shared goals and complementary schemes. This fact makes the double RTRS / ASC certification a competitive advantage for Argentine producers because it allows continuous improvement of management, transparency of processes and traceability of soy produced sustainably.

Source: Own elaboration based on AAPRESID (2021[52]), *Asociación Argentina de Productores en Siembra Directa*, https://www.aapresid.org.ar/ and RTRS (2021[53]), *Round Table on Responsible Soy Association*, https://responsiblesoy.org/soja-rtrs.

The production and distribution of coffee represents another promising value chain. The global market for coffee-related products is growing steadily, and product differentiation is based not only on the organoleptic attributes of the product but also on its environmental impact and sustainability scores. A complex system of quality labels, guides, classifications, rankings and networks is being developed to help consumers identify their products. In Central America, different strategies have focused on specialities and sustainable products. The Mesoamerican coffee chain is one of the strongest economically and socially, as well as one of the best organised within the regional food system. Constituted by approximately 380 000 producers (more than 90% small farmers), this chain occupied approximately 1.15 million ha. in the region in 2020 and it represented 2.3% of export earnings (USD 3.965 million), although in Honduras it represented 8.61% and in Guatemala almost 5% (Table 3.2). This value chain testifies to the development of a speciality, with a high level of sophistication in its primary production phases and collection and storage to obtain a differentiated high-quality product. It has advanced technology in the production phase, which is applied by the most innovative and largest producers. This scheme makes it possible to take advantage of an ecosystem of high-altitude forests, which is very relevant and of great value from a biodiversity point of view. The production areas have basic infrastructure and are relatively close to the US market, which is an important competitive advantage. Another peculiarity of the coffee chain is that it is networked with the Cafeteria Chain, which is rapidly evolving towards a service economy, as evidenced by the fact that more than 50% of the volume produced is certified, or that some countries and companies have escalated towards the most advanced segment, the management of brands and final consumption stores, the most outstanding case being the Federation of Coffee Growers of Colombia (500 000 associates) and its Juan Valdez brand (Box 3.4).

Both the soy and the coffee chains present different levels of complexity that vary in each country, as they follow specific technological trajectories that respond to their basic natural resources, as well as to their laws and institutional schemes. Both chains face severe environmental challenges and include thousands of companies that are subject to price volatilities and other instabilities that are typical of agricultural activity. Defending and developing these chains requires good public policies, regional standard development and new productive and trade agreements to avoid the commoditisation of specialities in the global markets. Co-ordination at the regional-sectoral level is key to adding value, developing regional linkages, increasing knowledge incorporation and sustainability. The agri-food sector in the region requires a set of co-ordinated policies that combine incentives to spur investments in innovative activities with subsidies to absorb the changes that are taking place at the global level.

Table 3.2. **Central American coffee producing countries: Harvested area, production, yields and number of producers, 2020**

Countries	Harvested Area (2020) Ha	Production (2020) Ton	Farms N°
Guatemala	422 445	225 000	125 000
Honduras	350 000	377 200	144 000
Nicaragua	126 154	150 615	44 519
Costa Rica	93 697	86 804	29 918
El Salvador	140 018	34 045	24 627
Panama	16 630.60	9 200	8 973
Total, Region	**1 148 944**	**884 033**	**377 037**

Source: Own calculations with data from: INE, 2020; USDA, 2020; ICO, 2021a; ICO, 2021b; INIDE, 2011; PROMECAFE, 2021; ICAFE, 2020; CSC, 2021; MIDA, 2020; ASAMBLEA NACIONAL, 2020; MIDA, 2020.

Box 3.4. **The Latin American experiences of the new trends Juan Valdéz and Britt**

The Colombian case

In 2002, the National Federation of Coffee Growers of Colombia created the "Juan Valdez" brand for its network of coffee shops and value-added businesses (Federación Nacional de Cafeteros de Colombia, 2019[54]). The objective of these coffee shops is to sell premium coffee to position the product as part of the heritage of Colombia. Following the popularity of the brand and its distribution in national stores, the distribution of Juan Valdez products expanded to Colombian retail and international markets. By 2019 Juan Valdez had 445 stores worldwide, of which 313 are in Colombia and 132 in 13 other countries (Federación Nacional de Cafeteros de Colombia, 2019[54]).

The products offered through these distribution channels are selected packaged coffees; premium, origin and specialty coffee; pods and drips (individual coffee sachets); and freeze-dried coffee (Juan Valdez, 2021[55]) (Portafolio, 2017[56]).

The Costa Rican case

Costa Rica has produced one of the best coffees in the world for more than a century. However, before Café Britt, all gourmet coffee was exported while low-quality coffee was distributed in the domestic market. Unlike most coffee that is sold commercially in non-coffee producing countries, Café Britt's coffee is grown, roasted and packaged in the country of origin, Costa Rica (El Financiero, 2016[57]).

In the 1990s Britt targeted air terminals by using a golf cart as a kiosk to sell brewed and bagged coffee. This tactic showed the potential of being present in airports, and in 2001, the company opened its first "Britt Shop". In 2017 Britt opened its first cafeteria, which grew to eight in Costa Rica and two abroad by 2019 (Fallas Villalobos, 2019[58]). This is in addition to the 135 establishments in terminal areas, which generate the highest income for the Costa Rican company. The products they offer are gourmet packaged coffee, origin, organic, espresso and capsules; as well as machinery to prepare coffee, among others (Mosere, 2021[59]).

The circular economy: New opportunities for value creation

The global green transition is no longer a distant goal. Nations are taking steps to achieve net-zero emissions and comply with the Paris agreement. While the transition to sustainable energy will result in important reductions in carbon emissions, it will not be enough to meet the global climate goals. Indeed, research has shown that relying solely on energy efficiency and switching to renewable energy will only address 55% of global GHG emissions. The remaining 45% are a direct result of the way products and food are made and used, but they can be significantly reduced through circular strategies (Ellen MacArthur Foundation, 2021[60]). Net zero is an ambitious target that cannot be achieved under the current economic model.

Building a sustainable world demands redesigning the economy fundamentally and replacing the actual linear approach of "take, make, waste", by creating a circular economy and promoting sustainability by design. This would reduce carbon, cut pollution and help protect biodiversity. The circular economy is a key element to address the climate crisis as it can both contribute to reducing emissions while increasing resilience to climate change.

The circular economy approach has been gaining momentum in the region since 2019. In the Forum of Environment Ministers of Latin America and the Caribbean, proposals to establish a Regional Coalition on Circular Economy were announced. The Coalition was officially created in 2021 to develop a regional circular vision and strategy for 2030 (Box 3.5) and national governments have implemented more than 80 public policy initiatives in LAC (e.g. the national circular economy strategy in Colombia or the Circular economy national plan in Uruguay).

Box 3.5. Regional Coalition on Circular Economy

Colombia, Costa Rica, Peru and the Dominican Republic are part of the first steering committee of the initiative that seeks to move towards a friendly economy where pollution is eliminated and natural systems are allowed to regenerate, helping to protect biodiversity and combat climate change.

The initiative, co-ordinated by the United Nations Environmental Programme (UNEP), is headed by a steering committee composed of four high-level government representatives who will be renewed every two years, starting with Colombia, Costa Rica, Peru and the Dominican Republic for the 2021-22 period.

The initiative has eight permanent strategic partners: the Climate Technology Centre and Network (CTCN), the Ellen MacArthur Foundation, the Inter-American Development Bank (IDB), the Konrad Adenauer Foundation (KAS), the Platform for Accelerating the Circular Economy (PACE), the United Nations Industrial Development Organization (UNIDO), the World Economic Forum (WEF) and UNEP.

The coalition aims to provide a regional platform to enhance inter-ministerial, multi-sectoral and multi-stakeholder co-operation, increase knowledge and understanding of the circular economy. It has already started working with LAC countries to develop a regional circular vision 2030.

Source: Circular Economy Coalition Latin America and the Caribbean (2021[61]), Governance Structure, https://www.coalicioneconomiacircular.org/en/elementor-7/inicio-english/

The circular economy is underpinned by three principles, all driven by upstream design and innovation: eliminate waste and pollution, keep products and materials in use, and regenerate natural systems. Environmental sustainability also means increasing efficiency in extracting and using resources in the economy and reducing the production of waste. In a circular economy, efforts should be done to improve efficiency and the useful life of materials by promoting durability and the capacity to repair, remanufacture, reuse and recycle goods. These changes are promoted through product design and business models, to ensure easier and more profitable repair, recycling, remanufacturing or shared use through services (Ellen MacArthur Foundation, 2013[62]).

A circular economy scenario is particularly relevant to LAC, given the economic weight of the extractive sectors. A scenario including an increase in recycling rates implies reduced extraction demand, but an increase in demand for services associated with waste management and remanufacturing of materials. Moreover, even if circularity is fully implemented, the demand for virgin materials will continue to increase (ECLAC, 2020[13]). These trends can be seen as an opportunity for the region. Greater circularity in the minerals and metals sector does not mean the disappearance of extractive activities, but a complement to them.

In the context of global economic transformation and the region's need for structural transformation, circular economy policies and investments could play a crucial role. By proposing the decoupling of economic growth from the exploitation of finite natural resources and energy use, the circular economy is considered a key tool to achieve the Sustainable Development Goals (SDGs) of the 2030 Agenda.

The circular economy is thus an important strategy to support regional development based on the expansion of manufacturing in the region but also the framework in which sustainable agriculture and bioeconomy could be fostered. LAC is facing a twin challenge of pursuing socio-economic development while reducing GHG emissions. In that context, Gramkow and Anger-Kraavi (2019[63]) highlighted that green fiscal stimulus in manufacturing sectors globally needs to be considered as one of the main policy measures helping with the transformation to a low-carbon economy, especially in the developing world. Recovery policies based on incentives for investment in low-carbon technologies in manufacturing sectors can bring about a significant reduction in CO_2 emissions while helping to improve economic performance by boosting activity, contributing to the diversification of the production structure and improving the trade balance. Environmental big push policies would also considerably expand the relative size of the industry in the economic structure. The value added by all manufacturing sectors rises the most in low-technology and intermediate-technology industries (Gramkow and Anger-Kraavi, 2019[63]; ECLAC, 2020[13]). This model shows that sound policies could help to tackle GHG emissions while contributing to structural change in the region.

Tackling structural inefficiencies across supply chains, the circular economy offers abundant value-creation opportunities at the industry level. Research suggests that transitioning to a circular economy could generate a net economic benefit of EUR 1.8 trillion for Europe by 2030 (Ellen MacArthur Foundation, 2021[64]). A transition to a circular economy would also create jobs in the region. In LAC, the adoption of a circular economy scenario would create a net total of 4.8 million jobs by 2030 (ILO/IDB, 2020[65]). Job creation in sectors such as the reprocessing of wood, steel, aluminium, and other metals would more than offset the losses associated with the extraction of minerals and other materials. This is because the value chain in reprocessing is longer and more employment-intensive than it is in mining (ECLAC and ILO, 2018[66]).

Conclusion

The COVID-19 crisis has demonstrated that the current productive structure in LAC is a limit to productivity growth, deeper regional integration and sustainability. The LAC region has not been able to achieve long-term productivity gains that allow it to sustain higher growth. This is mainly due to the region's poorly diversified productive structure, which is concentrated in sectors with low value-added. Most LAC countries participate in global production networks as suppliers of raw materials and basic manufacturing products, and only a few countries have diversified their productive structure and become critical actors within global production networks.

Regional integration remains an unexploited opportunity to diversify the productive structure and achieve higher productivity growth. Nevertheless, regional integration must go beyond market integration and aim to develop regional productive capacities and regional value chains. Major industrial-policy efforts will be required alongside the convergence between the existing integration mechanisms and institutions to overcome regional market fragmentation. In this sense, key specific sectors such as the pharmaceutical, automotive, energy, sustainable agriculture or the circular economy can lead the way. Similarly, regional integration and co-ordinated policy strategies will be key to ensuring the creation of digital opportunities that could transform the productive structure and the development of local and regional production capabilities while bridging existing digital divides (Box 3.6).

Box 3.6. **Key policy messages**

- Promote regional productive capacities and regional value chains.

- Push for further intraregional trade as it plays a strong role in economic diversification, the development of manufacturing capacities and the internationalisation of small and medium-sized enterprises.

- Go beyond market integration and trade performance. The development of regional productive capacities and regional value chains is key to boosting international productive linkages, fostering economic development and increasing the wellbeing of citizens.

- Foster industrialisation in the region based on production complementarities. This would expand intraregional trade of manufactured products and reduce dependency on commodity exports.

- Implement industrial and productive policies to strengthen existing capacities, generate new industries, promote regional production and research networks. Regionalisation and regional production networks offer the opportunity to foster productivity growth, higher wages and inclusive labour markets, while redefining the connection and integration of the region to international production and innovation hubs.

- Promote the convergence of integration mechanisms and institutions as it could provide an opportunity to boost investments, develop productive capacity and overcome regional market fragmentation.

- Promote digital transformation as it can play an important role in the region's recovery by addressing the persistent challenge of low productivity (OECD et al., 2020[18]). Despite the COVID-19 pandemic accelerating the process, incorporation of digital technologies in productive processes is still lagging behind in the region.

Box 3.6. **Key policy messages** (*cont.*)

Regional integration and co-ordinated policy strategies will be key to ensuring the creation of digital opportunities, while being a driving factor towards better social welfare and bridging digital divides.

- Aim COVID-19 recovery strategies with an emphasis on sustainability, green transition, a prominent role for industrial policy, and a big push towards greater national or regional self-reliance.

- Identify with relevant actors key sectors that could lead the way in integration and regional productive capabilities. Productive integration policy making requires an integrated approach, which is largely sector-specific. That makes it useful to focus on sectoral experiences in the region to draw lessons and identify future opportunities.

Notes

1. The importance of cross-industrial and cross-regional spill-over effects has gained increasing momentum in industrial organisation and economic development literatures (Gao, Pentland and Hidalgo, 2021[67]).

2. The Latin American pharmaceutical market has experienced consistent growth during the last five years, accounting for about 4% of global pharmaceutical market revenue in 2019.

3. This regulation was adopted by the resolution AFIP 3823/2015.

4. Currently, Colombia is the only Andean country that maintains an automotive sector of some relevance.

References

AAPRESID (2021), *Asociación Argentina de Productores en Siembra Directa*, https://www.aapresid.org.ar/. [52]

Amar, A. and F. García Díaz (2018), *Integración productiva entre la Argentina y el Brasil: Un análisis basado en metodologías de insumo-producto interpaís*, United Nations, https://www.cepal.org/sites/default/files/publication/files/43623/S1800116_es.pdf. [43]

Cimoli, Mario, et al. (2005), *Cambio estructural, heterogeneidad productiva y tecnología en América Latina*, United Nations, http://hdl.handle.net/11362/2800. [15]

Circular Economy Coalition Latin America and the Caribbean (2021), *Governance Structure*, https://www.coalicioneconomiacircular.org/en/elementor-7/inicio-english/. [61]

Closset, M. and V. Leiva (2021), *La especialización sectorial, un determinante clave de la brecha de productividad entre mipymes y grandes empresas: El caso de México*, United Nations, https://www.cepal.org/sites/default/files/publication/files/46815/S2100216_es.pdf. [16]

COMEX and ECLAC (2021), *Valor agregado y empleo inducido por el sector exportador de Costa Rica, Nota de política*, https://www.cepal.org/es/publicaciones/46922-valor-agregado-empleo-inducido-sector-exportador-costa-rica-nota-politica. [7]

Cullen International (2016), *Hacia la estrategia para el mercado único digital de América Latina*, Development Bank of Latin America (CAF), http://scioteca.caf.com/handle/123456789/997. [22]

Delgado, D. et al. (2020), "Personal safety during the COVID-19 pandemic: Realities and perspectives of healthcare workers in Latin America", *Int. J Environ. Res. Public Health*, 17 (2798), Vol. 17/8, http://dx.doi.org/10.3390/ijerph17082798. PMID: 32325718; PMCID: PMC7216115. [29]

Dossi, G. (1984), *Technical Change and Industrial Transformation: The theory and an Application to the semiconductor industry*, Palgrave Macmillan, http://dx.doi.org/10.1007/978-1-349-17521-5. [17]

ECLAC (2021), *Digital Technologies for a New Future*, United Nations, https://www.cepal.org/sites/default/files/publication/files/46817/S2000960_en.pdf. [24]

ECLAC (2021), *International Trade Outlook for Latin America and the Caribbean 2020: Regional integration is key to recovery after the crisis*, United Nations Publication, ECLAC, Santiago, https://www.cepal.org/sites/default/files/publication/files/46614/S2000804_en.pdf. [4]

ECLAC (2021), *Post Pandemic Covid-19: Enabling Latin America And The Caribbean To Better Harness E-Commerce and Digital Trade*, United Nations Publication, ECLAC, Santiago, https://www.cepal.org/sites/default/files/publication/files/46858/S2100269_en.pdf. [20]

ECLAC (ed.) (2021), *The Recovery Paradox in Latin America and the Caribbean Growth amid Persisting Structural problems:Inequality, poverty and low investment and productivity*, United Nations, https://www.cepal.org/sites/default/files/publication/files/47059/S2100378_en.pdf. [21]

ECLAC (2020), *Building a New Future: Transformative Recovery with Equality and Sustainability*, United Nations, ECLAC, https://www.cepal.org/sites/default/files/publication/files/46226/S2000665_en.pdf. [13]

ECLAC (2020), *Foreign Direct Investment in Latin America and the Caribbean 2020*, United Nations, https://www.cepal.org/en/https%3A//www.cepal.org/en/publications/type/foreign-direct-investment-latin-america-and-caribbean. [1]

ECLAC (2020), *International Trade Statistics Database*, United Nations Publications, Cepal, Satiago, https://comtrade.un.org. [2]

ECLAC (2020), *Sectors and Businesses Facing COVID-19: Emergency and reactivation*, United Nations, ECLAC, Santiago, https://www.cepal.org/sites/default/files/publication/files/45736/S2000437_en.pdf. [6]

ECLAC (2020), *The effects of the coronavirus disease (COVID-19) pandemic on international trade and logistics*, https://repositorio.cepal.org/bitstream/handle/11362/45878/1/S2000496_en.pdf. [5]

ECLAC (2020), *Universalizing access to digital technologies to address the consequences of COVID-19*, United Nations, https://www.cepal.org/sites/default/files/publication/files/45939/S2000549_en.pdf. [19]

ECLAC (2018), *Foreign Direct Investment in Latin America and the Caribbean 2018*, United Nations, ECLAC, https://www.cepal.org/sites/default/files/publication/files/43690/S1800683_en.pdf. [42]

ECLAC (2017), *Global Input-Output Tables: Tools for the analysis of the integration of Latin America with the world*, United Nations Publication, ECLAC, Santiago, https://www.cepal.org/en/events/global-input-output-tables-tools-analysis-integration-latin-america-world. [10]

ECLAC (2014), *Regional Integration: towards an inclusive value chain strategy*, United Nations, https://www.cepal.org/sites/default/files/publication/files/36734/S2014217_en.pdf. [3]

ECLAC (1959), *The Latin American Common Market*, United Nations, http://hdl.handle.net/11362/43910. [8]

ECLAC and ILO (2018), *Employment Situation in Latin America and the Caribbean: Environmental sustainability and employment in Latin America and the Caribbean*, United Nations, https://www.cepal.org/sites/default/files/publication/files/44186/S1800885_en.pdf. [66]

ECLAC and Internet & Jurisdiction (2020), *Internet & Jurisdiction and ECLAC Regional Status Report 2020*, United Nations, https://www.cepal.org/sites/default/files/publication/files/46421/S1901092_en.pdf. [23]

EIA (2018), *International Engergy Outlook 2018*, U.S. Energy Information Administration. [44]

El Financiero (2016), *Grupo Britt consolida su presencia en aeropuertos y llegará a nuevos países*, https://www.elfinancierocr.com/negocios/grupo-britt-consolida-su-presencia-en-aeropuertos-y-llegara-a-nuevos-paises/S7J4FTWLRFBMNIZZAXUMQL5O34/story/. [57]

Ellen MacArthur Foundation (2021), *Growth within: a circular economy vision for a competitive Europe*, https://ellenmacarthurfoundation.org/growth-within-a-circular-economy-vision-for-a-competitive-europe. [64]

Ellen MacArthur Foundation (2021), *The Big Food Redesign Study*, https://ellenmacarthurfoundation.org/the-big-food-redesign-study. [60]

Ellen MacArthur Foundation (2013), "Towards the circular economy", *Journal of Industrial Ecology 2*, pp. 23-44. [62]

Energy Policy Tracker (2021), *Report*, IISD International Institute for Sustainable Development, https://www.energypolicytracker.org/region/g20/. [27]

Eurostat (2021), *International trade in goods – a statistical picture*, https://ec.europa.eu/eurostat/statistics-explained/index.php?title=International_trade_in_goods_-_a_statistical_picture. [9]

Fallas Villalobos, C. (2019), *CEO de Britt confía en que abrirán más cafeterías dentro y fuera del país*, https://www.elfinancierocr.com/negocios/ceo-de-britt-confia-en-que-abriran-mas-cafeterias/HLEQPBABB5BU7A44P4KRVMPUKE/story/. [58]

FAO (2021), *FAOSTAT [online]*, http://www.fao.org/faostat/en/#home. [51]

FAO and ECLAC (2020), *Food systems and COVID-19 in Latin America and the Caribbean: Impact and risks in the labour market*, https://www.fao.org/3/ca9237en/ca9237en.pdf. [50]

Federación Nacional de Cafeteros de Colombia (2019), *Juan Valdez, 'La marca de todo un país'*, https://federaciondecafeteros.org/wp/listado-noticias/juan-valdez-la-marca-de-todo-un-pais/#:~:text=%C2%B7%20Juan%20Valdez%20ha%20conquistado%20el,132%20en%20otros%2013%20pa%C3%ADses (accessed on 2021). [54]

Feinberg and Majumdar (2001), "Technology Spillovers from Foreign Direct Investment in the Indian Pharmaceutical Industry", *Journal of International Business Studies*, Vol. 32/3, pp. 421-437, http://dx.doi.org/doi:10.1057/palgrave.jibs.8490975. [30]

Fraunhofer (2018), *Biological Transformation and Bioeconomy*, Fraunhofer, http://www.fraunhofer.cn/en/uploads/soft/190806/whitepaper-biological-transformation-and-bioeconomy.pdf. [48]

Gao, J., Z. Pentland and C. Hidalgo (2021), "Spillovers across industries and regions in China's regional economic diversification", *Regional Studies*, pp. 1-16, http://dx.doi.org/doi:10.1080/00343404.2021.1883191. [67]

Gramkow, C. and A. Anger-Kraavi (2019), "Developing green: a case for the Brazilian manufacturing industry", *Sustainibility*, Vol. 11/23, https://doi.org/10.3390/su11236783. [63]

Grupp, H. (1996), "Spillover effects and the science base of innovations reconsidered: an empirical approach.", *Journal of Evolutionary Economics*, pp. 175-197, http://dx.doi.org/doi:10.1007/BF01202593. [32]

Grupp, H. and M. Mogee (2004), "Indicators for national science and technology policy: how robust are composite indicators?", *Research Policy*, Vol. 33/9, pp. 1373-1384, http://dx.doi.org/10.1016/j.respol.2004.09.007. [31]

ILO/IDB (2020), *Jobs in a net zero emissions future in Latin America and the Caribbean*. [65]

IPBES (2019), *Global assessment report on biodiversity and ecosystem services of the Intergovernmental Science-Policy Platform on Biodiversity and Ecosystem Services*, https://doi.org/10.5281/zenodo.3553579. [26]

IRENA (2018), *Renewable Capacity Statistics*. [46]

Juan Valdez (2021), https://www.juanvaldezcafe.com/. [55]

MERCOSUR (2020), *Agenda Digital del Mercosur, 2018-2020*, https://cetic.br/media/docs/publicacoes/17/20200804155338/Agenda Digital del Mercosur 2018 2020%20Panorama de los Indicadores Disponibles.pdf. [25]

Mosere (2021), *Mosere: Spirit of taste*, https://mosere.co/cafe-pod. [59]

OECD (2007), *The Visible Hand of China in Latin America*, OECD Publishing, https://doi.org/10.1787/9789264028388-en. [11]

OECD et al. (2020), *Latin American Economic Outlook 2020: Digital Transformation for Building Back Better*, OECD Publishing, https://doi.org/10.1787/e6e864fb-en. [18]

Organization of Motor Vehicle Manufacturers (2021), *1950- 2020 Car production statistics*. [40]

PAHO (2010), *Resolution CD50.R9 Strengthening National Regulatory Authorities for Medicines and Biologicals, 2010*, PAHO, https://www.paho.org/en/documents/cd50r9-strengthening-national-regulatory-authorities-medicines-and-biologicals-2010. [37]

Paredes, J. (2017), *La Red del Futuro: Desarrollo de una red eléctrica limpia y sostenible para América Latina*, Inter-American Development Bank, http://dx.doi.org/10.18235/0000937. [45]

Pinto, A. (1970), *Naturaleza e implicaciones de la "heterogeneidad estructural" de la América Latina*, Fondo de Cultura Economica/ECLAC, http://hdl.handle.net/11362/2055. [12]

Porcile, G. and M. Cimoli (2013), *Tecnología, heterogeneidad y crecimiento: una caja de herramientas estructuralistas*, United Nations, https://www.cepal.org/sites/default/files/publication/files/4592/S2013731_es.pdf. [14]

Portafolio (2017), "¿Qué es el Café Drip, el nuevo ritual para una taza de café?", *Tendencias*, https://www.portafolio.co/tendencias/cafe-drip-el-nuevo-ritual-para-una-taza-de-cafe-503594. [56]

Rodríguez, A., A. Mondaini and M. Hitschfeld (2017), *Bioeconomía en América Latina y el Caribe: Contexto global y regional y perspectivas*, United Nations, https://www.cepal.org/sites/default/files/publication/files/42427/S1701022_es.pdf. [49]

RTRS (2021), *Round Table on Responsible Soy Association*, https://responsiblesoy.org/soja-rtrs. [53]

Shapiro, B. (1987), "Specialties versus Commodities. The Battle for Profit Margins", *Harvard Business School*, Revised April 1987. [47]

SIMI (2021), *Sistema integral de monitoreo de importaciones (SIMI)*, http://www.afip.gob.ar/simi/. [38]

Solano-Rodriguez, B. et al. (2019), *Implications of climate targets on oil production and fiscal revenues in Latin America and the Caribbean*, Inter-American Development Bank, http://dx.doi. org/10.18235/0001802.   [28]

Statista (2020), *Revenue of the worldwide pharmaceutical market from 2001 to 2020*, https://www. statista.com/statistics/263102/pharmaceutical-market-worldwide-revenue-since-2001/.   [34]

Sweet, C. (2017), "The Politics and Policis of Regulating Generics in Latin America: A Survey of Seventeen States", *Journal of Health Politics, Policy and Law*, Vol. 42/3, pp. 485-512, http://dx.doi.org/ doi:10.1215/03616878-3802953.   [35]

Sweet, C. (2013), "The Political Economy of Pharmaceuticals in Brazil", *Global Pharmaceuticals Politics and Production*, pp. 29-47, https://doi.org/10.1057/9781137315854_2.   [36]

US Commercial Service (2019), *International Healthcare Technologies Resource Guide*, https://www. trade.gov/healthcare-technologies-resource-guide.   [39]

Valverde, J. (2014), "Latin American pharmaceutical overview", *Pharmaceuticals, Policy and Law*, Vol. 16, pp. 179-206, http://dx.doi.org/doi:10.3233/PPL-140384.   [33]

Wilson, C. (2017), *Growing Together: Economic Ties between the United States and Mexico*, https://www. wilsoncenter.org/publication/final-report-growing-together-economic-ties-between-the-united-states-and-mexico. (accessed on March).   [41]

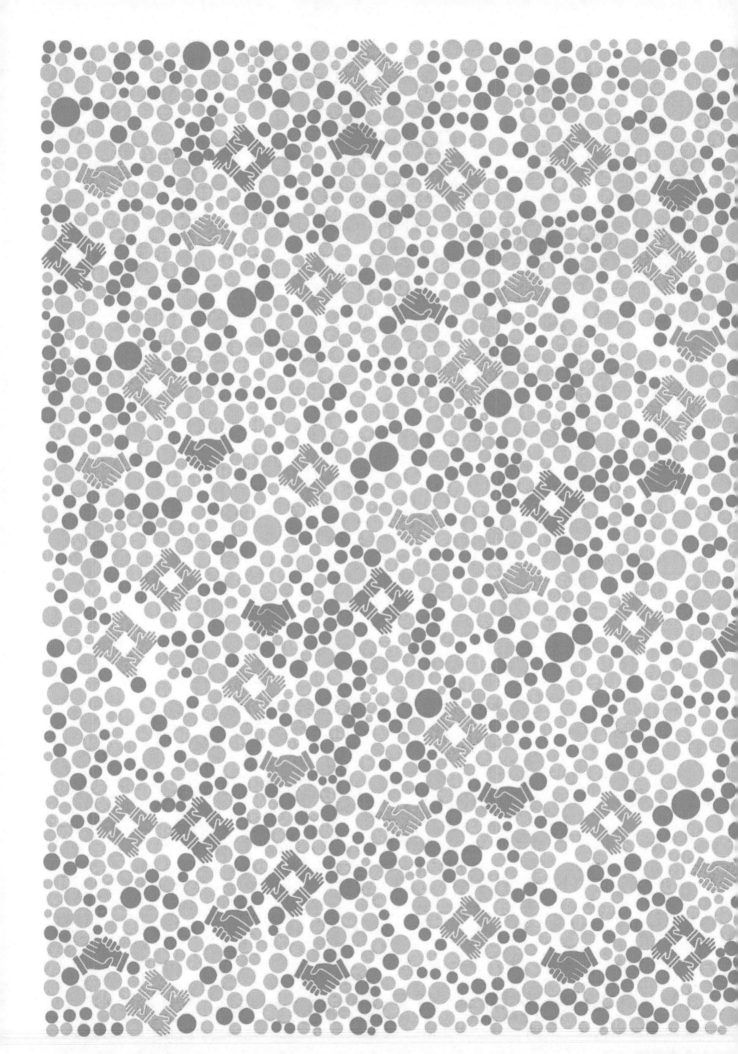

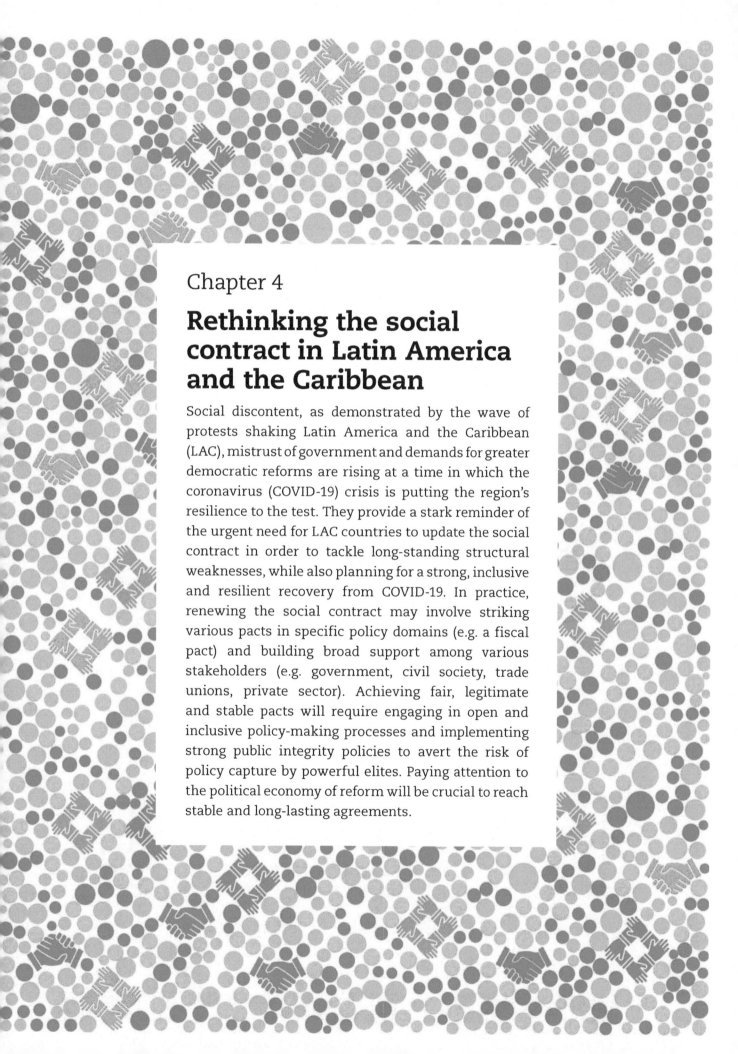

Chapter 4

Rethinking the social contract in Latin America and the Caribbean

Social discontent, as demonstrated by the wave of protests shaking Latin America and the Caribbean (LAC), mistrust of government and demands for greater democratic reforms are rising at a time in which the coronavirus (COVID-19) crisis is putting the region's resilience to the test. They provide a stark reminder of the urgent need for LAC countries to update the social contract in order to tackle long-standing structural weaknesses, while also planning for a strong, inclusive and resilient recovery from COVID-19. In practice, renewing the social contract may involve striking various pacts in specific policy domains (e.g. a fiscal pact) and building broad support among various stakeholders (e.g. government, civil society, trade unions, private sector). Achieving fair, legitimate and stable pacts will require engaging in open and inclusive policy-making processes and implementing strong public integrity policies to avert the risk of policy capture by powerful elites. Paying attention to the political economy of reform will be crucial to reach stable and long-lasting agreements.

Anewsocialcontracttoachieve astronginclusiveandresilientrecovery

Whyanewsocialcontract?

Torebuildtrust
andbridge
thegrowing
dividebetween
citizens
andpublic
institutions...

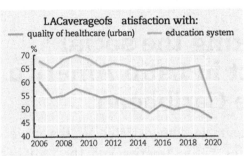

LACaverageofs atisfaction with:
— quality of healthcare (urban) — education system

...andto
mendthe
fractures
within
society

Only **12%**
ofLACcitizens
havetrustin
themajority
ofpeople

Whattypeofsocialcontractisneeded?

Onethatbuildsacross-cuttingpact...

across
socio-economic
groups

across
territories

across
generations

Howcanthiscontractbeimplemented?

Improvetheprocess
andthesequence
ofpolicyreformto
achieveconsensus

- Conciliate
- Contextualise
- Compensate
- Communicate

Overcomestructuralbarriersto
policyreformand
implementation

Fragmented
politics

Policy
capture

Poor
institutional
capacity

Frameitinalong-term,
nationaldevelopment
plan

Introduction

Times of crisis expose deeply ingrained structural vulnerabilities. This has been the case in Latin America and the Caribbean (LAC), where the impact of the coronavirus (COVID-19) has accentuated long-standing, multi-dimensional development challenges, putting the resilience of the region to the test. Indeed, the strong socio-economic impact of the pandemic is aggravating the four structural development traps already faced by LAC (OECD, 2020[1]; OECD et al., 2019[2]).

In this context, the foundations of the development model have proven to be weak and have been brought under particular scrutiny by citizens. Higher aspirations for better living conditions in pre-pandemic years already pointed to the need to rethink and redesign the pillars that had sustained socio-economic progress through the years of bonanza, since the mid-2000s. The rise of social discontent, marked by a wave of protests in late 2019, confirmed the need to reach a new, overarching consensus and bridge the divide between society and public institutions. While during COVID-19 there was an initial spike in confidence in many governments, spurred by their rapid reaction to counter the effects of the crisis, public trust and citizen satisfaction weakened as the pandemic unfolded, as evidenced by a new wave of protests throughout the region in 2020 and 2021.

Against this background, this chapter argues that there is a need for a renewed, post-pandemic social contract as a means to achieve greater well-being for all in LAC. A strong, inclusive and sustainable recovery from COVID-19 will require adopting bold measures and ambitious reforms. These will in turn require striking new and cross-cutting pacts around key policy areas, both to address the specific impact of the pandemic and to overcome structural development challenges in the region and advance towards the 17 Sustainable Development Goals in the 2030 Agenda for Sustainable Development (ECLAC, 2020[3]). Reforms will also require reaching a high degree of consensus among all parts of society and in the relevant legislative bodies to make reforms happen. In this perspective, governments should use the momentum provided by the crisis to rethink the social contract in a way that can address the impact of the pandemic and overcome structural vulnerabilities – the development traps of low productivity, high inequality and informality, deficient public services and institutions, and environmental challenges – that were accentuated by the COVID-19 crisis (OECD et al., 2019[2]).

The notion of the social contract is used in the literature for various purposes. *Latin American Economic Outlook 2021* (LEO) adopts a broad definition of the social contract, which is understood as the comprehensive yet intangible and implicit agreement that binds society together and exists within a certain set of formal and informal rules and institutions.

This chapter focuses on the issue of rethinking the social contract in LAC, addressing the following topics. First, it analyses the main reasons why there is a need to rethink the social contract in the region. Second, it explores critical questions that need to be addressed in order to set the foundations for a new social contract in LAC. In this sense, it starts by analysing what should be the main components of a renewed social contract, fit for purpose and adapted to the realities of the 21st century, from a multi-dimensional well-being perspective. Subsequently, the chapter focuses on the process, i.e. on how this new social contract can be achieved and made fair, legitimate and sustainable.

A new social contract in LAC: Why?

Multiple weaknesses point to the need to rethink the social contract in LAC. Before COVID-19 hit, rising social discontent, the increasing dissatisfaction with public services, and the decline in trust and legitimacy of public institutions were clear signs of the importance of renewing foundational agreements among citizens and between citizens and public institutions in the region (Larraín, 2020[4]).

Many of these trends were the result of long-standing structural challenges. LAC entered the COVID-19 crisis with the majority of countries facing major development traps, namely low potential growth (productivity trap), high vulnerability (social vulnerability trap), institutional weakness (institutional trap) and an environmentally unsustainable production model (environmental trap) (OECD et al., 2019[2]). These vulnerabilities aggravated and were aggravated by the impact of the pandemic.

In addition, embarking on a post-COVID-19 recovery will demand a strong and broad consensus across LAC societies to adopt the pending structural reforms necessary to tackle the impact of the crisis while overcoming the existing development traps. However, not all countries have the same starting conditions or are advancing towards a new social contract at the same speed. The heterogeneity of the region and the differentiated impact of the crisis must be taken into account when considering the agreements needed to underpin the recovery and build a better society for all, as well as the pace at which they can be implemented. The evolution of social contracts will depend on the opportunities created by the crisis, the structure of the political system, the effectiveness of mechanisms that hold the powerful to account and the emergence of political coalitions (Shafik, 2021[53]).

Against this background, the following section examines the main reasons why a new social contract is needed in LAC.

Social discontent is high and growing, with low levels of trust in institutions and satisfaction with public services

Despite the temporary recovery observed over 2018-20 (Figure 4.1, Panel A), opinion surveys show that confidence in government remained below the pre-2014 levels and that only about one in three citizens trusted public institutions. In 2020, episodes of mismanagement of public resources (e.g. vaccines and medical equipment) negatively affected citizens' view of their governments. In most LAC countries, satisfaction with the government's handling of the COVID-19 crisis was high in the early phase and then declined as the emergency progressed in August 2020 (Figure 4.1, Panel B). Most LAC countries adopted a cautious approach in March 2020 and enacted early lockdowns, even before the emergency reached the levels observed in the People's Republic of China and Europe. Moreover, governments' prominent role in the fight against the pandemic gave them renewed visibility and the unexpected and profound challenges to the status quo increased citizens' trust in governments as a result of a "rally-round-the-flag" effect (Kritzinger et al., 2021[143]).

As the crisis evolved, perceptions began to vary widely across the region. Opinion leaders' approval of their government's handling of the COVID-19 crisis declined in seven out of eight surveyed countries in LAC between April and August 2020 (Figure 4.1, Panel B) (ECLAC, 2021[5]). This trend is confirmed by another opinion survey showing a significant decrease in citizens' approval of the management of the crisis in Argentina, Colombia and Mexico between May and October 2020 (Estefan, Hadid and Georges, 2020[6]). Going forward, LAC governments adopting more (or less) ambitious vaccination and recovery programmes may experience a new surge (or decline) in confidence, as seen in the July 2021 survey in Chile following an ambitious vaccination programme. Other factors, including government change, may also shape citizens' trust (Figure 4.1, Panel B), together with perceptions of integrity, openness and fairness of public institutions and of the reliability of policies and responsiveness of public services (OECD, 2017[144]).

Figure 4.1. **Confidence in national government declined in recent years and picked up in 2020, but the approval of governments' handling of the COVID-19 crisis remained highly volatile**

Panel A. Confidence in national government, LAC average 2006-2020

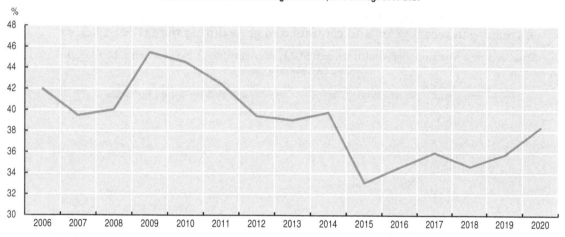

Panel B. Leaders' approval of their government's handling of the COVID-19 crisis, selected LAC countries, April to July 2021

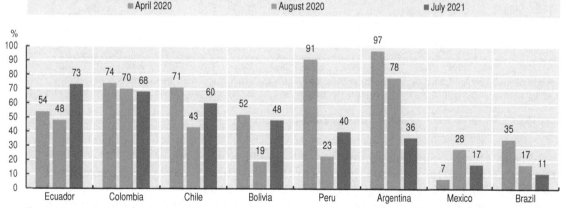

Notes: Panel A represents the unweighted LAC average of 16 LAC countries. It represents the share of respondents who answered "yes" to a question asking whether they have confidence in their national government. Data collection took place between August and November 2020 for most countries but lasted until January 2021 for Costa Rica, Jamaica and Peru. For Panel A, data for 2020 are missing for Guatemala, Honduras and Panama. For Panel B, respondents represent 371 Latin American opinion leaders and journalists who regularly share their opinions in Latin American media. Panel B shows the share of respondents who approved of their government's handling of the COVID-19 crisis.

Sources: Panel A: Gallup (2021[7]), *Gallup World Poll (database)*, https://ga.gallup.com; Panel B: ECLAC (2021[5]) *Social Panorama of Latin America 2020*, www.cepal.org/en/publications/46688-social-panorama-latin-america-2020, and Ipsos (2021[8]). *Percepciones de los líderes de opinión de Latinoamérica a un año y medio de pandemia*, www.ipsos.com/es-pe/percepciones-de-los-lideres-de-opinion-de-latinoamerica-un-ano-y-medio-de-pandemia.

StatLink  https://doi.org/10.1787/888934286787

Satisfaction with public services, including education and health, markedly decreased during the pandemic. Dissatisfaction continued to grow throughout the crisis, compounded by the difficulties to ensure continuity of schools' curricula during lockdowns, the increased childcare burden during school closures and the lack of resources to respond to the health crisis (Figure 4.2). Education systems in LAC were unprepared to handle massive distance learning. Low Internet penetration, poor digital skills and lack of information technology equipment and of an effective online learning support platform severely hampered students' ability to follow classes remotely in some countries (OECD et al., 2020[9]). These obstacles were especially severe for students attending disadvantaged schools or living in rural areas, reinforcing inequality of opportunity among students in the region (OECD, 2020[1]). Likewise, out-of-pocket (OOP) expenditures for health care continue to represent a high burden for families' budgets (Chapter 2).

Figure 4.2. Dissatisfaction with public services has been steadily increasing in recent years and continued to grow during the COVID-19 crisis

Share of people who are satisfied with the availability of quality health care and with the education system, LAC average, 2006-20

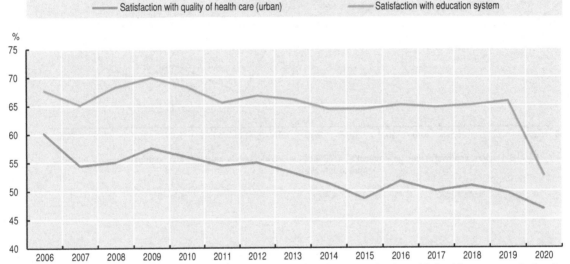

Notes: Unweighted LAC average including 16 LAC countries. 2020 data for satisfaction with health care are missing for Honduras and Panama. 2020 data for satisfaction with the education system are missing for Guatemala, Honduras and Panama.

Source: Gallup (2021[7]), *Gallup World Poll (database)*, https://ga.gallup.com.

StatLink 🔗📊 https://doi.org/10.1787/888934286255

Rising social aspirations compound citizen dissatisfaction in LAC. The digital transformation and the growing importance of "digital citizens" have played a significant role in shaping social aspirations. The expansion of smartphones and the emergence of new forms of communication have resulted in deep cultural change in LAC societies, especially among the young and urbanites. These people are often more educated and have higher aspirations than their parents, but face difficulties in terms of labour markets opportunities. These more connected urban youths now tend to compare their lifestyle with that of their international peers rather than with that of their parents' generation, and their unmet expectations can trigger disillusionment and anger (OECD et al., 2020[9] ; OECD, 2020[145]). A survey on politics and the strikes administered among Colombian youths between January 2020 and May 2021 showed that happiness had been replaced by sadness as the predominant sentiment among this group (Rosario University, 2021[10]).

Persistent inequalities and the perception that power and wealth are increasingly concentrated are key drivers of social discontent

The increase in social dissatisfaction seen in LAC before COVID-19 occurred in parallel with the economic slowdown in the region in past years, yet social discontent is driven by many factors beyond economic ones. The end of the commodity boom generated a slowdown in poverty reduction and a deterioration of living conditions, which are being further exacerbated by the pandemic. Notwithstanding this, other factors have also been key in the decline of trust and citizen satisfaction. The expansion of the vulnerable middle class during the early 2000s generated higher hopes not only for redistributive policies but also for the creation of quality jobs, universal access to quality public services, such as health care and education, efficient public institutions and greater representation. However, as the previous socio-economic progress was built on fragile foundations, in the last years, citizens have not seen their expectations met (OECD et al., 2019[2]). Experts in the region point to still-high social inequality, as well as the perception of widespread corruption, institutional weakness and poor state effectiveness to deliver results, as among the main drivers of the protests (Ipsos, 2019[11]). These factors concur in creating multiple dimensions of inequality beyond income, including an education system unable to offer equal opportunities for all; insufficient provision of taxes, transfers and social security to effectively decrease income inequality; and overrepresentation of well-off groups in policy and decision making spaces.

The perception of living in a highly unequal society is well grounded in reality and fuels social discontent. Despite the significant decline in income inequality since the onset of the commodity boom, the region remains among the most unequal in the world. In LAC, the richest 1% and 10% of the population possess 21% and 49% of the pre-tax national income, respectively, vs. around 13% and 38% in the Organisation for Economic Co-operation and Development (OECD) area (simple averages based on World Inequality Database, 2020[12]). Only the Middle East comes close to this level of inequality (World Inequality Database, 2020[12]; Busso and Messina, 2020[13]). During the pandemic, and in a context of rising poverty, the number of billionaires increased by 31 (from 76 to 107) in LAC, and their combined net worth increased by USD 196 billion (United States dollar) (López-Calva, 2021[14]). Despite motivational calls for collective mobilisation, the pandemic has imposed the greatest costs on those already worst off, including the elderly, youths, women and low-paid and informal workers (OECD, 2020[1]).

Some evidence also suggests that inequality reduction during the first decade of the 2000s was not as high as previously thought, since household surveys tend to underestimate the income of the richest households, which are more prone to elude income declarations for tax purposes (Lustig, 2020[15]). For instance, falling inequality trends in Brazil are less pronounced when combining different data sources (Morgan, 2018[16]). Similarly, adjusted income tax data for Chile show that concentration of income at the top 1% followed a U-shape rather than a decreasing trend between 1990 and 2017, with values at both ends hovering around 21% (Flores et al., 2020[17]). Comparing household and tax data in Uruguay shows that top income positions between 2009 and 2016 remained stable, while the equalising effect of income mobility was very modest (Burdin et al., 2020[18]).

As Latin America was unable to maintain the level of shared prosperity of the previous decade, the share of the population that perceived the income distribution to be fair has taken a dip since reaching its highest point in 2013 (Figure 4.3).

In parallel, the propensity to demonstrate grew in various LAC countries, and the number of actual protests and social discontent has increased since 2014 (Figure 4.3). Starting with Haiti in February 2019, the region was shaken by demonstrations throughout

2019, 2020 and 2021 in several countries, including Bolivia, Chile, Colombia, Cuba, Ecuador, Guatemala and Peru.

Beyond income inequality, rising social discontent is also a symptom of a growing frustration with the concentration of wealth and power in the region (López-Calva, 2020[21]). This generates the perception of being part of a system that is hopelessly rigged, especially among poor and vulnerable households that see no opportunities to improve their situation. In particular, the socio-economic progress experienced in the region in the past decades may have generated a "tunnel effect", as when drivers in a two-lane tunnel see the parallel lane starting to move while they remain stuck, or begin driving backwards (Hirschman and Rothschild, 1973[22]). The higher expectations of the vulnerable middle class have turned into social discontent.

The profound inequalities that permeate the region increase the perception that income is not fairly distributed (Figure 4.3) and grant elites unparalleled control over the political and economic agenda, perpetuating a culture of privilege and increasing the perception of policy capture (see the section Policy capture below). In 2020, 73% of Latin American citizens believed that their country was governed in the interests of a few powerful groups, representing the second highest recorded level since 2004 (after 79% in 2018) (Latinobarómetro, 2021[20]).

Figure 4.3. Street protests and the perception that income is not fairly distributed

Share of the population that believes income is fairly distributed and number of street protests (right axis), 2013-18

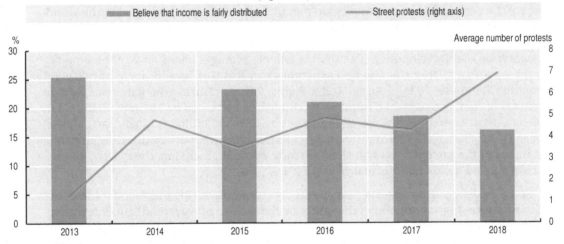

Note: Unweighted LAC average.
Source: Own elaboration based on Busso and Messina (2020[13]), *The Inequality Crisis: Latin America and the Caribbean at the Crossroads*, http://dx.doi.org/10.18235/0002629; CNTS (2020[19]), *Domestic Conflict Database*, www.cntsdata.com; Latinobarómetro (2021[20]), *Latinobarometro Survey 2020*, www.latinobarometro.org/latOnline.jsp.
StatLink ⟶ https://doi.org/10.1787/888934286806

Similarly, the perception of corruption and impunity remains high. Corruption has slightly increased in the region, in particular between the early 2000s and 2020 (Transparency International, 2021[23]). In 2019, elected politicians and public officers were seen as the most corrupt group. Moreover, more than half of the citizens believed that their government is performing poorly to tackle corruption effectively (Transparency International, 2019[24]). This perception directly affects the levels of trust in public institutions, the government, national courts and the police, while eroding their legitimacy in the eyes of their citizens. In terms of impunity, the region ranked relatively high in the Global Impunity Index in 2020, with most of the countries presenting medium and high impunity levels (CESIJ, 2020[130]).

A weakening of the ties that bind LAC citizens

A robust social contract relies not only on strong vertical trust in public institutions but also on solid horizontal connections among citizens. However, and in spite of the fact that the exceptional circumstances created by the pandemic demand more mutual help, the ties that bind LAC citizens remain fragile.

Social cohesion is weak at a time when collective action and social unity are most needed for the recovery from the pandemic. The five Latin American countries observed in the Ipsos Social Cohesion Index perform below the global average and, when comparing the social cohesion sub-indices by country, the sense of common good (helping others, respecting the laws, perception of corruption) is the lowest on average (Ipsos, 2020[26]) (Figure 4.4).

Figure 4.4. **Social cohesion is weak in selected Latin American countries**

IPSOS Social Cohesion Index, net sub-indices
("Solid sense of social cohesion" minus "Weak sense of social cohesion"), 2020

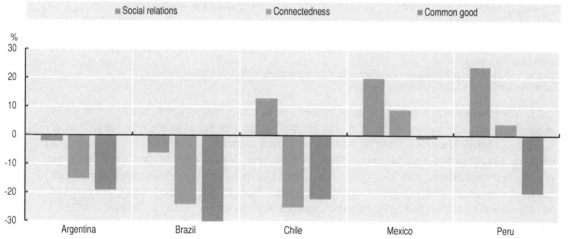

Note: The sub-indices show the share of people who have a "strong" or "solid" sense of social cohesion minus those who have a "weak" sense of social cohesion. The survey was conducted in 27 countries via the Ipsos Online Panel system between 25 September and 9 October 2020. Approximately 1 000+ individuals were surveyed per country, with the exception of Argentina and Mexico, which each had a sample of approximately 500+.

Source: IPSOS (2020[26]), *Social Cohesion in the Pandemic Age: A Global Perspective, October 2020,* www.ipsos.com/sites/default/files/ct/news/documents/2020-11/a_global_perspective_of_social_cohesion_in_the_pandemic_age.pdf.

StatLink ▨▨▨ *https://doi.org/10.1787/888934286825*

A weaker sense of unity and social cohesion is also illustrated by the decline in interpersonal trust among LAC citizens. Lack of interpersonal trust has characterised the region historically, with a notable decreasing trend after 2011 in parallel with the decline in confidence in government, reaching particularly low levels in 2020 (12%) (Figure 4.5).

Figure 4.5. **A lack of both interpersonal trust and trust in public institutions has characterised the LAC region in the past decade**

Share of the population with confidence in the majority of people and with a lot or some confidence in government, LAC average, 2002-20

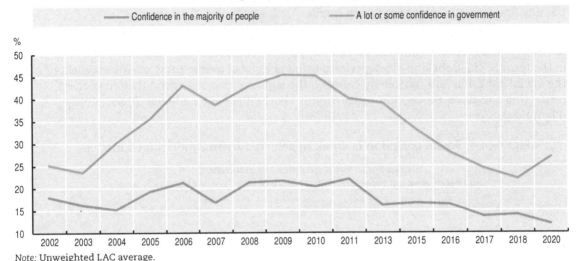

Note: Unweighted LAC average.

Source: Latinobarómetro (2021[20]), *Latinobarómetro Survey 2020*, www.latinobarometro.org/latOnline.jsp.

StatLink ⬛▤🔗 https://doi.org/10.1787/888934286844

In comparison with other regions in the world, LAC shows significantly lower levels of generalised interpersonal trust or horizontal trust, e.g. trust of people outside one's familiar or kinship circles. Only sub-Saharan Africa matches the low levels of horizontal trust in LAC (Mattes and Moreno, 2018[27]). However, levels of interpersonal trust are very heterogeneous across LAC countries, from 5% in Brazil to 21% in Uruguay in 2020 (Latinobarómetro, 2021[20]). High inequality and low interpersonal trust across LAC countries seem to be partially related (Mattes and Moreno, 2018[27]; Uslaner, 2002[28]). Violence is another factor affecting interpersonal trust and social cohesion in LAC (Box 4.1). Indeed, income inequality and the perceived threat of violence are tightly correlated in LAC and reflect a vicious cycle that also includes insecurity and low levels of development (Lloyd's Register Foundation/Gallup, 2019[29]).

Box 4.1. **Violence as an obstacle to achieving the social contract in LAC**

LAC remains the most violent region in the world, with negative consequences for its economic, social and institutional fabric. Nonetheless, there remains significant heterogeneity across countries in LAC, with Central America concentrating the highest homicide rates per 100 000 inhabitants (Figure 4.6). Crime and violence are also characterised by a degree of geographical concentration, and LAC cities tend to be more affected by the phenomena (Alvarado and Muggah, 2018[30]).

The direct costs of crime and violence were estimated at 3.5% of the region's gross domestic product for 17 LAC countries in 2010-14, but indirect problems also affect the social and institutional spheres (Jaitman et al., 2017[33]). Especially in Central America, the well-being of communities is negatively affected by the criminal activities of the gangs (maras), resulting in high school dropout rates among adolescents, self-restrictions on freedom of movement, greater intention to migrate and a wearing down of social cohesion, with negative consequences for

Box 4.1. **Violence as an obstacle to achieving the social contract in LAC** (*cont.*)

social and community networks (Raderstorf et al., 2017[34]; Maydeu-Olivares, 2016[35]). Crime and violence make it difficult for social activities, including sports and recreation, to function and result in community fragmentation, interpersonal distrust and diminished participation in democratic activities (Imbusch, Misse and Carrión, 2011[36]).

Figure 4.6. **LAC remains the most violent region in the world**

Homicide rate per 100 000 population, LAC countries and regional estimates, 2018 or latest

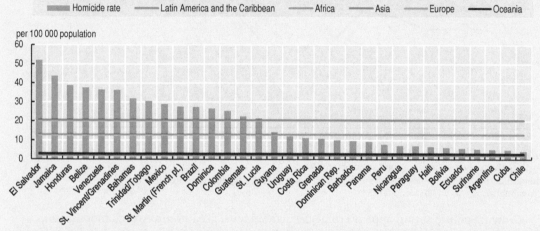

Note: Data for Bahamas, Belize, Dominica and Peru are from 2017; data for Bolivia, Cuba, Nicaragua, Saint Martin and Saint Vincent and the Grenadines are from 2016; data for Trinidad and Tobago are from 2015.

Sources: World Bank (2020[31]), *World Development Indicators (database)*, https://data.worldbank.org/indicator/VC.IHR. PSRC.P5; UNODC (2020[32]), *Victims of intentional homicide, 1990-2018*, https://dataunodc.un.org/data/homicide/ Homicide%20victims%20worldwide.

StatLink 📊 https://doi.org/10.1787/888934286863

At the same time, when citizens perceive that institutions are unable to guarantee their safety, they are less likely to support the political system and may resort to extra-legal violence (Cruz and Kloppe-Santamaría, 2019[37]).

Addressing insecurity is key to setting the basis for a new social contract. Taking a comprehensive approach to address violence is important to restore trust among citizens and *vis-à-vis* institutions, which can support social dialogue and the achievement of long-term and stable pacts among stakeholders. Moreover, focusing on crime prevention from cradle to adulthood can help reduce the insurgence of criminal behaviours. In particular, small-scale crime prevention interventions at the municipal level have generated positive results (Alvarado and Muggah, 2018[30]; Chioda, 2017[38]).

Increasing levels of polarisation and growing grassroots mobilisation, with less reliance on traditional channels of political participation

Politicisation, or identification with a political ideology, has increased in recent years in LAC in parallel with growing distrust towards political parties (Figure 4.7). Growing ideological orientation of citizens in recent years is especially evident in Argentina, Bolivia, Brazil, Colombia, Ecuador and Mexico. On the other hand, countries such as the Dominican Republic and Uruguay have shown higher and more stable levels of political engagement over time (Latinobarómetro, 2021[20]).

Figure 4.7. **On average, identification with a political ideology has increased in LAC in recent years, while confidence in political parties has declined**

Share of people who identify with a political ideology (left or right) and share of people who have "a lot" or "some" confidence in political parties (right axis), LAC average, 2002-20

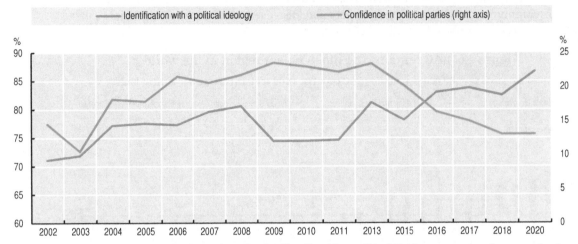

Notes: Unweighted LAC average. The share of people who identify with a political ideology represents those people who were able to place themselves on a left to right scale of 0 to 10.

Source: Latinobarómetro (2021[20]), *Latinobarómetro Survey 2020*, www.latinobarometro.org/latOnline.jsp.

StatLink ⬛🖳 *https://doi.org/10.1787/888934286882*

Growing politicisation appears to be associated with greater grassroots mobilisation, given the low trust in traditional parties, and points to a growing demand for change. Legislatures and political parties have the lowest levels of legitimacy among citizens in the region at 20% and 13%, respectively (Latinobarómetro, 2021[20]; Prats and Meunier, 2021[146]; González, 2020[147]). The two trends of increasing social discontent and political ferment converged in the social protests of 2019 and could reflect mobilisation at the grassroots level by an increasing share of the population that does not feel represented by traditional political channels.

Growing political activism can be a positive expression of political pluralism and encourage democratic renovation. Political activists and demonstrators in the recent protests have advocated for greater democratic reforms to counter the erosion of civic space, weakened checks and balances and attacks on human rights (openDemocracy, 2020[39]; Zovatto, 2020[40]). Moreover, when asked to comment on lessons learned from the COVID-19 crisis, a majority of respondents in ten LAC countries highlighted the need for greater government accountability and stronger human rights protection in their country (Acuña-Alfaro and Sapienza, 2021[41]). Demands for better and fairer institutions open a window of opportunity for discussing a new social contract (ECLAC, 2020[3]).

However, if not well channelled, higher politicisation risks resulting in higher polarisation – which could be exacerbated by COVID-19 – putting social cohesion to the test. In the recent round of elections, until 2021, dissatisfaction with the political system and the functioning of public institutions, as well as with the poor economic performance, resulted in "pendulum swings" and votes against traditional political elites. In some countries, this led to the emergence of anti-establishment candidates (Zovatto, 2019[42]; Malamud and Núñez, 2018[43]). In concomitance, religious groups, such as evangelical, are also gaining influence in the region and some are taking advantage of their proximity to the masses to spread political messages and weigh on the political agenda. Their influence was clear in the recent elections in some countries, and their worshipper base is growing throughout the region, currently accounting for 20% of the Latin American population (Malamud, 2018[44]).

Social media and digital platforms have also played a dual role in the rise of politicisation. On the one hand, the digital space has facilitated the rise and subsequent organisation of social movements. Especially thanks to social networks, activists are able to share their ideas, interact with like-minded people from all places and quickly organise demonstrations with millions of people without the need for financial support or intermediation (Billion and Ventura, 2020[45]). A survey conducted among Colombian youths between January 2020 and May 2021 showed that social networks (63%) were the most common channel of expression during the strikes, followed by street marches (53%) and debates with family (49%). Social networks, alongside protestors' own initiative, were also the most common way to convene the mobilisations (58%) (Rosario University, 2021[10]).

On the other hand, digital platforms facilitate the creation of homogeneous social networks that act as echo chambers or filter bubbles, insulating users from contrary perspectives (OECD et al., 2020[9]). They allow fake news to reach mass audiences and encourage social polarisation (Wardle and Derakhshan, 2017[46]; Marwick and Lewis, 2017[47]; Lazer et al., 2018[48]). As the most common type of COVID-19-related misinformation consists of false claims about actions or policies that public authorities are taking to address the pandemic, their spread risks further eroding the trust in institutions in LAC (Brennen et al., 2020[49]). Given the low reliability of messages circulating on Twitter in the region, they also risk undermining compliance with public norms (López-Calva, 2020[50]).

A number of megatrends provide further impetus for rethinking the social contract

A number of global megatrends are bringing about new challenges and opportunities. These trends are transforming LAC societies and hence must be integrated into a renewed social contract. Among these trends, the digital transformation, climate change and rising global movements for social and climate justice are some of the most relevant (Chapter 5).

First, the COVID-19 pandemic has given unprecedented impetus to the digital transformation. The spread of the Internet and the adoption of digital technologies have been pivotal in guaranteeing a certain continuity in business activity, government services and working and studying from home during lockdowns. However, the digital divide, notably the lack of high-speed broadband Internet and of appropriate digital skills, have prevented many, especially the most vulnerable, from reaping the benefits of these solutions (OECD, 2020[1]). For instance, more than six out of ten households with per capita income in the lower quintile of the income distribution do not have access to the fixed high-speed broadband Internet connection needed to support remote working and studying (Basto-Aguirre, Cerutti and Nieto-Parra, 2020[51]). Moreover, ensuring the safe and ethical management of data and guaranteeing digitally secure infrastructure are key for building trust and facilitating technology adoption (OECD et al., 2020[9]). Ensuring an inclusive and safe digital transformation is critical for the post-pandemic recovery period.

Second, the impacts of climate change are global in scope and unprecedented in scale, and action to confront them cannot be further delayed. Awareness about climate change risks has increased globally, and 41% of the world population sees it as a "very serious threat" to their country. Concerns about climate change in LAC are considerably higher than the world average. LAC stands out as the region second-most concerned about climate change after Southern Europe, with 71% and 73% of respondents in the two regions, respectively, saying that it is a serious threat for their country in the next 20 years. Chile, Colombia, Costa Rica and Ecuador are among the countries most concerned about climate change at the global level (Lloyd's Register Foundation, 2019[52]). Moreover, movements rallying for climate and environmental justice have gained momentum globally, including the LAC region. Nevertheless, climate activists are paying a high price across the world and particularly in Latin America. According to Global Witness, which tracks the killings of land and environmental defenders, 2019 showed the highest global number in a single year (212). Over two-thirds of the killings are taking place in Latin America. The region has consistently ranked as the worst-affected region since Global Witness began to publish data in 2012 (Global Witness, 2020[165]). Indigenous movements have been particularly vocal in LAC to advocate for more sustainable practices, in line with their *buen vivir* philosophy. Governments should build on this increased climate change awareness and invest in climate action as part of the COVID-19 recovery to bring the world closer to the Paris Agreement goal of, at most, a 2°C temperature rise before the end of the century. The entry into force of the Escazú Agreement is a promising step in the region, also for its provisions on human rights defenders in environmental matters.

Third, recent years have seen intense global mobilisations against racism and gender disparities in favour of social justice and human rights for Afrodescendants and women. The Black Lives Matter and the #MeToo movements have drawn considerable media attention to the issues of discrimination and gender-based violence. The Black Lives Matter protests in the United States inspired similar demonstrations in LAC, mainly in Brazil and Colombia, as well as the Caribbean islands, such as Jamaica and Trinidad and Tobago. Similarly, the considerable media exposure obtained by the #MeToo movement has garnered renewed support for feminist movements across LAC, although they existed well before the campaign. First in Argentina and later across the region, *#NiUnaMenos* has campaigned since 2015 to demand more protection for women's rights. Mass mobilisations resulted in government actions to stop gender-based violence in Peru in 2016, in Uruguay in 2018 and in Argentina in 2020. In Chile, increased awareness over representation issues is reflected in the gender-balanced body tasked with drafting a new Constitution, a global first. The awareness raised by these movements implies that a new social contract will need to put greater focus on empowerment, human rights and equality.

Defining a new concept of the social contract in LAC: What?

A challenging task for policy makers, analysts and observers alike will be to disentangle the dimensions that should be part of a renewed social contract.

This section analyses these issues in turn and looks into what should be the main ingredients of a new social contract in LAC by: i) revisiting the historical concept of the social contract and proposing the broad definition used in LEO 2021; ii) discussing the main dimensions along which it should be updated to be adequate for the post-pandemic world; and iii) offering a taxonomy of the main building blocks – guiding principles and specific policy areas – that should constitute the new social contract.

The concept of the social contract: Historical evolution and its current definition

The concept of the social contract stems from Western philosophers such as Grotius (1625), Hobbes (1651), Locke (1689), Hume (1740) and Rousseau (1762) and the subsequent contributions of 20th and 21st century philosophers and academics such as David Lewis (1969), John Rawls (1971, 1993), Robert Nozick (1974) and David Gauthier (1986). Early theories proposed by Hobbes, Locke and Rousseau differed in their conceptualisation but generally referred to the social contract as the rational agreement in which individuals surrender some of their freedoms to a central authority to leave the state of nature and become a civilised society. In this way, individuals agreed to give up part of their liberties and create a sovereign state that would ensure their rights and obligations, seeking equality of opportunities and the maximisation of society's well-being.

This initial idea of the social contract has been applied multiple times, and has progressively taken a more concrete content with the enlargement of the welfare state and the mobilisation of the labour movement. During the 19th century, labour and social reforms reinforced the rights of workers *vis-à-vis* their employers, and individuals became less responsible for their economic outcomes in favour of greater public-sector interventionism (Cosano, 2019[54]). Since then, the role of the state has expanded and included responsibilities not only on issues including protecting individuals from violence and assuring property rights but also embracing access to free markets, promoting economic growth and safeguarding citizens' well-being through a comprehensive social welfare system, among others (Manyika et al., 2020[55]).

In view of this evolution, LEO 2021 defines the social contract in broad terms as "the comprehensive yet intangible and implicit agreement that binds society together and exists within a certain set of formal and informal rules and institutions". Formal institutions include the written constitution, laws, policies and regulations enforced by official authorities. Informal institutions include (unwritten) social norms, customs and traditions.

This definition of the social contract first refers to it as "comprehensive", as it involves multiple actors. The role of the state – and its interaction with society – has evolved, and other players, such as the private sector and civil society, have become increasingly relevant and cannot be left outside an up-to-date notion of the social contract. The private sector is expected to engage in society further through greater Responsible Business Conduct (RBC), a role which is institutionalised as RBC standards become legitimate corporate norms and obligations (Granda Revilla, 2018[56]).

Moreover, the LEO definition of the social contract considers both "formal and informal rules and institutions". Formal rules are central, as they define the mutual rights and obligations of all key players (Kaplan, 2017[57]). Similarly, social contracts also arise from informal and customary institutions, such as values and shared norms (UNDP, 2018[58]).

The LEO definition also refers to the social contract as the agreement "that binds society together and exists...". This involves interactions between all parts of society and hence finding an equilibrium among them. This equilibrium is, in fact, a constant negotiation between societal actors and those in power, reflecting the distribution of power across all players in society (Loewe, Zintl and Houdret, 2020[59]). Reaching equilibrium in the social contract negotiation is critical, and social contracts will only prosper as members of society make important co-ordination efforts and find solutions to attain commonly desired outcomes while avoiding free-rider behaviour (Kaplan, 2017[57]; Vlerick, 2019[60]). Indeed, the social contract has also been defined as an "implicit self-policing agreement between members of society to co-ordinate on a particular equilibrium in the game of life" (Binmore, 1994[61]). However, individuals will only engage in social contracts if they perceive them as beneficial, fair and reliable, and while expectations from the social contract have increased, society's engagement depends highly on agreement and public justification (D'Agostino, 1996[62]).

Last, the LEO definition of the social contract is presented in broad terms and refers to "an intangible and implicit" agreement. While this acknowledges that the notion of the social contract goes beyond any agreement explicitly described in a tangible form, the LEO also acknowledges that a solid social contract is made up of, among other things, multiple specific social pacts in concrete policy areas (Box 4.2).

Box 4.2. **The social pacts within the social contract**

Social pacts refer to specific agreements in concrete policy areas that are agreed among various actors, such as civil society organisations, social partners and trade unions, as well as government and public institutions. Therefore, social pacts differ from collective bargaining (involving only two parties) and institutionalised tripartite agreements (where co-operation takes place within institutions) as they are broader, multi-stakeholder agreements around key policy issues (e.g. a fiscal pact or an environmental pact involving multiple players and interests). They take place at a certain moment in time, requiring the will of the parties (EurWork, 2019[63]).

Over time, social pacts have become powerful policy tools in dealing with economic and social challenges. In Europe, they were essential to reduce job losses and minimise social discontent, while in the Middle East they facilitated the democratisation process (Baccaro and Galindo, 2018[64]).

Social pacts depend on the international and economic environment in which they emerge (Baccaro and Galindo, 2018[64]). It is very likely that the current context in LAC will require solid social pacts, as countries will need to achieve broad consensus in key areas for a strong, inclusive and sustainable post-COVID-19 recovery. Social pacts, instead of unilateral decisions and reforms on the part of the government, may be able to reconcile various policy purposes, such as economic growth, social cohesion and equitable distribution, in an attempt to build larger consensus within societies (Baccaro and Galindo, 2018[64]). Likewise, social pacts can favour the involvement of all interested parties and reflect the diversity of opinions and interests, giving broader legitimacy to and supporting the greater sustainability of the decisions and reforms they involve.

Upcoming social pacts in the LAC region can play an important role in creating fairer social protection systems, reinvigorating productive strategies and the creation of good-quality jobs, or mobilising fiscal resources to finance the recovery. Hence, social pacts can provide the pillars for a new social contract aiming to bind society together and restore citizens' trust in public institutions.

Analytically, these pacts should involve elements of two dimensions: redistribution and recognition of rights and identities. Redistribution of resources and material opportunities and the recognition of the identities and rights of excluded or discriminated-against population groups are important components of a future social contract for inclusive well-being (Martínez Franzoni and Sánchez-Ancochea, 2020[65]; ECLAC, 2021[5]).

Updating the notion of the social contract for the post-pandemic world

The notion of the social contract should evolve, as major trends, including demographics, digital transformation and climate change, are transforming economies and societies.

The demographic dividend in the region will gradually fade, and the demographic structure will resemble that of advanced economies by 2050 (Berganza et al., 2020[66]). A new social contract must adapt to the consequences of population ageing, in particular through stronger social welfare systems.

As highlighted above, the digital transformation has also produced new inequalities and challenges. Less-skilled and medium-low skilled jobs are at greater risk of becoming automatised and disappearing in the near future. These challenges highlight the importance of building a digital transformation that works for all, including the tax implications of the digitalisation of the economy (OECD et al., 2020[9]; Cosano, 2019[54]; ECLAC/OEI, 2020[67]).

Climate change is arguably the most pressing challenge to sustainable development and hence needs to be a cornerstone of a renewed social contract to create a more equal, socially inclusive, low-carbon form of economic growth. The need to tackle the causes and consequences of climate change and environmental degradation has important consequences for the choice of sustainable modes of consumption and production. It also brings into the discussion of the social contract the dimension of inter-generational equity and solidarity.

Last, COVID-19 is bringing about deep transformations, and a new social contract should be designed with enough resilience and flexibility to adapt to rapidly changing realities, including more foresight and robust mechanisms for crisis prevention and management.

The building blocks of a new social contract

The building blocks of a new social contract should aim to be the pillars of a strong, inclusive and sustainable recovery from COVID-19 (Table 4.1). These building blocks result from two main dimensions. On the one hand, the social contract should be a transversal agreement across: i) socio-economic groups, through an intersectional approach mindful of income, gender, ethnic and racial differences, among others (Chapter 2); ii) territories, taking into account different local needs and opportunities and bridging territorial divides; and iii) generations, being aware that policy decisions must balance the interests of current and future generations and build on the notion of intergenerational solidarity. Taking into account these dimensions means that policies should be designed not only for these stakeholders but also with them, e.g. involving women in policy-making processes and supporting women's representation in decision-making bodies (see the section "Shaping a new social contract in LAC: How?" below).

On the other hand, a renewed social contract should help advance towards three key policy objectives whose relevance has been underscored by the crisis: i) resilient and sustainable productive strategies; ii) broader and more effective welfare systems by improving social protection systems and the delivery of quality public services; and iii) a more sustainable model of financing for development.

The intersection of these two axes creates specific areas for policy consensus: in practice, as mentioned above, the social contract is made up of specific social pacts in concrete policy domains (Table 4.1).

Good governance and mutual trust between the government and citizens, as well as with civil society and the private sector, is requisite for a solid social contract and hence represents a transversal pillar. The role of governance is further developed in the next section. International co-operation also plays an enabling role, supporting and facilitating the achievement of social pacts through the multilateral exchange of relevant experience, technical transfers and policy dialogue on an equal footing, notably to tackle the global commons and global public goods (Chapter 5). For instance, multilateral efforts will be crucial for the achievement of the 2030 Agenda, especially the goals related to climate change, biodiversity and ocean conservation. At the same time, some international alliances may support the achievement of national objectives, as in the case of the fight against domestic tax base erosion and profit shifting (BEPS) under the OECD/G20 Inclusive Framework on BEPS (OECD, 2019[68]).

Table 4.1. **The building blocks of a new social contract**

	A PACT		
	Across socio-economic groups (including income, gender, ethnic and racial)	**Across territories**	**Across generations**
Reinvigorating regional productive strategies	Creating better-quality jobs for all and embracing the digital transformation	Adapting productive strategies to local potential	Fostering green growth
Expanding the reach of social protection and public services	Strengthening social protection systems and public services	Ensuring wide territorial coverage	Restructuring pension systems and supporting children, youth, the disabled and the elderly with stronger welfare systems
Underpinning sustainable finance for development	Developing fairer and stronger tax systems and improving the effectiveness of public expenditure	Ensuring sound systems of transfers across territories and strengthening capacity to raise local revenues	Managing public debt in a sustainable and responsible manner

Stronger and more inclusive governance

Source: Authors' own elaboration.

A fundamental aspect of a robust, inclusive and sustainable recovery in the region will be advancing towards the accomplishment of solid fiscal pacts. This requires greater progressivity of the taxation system, higher tax compliance, and stronger tax administration with efficient tax expenditures. Before the pandemic, LAC already faced an institutional trap: citizens' growing distrust and dissatisfaction with public institutions and services negatively affected their tax morale, i.e. their willingness to pay taxes. This created a vicious circle, as low tax revenues limited the state's capacity to strengthen institutions and provide better-quality public services, further eroding social trust (OECD et al., 2019[2]). The impact of COVID-19 adds complexity, as it involves an enormous need for public resources to finance the recovery in a context of relatively low tax revenues, higher levels of indebtedness and narrower fiscal space (Chapter 1).

A broad consensus to determine sources of financing is needed, but a crisis may also be a favourable context to advance complex reforms and achieve intricate agreements. Crises increase the costs of delaying reform and may create disruptive distribution effects that facilitate reform by affecting existing rent-seeking coalitions or the status quo, creating a window of opportunity for reform (Dayton-Johnson, Londoño and Nieto Parra, 2011[70]).

Fiscal policy is perhaps the public policy area with the most interests at stake and thus illustrative of the critical importance of strengthening the process of dialogue and consensus building intrinsic to other types of reforms – i.e. pacts – needed for the recovery (Chapter 1).

Shaping a new social contract in LAC: How?

Achieving a renewed, post-pandemic social contract – or more specific social pacts in concrete policy areas – in LAC will require determination and engagement by all actors in society.

While there may be strong ambition and a widespread perception that a new, comprehensive agreement is needed, multiple barriers can hamper efforts, and a post-crisis context brings about particular challenges.

This section focuses on the "how" – the process of building a renewed social contract or advancing specific social pacts that are fair, legitimate and stable. This will demand: i) enhancing the inclusiveness of policy making to reach broad and representative consensus; ii) overcoming the barriers to policy reform and implementation; and iii) adopting a long-term horizon to make these agreements long lasting (Cabutto, Nieto-Parra and Vázquez-Zamora, 2021[163]).

Open and inclusive policy-making processes are key to achieving a new social contract that takes into account all points of view and promotes greater accountability

Strengthening open and inclusive policy making is key to designing policies and services that are transparent and take into account the needs of society as a whole. While a great deal of effort has been given to openness, i.e. providing citizens with information, governments should go beyond this. The share of LAC citizens that think that the freedom of political participation is completely or somewhat guaranteed in their country increased from 53% in 2007 to 66% in 2011, but has decreased ever since, reaching the lowest point in 2020 (45%) (Latinobarómetro, 2021[20]). Including a wide variety of voices in the policy-making process is required to develop truly inclusive policies. For the sake of equity, governments may need to make additional efforts to reach out to those segments of society unable or unwilling to participate in public debates (e.g. vulnerable, youth, new citizens) (OECD, 2009[71]; OECD, 2019[72]; OECD, 2020[145]).

The benefits of greater public engagement in policy making range from increasing accountability to strengthening policy evidence and tapping into social innovation. Open and inclusive policy making can result in greater accountability and civic capacity by widening the sphere of action in which citizens can influence the public process. As a result, it can also reduce implementation and compliance costs, as well as the risk of conflict during policy implementation or service delivery. By increasing social responsibility, it can galvanise citizens to take action in areas where success depends on changes in individual behaviour (e.g. climate change, social distancing rules during COVID-19). Open and inclusive policy making allows governments to understand better people's evolving needs and to address inequalities of voice and of access to both policy-making processes and public services. Last, it can help tackle complex issues in innovative ways by leveraging the information, ideas and resources held by businesses, civil society organisations and citizens (OECD, 2009[71]; OECD, 2020[148]; OECD, 2017[149]).

Ultimately, inclusive policy making can strengthen democracy, improve collective learning and experimentation and help rebuild trust between Latin American citizens and public institutions. Transparency and collective decision making can help lower concerns over undue influence in public policy by giving voice to a broader mix of underserved and excluded populations whose claims are often overwhelmed by powerful, well-organised interest groups. It can help channel the propositive potential of an active, informed and increasingly mobilised society, which has become more vocal in recent years (Naser, Williner and Sandoval, 2021[73]).

At the same time, inclusive and participative processes are important to ensure the policy commitment of various stakeholders over time. The benefit of inclusive policy making lies in the ability to achieve stable and lasting policies whose sustainability is not compromised by changes in government. For instance, Colombia's National System of Competitiveness and Innovation (*Sistema Nacional de Competitividad e Innovación*) is an institutional framework combining multilevel governance with the involvement of various actors outside the public sector, including civil society and the private sector. It seeks to set national policy objectives for innovation and competitiveness and to orient the activities of public entities, private firms and academia with a medium-to-long-term horizon.

The OECD has elaborated ten Guiding Principles for open and inclusive policy making that can help governments improve policy performance and service delivery (OECD, 2009[71]; OECD, 2001[150]) (Box 4.3).

Governments should carefully design their participatory strategies to ensure success. During the preparatory phase, the technical team should assess the feasibility of a participatory process, i.e. taking into account the availability of resources, the political will and the level of institutionalisation of participatory processes. Following this, the strategic phase should define the scale of the intervention and the actors involved and evaluate aspects of the socio-political context that may generate opportunities or risks for the strategy. In relation to the latter, during the elaboration phase, it is important to define the level of participation (e.g. informative, consultative, resolutive or co-management), which requires different methodological designs and techniques. After approval and implementation, it is crucial to systematise the inputs received, analyse their technical, political and economic feasibility and communicate to participants the accepted proposals. Last, the strategy should establish with monitoring and evaluation mechanisms the level of achievement of the objectives, activities and potential lessons learned, including through informal evaluations, participants' opinions and quantitative analyses (Naser, Williner and Sandoval, 2021[73]; OECD, 2001[150] ; OECD, 2021[151]).

While the forms of public engagement are varied, representative deliberative processes are one way of engaging various segments of society in participatory processes that focus on citizens' informed input. Deliberative processes can lead to better policy outcomes, enable policy makers to make hard choices and enhance trust between citizens and government. Deliberative processes are particularly apt for tackling issues that are values based, require trade-offs and demand long-term solutions (OECD, 2020[74]). They focus on finding common ground on political issues through a fair and reasonable discussion among citizens (Gastil and Levine, 2005[75]). They involve a randomly selected group of people who are broadly representative of a community[1] spending significant time learning and collaborating through facilitated deliberation to develop collective recommendations for policy makers on a specific issue (OECD, 2020[74]; Cesnulaityte, 2021[76]), as in the Itinerant Citizen Assembly of Bogotá.

At the multilateral level, there are several institutional frameworks promoting citizen participation. The OECD Recommendation of the Council on Open Government defines open government as "a culture of governance that promotes the principles of transparency, integrity, accountability and *stakeholder participation* in support of democracy and inclusive growth" (OECD, 2017[149]). To guarantee the participation of interested citizens, the Open Government Partnership (OGP) initiative promotes a proactive collaboration of government with citizens through multiple channels, including online consultations, public hearings and focus groups. These elements are key during the formulation and co-creation of an Open Government Action Plan, in which government and civil society define key national commitments to achieve better public services through a well-defined process (Naser,

Williner and Sandoval, 2021[73]). Of the 78 OGP member countries, 16 are from LAC. Of these, 15 already have a defined action plan (Open Government Partnership, 2021[77]).

Examples of participative and inclusive processes provide lessons for building new social pacts in LAC

Some notable examples of social pacts featuring participatory processes and consensus building include the current constitutional process in Chile, the Constitution of Mexico City, the Grenelle Environment Roundtables in France, the Moncloa Pacts and the Toledo Pact in Spain, the Economic Solidarity Pact in Mexico, the National Accord in Peru, as well as some particular cases of social pacts in the region, such as peace agreements.

The process (*proceso constituyente*) for the drafting of a new constitution in Chile has been hailed as a promising example of an inclusive legislative process. Following the 2019 protests and the national referendum of 25 October 2020, when a large majority of Chileans voted in favour of a new constitution, a Constitutional Convention (*Convención Constituyente*) responsible for drafting the new text was elected in 2021 (BCN, 2021[78]). This body, composed of 155 popularly elected representatives, is the first to respect gender parity, since half of the members are women. Moreover, seventeen seats are reserved for indigenous representatives. Last, the requisite of a two-thirds quorum for the approval of the new text aims to emphasise consensus building. Despite the focus on inclusiveness and representation, the low voter turnout registered during the election also points to the challenge of strengthening open and inclusive policy making, with an emphasis on engaging with citizens from disadvantaged neighbourhoods. However, social contracts can also be reached on a smaller scale, through a piecemeal approach, as in the case of the Constitution of Mexico City. The Lab for Mexico City set up the Constitución CDMX digital platform, which offered the public four ways to participate in the drafting process: 1) a survey, 2) online petitions, 3) collaborative drafting, and 4) an event register. These inputs were then reflected in the final draft (LabCDMX, 2016[152]).

The Grenelle Agreements (*Accords de Grenelle*) refer to the negotiations that took place in France among the government, labour unions and trade unions on 25-26 May 1968 amid the general strike of May 1968. Concluded on 27 May 1968 but rejected by workers, the agreements did not immediately enter into force, and the strike continued. However, they set the basis for, among other outcomes, an increase in the minimum wage, the establishment of labour union sections within enterprises and a reduced working day. Since these negotiations, "Grenelle" has been used to design debates and negotiations involving various parts of society aimed at reaching broad consensus, as with the Grenelle Environment Roundtable, which took place in 2007 under the initiative of the president and led to the adoption of a bill for environmental programming, known as the "Loi Grenelle 1", by the parliament in 2009 (OECD, 2016[79]). It was a unique multi-stakeholder initiative because it granted the public a central role in approving or rejecting proposals resulting from the deliberations of five collegial national working groups made up of trade unions, employers, non-governmental organisations, local authorities and public service representatives.

The Moncloa Pacts (*Pactos de la Moncloa*) were two social and economic agreements approved in 1977 in Spain to consolidate the transition to democracy and stabilise the economy affected by the 1973 oil crisis. They established a policy of economic recovery consisting of controlling public spending and inflation and reforming the tax administration. In social and political matters, they were decisive in ensuring civil and political rights, such as the rights of assembly and freedom of expression, as well as advancing women's rights by decriminalising adultery. These two pacts set a historical example of government and opposition forces working together to reach an understanding and abandoning the systematic confrontation that characterised that period. The climate of dialogue created through the Moncloa Pacts was critical for the elaboration of the Spanish constitution in 1978 (Cabrera, 2011[80]). The Toledo Pact was another remarkable and long-lasting agreement reached by the Spanish political parties in 1995 to address the instability faced by the pension and social security system. A similar negotiation between government, labour unions and trade unions in Mexico led to the adoption of the Economic Solidarity Pact (*Pacto de Solidaridad Económica*) of 1987. The Pact was successful in some domains such as ensuring economic stability, in particular regarding monetary stability by containing inflation.

The National Accord (*Acuerdo Nacional*) of Peru started in 2002 and developed and approved a set of long-term state policies for sustainable development on the basis of dialogue and consensus after a process of workshops, consultations and thematic and decentralised forums. Parties to the accord are the government, political parties with representation in the Congress and civil society organisations. The policies approved included engagements for strengthening democracy, guaranteeing equity and social justice, promoting competitiveness and developing efficient, transparent and decentralised public institutions (Acuerdo Nacional, 2014[69]). The National Accord informed the National Strategic Development Plan (*Plan Bicentenario: El Perú hacia el 2021*) and the sectoral and regional development plans that were dependent on it. However, stronger links between policy agendas and results-based budgeting are needed to ensure their coherent implementation (OECD, 2016[119]).

Past experiences associated with peace agreement processes in LAC, such as the cases of Colombia (2016) and Guatemala (1996), could shed light on some features of the architecture of these particular social pacts. The peace agreement methodology of having selected actors sitting at the same table with different and often conflicting interests to find shared solutions can certainly inspire the design of future social pact processes in the region while improving trust among citizens and in political institutions. This methodology could be complemented with a more participatory and open dynamic. Another key lesson to consider is the importance of anticipating during the dialogue process the stages that will take place after reaching each accord. This would ensure broad support coalitions, which are key for legitimising the results and mainstreaming their potential impact on people's well-being. Last, after reaching an agreement, political will and institutional capacities are fundamental to achieve its effective implementation and expected outcomes (Martínez Franzoni and Sánchez-Ancochea, 2020[65]).

Barriers that hinder consensus building and hamper policy reform and implementation must be overcome

There remain several challenges, on both the political and the technical levels, that block consensus building and hamper policy reform and implementation in LAC. These are therefore barriers to the success and sustainability of renewed social pacts and demand careful attention and specific policy responses.

The media and digital technologies and their role in facilitating inclusive policy-making processes and deliberation can be improved

Digital technologies and the Internet facilitate open and inclusive policy-making processes and public engagement. First, open government data can create a culture of transparency and promote accountability and access to information. By sharing information with citizens, open government can stimulate more civic engagement and oversight in areas susceptible to corruption – as observed in the early response to the COVID-19 pandemic (OECD and The GovLab, 2021[153]). Laws on access to information have been adopted in the region and are a necessary condition to ensure good governance and prevent corruption in the digital age as they set the rules for both proactive and reactive disclosure of information. However, the capacity to share information and data is necessary, albeit insufficient on its own. In addition, governments must provide the opportunity and tools to process the open data, and the ability and incentives for citizens and SMEs to act on and innovate with the information drawn from them. At the same time, digital technologies can benefit governments by facilitating interaction with stakeholders (online consultation) and citizen engagement in decision making (digitally-enabled decision making). Digital platforms can be a low-cost means for governments to interact with stakeholders in policy design, monitoring and implementation. Combined with investments in the development of infrastructure and digital talent and skills, the digital transformation can also help governments provide more inclusive public services, making public institutions more accessible and citizen centred (OECD et al., 2020[9]).

In the context of reduced trust in governments and public services, digital technologies and data can be critical to enable sound service design and delivery strategies that promote human-centric and joined-up public services that benefit all (OECD, 2020[155]; OECD, 2020[156]). This includes the adoption of *digital by design* principles in the implementation of public services, using digital technologies to breakdown policy and service siloes, unifying the experience of citizens with the public sector, reducing the burden of providing information that is already held by public sector organisations, and respecting individuals' preferences to access services through their preferred channel (e.g. in-person, digital, kiosks, telephone, etc). Finally, under a comprehensive service design and delivery approach in the digital age, governments accord a central role to citizens in expressing their preferences, needs and expectations, and reflect them into the design and delivery of public services, helping reduce the gap between citizens and the public sector through more pertinent and human-centric services (OECD, 2021[157]).

Alongside digital technologies, a pluralistic media play a significant role in shaping public opinion, channelling attention to important social issues and inspiring citizens to take action. However, Latin America shows some of the highest levels of media ownership concentration in the world (Rodríguez and Zechmeister, 2018[81]; Reporters without Borders, 2019[82]). The "limited pluralism" of the Latin American media environment means that the representation of diverse social, economic and political perspectives is often limited by industrial, commercial or government priorities (Segura and Waisbord, 2016[83]).

Lack of media pluralism and ownership concentration are important impediments to the creation of a healthy and informed debate in society and to exposing and drawing attention to governance abuses and resource misallocation. Countries in which press freedom is more restricted also tend to show higher levels of corruption in the public sector (Figure 4.8). Concerns about press freedom are on the rise in LAC, and the proportion of respondents who report having high trust in the media dropped to its lowest level in the 2016/17 round of the Americas Barometer (Rodríguez and Zechmeister, 2018[81]). Allowing greater competition in the media sector is a first step to enable a pluralistic and diverse debate in society (Mendel, Castillejo and Gómez, 2017[84]).

Figure 4.8. Greater restrictions on media freedom go hand in hand with higher corruption levels in the public sector

Reporters without Borders World Press Freedom Index (2021) vs. V-Dem public sector corruption index (2020)

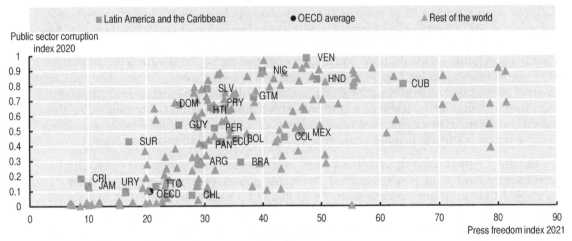

Notes: The World Press Freedom Index takes into account experts' responses to a questionnaire on countries' performance as regards pluralism, media independence and respect for the safety and freedom of journalists and combines them with quantitative data on abuses and acts of violence against journalists during the period evaluated. It ranges from 0 (best situation) to 100 (worst situation). The public sector corruption index ranges from 0 (least corrupt) to 1 (most corrupt). Rest of the world includes all countries except LAC countries.

Sources: Coppedge et al. (2021[85]), V-Dem 2020 Dataset v11.1, https://doi.org/10.23696/vdemds21; Reporters without Borders (2021[86]), 2021 World Press Freedom Index (database), https://rsf.org/en/ranking.

StatLink ᵅˢᵖ https://doi.org/10.1787/888934286901

Party fragmentation and polarisation can hamper consensus building, underscoring the need for strong intermediary structures

To achieve consensus and keep it once it has been reached, effective intermediary institutions are key to ensuring the long-term sustainability of a renewed social contract. By acting as interlocutors between citizens and the state, intermediary institutions, such as political parties, trade unions and associations, give individuals the opportunity to voice grievances and make public institutions more accountable (OECD, 2021[87]). Indeed, it is generally not possible for citizens to communicate directly with the state. These networks enable citizens to communicate their interests in a collective and organised way and also provide them with a form of group identity. This two-way dialogue can promote social cohesion and provide useful feedback to policy makers during the implementation and potential adjustment phase of a reform. On the other side, as seen in the loss of confidence in political parties in the region, the inability to affect change and mediate between citizens and the state may result in civic disengagement and mistrust in institutions.

Fragmentation and polarisation undermine the representative role of political parties

Party fragmentation and polarisation (covered above) can pose a challenge to finding compromise and common ground on salient political issues. This is a particularly critical issue in the context of the post-pandemic recovery, which will require broad consensus. In a context where electoral volatility is high due to fragmentation of the political landscape and there is uncertainty about parties' electoral prospects, parties' perception of the costs of polarisation decrease substantially (Moraes, 2015[88]). However, this strategy hampers consensus building and citizens' ability to understand programmatic politics (Carreras and Acácio, 2019[89]).

The proliferation of political parties in LAC is related to their crisis of legitimacy and representation. New political parties tend to appear when the demands of the population are not being answered or as a result of economic crises and corruption scandals that have caused the rejection of more traditional candidates (Cyr and Liendo, 2020[90]). The proliferation of political parties with effective representation in the legislative power characterises many LAC countries and may be posing a challenge to consensus building. On average, between 2005 and the latest elections, the number of effective legislative parties in LAC has risen (Figure 4.9). Some countries, including Brazil, Chile, Guatemala and Peru, have seen the number of parties with representation in congress increase signficantly, while others have seen a decline to fewer than two parties with large repesentation in the legislative power, which shows that the crisis of legitimacy can also lead to a stronger concentration of power in some countries.

The high heterogeneity affects not only the number of parties able to influence the policy-making process in LAC effectively but also the degree of polarisation and the level of inter-party competition. With low levels of polarisation, coalitions are more frequent, and fragmentation tends to decrease (Wills-Otero, 2020[93]). In some democracies, such as Chile, Costa Rica, Honduras and Uruguay, the patterns of inter-party competition have been much more stable, suggesting the need to avoid generalisations about volatility and system institutionalisation in the region (Carreras and Acácio, 2019[89]).

Figure 4.9. The crisis of legitimacy and representation of political parties in Latin America

Index of effective number of legislative parties in Latin America, 2005 vs. latest election, 2016-21

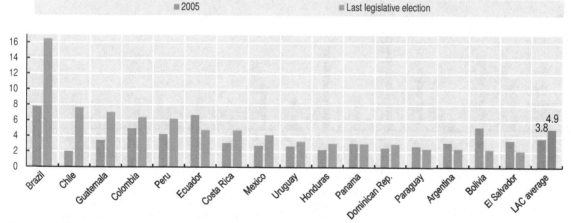

Notes: Index does not reflect the real number of parties but their effective number based on the share of seats each party holds. This is a measure of legislative fragmentation in the lower house (or national assembly). Higher values indicate that more parties have a number of seats in the legislature that allow them to have a say in the policy-making process. Calculations take into account the latest legislative elections, which took place between November 2016 (Nicaragua) and June 2021 (Mexico). Note that the 2015 reform of the electoral system in Chile may have affected the results for the country.
Source: Own elaboration based on the methodology by Laakso and Taagepera (1979[91]), "The 'effective' number of parties: A measure with application to West Europe", http://dx.doi.org/10.1177/001041407901200101; and Jones (2005[92]), *The Role of Parties and Party Systems in the Policymaking Process*, https://citeseerx.ist.psu.edu/viewdoc/download?doi=10.1.1.542.1866&rep=rep1&type=pdf.
StatLink  https://doi.org/10.1787/888934286920

The identity-based claims of under-represented and minority groups, such as indigenous or Afrodescendant peoples, have contributed to the emergence of new political parties, for instance in Bolivia, Colombia and Ecuador. Political decentralisation processes that took place in some LAC countries have further contributed to the proliferation of parties. These trends can be perceived as progress towards democratic consolidation and electoral competitiveness, as citizens are able to choose among a variety of political parties and voices, increasing inclusiveness and diversity and representation for minoritised groups. However, these trends can also lead to fragmentation by increasing co-ordination costs and intra-party competition, making effective governance more difficult. Similarly, given the low institutionalisation of political parties, these trends may be unable to channel citizens' interests effectively. Likewise, low levels of party support may also be dangerous for democratic legitimacy, especially when populist discourses proliferate (Cyr and Liendo, 2020[90]).

In around half of the LAC countries analysed, electoral volatility has increased recently with respect to the previous period, while in others it has declined, thanks to greater party system institutionalisation, as in Uruguay (Figure 4.10). Party proliferation and the fragmentation of political systems are contributing to electoral volatility (Mainwaring, 2018[94]), with the vote share of new and non-traditional parties increasing over time in both national and subnational elections (Cyr and Liendo, 2020[90]; Carreras and Acácio, 2019[89]; Laroze, 2019[95]; Gerring, 2005[96]). During the last decades, outsider leaders who are not compelled by strongly structured parties have increased their chances of being elected. New outsiders may also emerge and enter the political sphere as a consequence of the COVID-19 crisis (Murillo, 2020[97]).

Figure 4.10. **Electoral volatility in Latin America**

Pedersen index of electoral volatility in legislative elections, 1998-2017*

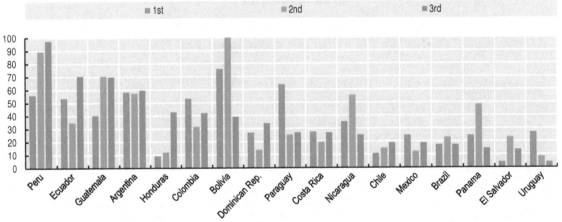

Note: *Figure compares the change in electoral volatility over four consecutive legislative elections over the period 1998-2017. The orange bar considers the change that took place around the early 2000s; the green bar considers the mid-2000s; the grey bar refers to the early 2010s. The Pedersen index ranges from 0 to 100, corresponding to the net shift in voting percentages: 0 signifies that no parties lost or gained vote (or seat) percentages; 100 means that all the votes (or seats) went to a new set of parties. The Pedersen index remains the gold standard measure to capture stability in aggregate patterns of inter-party competition, as it measures the degree of vote switching between political parties in two consecutive elections.
Source: Own calculations based on data from Roberts and Wibbels (1999[101]), "Party Systems and Electoral Volatility in Latin America" and (Cohen, 2018[102]), Latin American Presidential and Legislative Elections dataset, www.molliecohen.com/data.html.
StatLink ⟋⟍⟍ https://doi.org/10.1787/888934286939

High electoral volatility and weak party system institutionalisation destabilise democratic representation and hamper the process of holding parties accountable. High volatility and low institutionalisation can stifle consensus building and favour adoption of more radical policies, as parties become less concerned about their long-term reputation or constrained by their political organisation. They also hinder citizens' ability to understand programme-based politics and increase voter frustration. Lastly, high volatility undermines democractic representation, as it is harder for voters to hold parties and politicians accountable for their performance in office (Carreras and Acácio, 2019[89]).

As a consequence, distrust has proliferated among the electorate in several LAC countries (Wills-Otero, 2020[93]; Lupu, 2016[98]).

In addition, multiparty systems and presidentialism can be an unstable equation for democracy (Mainwaring, 1997[99]). With the proliferation of political parties in LAC, other government forms more inclined towards parliamentarism may favour the development of programme-based and more institutionalised parties (Croissant and Merkel, 2004[100]).

Policy capture may significantly undermine the outcome of public policies

In democracies, public consultation, lobbying or the financing of political parties and campaigns are legal and legitimate means through which interested parties can express their views and concerns. However, these practices can also give rise to "grey areas" where vested interests can exercise undue influence over public decision making at the expense of the public good. Policy capture is "the process of consistently or repeatedly directing public policy decisions away from the public interest towards the interests of a specific interest group or person" (OECD, 2017[103]; Carpenter and Moss, 2014[104]). Policy capture can take many forms, including through financing of political parties, media campaigns with manipulated information, aggressive lobbying and the revolving door between the private and the public sectors (Cañete Alonso, 2018[105]). The high levels of corruption and inequality, as well as the strong concentration of economic and media power, exacerbate the risk of policy capture in LAC, as they facilitate privileged groups' access to decision makers (OECD, 2017[103]; OECD et al., 2019[2]).

Capture has negative effects on the economy and society. It goes against the fundamental idea of democratic and fair decision making based on dialogue, consensus and openness, eroding social cohesion and trust in institutions. It also causes public resource misallocation, which is detrimental to productivity growth and can heighten inequalities.

Political finance and lobbying of public officials are the most common ways in which powerful groups can undermine the integrity of public decision making. Among the most paradigmatic examples of these mechanisms is the well-known Odebrecht scandal. With the exception of some countries in Central America, political finance is strongly regulated in LAC (International IDEA, 2020[106]), but an implementation gap still exists, and in 11 out of 12 countries surveyed, cash contributions were still allowed in 2018, making it easier to circumvent political finance regulations. Moreover, digital technologies and social media are creating "grey areas" that make tracking of digital advertisements for political parties and candidates more complex (OECD, 2021[107]). On the other hand, countries such as Argentina (2003), Colombia (2011), Chile (2014), Mexico (2010) and Peru (2003) have adopted laws or regulations on lobbying. Chile, Colombia and Mexico have a lobbyist register, and out of these, Colombia does not impose sanctions for non-compliance. Only four countries (Argentina, Chile, Mexico and Peru) require public officials' agendas to be public, and five countries (Argentina, Colombia, Costa Rica, Mexico and Peru) require disclosing the names of members of permanent advisory bodies (OECD, 2020[108]).[2] Early observations confirm that countries with a regulatory framework to enhance the transparency of lobbying activities, and policy making generally, ensured a greater degree of accountability in policy decisions during the COVID-19 crisis (OECD, 2021[107]).

A comprehensive system that fosters a culture of integrity and accountability in public decision making is key to mitigating the risk of policy capture. Four complementary strategies can help safeguard fair and inclusive policy making. First, ensuring transparency and access to timely, reliable and relevant information can facilitate participation and stakeholder engagement, as well as enable social control over public decision-making processes (OECD, 2017[103]). However, greater transparency should be accompanied by broader institutional reforms, especially in highly corrupt countries where information may even backfire and produce resignation, e.g. less civic engagement, or indignation (Bauhr and Grimes, 2014[109]; Corbacho et al., 2016[110]; Peiffer, 2018[111]). Second, it requires engaging stakeholders with diverging interests to help balance views and ensure a level playing field less prone to capture. This would also require reinforcing lobbying and political finance regulations. Third, competition authorities, regulatory agencies and supreme audit institutions can promote accountability in both the public and private sectors. Ultimately, appropriate organisational integrity policies can help identify and mitigate the risk of capture. Establishing clear standards of conduct, promoting a culture of integrity and ensuring a sound control and risk-management framework can make public organisations more resistant to capture (OECD, 2017[103]).

Behavioural research has produced a wealth of insights that policy makers can draw from to develop innovative and well-targeted integrity policies. Moving away from a narrow focus on deterrence and enforcement, these insights can help promoting values-based decisions in the public sector and society. For instance, behavioural research shows that inducing ethical reflection and preparing decision makers for ethical temptations can be more effective than over-strict control of a trust-based rule, which may drive people to disregard and break the rule (OECD, 2018[112]).

The political economy of reform plays a key role, particularly in the context of a post-crisis recovery

Policy-making processes are characterised by multiple actors with different time horizons, power and incentives (Spiller, Stein and Tommasi, 2008[113]). This complexity makes reforms hard to implement, despite their positive long-term effects, because they often entail the negotiation of some transitional or distributional costs. Good economic policies can yield poor results in their implementation phase if they fail to take these political economy constraints into account. First of all, reforms involve winners and losers. The latter have strong incentives to obstruct reforms going against their interests (Martínez Franzoni and Sánchez-Ancochea, 2020[65]). Second, reforms may have short-term costs despite their welfare-enhancing potential in the long term, making them less popular in the immediate term (Rodrik, 1996[114]; Williamson, 1994[115]; OECD, 2018[116]). Learning from previous reform episodes can be important for designing and carrying out successful reforms (Caldera Sánchez, de Serres and Yashiro, 2016[117]; OECD, 2010[118]; Tompson, 2009[25]).

Accounting for complementary policies to mitigate the distributional impact of a reform or offset its short-term costs is key to overcoming people's resistance. Designing appropriate compensation or cushioning schemes for those vulnerable groups likely to be negatively affected by the reform may be needed to win broad political support (OECD, 2018[116]; OECD, 2010[118]). For instance, as the region advances towards environment-related taxes, embedding income support schemes for poor households in wider energy subsidy reform packages can help mitigate the immediate negative effect on household finances of phasing out subsidies. Moreover, some reforms may be more effective when they are combined in packages that increase their synergies than when they are undertaken in isolation (Caldera Sánchez, de Serres and Yashiro, 2016[117]; Dayton-Johnson, Londoño and Nieto Parra, 2011[70]).

Given the growing distrust in institutions in LAC, a clear reform mandate and strong leadership are critical for the success of reforms. Without a clear electoral mandate for the government, reforms tend to happen only when there is evidence that current policies are not working, which may be the case in a post-crisis context. However, this approach risks making policies more reactive than proactive and tends to delay reforms until crises make them imperative (Rodrik, 1996[114]). Lack of mandate also undermines reform ownership and increases the likelihood that reforms will be unwound or reversed with changes in government, especially given the high electoral volatility and high party fragmentation observed in LAC. Strong leadership by a single policy maker or an institution also helps ensure that the reform momentum does not dissipate (OECD, 2018[116]; OECD, 2010[118]).

At the same time, in a context characterised by polarised political discourses and rising mis and dis-information on social media, evidence-based analysis and evaluation and effective communication are important to shed light on the benefits of a reform (Matasick, Alfonsi and Bellantoni, 2020[154]). Solid analysis and research by authoritative and non-partisan institutions are essential to build the case, especially in light of the low confidence in political parties and public institutions in LAC. This also requires investing in data collection, building strong and independent national statistical offices and committing to *ex-post* evaluation. An effective communication strategy based on audience insights and delivering targeted messages via a multitude of platforms is then important to raise awareness about the benefits of policy reform, which may often be less obvious than the disadvantages (OECD, 2018[116]; OECD DevCom, 2020[120]; OECD, 2010[118]; Tompson, 2009[25]). For instance, in some LAC countries progress should be made to raise awareness about the importance of progressivity and robust retirement schemes in view of population ageing (Chapter 2). Public institutions seeking to engage citizens with reform will need to invest in new communication skill sets and partnerships, choosing appropriate messengers and formats that can engage diverse audiences, on line – for example, on social media – and off line (OECD DevCom, 2020[120]; OECD, forthcoming[158]).

Appropriate sequencing and speed of reforms also play a crucial role for their successful implementation. For instance, it is generally advised that fiscal and monetary stabilisation, as well as institutional reforms, should precede more complex reforms, such as trade or capital account liberalisation (Nsouli, Rached and Funke, 2005[121]). Successful initial reforms can help increase support and facilitate the implementation of subsequent reforms. Appropriate sequencing should also avoid outbursts of inequality, which are likely to obstruct further advances in the reform process (Guriev, 2018[122]; Aristei and Perugini, 2014[123]). Moreover, the optimal speed of reforms is country specific, and the choice between pushing as many reforms as possible at once (big bang approach) and introducing them one after the other (unbundling strategy) is a critical one. Depending on the context, policy makers may prefer to bundle reforms into a comprehensive package so that losses from one reform are compensated by gains from others (Dayton-Johnson, Londoño and Nieto Parra, 2011[70]) or, if this is not possible, reach specific agreements and policy advances in areas where there is potential for accord.

The credibility of and commitment to the policy is also essential for the success of the reforms and the control of adjustment costs. Credibility is important for determining the size of the adjustment costs. When reforms are credible, early announcement of the policies will have the effect of aligning private agents' behaviour with the expected objectives of policy makers (Nsouli, Rached and Funke, 2005[121]). Policy commitment generates a stable policy environment in which political actors can reach policy agreements that survive government or cabinet turnover (Spiller, Stein and Tommasi, 2008[113]).

Last, timing is especially important, and while literature shows that reforms tend to be more frequent in negative times, the short-term challenges of reforms also tend to be larger in bad than in good economic times (Ciminelli et al., 2019[124]). Reforms undertaken during prosperous times may encounter higher opposition but also allow greater time for preparation, which may not be available during emergencies. Adjustment costs and compensation of losers also tend to be more affordable during good times (OECD, 2018[116]). Nonetheless, history shows that structural and regulatory reforms are more frequent during bad times (Ranciere and Tornell, 2015[125]). Examples include the reforms in Europe in the wake of the Eurocrisis or the trade reforms in LAC in the 1980s and 1990s.

Raising awareness of the sheer scale of the current crisis can increase public understanding of the need for significant changes. A well-managed crisis presents an enormous opportunity for countries to adopt challenging measures (IDB, 2020[126]; OECD, 2020[1]). A renewed social contract would entail moving from today's fragmented status quo to a new equilibrium based on equality of opportunities in the long run (Larraín, 2020[4]). A broader social contract would contribute to addressing the deep sense of discontent caused by increasing inequalities and outdated policies, bringing all actors into the discussion and reinforcing democratic institutions and the open market economy.

These considerations are particularly relevant in the post-pandemic context, where building back better will entail strong political impetus and wise management of the intricacies of the political economy of reform.

Low institutional capacities can result in poor policy implementation

Governments need to continue strengthening their core functions to ensure optimal policy impact. Important areas of work include promoting policy coherence and co-ordination, strengthening administrative capacity and skills, notably in subnational and local governments, simplifying administrative processes, reinforcing public procurement and investment, ensuring internal and external accountability and promoting a merit-based civil service. To a large degree, the quality of policy implementation depends on the strength of the judiciary and the bureaucracy, as well as on the resources and incentives available to them (Spiller, Stein and Tommasi, 2008[113]).

Public procurement can be a strategic tool to achieve the SDGs. Integrating economic, social and environmental policy objectives in public procurement processes - such as selection and contract award criteria, technical specifications, contract clauses - can provide companies with an incentive to align with the government agenda on sustainable development and RBC standards. For instance, ChileCompra introduced a programme to promote the participation of female-owned businesses in the public procurement market (OECD, 2020[159]).

Moreover, open contracting data can make governance more inclusive and democratic. For example, immediately after the COVID-19 outbreak, countries like Costa Rica, Ecuador, Paraguay and Peru set up transparency portals to disclose the information on procurements carried out in response to the COVID-19 emergency, including the information on the direct award procedures. Creating a culture of transparency, accountability and access to public information can also stimulate citizen participation in public procurement process. For instance, social witnesses in Mexico are required to participate in all stages of the federal public procurement procedures above certain thresholds as a way to promote public scrutiny. Peru launched a citizen control mechanism (*Monitores Ciudadanos de Control*) that allows citizens to visit construction sites at the beginning, during, and/or completion of public works in order to monitor the construction progress. Colombia introduced an anti-corruption mobile application called *Elefantes Blancos* in order to promote the citizen control of white elephant projects (neglected, abandoned or overbilled public works projects) (OECD, 2020[160]).

Policies will only attain their objectives if they are sustained by a strong institutional framework that is capable of providing accountability, inclusiveness, efficiency and accessibility (Staats, Bowler and Hiskey, 2008[127]). In this regard, an independent and reliable judicial system is crucial to maintain the checks and balances between the executive and legislative branches. A judiciary that ensures an impartial application of the rule of law and prevents violence from repeating itself will lay the grounds for sustainable economic development and a long-lasting democracy (Hilbink and Prillaman, 2002[128]).

During the last decade of the 20th century, countries in LAC lacked a strong institutional machinery and a reliable judiciary to guarantee the effective observance of human and civil rights conducive to economic growth. Echoing these problems, most countries in the region undertook a long process of institutional and judicial reform that continues today (DeShazo and Vargas, 2006[129]). Despite the efforts, impunity for perpetrators of past crimes, corruption and lack of political will, as well as limited resources, remain challenging problems across the region. An accurate diagnosis of the inefficiencies of each judicial system is necessary before implementing any reform in order to understand the causes behind past failures and limited results. The Global Impunity Index, which measures the functioning and structure of national security and justice systems, as well as the respect for human rights, locates LAC countries above the OECD average (Figure 4.11).

Figure 4.11. The level of impunity in LAC remains medium to high

Global Impunity Index 2020

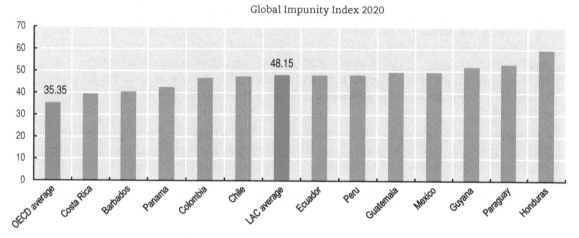

Notes: LAC average is a simple average of 12 countries. Owing to inconsistencies in the data, 2020 data are not available for Argentina, Brazil, Dominican Republic, El Salvador, Grenada, Nicaragua, Trinidad and Tobago and Venezuela. The Global Impunity Index ranges from 0 to 100, where 0 means the lack of impunity and 100 means the maximum level of impunity in a precise period of time.

Sources: CESIJ (2020[130]), *Global Impunity Index 2020 (GII-2020) (database)*, www.udlap.mx/cesij; CESIJ (2017[131]), *Global Impunity Index 2017 (GII-2017) (database)*, www.udlap.mx/cesij.

StatLink ᵇᵃᵇᵃᵇᵃ *https://doi.org/10.1787/888934286958*

The centre of government (CoG) also plays a key role in supporting the head of government and the cabinet of ministers. Among its functions, the CoG takes care of the co-ordination and monitoring of public policies to ensure that line ministries' actions are aligned with government priorities. The CoG is also responsible for strategic management and the design of policies for open government, good governance, accountability and transparency (OECD, 2020[108]).

Data-driven public sector and data governance in LAC

A data-driven public sector is key to governing data for the design, implementation, monitoring and evaluation of renewed social pacts. The COVID-19 crisis in LAC has demonstrated the potential of data to generate public value in several ways: i) anticipation and planning, e.g. to forecast the evolution of contagions and the occupation of intensive care units; ii) delivery, e.g. using data on informal workers to design targeted income support policies during lockdowns; and iii) monitoring and evaluation, e.g. using public procurement data to audit emergency purchases. Open and trustworthy data can also support the policy-making process and help build the case for complex reforms during the recovery. Going forward, it is important not only to invest in strengthening statistical systems but also to adopt an "open by default" approach across the whole of government. The latter approach focuses on enhancing the publication of open government data for re-use and value co-creation with the aim of increasing public-sector transparency and integrity, fostering development and social innovation, and fighting corruption (OECD, 2017[132]; OECD, 2020[133]).

However, results from the OECD Open, Useful and Re-usable data (OURdata) Index for LAC still show great disparities in relation to the publication of open government data and its use for accountability, policy making and service design and delivery (OECD, 2020[108]). Moreover, the OECD Digital Government Index 2019 shows that, among all participant countries including 7 LAC governments, achieving a data-driven public sector remains one of the key challenges for competent digital and data-driven governments (OECD, 2020[161]).

Governments should also take actions to ensure the efficient and ethical use of data in order to reap the benefits of the exponential generation of data in the digital age without compromising the privacy of citizens (OECD, 2020[133]; OECD, 2019[134]) or the exclusion of specific population groups due to biases in the generation of data or the development of algorithms (OECD, 2021[162]; OECD et al., 2020[9]). Poor data governance frameworks risk further eroding public trust in governments, which is already low in LAC. Progress in regulatory frameworks for data protection in LAC is mixed (OECD et al., 2020[9]; OECD, forthcoming[135]).

Moreover, despite advances, on average, LAC displays a basic level of digital security (IDB/OAS, 2020[136]). Going forward, it is crucial to guarantee the ethical and safe management of data, supported by effective privacy and digital security frameworks.

National strategies are a necessary instrument to ensure a coherent and long-term vision

To make the social contract sustainable over time requires careful planning and national strategies. National Development Plans (NDPs) are a vital policy instrument. NDPs are key to ensuring that the reforms contained in the new social contract are well designed and embrace a coherent, long-term vision. Dealing with increasingly complex and interconnected development challenges requires a clear and comprehensive logic in order to involve all government institutions at all levels over time. Key dimensions contributing to the effectiveness of NDPs are: i) clear goals and indicators to define priorities, allocate financial resources, monitor progress and identify gaps; ii) a solid legal framework to give the plan authoritative power; iii) a link with the national budget, allowing concrete assessment of policy feasibility; iv) inclusion of a subnational dimension and public participation in the creation of the plan, giving it greater legitimacy; v) a specialised agency responsible for formulating NDP to enhance commitment and expertise; and vi) monitoring and evaluation, which are fundamental for assessing implementation and enabling learning, prioritisation and policy improvement over time (OECD et al., 2020[9]).

Achieving the broader social contract may involve various social pacts, and NDPs can help sustain an integral vision across sectors. In the development of the social contract, it is important to consider the potential synergies between different policies, such as how social protection and labour market policies, as well as productive policies, can sustain the creation of formal, good-quality jobs that achieve wider societal well-being. Against a silo-based approach, NDPs are crucial to evaluate potential policy spillovers, co-ordinate across areas of intervention and set clear cross-cutting objectives to orient policy action, such as sustainability, inclusion and resilience (Soria Morales, 2018[137]; OECD, 2019[138]).

LAC governments are making many efforts in promoting a vision focused on people's well-being and sustainability, but more can be done to strengthen the non-economic aspects of NDPs, and to link the vision embodied in the NDPs with actual implementation processes (OECD, forthcoming[139]).

NDPs are key to ensuring coherence not only across sectoral policies but also across levels of government. NDPs can help foster alignment across national, regional and local policies and promote synergies among economic, social and environmental objectives in order to ensure an integrated approach to achieve Agenda 2030 (OECD, forthcoming[139]; Soria Morales, 2018[137]; OECD, 2019[138]). Multilevel planning is important to promote co-ordinated actions across levels of government (OECD, 2019[138]). In LAC, the revival of development planning since the early 2000s has been accompanied by growing subnational engagement, as opposed to the more centralised and top-down approach of the 1960s (Sandoval, Sanhueza and Williner, 2015[140]). This trend also offers spaces for stakeholder engagement and participation in the formulation, implementation and evaluation of development planning (Naser, Williner and Sandoval, 2021[73]). In LAC, around 35 NDPs have included a public consultation (ECLAC, 2021[141]). Examples of participatory planning processes include Ecuador's National Decentralised System of Participatory Planning (OECD, forthcoming[135]), Guatemala's K'atun Nuestra Guatemala 2032 NDP (Sandoval, Sanhueza and Williner, 2015[140]) and the Plan Estatal de Desarrollo 2013-2033 of the state of Jalisco, Mexico (Meza Canales, Gómez-Álvarez and Gutiérrez Pulido, 2016[142]).

Conclusions

The COVID-19 crisis aggravated existing structural vulnerabilities in LAC in a context of unmet citizen aspirations, deepening distrust of public institutions and social discontent, as seen in social protests. The region needs to update its social contract. This chapter suggests what a renewed social contract in LAC could look like and how to implement it.

The building blocks of a post-pandemic social contract should revolve around two interconnected dimensions. It should be a transversal agreement across: i) socio-economic groups, accounting for differences in terms of income, gender, ethnicity and race, among others; ii) territories, recognising specific local needs and opportunities and bridging territorial divides; and iii) generations, ensuring that policy decisions balance the interests of current and future generations and promote intergenerational solidarity. At the same time, it should advance towards: i) resilient and sustainable productive strategies that prioritise the creation of quality and green jobs and embrace the digital transformation; ii) broader and more effective social protection systems that strengthen targeting mechanisms, support formalisation and address challenges related to pension reforms (Chapter 2); and iii) more sustainable financing for a development model that allows for fiscal reforms addressing revenue and expenditure and that seeks to strengthen public debt management. The intersection of these objectives shows how the social contract is underpinned by more concrete and specific social pacts in various policy domains that each country must adapt to its specific needs and goals.

Paying attention to the process, from policy design to implementation, remains of utmost importance to create fair, legitimate and stable pacts. Open and inclusive policy-making processes help develop policies that address the needs of society as a whole and can generate greater accountability. However, challenges may hamper consensus building. First, lack of media pluralism and social media filter bubbles can prevent a healthy and informed debate in society around important policy reforms. Second, party proliferation in the highly volatile LAC electoral context increases the risk of polarised political campaigns and hinders consensus building. Third, lack of confidence in political parties due to their inability to effect change and mediate between citizens and the state may result in civic disengagement. Fourth, putting together various stakeholders with different time horizons, incentives and power may make it difficult to find compromise. For these reasons, the following policy messages are meant to guide policy makers along the path towards a new social contract in LAC and help them navigate the complex political economy reform (Box 4.3).

Box 4.3. **Key policy messages**

Strengthening inclusive policy-making processes to build consensus

- Build consensus by way of a transversal agreement across socio-economic groups, territories and generations to advance towards key policy objectives, including resilient and sustainable productive strategies, broader and more effective social protection systems and a more sustainable model of financing for development.

- Ensure good governance and mutual trust between the government and citizens, as well as with civil society and the private sector, for a solid social contract.

- Enhance the role of participatory processes in all stages of the policy-making process. The ten OECD Guiding Principles to strengthen open and inclusive policy making shed light on the importance of strong commitment; citizens' right to information; clarity of the process; adequate time for consultations and participation; efforts to make the process as inclusive as possible; adequate financial, human and technical resources; co-ordination within and across levels of government, as well as with external networks; government accountability; evaluation; and active citizenship (OECD, 2009[71]).

- Ensure a stronger role for deliberative practices, which involve a randomly selected group of people who are broadly representative of a community, and spend significant time learning and collaborating to develop collective recommendations for policy makers on a specific issue. This is especially valuable when dealing with issues that are values-based, require trade-offs and demand long-term solutions (Cesnulaityte, 2021[76]; OECD, 2020[74]).

- Foster the role of media and digital technologies to improve transparency, participation and accountability:

  o Reinforce the proactive publication of open data about government work and actions. Strengthening open government data policies, taking into account data re-usability, is a key step to enabling greater transparency and accountability vis-à-vis citizens, as well as to stimulate civic engagement and social oversight in areas particularly susceptible to corruption.

  o Tackling media concentration and lowering barriers to entry for new media can help the creation of a healthy and informed debate in society thanks to the representation of diverse social, economic and political perspectives (Mendel, Castillejo and Gómez, 2017[84]).

  o Streamline the use of digital technologies to communicate about the results of government initiatives and to support inclusive debates and provide additional channels for citizen engagement and participation (e.g. video-conferencing, social platforms, online forums).

  o Support the development of solid data governance foundations to enable the efficient and trustworthy access to, sharing and use of data by public sector organisations and across sectors (e.g. G2B). These data governance foundations include the definition of data ethical frameworks in the public sector in connection to the development and implementation of AI policies and initiatives by public bodies.

Box 4.3. **Key policy messages** (*cont.*)

- Make the most of national strategies or National Development Plans (NDPs) to ensure that social pacts embrace a coherent, long-term vision focused on improving people's well-being and sustainability in all its dimensions (OECD, forthcoming[139]). Clear goals and indicators, a link with the national budget, and monitoring and evaluation mechanisms are key characteristics contributing to the effectiveness of NDPs (OECD et al., 2020[9]; OECD et al., 2019[2]).

Overcoming the barriers to policy reform and implementation

- Define a well-established sequencing and pace of reforms, where successful initial reforms can help increase support and facilitate the implementation of subsequent reforms.

- Reinforce the role of political parties and innovative mechanisms of political intermediation to channel social demands and avoid opportunities for unfounded discourses.

- Fight policy capture through a comprehensive approach (OECD, 2017[103]), including complementary strategies to:

  o Ensure transparency and access to information to facilitate participation and social oversight over the policy-making process.

  o Encourage stakeholder engagement in order to level the playing field and make it less prone to capture.

  o Promote the accountability of decision makers through key institutions, including supreme audit institutions, competition authorities and regulatory agencies.

  o Mainstream sound organisational integrity policies to help identify and mitigate the risk of policy capture.

  These policy actions are in line with the OECD-LAC Action Plan on Integrity and Anti-Corruption.

- Take into account the political economy of reform, including the transitional or distributional costs that may increase resistance to some policies. In particular, for successful implementation, it is important to count on complementary cushioning schemes for vulnerable population groups negatively affected, as well as on a strong commitment to enhance reform credibility and sound evidence-based analysis supporting the case for reform.

- Strengthen institutional capacities for the successful implementation of reforms. Among others:

  o Promote the independence of the judiciary and grant it adequate resources to exploit its function in order to preserve the rule of law and a functioning democracy.

  o Focus on merit-based recruitment and improvements in results-based management to ensure an efficient civil service.

  o Simplify administrative processes, adopt service design and delivery approaches and move towards a digital government to help the public administration improve and speed up its internal processes, and make its services more human-centric and efficient.

  o Strengthen the national entity in charge of the implementation and monitoring of the social pacts (e.g. centre of government) by providing higher strategic management, among other tools.

Notes

1. Typically, the participants' selection method involves a civic lottery which combines random selection with stratification to assemble a small, but representative group of people (OECD, 2020[74]).

2. Data are drawn from the 2018 OECD *Questionnaire on Public Integrity in Latin America* covering 12 countries. Respondents were predominantly senior officials in central government, supreme audit institutions and electoral commissions.

References

Acuerdo Nacional (2014), *Políticas de Estado*, Secretaría Ejecutiva del Acuerdo Nacional, Lima, Peru, www.acuerdonacional.pe/politicas-de-estado-del-acuerdo-nacional/politicas-de-estado %e2%80%8b/politicas-de-estado-castellano/. [69]

Acuña-Alfaro, J. and E. Sapienza (2021), *COVID-19 and the Social Contract in Latin America: Citizens views of national responses one year on*, United Nations Development Programme Latin America and the Caribbean, New York, http://www.latinamerica.undp.org/content/rblac/en/home/ blog/2021/covid-19-y-el-contrato-social-en-america-latina--visiones-de-la-.html. [41]

Alvarado, N. and R. Muggah (2018), *Crime and Violence: Obstacles to Development in Latin American and Caribbean Cities*, Inter-American Development Bank, Washington, DC, http://dx.doi.org/10.18235/ 0001440. [30]

Aristei, D. and C. Perugini (2014), "Speed and sequencing of transition reforms and income inequality: A panel data analysis", *The Review of Income and Wealth*, Vol. 60/3, http://dx.doi. org/10.1111/roiw.12090. [123]

Baccaro, L. and J. Galindo (2018), *Are Social Pacts Still Viable in Today's World of Work?*, International Labour Organization, Geneva, https://www.ilo.org/wcmsp5/groups/public/---ed_dialogue/--- dialogue/documents/publication/wcms_648000.pdf. [64]

Basto-Aguirre, N., P. Cerutti and S. Nieto-Parra (2020), *COVID-19 can widen educational gaps in Latin America: Some lessons for urgent policy action*, VOXLACEA, Bogotá, https://vox.lacea.org/?q=blog/ covid19_widen_educational_gaps. [51]

Bauhr, M. and M. Grimes (2014), "Indignation or resignation: The implications of transparency for societal accountability", *Governance: An international journal of policy, administration, and institutions*, Vol. 27/2, pp. 291-320, http://dx.doi.org/10.1111/gove.12033. [109]

BCN (2021), *Proceso Constituyente*, Biblioteca del Congreso Nacional de Chile, Santiago, www.bcn.cl/ procesoconstituyente. [78]

Berganza, J. et al. (2020), "The end of the demographic dividend in Latin America: Challenges for economic and social policies", *Economic Bulletin*, No. 1/2020, Banco de España, Bilboa, Spain, https://repositorio.bde.es/handle/123456789/11806. [66]

Billion, D. and C. Ventura (2020), "¿Por qué protesta tanta gente a la vez?", *Nueva Sociedad (NUSO)* No. 286, https://nuso.org/articulo/por-que-protesta-tanta-gente-la-vez/. [45]

Binmore, K. (1994), *Playing Fair: Game Theory and the Social Contract: Volume 1*, The MIT Press, Cambridge, MA, https://mitpress.mit.edu/books/game-theory-and-the-social-contract- volume-1. [61]

Brennen, S. et al. (2020), "Types, sources, and claims of COVID-19 misinformation", *Reuters Institute for the Study of Journalism*, https://reutersinstitute.politics.ox.ac.uk/types-sources-and-claims- covid-19-misinformation. [49]

Burdin, G. et al. (2020), "Was falling inequality in all Latin American countries a data-driven illusion? Income distribution and mobility patterns in Uruguay 2009-2016", *IZA Discussion Paper*, No. 13070, IZA – Institute of Labor Economics, Bonn, Germany, https://www.iza.org/publications/dp/ 13070/. [18]

Busso, M. and J. Messina (2020), *The Inequality Crisis: Latin America and the Caribbean at the Crossroads*, Inter-American Development Bank, Washington, DC, http://dx.doi.org/10.18235/0002629. [13]

Cabrera, M. (2011), "Los Pactos de la Moncloa: Acuerdos políticos frente a la crisis", *Historia y política: Ideas, procesos y movimientos sociales*, pp. 81-110, https://dialnet.unirioja.es/servlet/ articulo?codigo=3741463. [80]

Cabutto, C., S. Nieto-Parra and J. Vázquez-Zamora (2021), "A post-pandemic social contract for Latin America: the why, the what, the how", *Vox Lacea (blog)*, http://vox.lacea.org/?q=blog/ social_contract_latam. [163]

Caldera Sánchez, A., A. de Serres and N. Yashiro (2016), "Reforming in a difficult macroeconomic context: A review of the issues and recent literature", *OECD Economics Department Working Papers*, No. 1297, OECD Publishing, Paris, https://doi.org/10.1787/5jlzgj45b3q0-en. [117]

Cañete Alonso, R. (2018), *Captured Democracies: A Government for the Few*, Oxfam International, Oxford, UK, https://www.oxfam.org/fr/node/8359. [105]

Carpenter, D. and D. Moss (2014), *Preventing Regulatory Capture: Special Interest Influence and How to Limit It*, Cambridge University Press, New York, https://doi.org/10.1017/CBO9781139565875. [104]

Carreras, M. and I. Acácio (2019), *Electoral Volatility in Latin America*, Oxford Research Encyclopedia: Politics, Oxford, UK, https://doi.org/10.1093/acrefore/9780190228637.013.1684. [89]

CESIJ (2020), *Global Impunity Index 2020 (GII-2020)*, Center of Studies on Impunity and Justice, UDLAP Jenkins Graduate School, University of the Americas Puebla, Puebla, Mexico, http://www.udlap.mx/cesij. [130]

CESIJ (2017), *Global Impunity Index 2017 (GII-2017)*, Center of Studies on Impunity and Justice, UDLAP Jenkins Graduate School, University of the Americas Puebla, Puebla, Mexico, http://www.udlap.mx/cesij. [131]

Cesnulaityte, I. (2021), "A deliberative wave for development?", *OECD Development Matters blog*, https://oecd-development-matters.org/2021/03/16/a-deliberative-wave-for-development/. [76]

Chioda, L. (2017), *Stop the Violence in Latin America: A Look at Prevention from Cradle to Adulthood*, World Bank, Washington, DC, https://openknowledge.worldbank.org/handle/10986/25920. [38]

Ciminelli, G. et al. (2019), "The political costs of reforms: Fear or reality?", *IMF Staff Discussion Note SDN/19/0*, https://www.imf.org/en/Publications/Staff-Discussion-Notes/Issues/2019/10/17/The-Political-Costs-of-Reforms-Fear-or-Reality-48735. [124]

CNTS (2020), *Domestic Conflict Event Database*, Cross-National Time-Series Data Archive, Databanks International, Jerusalem, http://www.cntsdata.com. [19]

Cohen, M. (2018), *Latin American Presidential and Legislative Elections (LAPALE) dataset*, http://www.molliecohen.com/data.html. [102]

Coppedge, M. et al. (2021), *V-Dem 2020 Dataset v11.1*, Varieties of Democracy Institute, University of Gothenburg, Gothenburg, Sweden, https://doi.org/10.23696/vdemds21. [85]

Corbacho, A. et al. (2016), "Corruption as a Self-Fulfilling Prophecy: Evidence from a Survey Experiment in Costa Rica", *American Journal of Political Science*, Vol. 60/4, pp. 1077-1092, http://www.jstor.org/stable/24877473. [110]

Cosano, P. (2019), "El Nuevo Contrato Social desde la perspectiva de la Ciencia Política", *Información Comercial Española (ICE): Revista de economía*, Vol. 911, https://doi.org/10.32796/ice.2019.911.6935. [54]

Croissant, A. and W. Merkel (2004), *Political Party Formation in Presidential and Parliamentary Systems*, Institute for Political Science of the University of Heidelberg, Heidelberg, Germany, https://library.fes.de/pdf-files/bueros/philippinen/50072.pdf. [100]

Cruz, J. and G. Kloppe-Santamaría (2019), "Determinants of support for extralegal violence in Latin America and the Caribbean", *Latin American Research Review*, Vol. 54/1, pp. 50-68, http://doi.org/10.25222/larr.212. [37]

Cyr, J. and N. Liendo (2020), *Party Change and Adaptation in Latin America*, Oxford Research Encyclopedia: Politics, Oxford, UK, http://dx.doi.org/10.1093/acrefore/9780190228637.013.1687. [90]

D'Agostino, F. (1996), *Free Public Reason: Making it Up as We Go*, Oxford University Press, Oxford, UK, https://philpapers.org/rec/DAGFPR. [62]

Dayton-Johnson, J., J. Londoño and S. Nieto Parra (2011), "The process of reform in Latin America: A review essay", *OECD Development Centre Working Papers*, No. 304, OECD Publishing, Paris, https://doi.org/10.1787/5kg3mkvfcjxv-en. [70]

DeShazo, P. and J. Vargas (2006), *Judicial Reform in Latin America: An Assessment*, Center for Strategic and International Studies (CSIS) and Justice Studies Center of the Americas (JSCA), Washington D.C. and Santiago, https://biblioteca.cejamericas.org/bitstream/handle/2015/5190/JudicialReforminLatinAmericaENGLISH_CEJA.pdf?sequence=1&isAllowed=y. [129]

ECLAC (2021), *Observatorio Regional de Planificación para el Desarrollo*, Instituto Latinoamericano de Planificación Económica y Social, Santiago, https://observatorioplanificacion.cepal.org/es/planning-development. [141]

ECLAC (2021), *Social Panorama of Latin America 2020*, Economic Commission for Latin America and the Caribbean, Santiago, https://www.cepal.org/en/publications/46688-social-panorama-latin-america-2020. [5]

ECLAC (2020), "Pactos políticos y sociales para la igualdad y el desarrollo sostenible en América Latina y el Caribe en la recuperación pos-COVID-19", *Informe Especial COVID-19*, No. 8, Economic Commission for Latin America and the Caribbean, Santiago, https://www.cepal.org/es/publicaciones/46102-pactos-politicos-sociales-la-igualdad-desarrollo-sostenible-america-latina [3]

ECLAC/OEI (2020), *Educación, juventud y trabajo: habilidades y competencias*, Economic Commission for Latin America and the Caribbean/Organization of Ibero-American States for Education, Science and Culture, Santiago, https://repositorio.cepal.org/handle/11362/46066. [67]

Estefan, F., G. Hadid and R. Georges (2020), "Measuring perceptions of democracy in Latin America during COVID-19", *Luminate blog*, https://luminategroup.com/posts/blog/measuring-perceptions-of-democracy-in-latin-america-during-covid-19. [6]

EurWork (2019), *Social Pact*, European Observatory of Working Life, Dublin, https://www.eurofound.europa.eu/observatories/eurwork/industrial-relations-dictionary/social-pact. [63]

Flores, I. et al. (2020), "Top incomes in Chile: A historical perspective on income inequality, 1964-2017", *Review of Income and Wealth*, Vol. 66, pp. 850-874, https://doi.org/10.1111/roiw.12441. [17]

Gallup (2021), *Gallup World Poll (database)*, Gallup Inc., Washington, DC, https://ga.gallup.com. [7]

Gastil, J. and P. Levine (eds.) (2005), *The Deliberative Democracy Handbook: Strategies for Effective Civic Engagement in the Twenty-First Century*, Jossey-Bass, San Francisco, CA, http://www.wiley.com/en-us/The+Deliberative+Democracy+Handbook%3A+Strategies+for+Effective+Civic+Engagement+in+the+Twenty+First+Century-p-9781118105108. [75]

Gerring, J. (2005), "Minor Parties in Plurality Electoral Systems", *Party Politics*, Vol. 11/1, pp. 79-107, https://doi.org/10.1177/1354068805048474. [96]

Global Witness (2020), *Defending Tomorrow*, Global Witness, London, www.globalwitness.org/en/campaigns/environmental-activists/defending-tomorrow/. [165]

González, S. (2020), "Testing the evidence, how good are public sector responsiveness measures and how to improve them?", OECD *Working Papers on Public Governance*, No. 38, OECD Publishing, Paris, https://doi.org/10.1787/c1b10334-en. [147]

Granda Revilla, G. (2018), "CSR in Europe: A new micro-social contract?", *Ramon Llull Journal of Applied Ethics* Iss. 9, pp. 75-94, https://search.proquest.com/openview/197477ab29a86c82217732da7230928c/1?cbl=2035658&pq-origsite=gscholar. [56]

Guriev, S. (2018), "Fairness and support for the reforms: Lessons from the transition economies", *SUERF Policy Note*, No. 24, European Money and Finance Forum, Vienna, http://www.suerf.org/docx/f_c5a4e7e6882845ea7bb4d9462868219b_1993_suerf.pdf. [122]

Hilbink, E. and W. Prillaman (2002), "The judiciary and democratic decay in Latin America: Declining confidence in the rule of law", *Latin American Politics and Society*, Vol. 44/1, http://dx.doi.org/10.2307/3177118. [128]

Hirschman, A. and M. Rothschild (1973), "The changing tolerance for income inequality in the course of economic development", *The Quarterly Journal of Economics*, Vol. 87/4, pp. 544-566, http://dx.doi.org/doi:10.2307/1882024. [22]

IDB (2020), *Emerging from the Pandemic Tunnel with Faster Growth: A Strategy for a New Social Compact in Latin America and the Caribbean*, Inter-American Development Bank, Washington, DC, http://dx.doi.org/10.18235/0002473. [126]

IDB/OAS (2020), *2020 Cybersecurity Report: Risks, Progress, and the Way Forward in Latin America and the Caribbean*, Inter-American Development Bank/Organization of American States, Washington, DC, http://dx.doi.org/10.18235/0002513. [136]

Imbusch, P., M. Misse and F. Carrión (2011), "Violence research in Latin America and the Caribbean: A literature review", *International Journal of Conflict and Violence*, Vol. 5/1, https://doi.org/10.4119/ijcv-2851. [36]

International IDEA (2020), *Political Finance Database (database)*, International Institute for Democracy and Electoral Assistance, Stockholm, https://www.idea.int/data-tools/data/political-finance-database. [106]

Ipsos (2021), *Percepciones de los líderes de opinión de Latinoamérica a un año y medio de pandemia*, www.ipsos.com/es-pe/percepciones-de-los-lideres-de-opinion-de-latinoamerica-un-ano-y-medio-de-pandemia. [8]

Ipsos (2020), *Social Cohesion in the Pandemic Age: A Global Perspective*, October 2020, Ipsos, Paris, https://www.ipsos.com/sites/default/files/ct/news/documents/2020-10/report-social-cohesion-and-pandemic-2020.pdf. [26]

Ipsos (2019), *La Crisis enAmérica Latina: Encuesta a líderes de opinión de Latinoamérica*, Ipsos, Paris, https://www.ipsos.com/sites/default/files/ct/news/documents/2019-12/la_crisis_en_america_latina.pdf. [11]

Jaitman, L. et al. (2017), *The Costs of Crime and Violence: New Evidence and Insights in Latin America and the Caribbean*, Inter-American Development Bank, Washington, DC, http://dx.doi.org/10.18235/0000615. [33]

Jones, M. (2005), *The Role of Parties and Party Systems in the Policymaking Process*, Paper prepared for Inter-American Development Bank Workshop on State Reform, Public Policies and Policy Making Processes, 28 February-2 March 2005, Washington, DC, https://citeseerx.ist.psu.edu/viewdoc/download?doi=10.1.1.542.1866&rep=rep1&type=pdf. [92]

Kaplan, S. (2017), *Inclusive Social Contracts in Fragile State in Transition: Strengthening the Building Blocks of Success*, Institute for Integrated Transitions, Barcelona, Spain, https://ifit-transitions.org/publications/inclusive-social-contracts-in-fragile-states-in-transition-strengthening-the-building-blocks-of-success/. [57]

Kritzinger, S. et al. (2021), "'Rally round the flag': the COVID-19 crisis and trust in the national government", *West European Politics*, Vol. 44/5-6, pp. 1205-1231, 10.1080/01402382.2021.1925017. [143]

Laakso, M. and R. Taagepera (1979), "The 'effective' number of parties: A measure with application to West Europe", *Comparative Political Studies*, Vol. 12/1, pp. 3-27, http://dx.doi.org/10.1177/001041407901200101. [91]

LabCDMX (2016), *Constitución CDMX*, Mexico City, Mexico, https://labcd.mx/experimentos/constitucion-cdmx/. [152]

Laroze, D. (2019), "Party collapse and new party entry", *Party Politics*, Vol. 25/4, pp. 559-568, https://doi.org/10.1177/1354068817741286. [95]

Larraín, G. (2020), *The Stability of the Social Contract in Chile: A paradoxical social explosion and its institutional responses*, OECD presentation, Facultad de Economía y Negocios de la Universidad de Chile, Santiago. [4]

Latinobarómetro (2021), *Latinobarómetro Survey 2020 (database)*, Corporación Latinobarómetro, Santiago, http://www.latinobarometro.org/latOnline.jsp. [20]

Lazer, D. et al. (2018), "The science of fake news", *Science*, Vol. 359/6380, pp. 1094-1096, https://science.sciencemag.org/content/359/6380/1094.full. [48]

Lloyd's Register Foundation (2019), *Lloyd's Register Foundation World Risk Poll (database)*, Lloyd's Register Foundation, London, https://wrp.lrfoundation.org.uk/explore-the-poll/the-majority-of-people-around-the-world-are-concerned-about-climate-change/. [52]

Lloyd's Register Foundation/Gallup (2019), *The Lloyd's Register Foundation World Risk Poll: Full report and analysis of the 2019 poll*, Lloyd's Register Foundation/Gallup Inc., London/Washington, DC, https://wrp.lrfoundation.org.uk/LRF_WorldRiskReport_Book.pdf. [29]

Loewe, M., T. Zintl and A. Houdret (2020), "The social contract as a tool of analysis: Introduction to the special issue on 'Framing the evolution of new social contracts in Middle Eastern and North African countries'", *World Development*, https://www.die-gdi.de/en/others-publications/article/the-social-contract-as-a-tool-of-analysis-introduction-to-the-special-issue-on-framing-the-evolution-of-new-social-contracts-in-middle-eastern-and-north-african-countries/. [59]

López-Calva, L. (2021), "COVID-19 and Wealth at the Top: More and Wealthier Billionaires After the Crisis in LAC", *Director's Blog: Graph for Thought*, http://www.latinamerica.undp.org/content/rblac/en/home/presscenter/director-s-graph-for-thought/covid-19-and-wealth-at-the-top--more-and-wealthier-billionaires-.html. [14]

López-Calva, L. (2020), *Reflexiones sobre papel de fallas de gobernanza en disturbios sociales en América Latina*, Inter Press Service, Panama, http://www.ipsnoticias.net/2020/03/reflexiones-papel-fallas-gobernanza-disturbios-sociales-america-latina/. [21]

López-Calva, L. (2020), "Where the pandemic meets the infodemic: The challenge of misinformation in the fight against COVID-19 in LAC", *Director's Blog: Graph for Thought*, http://www.latinamerica.undp.org/content/rblac/en/home/presscenter/director-s-graph-for-thought/where-the-pandemic-meets-the-infodemic--challenge-of-misinformat.html. [50]

Lupu, N. (2016), *Party Brands in Crisis: Partisanship, brand dilution, and the breakdown of political parties in Latin America*, Cambridge University Press, New York, http://www.cambridge.org/core/books/party-brands-in-crisis/FF3A9C59D329AE74A5712254DF2C5BAF. [98]

Lustig, N. (2020), "The 'missing rich' in household surveys: causes and correction approaches", *Society for the Study of Economic Inequality Working Paper Series*, No. 2020-520, Society for the Study of Economic Inequality, London, http://www.ecineq.org/milano/WP/ECINEQ2020-520.pdf. [15]

Mainwaring, S. (ed.) (2018), *Party Systems in Latin America: Institutionalization, Decay, and Collapse*, Cambridge University Press, Cambridge, UK, http://dx.doi.org/doi:10.1017/9781316798553.　[94]

Mainwaring, S. (1997), "Presidentialism, multiparty systems, and democracy: The difficult equation", *Helen Kellogg Institute for International Studies, University of Notre Dame, Notre Dame, IN*, Vol. Working Paper - 144, https://kellogg.nd.edu/documents/1338.　[99]

Malamud, C. (2018), "The political expansion of evangelical churches in Latin America", *Elcano Royal Institute*, http://www.realinstitutoelcano.org/wps/portal/rielcano_en/contenido?WCM_GLOBAL_CONTEXT=/elcano/elcano_in/zonas_in/latin+america/ari131-2018-malamud-political-expansion-evangelical-churches-latin-america.　[44]

Malamud, C. and R. Núñez (2018), "The anger vote: The new (or not so new) Latin American electoral phenomenon", *Elcano Royal Institute*, http://www.realinstitutoelcano.org/wps/portal/rielcano_en/contenido?WCM_GLOBAL_CONTEXT=/elcano/elcano_in/zonas_in/ari107-2018-malamud-nunez-anger-vote-latin-american-electoral-phenomenon.　[43]

Manyika, J. et al. (2020), *The Social Contract in the 21st Century: Outcomes so far for Workers, Consumers and Savers in Advanced Economies*, McKinsey Global Institute, http://www.mckinsey.com/industries/public-and-social-sector/our-insights/the-social-contract-in-the-21st-century#.　[55]

Martínez Franzoni, J. and D. Sánchez-Ancochea (2020), *Pactos sociales al servicio del bienestar en América Latina y el Caribe: ¿qué son y qué papel tienen en tiempos de crisis?*, Economic Commission for Latin America and the Caribbean, Santiago, http://www.cepal.org/es/publicaciones/46527-pactos-sociales-al-servicio-bienestar-america-latina-caribe-que-son-que-papel.　[65]

Marwick, A. and R. Lewis (2017), *Media Manipulation and Disinformation Online*, Data & Society Research Institute, New York, https://datasociety.net/library/media-manipulation-and-disinfo-online.　[47]

Matasick, C., C. Alfonsi and A. Bellantoni (2020), "Governance responses to disinformation: How open government principles can inform policy options", *OECD Working Papers on Public Governance*, No. 39, OECD Publishing, Paris, https://doi.org/10.1787/d6237c85-en.　[154]

Mattes, R. and A. Moreno (2018), *Social and Political Trust in Developing Countries: Sub-Saharan Africa and Latin America*, Oxford University Press, Oxford, UK, http://dx.doi.org/10.1093/oxfordhb/9780190274801.013.10.　[27]

Maydeu-Olivares, S. (2016), *Violence: Central America's Achilles Heel*, Barcelona Centre for International Affairs, Barcelona, Spain, http://www.cidob.org/ca/publicacions/series_de_publicacio/notes_internacionals/n_142_la_violencia_el_talon_de_aquiles_de_centroamerica/violence_central_america_s_achilles_heel.　[35]

Mendel, T., Á. Castillejo and G. Gómez (2017), *Concentration of Media Ownership and Freedom of Expression: Global Standards and Implications for the Americas*, UNESCO Montevideo Office/Regional Bureau for Science in Latin America and the Caribbean, Montevideo, https://unesdoc.unesco.org/ark:/48223/pf0000248091.　[84]

Meza Canales, O., D. Gómez-Álvarez and H. Gutiérrez Pulido (2016), *La Planificación Participativa Desde lo Subnacional: El Caso de Jalisco, México*, United Nations Development Programme/State of Jalisco, Mexico, http://www.latinamerica.undp.org/content/rblac/es/home/library/democratic_governance/la-planificacion-participativa-desde-lo-subnacional--el-caso-de-.html.　[142]

Moraes, J. (2015), "The electoral basis of ideological polarization in Latin America", *Working Paper*, No. 403, Kellogg Institute for International Studies, University of Notre Dame, Notre Dame, IN, https://kellogg.nd.edu/documents/1721.　[88]

Morgan, M. (2018), "Falling inequality beneath extreme and persistent concentration: New evidence for Brazil combining national accounts, surveys and fiscal data, 2001-2015", *WID.world Working Paper Series*, No. 2017/12, World Inequality Database, https://wid.world/document/extreme-persistent-inequality-new-evidence-brazil-combining-national-accounts-surveys-fiscal-data-2001-2015-wid-world-working-paper-201712/.　[16]

Murillo, M. (2020), *Coming next to Latin America: Even more political fragmentation*, Americas Quarterly, New York, http://www.americasquarterly.org/article/coming-next-to-latin-america-even-more-political-fragmentation/.　[97]

Naser, A., A. Williner and C. Sandoval (2021), *Participación Ciudadana en los Asuntos Públicos: Un Elemento Estratégico para la Agenda 2030 y el Gobierno Abierto*, Economic Commission for Latin America and the Caribbean, Santiago, https://repositorio.cepal.org/bitstream/handle/11362/46645/1/S2000907_es.pdf.　[73]

Nsouli, S., M. Rached and N. Funke (2005), "The speed of adjustment and the sequencing of economic reforms: Issues and guidelines for policymakers", *International Journal of Social Economics*, Vol. 32/9, pp. 740-766, https://doi.org/10.1108/03068290510612566.　[121]

OECD (2021), *Guía sobre Gobierno Abierto para Funcionarios Públicos Peruanos*, OECD Publishing, Paris, www.oecd.org/gov/open-government/guia-de-la-ocde-sobre-gobierno-abierto-para-funcionarios-publicos-peruanos.htm. [151]

OECD (2021), *Government at a Glance 2021*, OECD Publishing, Paris, https://doi.org/10.1787/1c258f55-en. [157]

OECD (2021), *Good Practice Principles for Data Ethics in the Public Sector*, OECD Publishing, Paris, www.oecd.org/gov/digital-government/good-practice-principles-for-data-ethics-in-the-public-sector.pdf. [162]

OECD (2021), *Lobbying in the 21st Century: Transparency, Integrity and Access*, OECD Publishing, Paris, https://dx.doi.org/10.1787/c6d8eff8-en. [107]

OECD (2021), *Perspectives on Global Development 2021: From Protest to Progress?*, OECD Publishing, Paris, https://dx.doi.org/10.1787/405e4c32-en. [87]

OECD (2020), "Inclusive social dialogue and citizen engagement to enhance social cohesion and ownership of recovery measures", *Informality and Social Inclusion in Times of Covid-19*, OECD-LAC Virtual Social Inclusion Ministerial Summit, OECD Publishing, Paris, www.oecd.org/latin-america/events/lac-ministerial-on-social-inclusion/2020-OECD-LAC-Ministerial-Inclusive-social-dialogue-and-citizen-engagement-to-enhance-social-cohesion-background-note.pdf. [148]

OECD (2020), "Digital Government Index: 2019 results", *OECD Public Governance Policy Papers*, No. 03, OECD Publishing, Paris, https://doi.org/10.1787/4de9f5bb-en. [155]

OECD (2020), *Digital Government in Chile – Improving Public Service Design and Delivery*, OECD Digital Government Studies, OECD Publishing, Paris, https://doi.org/10.1787/b94582e8-en. [156]

OECD (2020), *Integrating Responsible Business Conduct in Public Procurement*, OECD Publishing, Paris, https://doi.org/10.1787/02682b01-en. [159]

OECD (2020), "Public procurement and infrastructure governance: Initial policy responses to the coronavirus (Covid-19) crisis", *OECD Policy Responses to Coronavirus (COVID-19)*, OECD Publishing, Paris, www.oecd.org/coronavirus/policy-responses/public-procurement-and-infrastructure-governance-initial-policy-responses-to-the-coronavirus-covid-19-crisis-c0ab0a96/. [160]

OECD (2020), "Digital Government Index: 2019 results", *OECD Public Governance Policy Papers*, No. 03, OECD Publishing, Paris, https://doi.org/10.1787/4de9f5bb-en. [161]

OECD (2020), *COVID-19 in Latin America and the Caribbean: Regional socio-economic implications and policy priorities, Updated 8 December 2020*, OECD Publishing, Paris, http://www.oecd.org/coronavirus/policy-responses/covid-19-in-latin-america-and-the-caribbean-regional-socio-economic-implications-and-policy-priorities-93a64fde/. [1]

OECD (2020), *Government at a Glance: Latin America and the Caribbean 2020*, OECD Publishing, Paris, https://dx.doi.org/10.1787/13130fbb-en. [108]

OECD (2020), *Innovative Citizen Participation and New Democratic Institutions: Catching the Deliberative Wave*, OECD Publishing, Paris, https://dx.doi.org/10.1787/339306da-en. [74]

OECD (2020), "The OECD Digital Government Policy Framework: Six dimensions of a Digital Government", *OECD Public Governance Policy Papers*, No. 02, OECD Publishing, Paris, https://dx.doi.org/10.1787/f64fed2a-en. [133]

OECD (2020), *Governance for Youth, Trust and Intergenerational Justice: Fit for All Generations?*, OECD Public Governance Reviews, OECD Publishing, Paris, https://doi.org/10.1787/c3e5cb8a-en. [145]

OECD (2019), "Engaging Citizens for Sustainable Development in the Ibero-American Region", *Joint Policy Note*, September 2019, OECD Development Communication Network/Ibero-American General Secretariat, http://www.oecd.org/dev/pgd/Engaging Citizens for Sustainable Development in IberoAmerica 0919.pdf. [72]

OECD (2019), *International collaboration to end tax avoidance*, OECD Publishing, Paris, http://www.oecd.org/tax/beps/. [68]

OECD (2019), "Recommendation of the Council on Policy Coherence for Sustainable Development (PCSD)", *OECD/LEGAL/0381*, https://legalinstruments.oecd.org/en/instruments/OECD-LEGAL-0381. [138]

OECD (2019), *The Path to Becoming a Data-Driven Public Sector*, OECD Digital Government Studies, OECD Publishing, Paris, https://dx.doi.org/10.1787/059814a7-en. [134]

OECD (2018), *Behavioural Insights for Public Integrity: Harnessing the Human Factor to Counter Corruption*, OECD Public Governance Reviews, OECD Publishing, Paris, https://dx.doi.org/10.1787/9789264297067-en. [112]

OECD (2018), *Good Jobs for All in a Changing World of Work: The OECD Jobs Strategy*, OECD Publishing, Paris, https://doi.org/10.1787/9789264308817-en. [116]

OECD (2017), *Compendium of Good Practices on the Use of Open Data for Anti-corruption: Towards data-driven public sector integrity and civic auditing*, OECD Publishing, Paris, http://www.oecd.org/gov/digital-government/g20-oecd-compendium.pdf. [132]

OECD (2017), *Preventing Policy Capture: Integrity in Public Decision Making*, OECD Public Governance Reviews, OECD Publishing, Paris, https://dx.doi.org/10.1787/9789264065239-en. [103]

OECD (2017), *Trust and Public Policy: How Better Governance Can Help Rebuild Public Trust*, OECD Public Governance Reviews, OECD Publishing, Paris, https://doi.org/10.1787/9789264268920-en. [144]

OECD (2017), *Recommendation of the Council on Open Government*, OECD/LEGAL/0438, https://legalinstruments.oecd.org/en/instruments/OECD-LEGAL-0438. [149]

OECD (2016), *Multi-dimensional Review of Peru: Volume 2. In-depth Analysis and Recommendations*, OECD Development Pathways, OECD Publishing, Paris, https://doi.org/10.1787/9789264264670-en. [119]

OECD (2016), *Pilot Database on Stakeholder Engagement Practices in Regulatory Policy*, OECD Publishing, Paris, http://www.oecd.org/gov/regulatory-policy/pilot-database-on-stakeholder-engagement-practices.htm. [79]

OECD (2010), *Making Reform Happen: Lessons from OECD Countries*, OECD Publishing, Paris, https://dx.doi.org/10.1787/9789264086296-en. [118]

OECD (2009), *Focus on Citizens: Public Engagement for Better Policy and Services*, OECD Studies on Public Engagement, OECD Publishing, Paris, https://dx.doi.org/10.1787/9789264048874-en. [71]

OECD (2001), *Citizens as Partners: OECD Handbook on Information, Consultation and Public Participation in Policy-Making*, OECD Publishing, Paris, https://doi.org/10.1787/9789264195578-en. [150]

OECD (forthcoming), *How's Life in Latin America? Measuring well-being for policymaking*, OECD Publishing, Paris. [139]

OECD (forthcoming), *Public Communication: The Global Context and the Way Forward*, OECD Publishing, Paris. [158]

OECD (forthcoming), *Multi-Dimensional Country Review of Ecuador: Phase I*, OECD Publishing, Paris. [135]

OECD and The GovLab (2021), *Open data in action: initiatives during the initial stage of the COVID-19 pandemic*, OECD Publishing, Paris, www.oecd.org/gov/digital-government/open-data-in-action-initiatives-during-the-initial-stage-of-the-covid-19-pandemic.pdf. [153]

OECD DevCom (2020), *SDG Communicator: Toolkit*, OECD Development Communication Network, Paris, https://sdg-communicator.org/toolkit/. [120]

OECD et al. (2020), *Latin American Economic Outlook 2020: Digital Transformation for Building Back Better*, OECD Publishing, Paris, https://dx.doi.org/10.1787/e6e864fb-en. [9]

OECD et al. (2019), *Latin American Economic Outlook 2019: Development in Transition*, OECD Publishing, Paris, https://dx.doi.org/10.1787/g2g9ff18-en. [2]

Open Government Partnership (2021), *Members*, Open Government Partnership, New York, http://www.opengovpartnership.org/our-members. [77]

openDemocracy (2020), *2019: Protests and disruptive changes in Latin America*, openDemocracy, London, http://www.opendemocracy.net/en/democraciaabierta/2019-movilizaciones-ciudadanas-y-cambios-disruptivos-en-am%C3%A9rica-latina-en/. [39]

Peiffer, C. (2018), "Message Received? Experimental Findings on How Messages about Corruption Shape Perceptions", *British Journal of Political Science*, Vol. 50/3, pp. 1207–1215, https://doi.org/10.1017/S0007123418000108. [111]

Prats, M. and A. Meunier (2021), "Political efficacy and participation: An empirical analysis in European countries", *OECD Working Papers on Public Governance*, No. 46, OECD Publishing, Paris, https://doi.org/10.1787/4548cad8-en. [146]

Raderstorf, B. et al. (2017), "Beneath the Violence: How insecurity shapes daily life and emigration in Central America", *Rule of Law Working Paper*, Latin America Public Opinion Project/The Inter-American Dialogue, Washington, DC, http://www.thedialogue.org/analysis/beneath-the-violence-how-insecurity-shapes-daily-life-and-emigration-in-central-america/. [34]

Ranciere, R. and A. Tornell (2015), "Why do reforms occur in crises times?", *Working Paper*, Economics Department, University of California at Los Angeles, Los Angeles, CA, http://www.econ.ucla.edu/people/papers/Tornell/Tornell702.pdf. [125]

Reporters without Borders (2021), *2021 World Press Freedom Index (database)*, Reporters without Borders, Paris, https://rsf.org/en/ranking. [86]

Reporters without Borders (2019), "Latin American media: Under control of families, economic and political elites", *Media Ownership Monitor América Latina*, https://rsf.org/en/news/latin-american-media-under-control-families-economic-and-political-elites. [82]

Roberts, K. and E. Wibbels (1999), "Party systems and electoral volatility in Latin America: A test of economic, institutional, and structural explanations", *The American Political Science Review*, Vol. 93/3, pp. 575-590, http://dx.doi.org/10.2307/2585575. [101]

Rodríguez, M. and E. Zechmeister (2018), *Media Pluralism, Public Trust, and Democracy: New Evidence from Latin America and the Caribbean*, Center for International Media Assistance National Endowment for Democracy, Washington, DC, http://www.cima.ned.org/publication/media-pluralism-public-trust-democracy-new-evidence-latin-america-caribbean/. [81]

Rodrik, D. (1996), "Understanding Economic Policy Reform", *Journal of Economic Literature*, Vol. 34/1, pp. 9-41, http://www.jstor.org/stable/2729408. [114]

Rosario University (2021), *Panorama Regional de la Tercera Medición de la Gran Encuesta Nacional sobre Jóvenes*, Cifras y Conceptos, Rosario University, El Tiempo, http://www.urosario.edu.co/Periodico-NovaEtVetera/Documentos/079-21-Presentacion-de-resultados-finales_V6/. [10]

Sandoval, C., A. Sanhueza and A. Williner (2015), *La Planificación Participativa para Lograr un Cambio Estructural con Igualdad: Las estrategias de participación ciudadana en los procesos de planificación multiescalar*, Economic Commission for Latin America and the Caribbean, Santiago, http://www.cepal.org/sites/default/files/publication/files/39055/S1501278_es.pdf. [140]

Segura, M. and S. Waisbord (2016), *Media Movements: Civil Society and Media Policy Reform in Latin America*, Zed Books, London, http://www.bloomsbury.com/uk/media-movements-9781783604623. [83]

Shafik, M. (2021), "What We Owe Each Other: A New Social Contract for a Better Society", *The Forum Network*, OECD Publishing, Paris, www.oecd-forum.org/posts/what-we-owe-each-other-a-new-social-contract-for-a-better-society-by-minouche-shafik. [53]

Soria Morales, E. (2018), "Why is policy coherence essential for achieving the 2030 Agenda?", *UN System Staff College blog*, http://www.unssc.org/news-and-insights/blog/why-policy-coherence-essential-achieving-2030-agenda/. [137]

Spiller, P., E. Stein and M. Tommasi (2008), "Chapter 1. Political Institutions, Policymaking, and Policy: An Introduction", *Policymaking in Latin America: How politics shapes policies*, Inter-American Development Bank, Washington, DC, https://publications.iadb.org/publications/english/document/Policymaking-in-Latin-America-How-Politics-Shapes-Policies.pdf. [113]

Staats, J., S. Bowler and J. Hiskey (2008), "Measuring Judicial Performance in Latin America", *Latin American Politics and Society*, Vol. 47/4, pp. 77-106, https://doi.org/10.1111/j.1548-2456.2005.tb00329.x. [127]

Tompson, W. (2009), *The Political Economy of Reform: Lessons from Pensions, Product Markets and Labour Markets in Ten OECD Countries*, OECD Publishing, Paris, https://dx.doi.org/10.1787/9789264073111-en. [25]

Transparency International (2021), *Corruption Perceptions Index 2020: Americas*, Transparency International, Berlin, http://www.transparency.org/en/news/cpi-2020-americas. [23]

Transparency International (2019), *Global Corruption Barometer Latin America and the Caribbean 2019: Citizen's views and experiences of corruption*, Transparency International, Berlin, https://images.transparencycdn.org/images/2019_GCB_LatinAmerica_Caribbean_Full_Report_200409_091428.pdf. [24]

UNDP (2018), *Forging Resilient Social Contracts: Preventing Violent Conflict and Sustaining Peace*, United Nations Development Programme, Oslo Governance Centre, Oslo, http://www.undp.org/content/undp/en/home/librarypage/democratic-governance/oslo_governance_centre/forging-resilient-social-contracts--preventing-violent-conflict-.html. [58]

UNODC (2020), *Victims of intentional homicide, 1990-2018 (database)*, United Nations Office on Drugs and Crimes, Vienna, https://dataunodc.un.org/data/homicide/Homicide%20victims%20worldwide. [32]

Uslaner, E. (2002), *The Moral Foundations of Trust*, Cambridge University Press, Cambridge, UK, http://dx.doi.org/10.1017/CBO9780511614934. [28]

Vlerick, M. (2019), "The evolution of social contracts", *Journal of Social Ontology*, Vol. 5/2, pp. 181-203, https://doi.org/10.1515/jso-2019-0041. [60]

Wardle, C. and H. Derakhshan (2017), *Information Disorder: Toward an interdisciplinary framework for research and policy making*, Council of Europe, Strasbourg, France, https://rm.coe.int/information-disorder-toward-an-interdisciplinary-framework-for-researc/168076277c. [46]

Williamson, J. (ed.) (1994), *The political economy of policy reform*, Institute for International Economics, Washington, DC, http://www.piie.com/bookstore/political-economy-policy-reform. [115]

Wills-Otero, L. (2020), *Party Systems in Latin America*, Oxford University Press, Oxford, UK, https://oxfordre.com/politics/view/10.1093/acrefore/9780190228637.001.0001/acrefore-9780190228637-e-1683. [93]

World Bank (2020), *World Development Indicators (database)*, World Bank, Washington, DC, https://data.worldbank.org/indicator/VC.IHR.PSRC.P5. [31]

World Inequality Database (2020), *World Inequality Database*, https://wid.world/. [12]

Zovatto, D. (2020), "The rapidly deteriorating quality of democracy in Latin America", *The Brookings Institution*, http://www.brookings.edu/blog/order-from-chaos/2020/02/28/the-rapidly-deteriorating-quality-of-democracy-in-latin-america/. [40]

Zovatto, D. (2019), "Latin America: political change in volatile and uncertain times", *International Institute for Democracy and Electoral Assistance*, http://www.idea.int/news-media/news/latin-america-political-change-volatile-and-uncertain-times. [42]

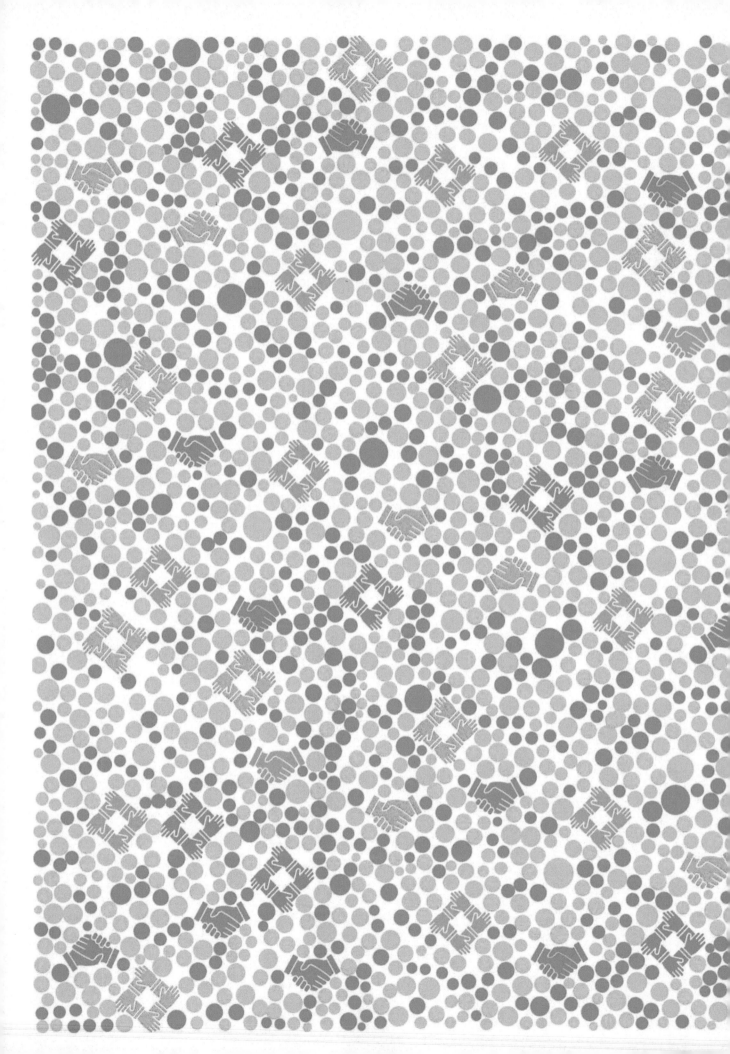

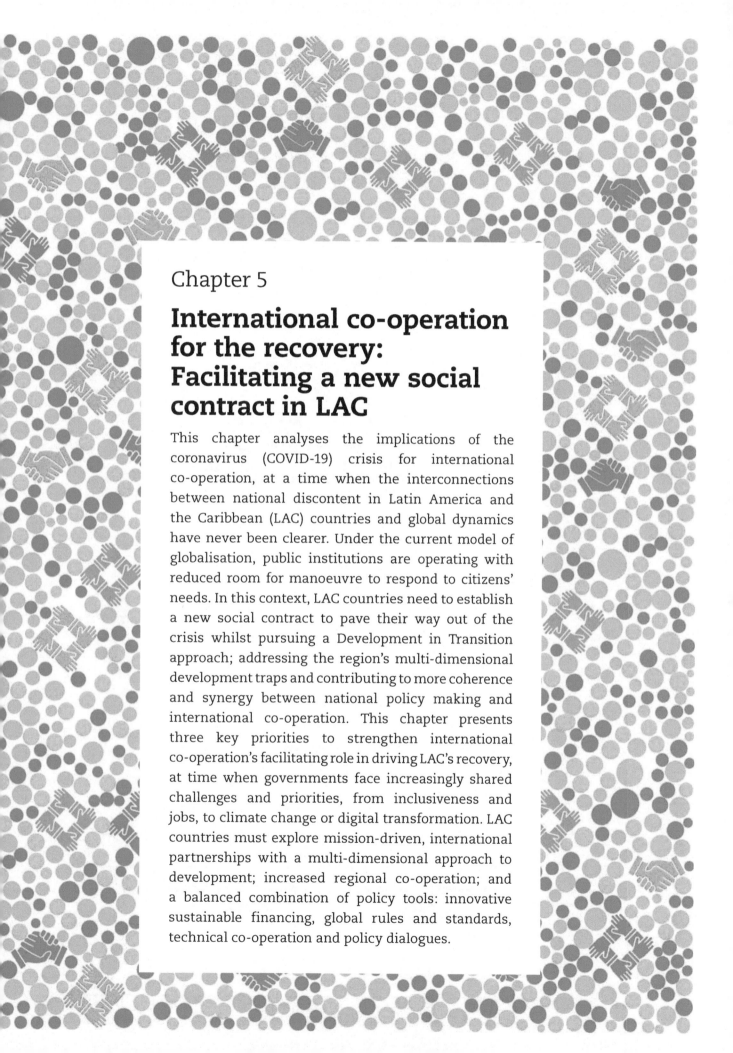

Chapter 5

International co-operation for the recovery: Facilitating a new social contract in LAC

This chapter analyses the implications of the coronavirus (COVID-19) crisis for international co-operation, at a time when the interconnections between national discontent in Latin America and the Caribbean (LAC) countries and global dynamics have never been clearer. Under the current model of globalisation, public institutions are operating with reduced room for manoeuvre to respond to citizens' needs. In this context, LAC countries need to establish a new social contract to pave their way out of the crisis whilst pursuing a Development in Transition approach; addressing the region's multi-dimensional development traps and contributing to more coherence and synergy between national policy making and international co-operation. This chapter presents three key priorities to strengthen international co-operation's facilitating role in driving LAC's recovery, at time when governments face increasingly shared challenges and priorities, from inclusiveness and jobs, to climate change or digital transformation. LAC countries must explore mission-driven, international partnerships with a multi-dimensional approach to development; increased regional co-operation; and a balanced combination of policy tools: innovative sustainable financing, global rules and standards, technical co-operation and policy dialogues.

Newpartnershipstofacilitate therecoveryinLAC

Boldinternationalpolicyactionsarerequiredtoadvance towardsanewsocialcontract

Mostcitizensunderstandco-operationisthewayforward

70%ofLatinAmericans thinkitisessentialfor countriestowork togethertomanage globaltrends

81% ofpeoplein advancedeconomies supportmultilateralism

Almost **50%** ofLatinAmericansreport thattheCovid-19crises convincedthemthatmore co-operationbetween countriesisneeded

How?

Structuring international co-operationthrough **mission-driven partnerships**

\+

Promoting **regional co-operationas** akeybuildingblock

Byfosteringintegratedapproachesforabalanceduseoftools, suchas:

Sustainable financing

Globalrules, standardsandpolicy dialogue

Technicalco-operation forcapacitybuilding

Introduction

The global reach of the pandemic has shown that, as governments' room for manoeuvre weakens when faced with global challenges, national responses are not enough. Meanwhile, multilateralism has been at the forefront during this crisis, showing its power for collective action but also exposing its constraints. In Latin America and the Caribbean (LAC), the crisis has stressed what previous social outbreaks had demonstrated: the increasing interconnection between national and international development challenges requires a change of mind-set with regards to international co-operation, multilaterally and within LAC.

In this context, the Development in Transition (DiT) framework presented in the *Latin American Economic Outlook 2019* gains renewed relevance and impetus (OECD et al., 2019[1]). DiT proposes to look at development from a multi-dimensional lens; it calls for going beyond gross domestic product (GDP) and using indicators that reflect countries' development levels to inform policy design, implementation, monitoring and evaluation. Moreover, DiT proposes a renewed role for international co-operation as a "facilitator" for the transformation of LAC's structural challenges into development opportunities supporting the region achieving the 2030 Agenda.

On one hand, this more targeted approach would more effectively support LAC in redefining its social contract to address the region's development traps of low productivity, social vulnerability, institutional weaknesses and environmental sustainability, all of which have been exacerbated during the pandemic.

On the other hand, LAC's exit from the crisis through a new social contract is an opportunity to put international co-operation's facilitating role into full practice, including by ensuring coherence across national, regional and global actions. The social contract, understood as an equilibrium between societal actors and those in power, reflects the distribution of power in state-society relations (Loewe, Zintl and Houdret, 2020[2]) and consists of specific pacts that attain all areas of development: environmental, social, productive and institutional (Chapter 4). A new social contract would entail moving from today's fragmented status quo to a new equilibrium, grounded on equality of opportunities for all citizens in all countries in the long run (Larrain, 2020[3]). The issues addressed in specific social pacts are directly or indirectly linked to international development dynamics (e.g. offshoring) and co-operation actions to address them (e.g. global taxation). A renewed international co-operation should better grasp these interconnections and comprise them in renewed partnerships to address the multi-dimensional nature of global development through equally multi-dimensional responses.

First, this chapter puts forward what the COVID-19 crisis has exposed: it shows how long-standing global dynamics coupled with structural domestic challenges are a perfect storm that can lead to a new rise in social protest, and the need therefore for LAC countries to engage in building a new social contract. It argues why the DiT framework is highly relevant to re-envision international co-operation with LAC to support the region's recovery. The chapter then moves on to analysing what type of international partnerships could enable a new social contract in LAC, including the innovative practices that could be explored to this end. Notably it proposes to explore the value of (1) multi-stakeholder and multi-dimensional mission-driven partnerships and (2) of enhanced regional co-operation, as well as (3) identifying a comprehensive and balanced use of three key tools to ensure policy coherence and improved results; innovative sustainable financing for development, global rules and standards, and technical co-operation. The chapter concludes by putting forward practical policy proposals for post-COVID-19 partnerships.

What the COVID-19 crisis has revealed: Long-standing global dynamics and the emergence of new challenges require adapting international co-operation

The COVID-19 crisis has put a strain on LAC's structural development vulnerabilities. The pandemic hit LAC when the region was already under a declining process of low potential growth, persistent inequalities, increasing poverty and social tensions, all coupled with an increasing environmental decline. The health-related needs created by the pandemic revealed the insufficient and unequal coverage of national health systems, while the economic shock affected poor and vulnerable workers, particularly informal ones who worryingly represent 58% of the Latin American labour force (with 65% of total workers receiving no form of social protection) (OECD et al., 2019[1]).

Meanwhile, the international community's efforts to put solidarity at the forefront of its response to the global sanitary and economic crisis have been limited. Innovative thinking and action to offset international co-operation's lack of flexibility and ability to adapt to the pandemic are underway, but more efforts are needed to explore innovative practices to transform international co-operation such as bringing in citizens' voices, involving a broader range of key stakeholders and giving room to innovative policy thinking for the recovery.

COVID-19 has made clear that countries cannot face global challenges alone and that an increasing number of shared global challenges influence national discontent in LAC countries. Even before the COVID-19 outbreak, growing social discontent had resulted in protests in several Latin American countries. Chile, Colombia and Ecuador saw a rise in protests. National expressions of discontent in LAC are mostly linked with national governments' responses to structural vulnerabilities, and with international financial markets, global inequality and environmental challenges. Public institutions, for example, have failed to respond fully to citizens' increasing demands, creating distrust and low satisfaction with public services. From 2006 to 2020, the share of the LAC population satisfied with the quality of healthcare services fell from 57% to 47%, well below the Organisation for Economic Co-operation and Development (OECD) average of around 70%. Likewise, only 38% of the population has confidence in the national government (Nieto Parra and Da Costa, 2021[4]).

Alongside domestic challenges, in 2019, worldwide protests emerged as a common movement against "the system"; one that weakened the role of the state, international institutions and the participation of social movements. The globalisation process since the fall of the Berlin Wall has been fixated on market forces as key to a peaceful and co-operative world order, having the twin effects of weakening the capacity of states to regulate the global economy and of frustrating social forces. Social unrest is therefore the result of the decoupling of the global economy from its socio-political context and of the lack of horizontal inter-social linkages in the inter-state system (Badie, 2020[5]).

Moreover, economic global asymmetries, such as economic concentration, global value chains, financial centres or digital networks are becoming harder to ignore, as they all contribute to a growing polarisation, and serve as vehicles for seizing economic advantage (Pisani-Ferry, 2021[6]). Understanding these asymmetries and how they affect national discontent will be critical in defining a new international co-operation system.

Instability in certain LAC countries has spillovers in the rest of the region and the world. An example is the refugee and migrant crisis stemming from several LAC countries and its impacts on countries unprepared to act as host countries. In addition, the lack of accountability and the weakness of public institutions, along with the lack of citizen trust, create a favourable context for the depredation of environmental public goods.

For instance, deforestation of the Amazon Rainforest rose by 17% in 2020, with 2 500 major fires across the Amazon (Amazon Conservation, 2020[7]).

Rising discontent, particularly in LAC, is likely to surge after the pandemic. Ongoing social distancing measures may have a mitigating effect on protests, but these and other responses to the pandemic may also cause scarring social effects, increasing the likelihood of social unrest, as recently seen in Chile, Paraguay (Mander, 2021[8]) and Colombia (BBC, 2021[9]). In fact, historical evidence has shown a positive cross-sectional relationship between epidemics and social unrest. Recent trends in social unrest immediately before and after the COVID-19 outbreak are consistent with these findings (Fund, 2021[10]). This hypothesis is reinforced by the rise in income inequality experienced during the pandemic in LAC, where 22 million more people became poor in 2020 (ECLAC, 2021[11]), while the fortunes of 73 billionaires swelled by USD 48.2 billion (United States dollars) (Oxfam, 2020[12]).

COVID-19 forces a collective lucidity about the depth of global interdependence, the fact that the world is only as resilient as the least resilient country and person, and the fact that the world is reaching tipping points in multiple dimensions (UN, 2020[13]). The strain on the planet mirrors that in societies, and these imbalances reinforce each other, amplifying development challenges (UNDP, 2020[14]).

Most Latin Americans consider international co-operation part of the solution. The effects of the coronavirus outbreak have raised awareness among citizens about the need for more international co-operation, making it a popular and legitimate claim for the region. Almost 50% of Latin Americans surveyed are in favour of more co-operation after COVID-19, and 70% think that it is essential to deal with current global challenges (Figure 5.1). Around the world, it has become clear that countries cannot face global challenges alone. Citizens are increasingly aware of this: 81% of people in advanced economies support multilateralism, reinforcing the idea that countries should act as part of a global community that works together to solve shared problems (Pew Research Center, 2020[15]).

Figure 5.1. **Perceptions of Latin American and Caribbean citizens towards international co-operation**

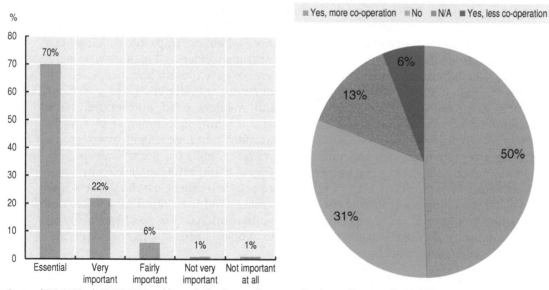

Panel A. How important - or not - is it for countries to work together to manage the above trends?

Panel B. Has COVID-19 changed your views on co-operation between countries?

■ Yes, more co-operation ■ No ■ N/A ■ Yes, less co-operation

Source: (UN, 2020[16]), *UN75 2020 and beyond: Shaping our future together,* https://un75.online/es/data/.

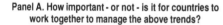 StatLink *https://doi.org/10.1787/888934286977*

Recognising the increasing linkages across domestic policies and global dynamics, international co-operation appears an essential tool to realise the full potential of a new social contract in LAC. A new social contract should address domestic and global challenges, balancing the market results of global interdependent economies and their interrelation with national political agendas, guided by the Sustainable Development Goals (SDGs) of the United Nations 2030 Agenda for Sustainable Development and its pledge to leave no one behind (UN, 2020[13]). To this end, actors at various levels, including local, national, regional and international, need to reflect on how best to place an equitable, ecological and social transition at the heart of international efforts, moving beyond current models of co-operation, growth and development.

In this context, the DiT framework offers a new narrative and useful approach to initiate such a reflection. Better understanding current needs and challenges faced by LAC countries and better delineating the new social contract's interrelations with international dynamics are at the forefront of a debate on what international co-operation and partnerships are required for LAC in the post-COVID-19 world. Pursuing innovative financial approaches, transforming linear approaches to multi-dimensional ones, finding new tools and updating governance agreements become necessary to tackle a growing set of shared and interconnected challenges also affecting LAC countries.

The Development in Transition policy framework is more relevant in times of COVID-19

The dramatic effects of the COVID-19 crisis in LAC evidence the roots of the widespread social discontent in the region and the inadequacy of prevailing standards of international co-operation that focus on GDP as a unique measure of development progress. With only 8.4% of the global population, and 28 of the 33 countries in the region being middle-income countries (MICs), LAC accounts for 30% of total COVID-19 deaths (UNDP, 2020[17]), proving that decision making based on average GDP per capita overlooks structural inequalities and development challenges that go beyond income. Focusing on LAC countries' level of GDP not only contradicts the SDGs' comprehensive conception of development but is also proven limited by the exposed fragilities of these countries in dealing with the pandemic, despite their relatively higher income levels compared to low-income countries (LICs).

At the core of the DiT framework is the call for going beyond GDP as a measure of development, adopting multi-dimensional development approaches and making international co-operation a facilitator to transform development traps into development opportunities. It identifies four main development traps hindering LAC's development transition, which reinforce each other, and have been exposed and deepened by the current crisis (OECD et al., 2019[1]). The productivity trap explains why the most vulnerable companies, mainly micro, small and medium-sized enterprises, have been the most affected during the pandemic, with 2.7 million companies closing in 2020 (ECLAC, 2021[11]). At the same time, the persistent heterogeneity in the region's productive structure increases its reliance on resource-intensive sectors, deepening the environmental trap. The social vulnerability trap is behind the pandemic's unequal socio-economic impact, which left 22 million more people living below the poverty line and affected the living conditions of the 40% of workers and their families who are not protected by any form of social security. Last, the institutional trap has been widened by the low capacity of public services to respond to people's needs during the pandemic, heightening social discontent.

The recovery process presents a unique chance for LAC to put international co-operation's facilitating role into full practice and transform the vicious cycle of development traps into opportunities for more inclusive and sustainable development models. A comparison of various recovery scenarios indicates that an exit strategy that includes a big boost for environmental sustainability, in the context of an international co-operation agreement, would have a significant positive impact on LAC's carbon dioxide emissions (-23% by 2030). It would also have an impact on GDP growth (approximately 2.5% more than in COVID-19 scenario), inequality (approximately 0.5% less than in COVID-19 scenario) and employment (approximately 0.75% more than in COVID-19 scenario) (ECLAC, 2020[18]).

International co-operation is therefore essential, but not any co-operation. The DiT framework calls for international co-operation to act as a facilitator to help build stronger capacities in LAC countries by promoting nationally driven processes based on national development plans, aligning national and global priorities, and promoting LAC's active participation in the global agenda (OECD et al., 2019[1]). A facilitating role can also bolster the use of diverse co-operation tools, such as increased technical co-operation based on knowledge, South-South and triangular co-operation, and whole-of-government approaches. Last, through equal-footing policy partnerships and multi-stakeholder co-operation, a facilitating role would foster a more inclusive way of working (Table 5.1).

Table 5.1. **Key dimensions for rethinking international co-operation as a facilitator for sustainable development in LAC**

Dimensions	Description
Working inclusively	Engaging countries at all development levels on an equal footing as peers, to build and participate in multilateral and multi-stakeholder partnerships to tackle shared multi-dimensional development challenges with multi-dimensional responses.
Building domestic capacities	Strengthening countries' capacities to design, implement and evaluate their development policy priorities and plans, encouraging alignment between domestic and international priorities and ensuring integrated approaches to more complex and interlinked challenges.
Operating with more tools and actors	Expanding instruments for greater international co-operation, such as knowledge sharing, policy dialogues, capacity building, technology transfers, and including more actors, such as public actors, in a whole-of-government approach.

Source: (OECD et al., 2019[1]), *Latin American Economic Outlook 2019: Development in Transition*, https://doi.org/10.1787/g2g9ff18-en.

To transform the development paradigm in the region, international co-operation must help countries tackle the effects of globalisation on national political agendas. There are many shared challenges for which domestic policies are insufficient: pandemic prevention and control, climate change, digital transformation and – very important in the case of LAC – debt management. This is not only legitimate from the standpoint of citizens and beneficial for LAC's development transition but also necessary for the provision of global public goods.

The urgent need to adapt multilateralism

The outbreak of COVID-19 as a global health emergency and the resulting socio-economic crisis have given rise to new forms of transnational solidarity and partnerships. However, the international community also acknowledges that the initiatives and responses have not been enough and are, in many cases, thwarted by established international rules and governance that impede facing a crisis of global dimensions.

This is the case with Special Drawing Rights (SDR) allocations. Despite the emergence of the need to improve co-operation in relation to debt sustainability, international rules and governance structure impede comprehensive support to the region through this mechanism. This is especially important for LAC since all countries in the region have increased their levels of indebtedness owing to the pressure on fiscal systems. In the current context, it is expected that indebtedness will have increased from an already high 68.9% to 79.3% of GDP between 2019 and 2020 at the regional level, making LAC the most indebted region of the developing world and the one with the highest external debt service in relation to exports of goods and services (57%) (ECLAC, 2021[19]).

Notwithstanding the relief and immediate liquidity provided by the Debt Service Suspension Initiative (DSSI), this is not enough for the current needs of the region. Global rules do not foresee an egalitarian distribution of SDRs, nor a distribution based on the needs of each country, but in proportion to their existing quotas in the International Monetary Fund (IMF). This can be problematic in the face of a global crisis like the current one. In fact, the region was granted 6.7% of the new allocation of SDRs amounting close to USD 50 billion in additional international reserves for LAC economies (CGD, 2021[20]). This has benefited several LAC economies, including highly indebted ones, but the new SDR allocation would have more impact if complemented with a reallocation of existing SDRs to MICs in LAC. In addition, multi-stakeholder international co-operation is of utmost importance, since many MICs' debt is mostly owed to private creditors.

With a crisis of global dimensions, international rules and global governance can play a significant role in enabling international co-operation for a fast, inclusive and resilient recovery. Integrated responses are therefore essential when facing challenges that are multi-dimensional, interconnected and globally shared. Unregulated global megatrends, a weakened global governance and asymmetric and top-down decision making in international co-operation are still some of the barriers preventing multilateralism from effectively helping countries facing today's global challenges.

Accelerated change has become the *leitmotif* of our times. In the international sphere, this is evidenced by growing unregulated megatrends, such as climate change, offshoring, financialisation and digitalisation of the economy, and their challenges for international taxation. Despite efforts through the current global governance architecture, these phenomena are still largely unregulated and steered mainly by factual powers and market dynamics, undermining the achievement of the SDGs and current efforts to end the pandemic. A clear example in the context of COVID-19 is that of the financialisation of private pharma. Main pharma companies have been reducing research investment while increasing spending in share buybacks, a strategy used to boost stock price that undermines necessary scientific findings to ensure global health (Mazzucato, 2018[21]).

The exponential growth of these global dynamics weakens global governance. The development and roll out of COVID-19 vaccines globally offers the sharpest example of this. While the international vaccine purchase and distribution platform COVID-19 Vaccines Global Access (COVAX) represents a momentous step forward, its impact has been offset by massive bilateral advance-purchase agreements by rich countries that could afford to bet on multiple vaccines (Mazzucato et al., 2020[22]). In addition, the refusal of most developed countries of requests by many developing countries to allow for a Trade-Related Aspects of Intellectual Property Rights (TRIPS) waiver for COVID-19 vaccines in the World Trade Organization (WTO), is hindering opportunities to scale up production and address emerging variants (Johns Hopkins, 2020[23]). As a result, COVID-19 vaccine contracts are unequally distributed across the globe.

These dynamics are sustained by asymmetric and top-down decision making at the international level. Developing countries have found their voice in the Bretton Woods organisations to be limited, even as their number grew substantially in the years following the end of the Second World War (OECD, 2021[25]). As argued by the Group of 24, MICs – a category to which most LAC countries belong – have not received sufficient allocations, and their voices have not yet been heard in the context of these institutions, which have been accused of operating on a one dollar-one vote basis (Singer, 1995[26]). The refusal by developed countries to the TRIPS waiver is only one example. Another case in the context of the current crisis is the IMF's SDR allocations. In many ways, discontent is a global phenomenon that underlines the need for fairer, more inclusive and more effective systems of international co-operation (Pezzini and Pick, 2021[27]).

Effectiveness and legitimacy are intertwined: as the successful co-operation of the international scientific community on COVID-19 demonstrates, it is not possible to devise solutions to global challenges without the inputs and expertise of countries around the world. Multilateral institutions need to further promote a process of experimentalism to empower a broader variety of actors, employ a broader set of modalities and be guided by a wider range of voices, including those of the discontented themselves (Pezzini and Pick, 2021[27]).

To make a difference, reforms pushed by international co-operation should go beyond reconstruction and recovery. Rather, they should focus on transforming globalisation to maximise its contribution to inclusive, resilient and sustainable development in LAC (Nieto Parra and Da Costa, 2021[4]).

Moreover, a recovery process will need a transformative consensus not only at the national and subnational levels but also in the regional and multilateral spheres. The broad multi-stakeholder mobilisation that a new social contract in LAC will entail should be bottom up, to enrich international development with the participation of representative collective groups of civil society (Figure 5.2). This should enable overcoming development traps and social discontent in LAC and allow the region to achieve a new social contract that puts people first and provides public goods at the global level.

Figure 5.2. **A vicious circle between global and national development dynamics in LAC**

Source: Own elaboration.

It is time to rethink systems, not just fix them. International efforts triggered during the COVID-19 pandemic, analysed next, reflect some changes in this direction, as well as pending issues. A lot can be learned from both to build forward better in the frame of a new social contract.

The international response to the crisis has not been enough

Overcoming LAC's vulnerability traps and offsetting the negative impacts of global megatrends in the region as countries in LAC prepare for the recovery demand an international co-operation system and a dynamic multilateralism that react swiftly, efficiently and with a long-term multi-dimensional perspective (OECD et al., 2019[1]). Seizing this window of opportunity will require assessing what worked and did not work during the pandemic. This section summarises the main findings on financial and non-financial co-operation, co-operation with the private sector and regional co-operation, including by shedding some light on innovative practices taking place during the pandemic.

International financial assistance during the pandemic

International financial assistance has been multiplied since the beginning of the COVID-19 outbreak, even when the crisis affected developed economies. Multilateral institutions, development banks, bilateral co-operation donors and the private sector have made outstanding efforts in tackling the pandemic and speeding up economic recovery. An analysis of total funding announcements responding to the pandemic and its impacts between 1 January 2020 and 28 February 2021 shows that more than USD 20.7 trillion have been pledged (DEVEX, 2021[28]). Funding levels and focus areas are unclear and difficult to track and determine, including how much was actually disbursed and how much is extra-budgetary or reallocated from existing programmes (OECD, 2020[29]).

Despite the fact that LAC has worsened its already critical fiscal deficit, becoming the most indebted region in the world, the region benefits from a relatively small share of global development co-operation efforts. Within the developing world, the LAC region faced the worst crisis on historical record and the sharpest contraction (close to -7% and -20% in GDP and investment growth, respectively, in 2020) (ECLAC, 2021[30]). Total fiscal expenditure rose in order to face the impacts of the COVID-19 crisis on poor households and other vulnerable populations, as well as the private sector, while fiscal revenues fell, resulting in an increase in the overall fiscal deficit from -3.0% of GDP in 2019 to slightly below -7% of GDP in 2020 (ECLAC, 2021[31]).

An analysis of co-operation flows shows that LAC's recovery relies more on support from regional development banks and receives relatively less support from traditional partners and non-traditional ones like the private sector (DEVEX, 2021[28]). For instance, the Inter-American Development Bank (IADB) is the second largest contributor in LAC, while it is 12th in the world. Furthermore, while the European Union and the European Investment Bank are the third and fourth largest contributors in the world, they hold 13th and 11th place in LAC, respectively. The private sector is the seventh largest contributor worldwide, although it is only 24th in LAC.

A look at the focus areas shows that, as in the rest of the world, co-operation and other sources of financing with LAC has prioritised the economic recovery and the immediate response, but has also given greater consideration for vulnerable populations compared to the rest of the world, although other key issues for the social pact are unclear. The economic response takes 60% of worldwide international efforts and 37% of that directed towards LAC. In the region, funding aimed to vulnerable populations holds second place (17%), followed by immediate response (14%), health systems (11%) and gender (7%) (Figure 5.3).

Figure 5.3. **Total funding by policy area in LAC**

1 January 2020 to 7 March 2021 (USD million)

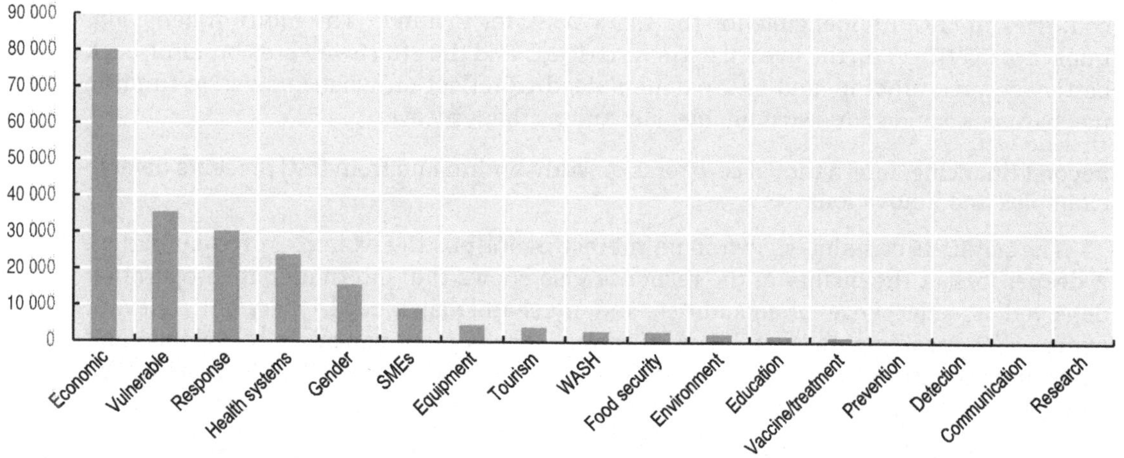

Note: SMEs = small and medium-sized enterprises. WASH = water, sanitation and hygiene.
Source: (DEVEX, 2021[28]), *Funding the response to COVID-19: Analysis of funding opportunities*, www.devex.com/news/interactive-who-s-funding-the-covid-19-response-and-what-are-the-priorities-96833.
StatLink ᵐˢᵖ *https://doi.org/10.1787/888934286996*

Official development assistance (ODA) reached an all-time high in 2020, and the Group of Twenty (G20) has put in place important measures to increase financing for developing countries in the context of Bretton Woods institutions. Foreign aid from the Development Assistance Committee (DAC) donors rose to USD 161.2 billion in 2020, up 3.5% in real terms from 2019, boosted by additional spending mobilised to help developing countries grappling with the COVID-19 crisis (OECD, 2021[32]). ODA contributions to multilateral organisations, which represent about a third of total ODA, increased by 9% globally in 2020 compared with 2019 (OECD, 2020[29]). Nevertheless, these levels include a rise in the proportion of loans and equity investment versus grants by some donor countries (OECD, 2021[33]). ODA plays an essential and unique role in supporting developing countries to face and cope with challenges, focusing on people's welfare, going where other (private) finance does not, and has been a relatively stable and predictable resource in times of crisis. Yet, ODA cannot respond to the COVID-19 crisis alone.

LAC countries have turned to development banks and benefited from the rapid credit and financing lines put in place to respond to the pandemic that impose no conditions on borrowing countries. Among the positive news from the G20's communiqué of 7 April 2021, it is important to mention the agreement to issue USD 650 billion in SDRs, the global reserve asset of the IMF. In addition, extensions of the DSSI and the G20's Common Framework for Debt Treatments and the Catastrophe Containment and Relief Trust provide grants to particularly hard-hit low-income countries (LICs) (Ocampo, 2021[34]).

Despite these efforts, the amount of co-operation has been insufficient (Kharas and Dooley, 2020[35]; OECD, 2021[32]; Ocampo, 2020[36]). The financing lines granted by the IMF to LAC countries to cope with the effects of the pandemic have covered, on average, only between 23.1% and 32.3% of the financing needs of the countries requesting support (ECLAC, 2021[31]). Meanwhile, the financing committed by the World Bank and the IADB, equivalent to USD 8 billion and USD 7.7 billion, respectively, has been less than that granted by the subregional development banks, namely the Development Bank of Latin America (CAF), the Central American Bank for Economic Integration (CABEI) and the Caribbean Development Bank (CDB), estimated at USD 12.3 billion (Bárcena, 2021[38]; ECLAC, 2021[30]).

Financial co-operation has been particularly insufficient in responding to the needs of MICs. Unlike the effects of COVID-19, the architecture of international co-operation distinguishes between income levels, prioritising low-income countries. Therefore, most countries in LAC are ineligible for the G20's DSSI, for instance. The multi-dimensional impact of COVID-19 on the lives of Latin Americans and the efforts towards building back better requires funding, and LAC partners need to reflect on what innovative funding mechanisms could spur a sustainable, just and resilient recovery.

Beyond financing, international co-operation with, within and from LAC presents diverse examples and innovations

The COVID-19 crisis has shown some interesting and positive examples of co-operation. A deeper look at the quality of the response also shows that international co-operation deployed a wide range of modalities and mechanisms. Indeed, there are relevant experiences involving multilateral institutions, development banks and developed and developing countries in terms of technical co-operation, whole-of-government-approach co-operation, multi-stakeholder co-operation, knowledge transfer and capacity building.

Regarding technical co-operation, LAC has tapped into its experience with South-South co-operation. For instance, Argentina and Mexico exchanged non-financial co-operation to speed up administrative processes to approve and administer the Sputnik-V vaccine (El País, 2021[40]) and collaborated to co-produce and distribute the AstraZeneca vaccine in LAC. Venezuela donated 136 000 litres of oxygen to the state of Amazonas in Brazil when it faced a shortage treating a spike in COVID-19 patients (Reuters, 2021[41]). Argentina and Chile are working together to strengthen their small and medium-sized enterprise (SME) sectors by supporting their digitalisation process and improving their participation in the public procurement market.

Beyond LAC, Southern partners have also displayed innovative examples of solidarity. For example, Morocco supported El Salvador with financial support to build a national network of medical oxygen within its national health system.

The region has also seized opportunities to adapt triangular co-operation initiatives to the pandemic context. Triangular co-operation offers an opportunity to jointly address the global pandemic, by learning from different regions' experience of addressing COVID-19's impacts. For instance, Uruguay is preparing and adapting a triangular co-operation initiative with Spain to provide technical assistance to Bolivia to assess their situation in relation to telemedicine software. The German Regional Fund for Triangular Co-operation with LAC has also refocused programmes in light of the pandemic. The EU, through its Triangular Co-operation Facility for LAC, has given priority to the initiatives presented to the ADELANTE Window 2021 that aimed to respond to development challenges related to circumstances arising from the COVID-19 pandemic crisis.

Regional development banks and traditional development co-operation partners have also provided strategic support for capacity building. The Inter-American Bank (IADB) provided financial assistance to develop mechanical ventilator prototypes in Colombia at low cost and with easily available materials and supplies. In El Salvador, Luxembourg supported the creation of the first university hospital within the national hospital. The CAF strengthened capabilities in Dominican Republic to improve the Emergency Operations Centre, and the IADB provided assistance to build Costa Rica's Accountability Platform, where citizens can access the details of public investments in response to the pandemic.

Innovative examples of co-operation and transformational proposals for multilateral co-operation have also stemmed from LAC during the pandemic. For instance, Cuban doctors assisted Italy and South Africa through the country's international medical programme (Bhattacharya and Sabin Kahn, 2020[42]). Costa Rica launched two ambitious co-operation initiatives at the multilateral level. First, the COVID-19 Technology Access Pool (C-TAP) in the context of the World Health Organization (WHO) facilitates timely, equitable and affordable access to COVID-19 health products by sharing intellectual property and know-how of COVID-19 therapeutics, diagnostics, vaccines and other health products. Second, the Fund to Alleviate COVID-19 Economics (FACE) – an alternative to current co-operation frameworks. This initiative seeks to provide developing countries with the funds to cope with the socio-economic effects of COVID-19 on the economy and on people, on concessional and solidarity-based terms (Box 5.1).

Some partners have also promoted a whole-of-government-approach to co-operation to tackle the first stages of the recovery phase effectively. CAF is working with Paraguay on a multi-dimensional programme directed towards funding the Ñapu'ã Paraguay Plan for Economic Recovery. This plan includes a countercyclical agenda with three guidelines: i) social protection; ii) public investment for employment and credits for development; and iii) reforms for the transformation of public institutions (CAF, 2021[43]). A whole-of-government-approach has also been adopted by Team Europe, kick-started by the Mesas COVID-19 initiative.

Box 5.1. **Fund to Alleviate COVID-19 Economics**

The Fund to Alleviate COVID-19 Economics (FACE) was first proposed by the government of Costa Rica in the framework of the 75th United Nations General Assembly as a vehicle for international solidarity in view of the economic recession caused by the pandemic and as an instrument to drive a sustainable recovery (ECLAC, 2020[44]).

The fund of USD 500 million for one-off support is financed with 0.7% of the GDP of the world's largest and strongest economies – those that account for 80% of global GDP – to be intermediated by one or several multilateral development banks as concessional loans to developing countries.

Funds will be lent under favourable conditions and on solidarity-based terms. A 50-year repayment period, a 5-year grace period and a 0% fixed interest rate. To contribute to these special circumstances, financial organisations would not charge any fees for the intermediation and administration of FACE resources. Allocation of FACE resources would not be subject to traditional monetary or structural conditions but would consider norms of good governance and a committed fight against corruption.

The fund would be equivalent to 3% of the GDP of beneficiary countries, a figure representative of the drop in tax income plus the extra budgetary costs of addressing the pandemic. The funds would be lent for a long term and at fixed rates, to provide financing to developing countries that have limited policy tools for responding to the crisis.

Outlays of the resources would be fully aligned with the fulfilment of the 2030 Agenda and the SDGs in order to build resilience and achieve the goals of multilateral environmental agreements, such as the Nationally Determined Contributions, to accelerate progress towards sustainable development in this Decade of Action.

Incipient international collaboration with the private sector has been strengthened

As COVID-19 spread and its global impact on health and the economy became more evident, some multinational companies sought to complement government efforts to fight the pandemic. Information and communications technology companies, such as AT&T and Telefónica, worked in collaboration with LAC governments to support distance education initiatives during school closures. Efforts towards greater financial inclusion through innovative digital finance initiatives meant providers could move swiftly to facilitate digital payments, including in support of social protection programmes, which research indicates reduced the unbanked population throughout Latin America by 25% (Americas Market Intelligence, 2020[45]). Many companies embraced a responsibility to act, exemplified by private-sector initiatives across the region (OECD, 2021[46]), ranging from pivoting supply chains to producing essential products, maintaining supply of essential services and offering free or flexible payments.

At the international level, the private sector is working with the International Trade Centre, the IADB, the United Nations Development Programme and others to support the economic recovery by implementing the Trade Facilitation Agreement (TFA). The TFA is a driver for growth, based on best practices agreed by WTO members. National trade facilitation committees have proven to be a key driver for growth in developing economies, increasing the dialogue with governments. In addition, several donors and organisations, such as the Global Alliance for Trade Facilitation, are actively looking for partners to pilot reform projects in LAC.

Current recovery initiatives are an important opportunity to realise pending reforms and invest in strategic sectors, such as public health, as future growth drivers. In that vein, in collaboration with governments, many companies have sought to identify and support initiatives that have an immediate impact and are in line with longer-term growth strategies. During the COVID-19 crisis, many countries openly engaged with regional and international institutions and mitigated the negative effects through dialogue with the private sector (e.g. facilitating trade of essential products). There is an opportunity to build on this foundation to design longer-term plans for modernisation, digitalisation and regulatory reform in the region. Examples in the promotion of digitalisation encompass the digital expedited digitalised customs procedures, labour policies allowing for remote working, reduced reporting requirements and additional spectrum availability (OECD, 2021[39]).

Regional policy partnerships in and beyond LAC in the face of COVID-19

Co-operation networks, platforms and integration institutions in LAC have activated response strategies to face the immediate impacts of the pandemic. One of the most salient is the General Secretariat of the Central American Integration System (SICA). Its member countries agreed on a Regional Contingency Plan to face COVID-19 (with 85% completed in the first nine months of execution) and launched a Regional COVID-19 Observatory. SICA also receives support from the European Union to implement its Recovery, Social Reconstruction and Resilience Plan for Central America and the Dominican Republic (Box 5.2).

Box 5.2. Plan 3R: Recovery, Social Reconstruction and Resilience Plan for Central America and the Dominican Republic

Given the huge economic and social impact of the COVID-19 crisis in Central America and the Dominican Republic, the Council for Central American Social Integration (CIS) approved the Second Special Declaration in April 2020, "United for the recovery and social reconstruction of the SICA region". It identifies the urgent need to design mechanisms to mitigate the damage and establish the foundations for a sustainable social recovery and reconstruction, addressing factors that have undermined the region's resilience.

The CIS instructed the Secretariat for Central American Social Integration to develop an articulated response and prepare a Recovery, Social Reconstruction and Resilience Plan for Central America and the Dominican Republic, with the support of the EU EUROsociAL+ programme in alliance with specialised UN agencies (EUROsociAL, 2021[47]).

Box 5.2. **Plan 3R: Recovery, Social Reconstruction and Resilience Plan for Central America and the Dominican Republic** *(cont.)*

The plan includes a set of strategic projects under three areas of intervention: i) social protection; ii) employment; and iii) informal settlements and sustainable urban development. Each involves strategic and transformative actions to provide wide-ranging responses to problems that have been prioritised by Central American countries, hence promoting their reactivation and recovery. The projects seek to create the conditions for more resilient, socially just and environmentally sustainable societies.

The experience of the plan shows the relevance of regional frameworks and policies to support resilience and to guide national recovery plans, strengthening and renewing the social pacts necessary for their implementation.

Nevertheless, the pandemic has not yet turned into an opportunity for LAC as a whole to take broader regional solidarity actions, speak as one voice in the multilateral sphere and push forward a transformative regional co-operation strategy towards inclusive and sustainable development pathways. Nor have all LAC countries been able to align support around the more transformative proposals that originated in the region during the pandemic, such as Costa Rica's FACE and C-TAP. The insufficient political alignment of LAC governments to boost a regional response contrasts with citizens' will, given that 61.8% of people declare being somewhat or very in favour of the political integration of their country with others in the region (Figure 5.4).

Figure 5.4. **Perceptions of political integration in Latin America (in favour or against)**

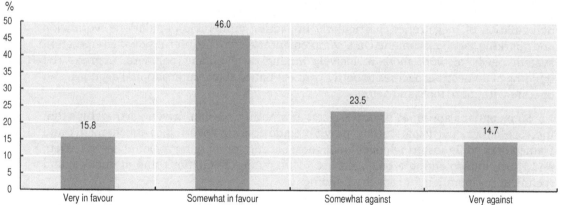

Source: (Nieto Parra and Da Costa, 2021[4]), "Desarrollo en Transición en América Latina en tiempos de la COVID-19", *Documentos de Trabajo Fundación Carolina.*
StatLink ▦▒▦ *https://doi.org/10.1787/888934287015*

LAC countries should react to expressions of social discontent and seek citizens' support for further regional co-operation. The region could develop a regional development agenda with ambitious political and operational agreements that include multi-stakeholder dialogues. Regional co-operation would increase the magnitude of policy responses towards the recovery. On one hand, it would help positioning the region's needs and specificities in the global context in negotiation and governance frameworks. On the other hand, it would contribute to align country efforts towards increased regional integration that could help countries better respond to the recovery agendas. Regional co-operation that adequately underpins the negotiations of the social contract would allow for the creation of fairer social protection systems, the mitigation of climate change impacts, and the promotion of regional value chains to boost productivity and innovation, which are the focus of the forthcoming section.

An encouraging sign in the context of the recovery, is the approval of a regional Sanitary Self-Sufficiency Plan by the 33 LAC countries gathered in the recent IV Summit of Heads of State and Government of the Community of Latin American and Caribbean States (UN, 2021[48]). This plan, which counts with the support of ECLAC, will address research, development and production capabilities for vaccines and medicines at the regional level. This will strengthen the region's scientific and sanitary sovereignty and address key drivers of the region's structural vulnerabilities through regional integration and co-operation.

What kind of international partnerships could facilitate efforts towards a new social contract in LAC?

The world is rapidly approaching the end of the 2030 Agenda with few results to match its initial ambition. The COVID-19 crisis has accentuated the difficulties to meet the SDGs. International action should take a more ambitious stance if the world is to get closer to these goals. Countries in the LAC region are no different. The post-COVID-19 context demands new ways of engagement with and, very importantly, within the region. A new social contract encompassing socio-economic groups (including income, race, ethnicity and gender), sectors, territories and generations can provide the pillars for a new development pathway that binds society together and restores citizens' trust in national and international public institutions

International co-operation efforts need to address the weakened global governance institutions and asymmetric, top-down decision-making structures that lead to greater deregulation of megatrends, particularly impacting vulnerable populations worldwide and sparking social discontent. On a complementary side, the international co-operation system needs to work more inclusively among development partners, upgrade the building of domestic capacities to better connect national and international agendas, and operate with more tools and actors.

Some options appear as priorities. First, promoting mission-driven partnerships that increase citizen participation and provide equal footing governance mechanisms and frameworks while fostering policy dialogues; second, reinforcing regional co-operation; and third, implementing a balanced use of financing, regulations and standards, and technical co-operation for capacity building.

This section presents practical policy considerations and options for a continued update of international co-operation schemes with and within LAC to build forward better.

Mission-driven international partnerships

Mission-driven international partnerships entail thinking beyond currently defined areas and institutions to encompass all relevant resources, tools and actors in issue-based coalitions that achieve measurable development results. First, in terms of purpose or objectives, international partnerships can be driven by multi-dimensional missions or development objectives, rather than structured according to sectors or institutions, therefore allowing for policy coherence across efforts. Second, in terms of tools, all relevant resources, for instance financing, knowledge and technology, should be deployed, ensuring a whole-of-government approach as proposed in the DiT framework. Third, in terms of participation, led by clear political will and bottom-up endorsement, and supported by relevant research and accountability mechanisms, new partnerships will be a key driver of the virtuous cycle at the multilateral level to ensure the attainment of the SDGs and, particularly relevant in the case of LAC, the effective implementation of a new social contract. Innovative experiences have multiplied during the pandemic, reflecting this vision (Box 5.3).

Box 5.3. Team Europe: A mission-driven initiative created in the context of COVID-19

Team Europe was born out of the extraordinary conditions created in 2020 by the COVID-19 pandemic as a united European response to the major needs emerging in partner countries. Team Europe strengthens the European Union's contribution through improved co-ordination and coherence. It combines the collective development resources of the European Union, EU member states, the European Investment Bank and the European Bank for Reconstruction and Development. Members of Team Europe work together in an inclusive and co-ordinated manner to support partners.

The Team Europe COVID-19 response for LAC included a redirection of existing programmes and funds where possible and an acceleration of payments at both the country and multi-country levels. The initial Team Europe scheme concerned around EUR 900 million (Euros) for LAC.

From April 2020 onwards, the European Union launched a pilot exercise of Team Europe country roundtables in Argentina, Costa Rica and Ecuador. Under the co-leadership of the EU Delegation and the partner government, these meetings gather a wide range of national stakeholders and representatives of the EU member states active in the country, European Commission-supported programmes and the local administration to discuss how better to join forces and provide coherent EU support to COVID-19 management and recovery in the country. In this way, Team Europe acts in line with partner countries' development needs and priorities and facilitates the transition to inclusive and sustainable economies and societies, promoting digitalisation for development, boosting resilience and reducing the risk of future crises.

The so-called "Team Europe Initiatives" will be integrated into the 2021-27 EU Multi-annual Indicative Programme. Underpinned by strategic policy dialogue, they will aim to support transformational change by delivering concrete results for partner countries. They will draw on the best mix of support modalities and will be grounded at the most appropriate level. The purpose is to maximise the impact and the transformational effect of European funds by merging the capacities of EU member states, the European Commission and their various institutions. Doors are also open to other partners or development institutions to join in.

Structuring international co-operation through mission-driven partnerships can help grasp the multi-dimensionality of development and promote greater policy coherence (SDG 17). Focusing efforts on solving wicked development issues can be a catalyst for the international architecture to adopt more flexible approaches focused on results. It is essential to promote cross-sectoral approaches and a better understanding of the many dimensions of development to create synergies between policies across sectors and levels and as many win-win scenarios as possible. These synergies we refer to are horizontal (e.g. the different pillars of the social contract) as well as vertical (between global, regional, national and subnational levels of governance) (Knoll, 2014[49]).

Focusing on a specific mission can also drive a more flexible use of more tools and help create new ones. LAC needs a broader set of tools beyond traditional ones, including a more technical conversation amongst partners based on knowledge sharing, policy dialogue, capacity building exchanges, technology transfers and South-South and triangular co-operation (OECD et al., 2019[1]). Further, new tools from other forms of partnerships, for example public-private ones, could be embedded in new international partnerships, by way of the whole-of-society platforms that should structure these international policy making processes. Enabling and steering multi-level and multi-stakeholder participation is therefore key.

Mission-driven partnerships could be at the heart of experimenting new ways of involving citizens in international co-operation efforts. Several strategic considerations should be examined to put these mission-driven partnerships into practice more broadly. Key questions include: What benefits does this new approach bring compared to current mechanisms? Who should participate in the policy-making process and define the mission that will lead international partnerships forward? When and how should the various stakeholders be included?

Whole-of-government approaches are still needed, but the current context calls for whole-of-society approaches to international co-operation. A combination of political will at the highest level and opening the floor in the policy-making process of international co-operation to non-state and subnational actors is complex. Still, there is a lot to be gained if LAC countries harness the opportunities of the broad negotiations that new social contracts entail and successfully scale them up in international arenas. The active participation of representative groups of civil society, the private sector, subnational governments and the academy in the agenda-setting process of international co-operation would positively politicise and increase the legitimacy of its mission, turning it into an opportunity to connect global governance more closely to citizens' daily concerns. These actors have on-the-ground projects that provide them with street-level information and implementation insights that could be useful to multilateral policy makers (Chatham House, 2021[50]). Furthermore, they are generally more effective implementers than traditional co-operation actors. This co-operation architecture would foster much-needed horizontal inter-social linkages (Badie, 2020[5]).

A reflection needs to take place on what the new mechanisms of participation would look like, and how they could guarantee inclusive and effective policy dialogue. Multi-stakeholder platforms should be organised with a clear objective and should undertake efforts to ensure the participation of under-represented groups. This is especially important in LAC, given its high and multiple inequalities, which create varying capabilities for representation across various types of actors. Renewed platforms should avoid clustering constituencies, including in the private sector, without considering power imbalances. For instance, SMEs represent 99% of businesses and micro enterprises concentrate most enterprise closures and job losses during COVID-19 (ECLAC, 2021[51]).

Renewed international partnerships should create the appropriate institutional mechanisms to continue improving the transparency of decision making, increasing national and international policy coherence and facilitating implementation. Transparency and accountability would promote greater policy coherence. Some lessons indicate that bottom-up processes work best when structured with an empowered referee, built-in accountability mechanisms and key powerbrokers committed to the process and willing to implement its decisions (Chatham House, 2021[50]).

The post-COVID-19 development narrative needs to cast away old top-down practices and incorporate Southern perspectives and non-state actors that endow international co-operation with local level context and knowledge (Bhattacharya and Sabin Kahn, 2020[42]). More participatory international partnerships are especially important for frontier policy issues such as the ones posed by global megatrends. Effective governance of climate change, international migration, the digitalisation of the economy and other issues on a pressing implementation track requires significant social change, a dialogue on equal footing and bottom-up collaboration that provides multilateral policy makers with early and relevant insights (Chatham House, 2021[50]).

Regional co-operation to leverage the voice of the region in the world

Regional initiatives have a significant role to play to support national efforts towards a new development model, embrace megatrends like digital transformation as tools for recovery and create resilience in the face of future crises. Regional collaboration is a unique space within which states facing similar challenges can share best practices and guidance on how to design policies and compare results and outcomes.

LAC governments should leverage their structural development traps exposed by COVID-19 as a catalyst to overcome the causes of the current "Latin American vacuum". This vacuum refers to the deliberate absence of collective action by the region, which could exacerbate its present weak international influence (Gonzalez et al., 2021[52]). LAC has been losing its capacity to co-operate and act collectively at the regional and global level, having dismantled part of its regional organisations because of political polarisation and fragmentation (Sanahuja, 2020[53]). This is evidenced in the case of the four-year impasse of the Community of Latin American and Caribbean States (CELAC), which hosted its latest Meeting of Heads of State in September 2021. This polarisation has hindered a united voice in the multilateral sphere, as well as the sustainability of ongoing regional and sub-regional endeavours.

Some examples from outside the region could help envisage the type of endeavours that lie ahead for LAC governments in the regional sphere. In 2020, the European Union approved the largest stimulus package in its history. The European Union's long-term budget, coupled with Next Generation EU fund (the temporary instrument designed to boost the recovery), will be the largest stimulus package ever financed through the EU budget (EU, 2020[54]). A total of EUR 1.8 trillion will help rebuild a post-COVID-19 Europe with the mission of making it greener, more digital and more resilient. More than 50% of the amount will support modernisation through: i) research and innovation (Horizon Europe); ii) fair climate and digital transitions (Just Transition Fund and Digital Europe Programme); and iii) preparedness, recovery and resilience (Recovery and Resilience Facility, rescEU and EU4Health). In addition, the package pays attention to modernising traditional policies, such as the cohesion and common agricultural policies, fighting climate change (30% of EU funds), biodiversity protection and gender equality.

The African Union has mobilised its recovery strategy around its continental development framework, the Agenda 2063 (African Union, 2021[55]). This framework aims to deliver inclusive and sustainable development and is a concrete manifestation of the pan-African drive for unity, self-determination, freedom, progress and pursuit of collective prosperity. The agenda is a 50-year vision that encapsulates Africa's Aspirations for the Future and identifies key flagship programmes that can boost Africa's economic growth and development. The agenda identifies key activities to be undertaken through its ten-year implementation plans, which will ensure that it delivers both quantitative and qualitative Transformational Outcomes for Africans.

The Association of South East Asian Nations (ASEAN) launched a rapid assessment of COVID-19 impact on livelihoods across the region and an ASEAN Comprehensive Recovery Framework (ACRF). The ASEAN recognised that addressing the crisis requires both co-ordinated actions within the region and co-operation with its partners. The ACRF serves as the consolidated exit strategy from the COVID-19 crisis. It articulates the ASEAN response through the stages of recovery, focusing on key sectors and segments of society most affected by the pandemic, setting broad strategies and identifying measures for recovery in line with sectoral and regional priorities. Its approach to recovery is proactive, all-encompassing (whole-of-community), flexible and agile. An implementation plan has also been developed (ASEAN, 2020[56]).

Regional co-ordination is critical to strengthening the voice of LAC countries in the international arena, as well as its capacities to deal with the region's structural vulnerabilities in an interconnected world. "Minilateral agreements"[1] have helped blocks of like-minded parties bolster their diplomatic leverage within complex governance negotiations (Chatham House, 2021[50]). This has been the case with the Alliance of Small Island States during multilateral climate negotiations. LAC countries should emulate this strategy on issues where further support from the international community would be desirable, such as debt sustainability, tax evasion and international migration. Moreover, more integration and co-ordination would also help to align international efforts towards key strategic priorities and shared challenges for the region, such as investments at the regional level that promote regional integration. This might be the time for the international community to innovate regarding foreign debt instruments, especially given the investments needed to pursue the SDGs and the 2030 Agenda (Chapter 1).

LAC could be a fertile ground to leverage renewed regional partnerships. The region can learn from past regional and subregional experiences and co-ordinate current processes accordingly. LAC has a wide range of co-operation mechanisms and integration processes, with diverse memberships, capacities and mandates. However, regional partnerships in LAC should avoid overlapping by making current mechanisms and processes converge through the "3M *governance approach*", multilevel, multilateral and multi-stakeholder (Bianchi and Lara, 2021[57]). This regional convergence should innovate purposefully in integrating LAC's non-state actors, subnational governments and development banks from the start in tailored co-operation schemes that are functional for each partnership's mission. Regional institutions with financial and knowledge capacities will be critical in leading these processes.

Social participation experiences at the subregional level in LAC can provide useful lessons on strategies to involve under-resourced and under-represented groups. From the Southern Common Market MERCOSUR's Social Summits and Youth Parliaments to SICA's Regional Forum and Youth Meetings, the region has different approaches to participatory regional policy making that can be harnessed in a regional recovery strategy that puts people first. The results attained by the current flagship participatory instrument of the region, the Escazú Agreement on human rights and the environment (Box 5.4), should be closely monitored to ensure ongoing learning for participatory regional co-operation. Further, regional co-operation with civil society organisations can help protect human rights and strengthen civil society organisations, as is the case of the joint plan between OXFAM and the Inter-American Commission on Human Rights signed in 2019 (Oxfam International, 2020[58]).

> ### Box 5.4. **The participatory experience of the Escazú Agreement**
>
> The Regional Agreement on Access to Information, Public Participation and Justice in Environmental Matters in Latin America and the Caribbean, better known as the Escazú Agreement, stands out for civil society's broad participation in both its promotion and its negotiation process (Naser, Williner and Sandoval, 2021[59]). Adopted in Escazú, Costa Rica in March 2018 after a four-year negotiation process with the technical support of ECLAC, the agreement has been signed by 24 LAC countries and ratified by 12, entering into force on 22 April 2021.
>
> During the preparatory stage of the negotiation process (2012-14), member countries agreed on the Modalities for the participation of the public in the Negotiation Committee. The mechanism comprised three participation tiers (attendance, reporting and making statements) and formally ensured public participation through two representatives who had four substitutes. These were elected according to an agreed voting system.
>
> Participation is also deeply entrenched in the text of the agreement, as public participation is one of the three rights regulated by it. Through its articles, the document establishes the principles, subjects and characteristics of participation, imposing high standards on countries that adopt it. This regional agreement follows Principle 10 of the Rio Declaration on Environment and Development (1992), which established that "the best way to deal with environmental issues is with the participation of all interested citizens".

Enabling a new social contract through a balanced use of tools: Sustainable financing, global rules and standards, and technical co-operation for capacity building

As proposed by the DiT framework, international co-operation as a facilitator implies, among others, using diverse co-operation tools (OECD et al., 2019[1]). Concretely, in the scenario of an exit from the COVID-19 crisis through a new social contract, development partners need to encourage international partnerships that provide the best combination of tools to ensure coherence across national and international policies.

Strengthened political and policy dialogues should underpin mission-driven partnerships with and within the region to ensure a comprehensive and integrated approach that includes the following main tools (Table 5.2): i) sustainable financing; ii) global rules and standards; and iii) enhanced technical co-operation for capacity building. Further, these tools should be implemented towards achieving the more specific social pacts underpinning the social contract (e.g. expanding the reach of social protection and public services, reinvigorating regional productive strategies) and others with a global scope (e.g. mainstreaming environmental sustainability) including an intersectional perspective that goes across socioeconomic groups (including income, gender, ethnic and racial), generations and territories. Strengthening political and policy dialogues involving discussions across these tools is critical to ensure a mission-driven approach that integrates them and considers their interconnections, as most of the time these tools are designed and implemented separately.

Table 5.2. **Integrated approaches for international co-operation to enable a new social contract in LAC**

	Mainstreaming environmental sustainability	Expanding the reach of social protection and public services	Reinvigorating regional productive strategies
Sustainable financing	Mainstream environmental sustainability across financing instruments.	Ensure debt repayment schemes do not compromise expanding the reach of social protection and public services delivery.	Ensure sufficient public and private financing for strategic productive.
Global rules and standards	Adopt environmental regulations and standards, following the principle of common but differentiated responsibilities.	Adopt international regulations for the cross-border transfer of social security contributions and a global corporate tax rate. Agree on international standards for social protection, fair labour, taxation, international migration, etc.	Agree and implement rules conducive to LAC's productive diversification.
Technical co-operation for capacity building	Provide technical co-operation on sustainability practices, research and knowledge; promote policy dialogues with a focus on environmental sustainability.	Exchange policy experiences on social protection and public services delivery; foster capacity building in public institutions, including by enhancing understanding of the interconnections across national development strategies and global dynamics.	Transfer knowledge and technology to increase productivity; boost policy dialogues at regional and global levels to foster regional value chains.

Strengthen political and policy dialogues
with a balanced and integrated use of tools

Source: Own elaboration.

Sustainable finance for development

Sustainable finance for development remains an essential tool for international co-operation with the region, particularly for the post-COVID-19 recovery. Capacity to mobilise domestic and external resources remains a key challenge for countries in LAC. Domestic resource mobilisation remains low, at 22.9% of GDP, compared to 33.8% in OECD countries (OECD et al., 2021[60]). Further, accessing international development finance is a key element to enable a new social contract in the region promoting inclusive and sustainable development. This is especially essential given the economic and financial shock the COVID-19 crisis has inflicted in LAC, by reducing its already weak fiscal capacity and liquidity.

Financial challenges for a new social contract should be addressed considering the previous financial inflow structure of the region and acting upon projected tendencies. Most of the inflows of external financing received by LAC economies are from foreign direct investment (FDI), representing more than 3% of the region's GDP. The dynamics of financial flows to LAC show that the share of private flows in total financial flows to the region has increased in contrast to ODA, which has declined to represent less than 1% of GDP in the region (ECLAC, 2021[31]), falling short of the spending needs to achieve the SDGs by 2030. During 2020, the different sources of external financing evolved differently. ODA rose globally, remittances to LAC increased by 6.5% (World Bank, 2021[61]), but FDI, the region's main external financing resource, fell 34.7%, going back to 2005 levels (ECLAC, 2021[30]).

Diversifying external financing, pushing forward innovative finance mechanisms and channelling financing towards overcoming multi-dimensional development traps and attaining the SDGs, should be a priority for LAC and its partners. Governments from the region and intergovernmental organisations should put forward further external financing innovations for building a sustainable recovery, by boosting public finance and leveraging private finance towards achieving the SGDs and the 2030 Agenda. In particular, efforts should be devoted to catalysing the important volumes of private assets, such as pension funds or insurance companies. FDI and other sources of investment should be channelled into sectors that can promote a new development pattern, boost competitiveness and employment and reduce the environmental footprint. For instance, promising sectors include renewable energy, sustainable mobility in cities, the digital revolution to universalise access to technology, the health-care manufacturing industry, the bioeconomy and ecosystem services, the care economy, the circular economy and sustainable tourism (ECLAC, 2021[62]).

Innovation efforts should focus on increasing climate finance, which currently falls short. As of September 2020, Brazil, Chile, Colombia and Mexico lead the region in relation to sustainable finance markets, with green bonds issuance and active dialogue with investors and financial institutions on sustainable practices. The total amount of climate change finance needed to fund both mitigation and adaptation measures post-2020 has been estimated at more than USD 100 billion annually, an ambitious global goal for facing current scenarios (The Independent Expert Group on Climate Finance, 2020[63]). Despite the financing gap, a promising trend appears. During 2020, the volume of green, social and sustainable bonds issued in the region doubled to USD 12 693 billion. This growth is attributable to the first social bond issues, which totalled USD 3 876 billion, and the first sustainable bond issues, which amounted to USD 1 689 billion (ECLAC, 2021[19]).

The region needs to contribute to and harness ongoing innovative efforts in terms of finance for development. The interlinkages across domestic and global challenges – including inclusiveness and jobs, global health, digital transformation or climate change – make it even more relevant for LAC to join efforts in mobilising private investment in line with the region's development objectives in a coherent manner. Positive innovations are already emerging. These include development of blended finance mechanisms, such as the Latin American Investment Facility (LAIF) and the European Union's Caribbean Investment Facility (CIF). Another innovative example is the UN Net Zero Asset Owner Alliance, whose members – representing a USD 6.6 trillion united investor action – commit to transitioning their investment portfolios to net-zero GHG emissions by 2050 consistent with a maximum temperature rise of 1.5°C above pre-industrial temperatures (UNEFPI, 2019[64]). Finally, LAGREEN, the first Latin American green bond fund created by EU's LAIF, the German Co-operation Ministry and the German Development Bank, will leverage an approximate EUR 450 million investment (EC, 2020[65]).

A co-ordinated solution for managing the challenge of debt should be a priority, especially considering the investments to be made in the medium and long term to attain the SDGs. The *Forum of the Countries of LAC on Sustainable Development 2021* (hereafter, The Forum) made key agreements on the international financial measures needed to address LAC countries' limited fiscal space and high debt levels, which take into account the heterogeneity of countries in the region. The Forum called on UN member states and international financial institutions to provide more liquidity in the financial system, especially in all developing countries (ECLAC, 2021[66]).

Regional institutions and experts call for leveraging the current policy space to drive reform of the international debt architecture and to integrate short-term measures into financing for a development strategy focused on building forward better (ECLAC, 2021[30]; Ocampo, 2021[34]). This could include the creation of a multilateral sovereign debt restructuring mechanism and the establishment of a multilateral credit rating agency (ECLAC, 2021[30]). Other proposals for the long term include eliminating the dual IMF accounting and consolidating regular and SDR accounts so that unused SDRs could be considered deposits by countries into the fund, which the institution can then use to finance its programmes. Future financial instruments should also consider improving countries' capacity for debt repayment and avoid an unsustainable indebtedness that compromises the expansion of social protection and public services by, for instance, linking loan repayments to each country's exposure and vulnerability to disasters (as do current hurricane clauses) (Nieto Parra and Da Costa, 2021[4]). Last, sovereign debt issues should be managed with a long-term view through the design of an institutional mechanism to facilitate sovereign debt restructuring (Ocampo, 2021[34]). Environmental sustainability should be mainstreamed across innovative debt mechanisms, for instance through SDG and green bonds and debt-swaps (Nieto Parra and Da Costa, 2021[4]).

LAC countries represented in the Forum also stressed the importance of addressing the specific needs of MICs through innovative financing for development. MICs (also HICs) of the region need an accurate response that goes beyond current graduation criteria and takes into account their structural vulnerabilities. One of the latest proposals looks to implement an ambitious idea, Global Public Investment (GPI) (Box 5.5) (Glennie, 2020[67]).

Box 5.5. Global Public Investment

The pandemic has highlighted the profound funding challenges that prevent the international community from securing essential global public goods and realising sustainable development. The post-COVID-19 period will provide a unique opportunity to gather momentum behind a paradigm shift in how concessional international public finance can complement other sources of finance in promoting sustainable development; securing global public goods, services and infrastructure; and protecting the global commons.

Global Public Investment (GPI) is a new approach to concessional international public finance for the 21st century (Glennie, 2020[67]). Building on the SDGs, where development is understood in its diversity and multi-dimensionality, and the push in LAC towards DiT, the GPI approach suggests a framework based on sustained co-responsibility. Under this framework, all countries would work together: all would contribute on an ongoing basis, and all would be eligible to receive, based on assessed requirements. As co-contributors, all countries would play a role in deciding how the funds are allocated. For the world to move closer to the internationally agreed development goals, multiple types of financing need to be maximised. Domestic resources (including taxation), private financing, philanthropic funds and remittances are all crucial, but the concessional international public funding component is also critical and needs to evolve to fit modern expectations of governance and objectives. That is what the GPI approach offers.

GPI proposes five broad evolutions (or paradigm shifts) in ambition, function, geography, governance and narrative. It comprises four fundamental pillars: i) universal contributions; ii) ongoing commitments; iii) representative control; and iv) co-creation between governments and peoples of the world.

This new approach to finance could be a strategic tool, especially for LAC countries, as many are reaching the upper middle-income and high-income thresholds. Instead of "graduation", which would affect progress in many LAC countries, GPI proposes "gradation" whereby all countries continue to receive financial support depending on their specific needs. This new approach would also allow the region to create forms of wealth redistribution to tackle the growing problem of inequality.

Global rules and standards

Promoting inclusive and sustainable development requires that regional and international partnerships take integrated approaches that combine financing and knowledge transfer with the creation and implementation of global rules and standards pertinent to facing global shared challenges. The cross-border nature of major development issues not only calls for the improvement of national capacities but equally, or even more importantly, it requires multilateral agreements on shared policy criteria and actions that reduce global inequality and promote policy coherence across national, bilateral and multilateral levels.

For instance, eradicating tax evasion is a requirement for the attainment of new social contracts in LAC that demands cross-border rules. In 2018, tax evasion amounted to USD 325 billion, which equated to 6.1% of LAC's GDP that year (Pezzini, 2020[68]; UN, 2020[69]). Untaxed resources unfairly reproduce the region's high income and wealth inequality levels and withhold funds needed to invest in an inclusive and sustainable recovery. Promising outcomes stem from recent agreements for the adoption of a global corporate tax rate and from ongoing work by the OECD through instruments such as the Common Reporting Standard (OECD, 2021[70]), the Inclusive Framework on Base Erosion and Profit Shifting and the LAC Fiscal Initiative. Regional and global standards would help foster the implementation of gender-oriented tax policies and other innovative policy actions in the taxing field (Chapter 1).

LAC's development success through a new social contract relies on the capability of the multilateral system to regulate this and other global megatrends, such as digitalisation, inequality and climate change, through innovative collective action. In turn, the region will be better equipped to contribute to the attainment of the SDGs and the provision of regional and global public goods.

Technical co-operation for capacity building

Technical co-operation remains essential, particularly in exiting this crisis through new social contracts. International co-operation efforts could include transferring capacities on innovative options for the reduction of social protection gaps – particularly for the poor and extremely poor, informal workers, those vulnerable to climate change, women and migrants – and exchanging experiences on how to improve the quality and coverage of basic public services, for example, through digitalisation. In the productive sphere, renewed partnerships should promote spaces for political and policy discussion at the regional level on regional value chains and the diversification of the productive matrix to help LAC countries increase manufacturing capacities, improve preparedness and resilience for future pandemics, and accelerate industrialisation, including in the health sector. Technology and knowledge transfer will be fundamental instruments.

This crisis has shown that national development strategies cannot be conceived in a national vacuum. For developing countries to reduce their exposure to external shocks and improve their fiscal or socio-economic capacities, these strategies will have to grasp global challenges better. Policy dialogue, training, exchange of knowledge and best practices, and technical co-operation, particularly through South-South and triangular co-operation, could provide valuable lessons in this regard (Nieto Parra and Da Costa, 2021[4]).

Capacity building should also follow a multilevel, multilateral and multi-stakeholder approach. National governments, as well as subnational governments, civil society, the productive sector and organised vulnerable groups, should take part in capacity-building programmes. Multilateral roundtables that favour mutual learning and monitoring can function as an effective mechanism to advance more impactful knowledge sharing at the international level.

European Union-LAC partnerships to build forward better

The European Union is a key interregional partner of LAC, as seen during the pandemic. The European Union has signed association, free trade or political and co-operation agreements with 27 of the 33 LAC countries and is LAC's largest provider of development co-operation, its third largest trade partner and its first foreign investor (EEAS, 2019[71]).

However, there is a need to continue strengthening and modernising the bi-regional partnership. In April 2019, the European Commission released a communication to revitalise political dialogue by joining forces for a common future through four mutually reinforcing priorities: prosperity, democracy, resilience and effective global governance (EEAS, 2019[71]). The document stated that the rapidly evolving geopolitical environment introduces new challenges and opportunities to which the European Union and LAC should respond by working together to preserve multilateralism and a rules-based global order (EEAS, 2019[71]).

LAC and the European Union should seize the global momentum created by the pandemic to continue crafting a partnership that provides strategic autonomy for both regions, a space for policy dialogue, regulatory convergence and, in the case of LAC, a productive transformation to change the economic model and a reconstruction of the social contract (Sanahuja and Rodríguez, 2021[72]). It is important to sustain the European Union's support, through capacity building and policy dialogue, to the revision of national social contracts in LAC, as with EUROsociAL's co-operation directed towards Chile's constitutional process and towards Argentina and Costa Rica in the creation and strengthening of their own Economic and Social Councils. Triangular co-operation will be a key instrument for the bi-regional partnership, facilitated by the programme ADELANTE 2 and its 2021-2024 Triangular Co-operation Window.

Mission-driven partnerships between LAC and the European Union should further ensure a multi-dimensional and universally coherent approach to the region's development traps and foster a stronger and co-ordinated voice to address common issues in the multilateral sphere. The new generation of Association Agreements might be a key instrument in the implementation of these renewed partnerships, as they cover all areas of the bi-regional relation (co-operation, political dialogue, trade, investment) in one document, thereby helping identify synergies and promoting greater national and international policy coherence. Team Europe is an institutional innovation that will facilitate this process.

Conclusions

International co-operation is indispensable for Latin America to exit the COVID-19 crisis, set the region on the path towards achieving the SDGs, complete and foster national efforts. There is a need to create a new social contract to allow LAC countries to break the vicious circles created by development traps and reinforce international co-operation's facilitating role – as stated in the DiT framework – in a context of increased interconnection between the national and international spheres.

The pandemic proved that the region is a fertile ground to realise international co-operation's facilitating role, but there is space to improve collaboration. LAC shows a wide range of North-South, South-South, triangular, multi-stakeholder and even South-North initiatives that have addressed key challenges during the pandemic and towards the recovery stage by providing not only financial support, but also technical assistance and exchange of experiences. Nevertheless, the crisis also showed that the region still lacks bolder regional co-operation and co-ordination, as well as international financial and non-financial co-operation initiatives to ensure its long-term recovery.

This moment brings an opportunity to strengthen regional and international co-operation with and within LAC, revaluing and renewing multilateralism. This critical juncture, coupled with the need for LAC countries to build a new social contract, calls for defining new partnerships. These new partnerships need to face the issues that are blocking the full potential of international co-operation. This includes the need for increased participation of citizens, for equal-footing governance mechanisms and frameworks, including strengthened regional co-operation, and addressing the current levels of fragmentation between institutions and between tools.

Mission-driven partnerships could be an innovative approach to experimenting new ways of integrating all relevant resources, tools and actors in issue-based coalitions that achieve measurable development results. This could enable greater policy coherence across international co-operation efforts, foster a whole-of-society approach to the design and implementation of international partnerships, and promote a virtuous cycle at the multilateral level to ensure the attainment of the SDGs and the effective implementation of a new social contract. Leveraging regional co-operation efforts and networks towards increased regional integration appear as a key step forward. Finally, equally relevant would be to explore how best to take holistic approaches that consider different tools to solve multi-dimensional challenges. Efforts would need to be put in place to find the right balance across sustainable finance, global rules and standards, and technical co-operation for capacity building, in order to face global shared challenges. Well-articulated political and policy dialogues are a necessary condition to underpin the above-mentioned efforts.

LAC can contribute to strengthen and experiment new forms of multilateralism by boosting policy dialogues within the region and beyond through equal-footing international policy partnerships that put people and policy first. The LAC-European Union partnership is a privileged policy space to implement this agenda, as it has already taken decisive steps in this direction.

Box 5.6. **Key policy messages**

- The COVID-19 crisis revealed the interconnection between unregulated global megatrends and national discontent in Latin America.

- The consolidation of a Development in Transition approach can contribute to boosting a multi-dimensional agenda for the recovery in LAC that considers the interrelation between policy areas, actors and governance levels.

- The multi-dimensional nature of global development calls for multi-dimensional responses, including efforts to measure development beyond GDP, both nationally and internationally, providing a renewed guidance for co-operation efforts.

- International co-operation can facilitate and complement domestic efforts to define and implement a new social contract in the region, allowing to break the vicious circle created by LAC development traps.

- The pandemic has scaled up efforts by LAC countries and international partners with important lessons for international co-operation's facilitating role (particularly through technical South-South and triangular co-operation). Still, there have been significant gaps in financing and in policy co-ordination at the regional and multilateral spheres.

- Mission-driven partnerships can promote more participatory and equal multilateral governance. They can increase citizens' participation and ensure policy coherence at the national, regional and international level, as well as across social, environmental and economic objectives. These are critical elements of a global enabling environment for exiting the crisis with more inclusive and sustainable development models.

- Strengthening regional co-operation will be key to enhancing the region's voice in the international arena, as well as its capacities to deal with its development traps in an interconnected world.

Box 5.6. **Key policy messages** *(cont.)*

- Strengthening the political and policy dialogue will be crucial towards building new social contracts for the recovery in the region.
- Within these dialogues, balancing the three key tools of 1) sustainable finance; 2) global rules and standards; and 3) technical co-operation for capacity building will be crucial to ensuring coherence across national and international policies and facilitating a new social contract.
- Renewed political and policy dialogue and co-operation between LAC and the European Union could provide both regions with strategic autonomy and mutual learning to tackle common development challenges. It could also provide LAC with the resources and capabilities to transform its economic model and reconstruct its social contract.

Note

1. Minilateral agreements or small-group voluntary commitments can provide pathways to achieving global norms (Chatham House, 2021[50]).

References

African Union (2021), *Agenda 2063: The Africa We Want*, African Union Commission, Addis Ababa, https://au.int/en/agenda2063/overview. [55]

Amazon Conservation (2020), *MAAP #129: Amazon Fires 2020 – Recap of Another Intense Fire Year*, Amazon Conservation Association, New York, https://www.amazonconservation.org/2020-fires-recap/. [7]

Americas Market Intelligence (2020), *The Acceleration of Financial Inclusion during the COVID-19 Pandemic*, study by Americas Market Intelligence commissioned by Mastercard, https://newsroom.mastercard.com/latin-america/files/2020/10/Mastercard_Financial_Inclusion_during_COVID_whitepaper_EXTERNAL_20201012.pdf. [45]

ASEAN (2020), *ASEAN Comprehensive Recovery Framework and its Implementation Plan*, Association of South East Asian Nations, https://asean.org/asean-comprehensive-recovery-framework-implementation-plan/. [56]

Badie, B. (2020), *Inter-socialités. Le monde n'est plus géopolitique*, CNRS Editions. [5]

Bárcena, A. (2021), *Retos de financiación para sostener una política fiscal expansiva y ampliar el espacio fiscal para una recuperación transformadora en los países de ingresos medios*, Comisión Económica para América Latina y el Caribe (CEPAL), https://www.cepal.org/sites/default/files/presentations/webinar_3-_210423_final_alicia_barcena_ffd._viernes_23_de_abril.pdf. [38]

BBC (2021), *Why Colombia's protests are unlikely to fizzle out*, British Broadcasting Corporation, https://www.bbc.com/news/world-latin-america-56986821. [9]

Bhattacharya, D. and S. Sabin Kahn (2020), *COVID-19: A game changer for the Global South and international co-operation?*, OECD Publishing, https://oecd-development-matters.org/2020/09/02/covid-19-a-game-changer-for-the-global-south-and-international-co-operation/. [42]

Bianchi, M. and I. Lara (2021), *Gobernanza Regional 3M: Hacia una convergencia del multilateralismo en América Latina en tiempos pandémicos*, Colabora.lat, https://colabora.lat/wp-content/uploads/2021/04/PAPER-BIANCHI-LARA.pdf. [57]

CAF (2021), *Se aprueban USD 250 millones para apoyar el plan de reactivación económica del Paraguay*, CAF, Banco de Desarrollo de América Latina, https://www.caf.com/es/actualidad/noticias/2021/03/caf-destinara-usd-250-millones-para-apoyar-el-plan-de-reactivacion-economica-del-paraguay/?parent=2198. [43]

CGD (2021), *SDRs and Fiscal Space*, XXXIII Regional Seminar on Fiscal Policy ECLAC, https://www.cepal.org/sites/default/files/presentations/mark_plant.pdf. [20]

Chatham House (2021), *Reflections on building more inclusive global governance – Ten insights into emerging practice*, https://www.chathamhouse.org/2021/04/reflections-building-more-inclusive-global-governance/03-ten-insights-reflections-building. [50]

DEVEX (2021), *Funding the response to COVID-19: Analysis of funding opportunities*, https://www.devex.com/news/interactive-who-s-funding-the-covid-19-response-and-what-are-the-priorities-96833 (accessed on 15 March 2021). [28]

EC (2020), *Team Europe: A new Green Bond fund for Latin America*, European Commission, https://ec.europa.eu/international-partnerships/news/team-europe-new-green-bond-fund-latin-america_en. [65]

ECLAC (2021), *Development in transition: Concept and measurement proposal for renewed cooperation*, United Nations Publication, Santiago, https://www.cepal.org/en/publications/47167-development-transition-concept-and-measurement-proposal-renewed-cooperation-latin. [31]

ECLAC (2021), *Economic Survey of Latin America and the Caribbean*, United Nations Publication, Santiago, https://www.cepal.org/en/pressreleases/latin-america-and-caribbean-will-grow-59-2021-reflecting-statistica. [62]

ECLAC (2021), *Financing for development in the era of COVID-19 and beyond*, United Nations Publication, Santiago, https://www.cepal.org/en/publications/46711-financing-development-era-covid-19-and-beyond. [30]

ECLAC (2021), *Intergovernmentally agreed conclusions and recommendations of the Fourth Meeting of the Forum of the Countries of Latin America and the Caribbean on Sustainable Development*, Economic Commission for Latin America and the Caribbean, https://foroalc2030.cepal.org/2021/en/documents/intergovernmentally-agreed-conclusions-and-recommendations-fourth-meeting-forum-countries. [66]

ECLAC (2021), *Mipymes y el COVID-19*, United Nations Publication, Santiago, https://www.cepal.org/es/euromipyme/mipymes-covid-19. [51]

ECLAC (2021), *Panorama Fiscal de América Latina y el Caribe, 2021*, United Nations Publication, Santiago, https://repositorio.cepal.org/bitstream/handle/11362/46808/1/S2100170_es.pdf. [19]

ECLAC (2021), *Social Panorama of Latin America 2020*, United Nations Publication, Santiago, https://www.cepal.org/en/publications/46688-social-panorama-latin-america-2020. [11]

ECLAC (2020), *Construir un nuevo futuro. Una recuperación transformadora con igualdad y sostenibilidad*, United Nations Publication, Santiago, https://repositorio.cepal.org/bitstream/handle/11362/46225/1/S2000667_es.pdf. [18]

ECLAC (2020), *Costa Rica Presents a Proposal for a COVID-19 Economic Relief Fund*, United Nations Publication, Santiago, https://www.cepal.org/en/pressreleases/costa-rica-presents-proposal-covid-19-economic-relief-fund. [44]

EEAS (2019), *Joint Communication to the European Parliament and the Council European Union, Latin America and the Caribbean, Joining Forces for a Common Future*, https://eeas.europa.eu/sites/default/files/joint_communication_to_the_european_parliament_and_the_council_-_european_union_latin_america_and_the_caribbean_-_joining_forces_for_a_common_future.pdf. [71]

El País (2021), *La conexión México-Buenos Aires-Moscú: así se disparó la Sputnik V en América Latina*, El País, https://elpais.com/sociedad/2021-02-03/la-conexion-mexico-buenos-aires-moscu-asi-se-disparo-la-sputnik-v-en-america-latina.html. [40]

EU (2020), *Recovery plan for Europe*, European Union, https://ec.europa.eu/info/strategy/recovery-plan-europe_en. [54]

EUROsociAL (2021), *Plan for the recovery, social reconstruction and resilience of Central America and the Dominican Republic*, https://eurosocial.eu/en/eurosocial-tv/plan-para-la-recuperacion-reconstruccion-social-y-resiliencia-de-centroamerica-y-republica-dominicana/. [47]

Fund, I. (ed.) (2021), *Social Repercussions of Pandemics*, IMF Working Papers, https://www.imf.org/en/Publications/WP/Issues/2021/01/29/Social-Repercussions-of-Pandemics-50041. [10]

Glennie, J. (2020), *The Future of Aid, Global Public Investment*, Routledge, https://www.routledge.com/The-Future-of-Aid-Global-Public-Investment/Glennie/p/book/9780367404970. [67]

Gonzalez, G. et al. (2021), "Coyuntura crítica, transición de poder y vaciamiento latinoamericano", *Revista Nueva Sociedad*, Vol. 291, pp. 49-65. [52]

Johns Hopkins (2020), *WTO TRIPS Waiver for COVID-19 Vaccines*, Johns Hopkins Bloomberg School of Public Health, https://www.jhsph.edu/covid-19/articles/wto-trips-waiver-for-covid-19-vaccines.html. [23]

Kharas and Dooley (2020), *Sustainable development finance proposals for the global COVID-19 response*, Brookings: Global Working Papers, https://www.brookings.edu/research/sustainable-development-finance-proposals-for-the-global-covid-19-response/. [35]

Knoll, A. (2014), "Bringing policy coherence for development into the post-2015 agenda – Challenges and prospects", ECDPM, Discussion paper, https://ecdpm.org/wp-content/uploads/DP-163-Policy-Coherence-for-Development-Post-2015-Agenda-Challenges-Prospects-2014.pdf. [49]

Larrain, G. (2020), *The Stability of the Social Contract in Chile: A paradoxical social explosion and its institutional responses*, OECD presentation, Facultad de Economía y Negocios de la Universidad de Chile. [3]

Loewe, M., T. Zintl and A. Houdret (2020), "The social contract as a tool of analysis: Introduction to the special issue on Framing the evolution of new social contracts in Middle Eastern and North African countries", *World Development*, http://www.die-gdi.de/en/others-publications/article/the-social-contract-as-a-tool-of-analysis-introduction-to-the-special-issue-on-framing-the-evolution-of-new-social-contracts-in-middle-eastern-and-north-african-countries/. [2]

Mander, B. (2021), "Protesters take to Paraguay's streets as Covid cases climb", *Financial Times*, https://www.ft.com/content/425f05d0-0931-4394-b559-bf6b9beed3f9. [8]

Mazzucato, M., H. Lishi Li and E. Torreele (2020), *Designing vaccines for people not profits*, Project Syndicate, https://www.project-syndicate.org/commentary/covid-vaccines-for-profit-not-for-people-by-mariana-mazzucato-et-al-2020-12. [22]

Mazzucato, M. (2018), *The Entrepeneurial State. Debunking public vs private sector myths*. [21]

Naser, A., A. Williner and C. Sandoval (2021), *Participación ciudadana en los asuntos públcos: un elemento estratégico para la Agenda 2030 y el gobierno abierto*, https://www.cepal.org/sites/default/files/publication/files/46645/S2000907_es.pdf. [59]

Nieto Parra, S. and R. Da Costa (2021), "Desarrollo en Transición en América Latina en tiempos de la COVID-19", *Documentos de Trabajo Fundación Carolina*. [4]

Ocampo, J. (2021), *"Significant but insufficient progress in financial support for developing countries"*, OECD Development Matters, https://oecd-development-matters.org/2021/04/13/significant-but-insufficient-progress-in-financial-support-for-developing-countries/. [34]

Ocampo, J. (2020), *UNDP LAC C19 PDS No. 7, International financial cooperation in the face of Latin America's economic crisis*, United Nations Development Programme, https://www.latinamerica.undp.org/content/rblac/en/home/library/crisis_prevention_and_recovery/la-cooperacion-financiera-internacional-frente-a-la-crisis-econo.html. [36]

OECD (2021), *Automatic Exchange Portal, Online support for the implementation of automatic exchange of information in tax matters*, OECD Publishing, Paris, https://www.oecd.org/tax/automatic-exchange/common-reporting-standard/. [70]

OECD (2021), "Business Insights on Emerging Markets 2021", OECD Emerging Markets Network, OECD Development Centre, Paris, http://www.oecd.org/dev/oecdemnet.htm [39]

OECD (2021), *Business Sustainability in Emerging Markets*, OECD Publishing, Paris, https://www.oecd.org/dev/EMnet_Policy_Note_Business_Sustainability_Emerging_Markets.pdf. [46]

OECD (2021), *COVID-19 spending helped to lift foreign aid to an all-time high in 2020 but more effort needed*, OECD Publishing, Paris, https://www.oecd.org/newsroom/covid-19-spending-helped-to-lift-foreign-aid-to-an-all-time-high-in-2020-but-more-effort-needed.htm. [32]

OECD (2021), *Development co-operation during the COVID-19 pandemic: An analysis of 2020 figures and 2021 trends to watch*, OECD Publishing, Paris, https://www.oecd-ilibrary.org/sites/2dcf1367-en/1/3/1/1/index.html?itemId=/content/publication/2dcf1367-en&_csp_=177392f5df53d89c9678d0628e39a2c2&itemIGO=oecd&itemContentType=book&_ga=2.80395223.1975534698.1630687949-1355889696.1626703359. [33]

OECD (2021), *Perspectives on Global Development 2021: From Protest to Progress?*, OECD Publishing, Paris, https://doi.org/10.1787/405e4c32-en. [25]

OECD (2020), "COVID-19 in Latin America and the Caribbean: Regional socio-economic implications and policy priorities", *OECD Policy Responses to Coronavirus (COVID-19)*, http://www.oecd.org/coronavirus/policy-responses/covid-19-in-latin-america-and-the-caribbean-regional-socio-economic-implications-and-policy-priorities-93a64fde/. [73]

OECD (2020), *Development Co-operation Report 2020: Learning from crises, building resilience*, OECD Publishing, Paris, https://doi.org/10.1787/20747721. [29]

OECD et al. (2021), *Revenue Statistics in Latin America and the Caribbean 2021*, OECD Publishing, Paris, https://doi.org/10.1787/96ce5287-en-es. [60]

OECD et al. (2019), *Latin American Economic Outlook 2019: Development in Transition*, OECD Publishing, Paris, https://doi.org/10.1787/g2g9ff18-en. [1]

Oxfam (2020), *Latin American billionaires surge as world's most unequal region buckles under coronavirus strain*, https://www.oxfam.org/en/press-releases/latin-american-billionaires-surge-worlds-most-unequal-region-buckles. [12]

Oxfam International (2020), *IACHR and Oxfam Sign Agreement for Cooperation in Latin American and Caribbean Human Rights Crises*, https://www.oxfam.org/en/press-releases/iachr-and-oxfam-sign-agreement-cooperation-latin-american-and-caribbean-human-rights. [58]

Pew Research Center (2020), *Summer 2020 Survey September 21*, https://www.pewresearch.org/global/wp-content/uploads/sites/2/2020/09/PG_2020.09.21_UN-Multilateralism_TOPLINE.pdf. [15]

Pezzini, M. (2020), *Citizens' raising expectations: A call to rebuild the social contract?, in "Trapped in the middle? Developmental Challenges for Middle-Income Countries"*, Oxford University Press. [68]

Pezzini, M. and A. Pick (2021), *"From protest to progress?"*, OECD Development Matters, https://oecd-development-matters.org/2021/07/21/from-protest-to-progress/. [27]

Pisani-Ferry, J. (2021), *Global asymmetries strike back*, Bruegel Essay and Lecture Series, https://www.bruegel.org/wp-content/uploads/2021/08/Asymmetries_essay-2508-online.pdf. [6]

Reuters (2021), "Oxygen from Venezuela arrives in Amazon city for COVID-19 patients", https://www.reuters.com/article/us-health-coronavirus-brazil-amazon-idUSKBN29P1U4. [41]

Sanahuja, J.A. (2020), *América Latina y la Unión Europea: agendas sociales, competencia geopolítica y COVID-19*, Araucaria. Revista Iberoamericana de Filosofía, Política, Humanidades y Relaciones Internacionales, https://www.academia.edu/44460023/Am%C3%A9rica_Latina_y_la_Uni%C3%B3n_Europea_agendas_sociales_competencia_geopol%C3%ADtica_y_COVID_19. [53]

Sanahuja, J.A. and J.D. Rodríguez (2021), *El Acuerdo MERCOSUR-Unión Europea: Escenarios y opciones para la autonomía estratégica*, https://www.fundacioncarolina.es/wp-content/uploads/2021/06/AC-20.2021.pdf. [72]

Singer, H. (1995), *"Half a century of economic and social development policies of the UN and Bretton Woods institutions"*, The Pakistan Development Review, Vol. 34/4 Part 1, http://www.jstor.org/stable/41260131 (accessed on 17 February 2021). [26]

The Independent Expert Group on Climate Finance (2020), *Delivering on The $100 Billion Climate Finance Commitment and Transforming Climate Finance*, https://www.un.org/sites/un2.un.org/files/100_billion_climate_finance_report.pdf. [63]

UN (2021), *La CELAC aprueba un proyecto para reducir la dependencia externa en el sector de la salud*, https://news.un.org/es/story/2021/09/1496932. [48]

UN (ed.) (2020), *UN75 2020 and beyond: Shaping our future together*, United Nations, https://un75.online/es/data. [16]

UN (2020), *Development Policy and Multilateralism after COVID-19*, United Nations, https://www.un.org/development/desa/dpad/wp-content/uploads/sites/45/CDP-Covid-19-and-Multilateralism.pdf. [13]

UN (2020), *La evasión fiscal en América Latina, un obstáculo para la recuperación de la crisis del coronavirus*, United Nations, https://news.un.org/es/story/2020/07/1477031. [69]

UNDP (2020), *Human Development Report 2020: The Next Frontier, Human Development and the Anthropocene*, United Nations Development Programme, http://hdr.undp.org/en/content/human-development-report-2020. [14]

UNDP (2020), *Lo que sabíamos entonces, lo que sabemos ahora: Mirando hacia atrás el COVID-19 en 5 gráficos*, United Nations Development Programme, https://www.latinamerica.undp.org/content/rblac/es/home/presscenter/director-s-graph-for-thought/what-we-knew-then--what-we-know-now--looking-back-on-covid-19-in.html. [17]

UNEFPI (2019), *The Net-Zero Asset Owner Alliance FAQ*, https://www.unepfi.org/wordpress/wp-content/uploads/2019/09/AOA_FAQ.pdf. [64]

World Bank (2021), *Defying Predictions, Remittance Flows Remain Strong During COVID-19 Crisis*, https://www.worldbank.org/en/news/press-release/2021/05/12/defying-predictions-remittance-flows-remain-strong-during-covid-19-crisis. [61]

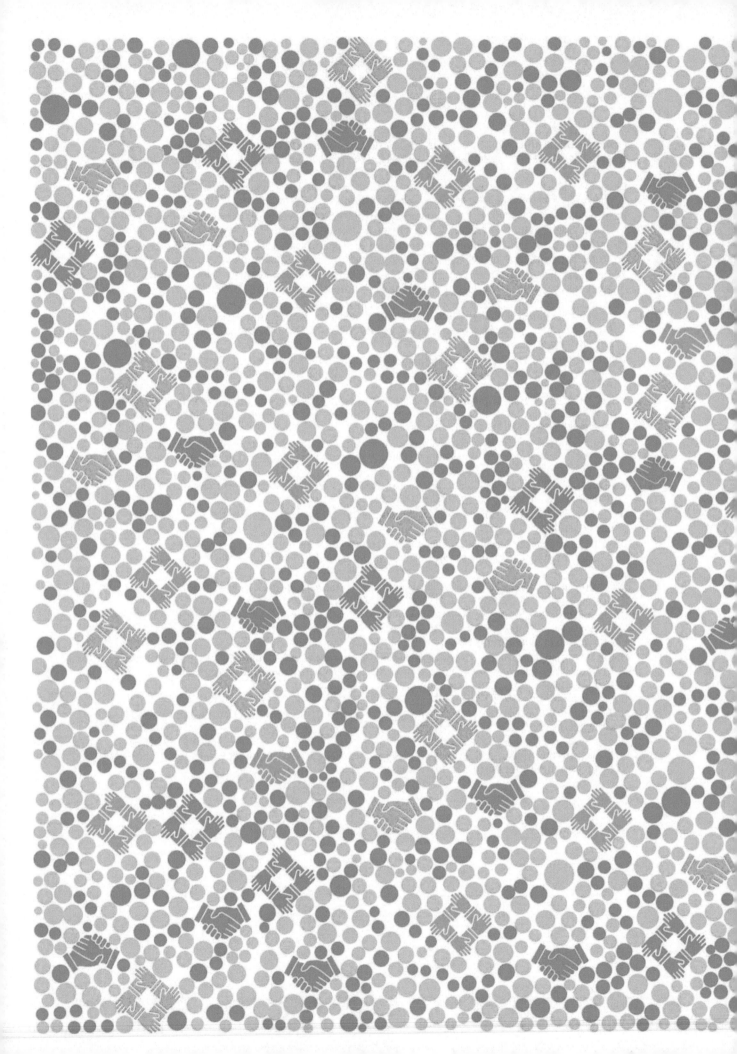

Chapter 6

Special feature: The Caribbean

Before the COVID-19 pandemic, the economies of the Caribbean countries were characterised by modest economic growth, high indebtedness, significant vulnerability to different hazards – notably natural hazards – and dependence on tourism and food imports.

Although there are heterogeneities across Caribbean countries, most of them share structural challenges that have been aggravated by the pandemic. This chapter explores the main impacts of the crisis on the Caribbean sub-region, focusing on how this has affected structural vulnerabilities and analysing the policy response to the crisis and the main strategic areas of policy action to build a recovery that is resilient, inclusive and sustainable.

RecoverypoliciesintheCaribbeanmust addresspendingeconomic,social andenvironmentalchallenges

Structuralchallengeshavebeenaggravatedbythe COVID-19crisis

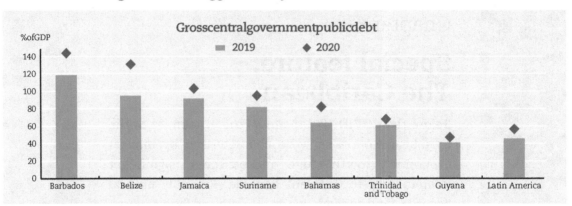

Grosscentralgovernmentpublicdebt
%ofGDP
■ 2019 ◆ 2020

Schoolshavebeenclosedforalongperiod,withsignificantsocio-economicimpact

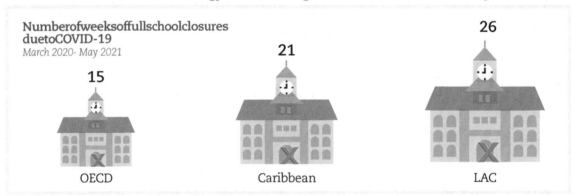

Numberofweeksoffullschoolclosures
dueto COVID-19
March 2020- May 2021

15 — OECD
21 — Caribbean
26 — LAC

Fiscalspacetoaddresstherecoveryislimited

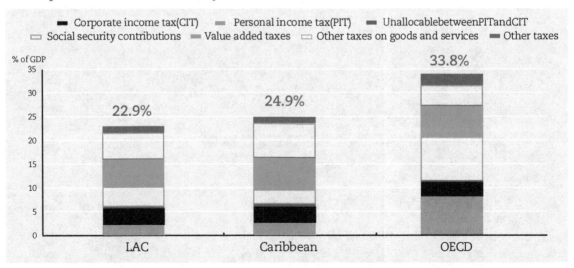

■ Corporate income tax(CIT) ■ Personal income tax(PIT) ■ UnallocablebetweenPITandCIT
□ Social security contributions ■ Value added taxes □ Other taxes on goods and services ■ Other taxes

% of GDP

LAC 22.9%   Caribbean 24.9%   OECD 33.8%

Structural challenges in the Caribbean have been aggravated by the impact of the coronavirus pandemic

The coronavirus pandemic (COVID-19) has had a large-scale effect on the Caribbean economies that has particularly aggravated long-standing vulnerabilities such as slow economic development, low tax revenues and high debt levels.

In terms of economic development, growth in 2021 is forecast to reach 5.2%, which will not be sufficient to compensate for the 7.6% contraction of 2020 and regain the level of output recorded in 2019. Economic growth will be heterogeneous across the sub-region economies, although practically all of them will register growth in 2021 (Figure 6.1).

Figure 6.1. **The Caribbean: GDP growth rate in 2020 and projections for 2021 and 2022**

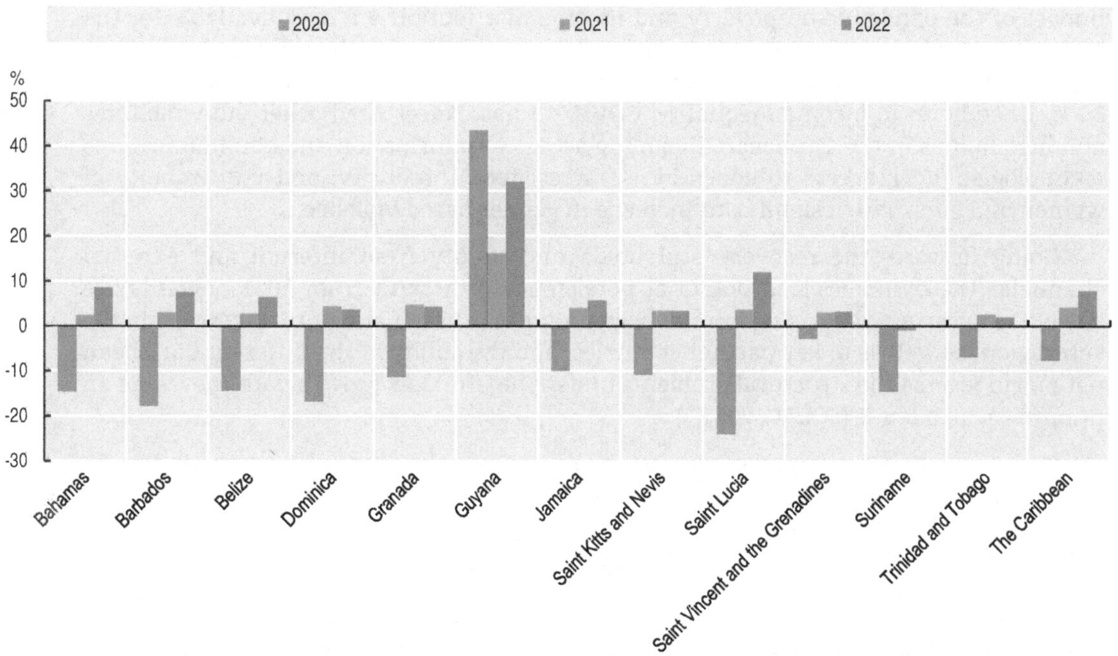

Source: ECLAC (2020[1]), *Fiscal Panorama of Latin America and the Caribbean 2020: Fiscal Policy Amid the Crisis Arising from the Coronavirus Disease (COVID-19) Pandemic*.
StatLink ᵇᵇᵇ *https://doi.org/10.1787/888934287034*

Economic activity in the Caribbean has been hit by several external shocks (ECLAC, 2020[2]). First, a decline in the economic activity of the region's main trading partners and a collapse in international trade (Chapter 1). Second, a temporary decline in commodity prices (Chapter 1). The Caribbean countries (except Trinidad and Tobago) have benefited from temporary falls in agricultural and energy prices. As a result, most of the countries of the sub-region have been able to absorb the shocks they were experiencing through other channels. However, commodity prices are back to their pre-crisis levels – and even higher – reducing any possible benefits. Third, there has been a decline in remittances. The Eurozone and the United States are the main destinations for migrants from the Caribbean. The sub-region economies most affected by the drop in remittances have been Haiti, where they account for 33% of GDP, Jamaica, where they represent 16%, and Saint Vincent and the Grenadines, Dominica and the Dominican Republic, where remittances represent between 5% and 10% of GDP. Fourth, there has been a lower demand for tourism services and tourist activity could take several years to return to 2019 levels. In the short term, there is a gradual recovery as borders open, but flows will be much lower than before the pandemic. There will also be a fear of potential infection during the trip, accompanied by uncertainty about hospital capacities in destination countries and about new border closures, all of which may lead tourists to postpone travel.

The pandemic is having a negative impact in key Caribbean economic sectors (ECLAC, 2021[3]) .These include tourism, aviation, lodging, restaurants, entertainment and commerce, with less on supermarkets, pharmacies and other nationally considered "essential" services. Non-essential product industries also face problems arising from the lockdown measures that meant the suspension of their activities. Businesses' income has declined significantly, making access to credit difficult and in many cases leading to definitive closures. In some countries, construction has also been hit hard by stoppages and the considerable uncertainty surrounding new projects (ECLAC, 2021[4]) .

The economic shock is expected to cause greater income inequality in all the countries of the Caribbean. Given the limited availability of data in the sub-region, estimates on the impact of the pandemic on poverty and income distribution are only available for the Dominican Republic. For 2020, it is estimated that poverty rose there by 4.4 percentage points, extreme poverty by 2.2 percentage points and the Gini index by between 3% and 3.9%. In addition to income inequality, COVID-19 has exacerbated other vulnerabilities and inequalities in the Caribbean, including access to information and communications technologies (ICT); access to education services; food insecurity; and vulnerability of women and girls, with a significant increase in gender-based violence.

Going forward, the recovery still holds uncertainty from internal and external channels. The dynamics and potential persistence of growth from 2021 onwards are subject to uncertainties arising from uneven progress in vaccination processes within the sub-region, as well as in key partner countries, and the ability of the different Caribbean nations to reverse the structural problems underlying the slow growth path they were on prior to the pandemic (ECLAC, 2021[5]).

Governments must face the complex challenge of supporting the recovery despite a low fiscal space that gives rise to structural challenges such as raising tax revenues and dealing with high levels of public debt. Although with strong heterogeneity, in all of the Caribbean economies fiscal balances (and primary balances) worsened in 2020. For instance, in Belize, the overall fiscal deficit deteriorated from -3.5% of gross domestic product (GDP) in 2019 to -11.4% of GDP in 2020. On a smaller scale, Suriname's overall deficit passed from -9.8% of GDP in 2019 to -10.0% of GDP in 2020. Primary balances also worsened in most of the economies except in Barbados and Jamaica. The larger primary deficit and the fall in GDP also exacerbated negative debt dynamics (ECLAC, 2021[6]).

As a result of the pandemic, there was a considerable increase in debt levels in the Caribbean, which is one of the most indebted regions in the world. Of the seven countries where data were available, three had debt-to-GDP ratios of over 100% at the end of 2020, including Barbados (144%), Belize (131%) and Jamaica (103%) (Figure 6.2). Debt increases for 2020 also varied by country; in economies such as Barbados and Belize debt increased by more than 25 percentage points of GDP, while in Trinidad and Tobago and Guyana by less than 10 percentage points. (ECLAC, 2021[6]).

Debt was already a major challenge for the Caribbean before the pandemic. Policy missteps and fiscal profligacy have not necessarily been the root causes of debt accumulation in the sub-region, but rather the result of the impacts of negative external economic shocks, extreme events and climate change challenges (ECLAC, 2020[12]). High indebtedness has translated into high debt service that consumes a significant part of tax revenue. In the 2009-18 period, average debt service, as a percentage of government income, exceeded 40% in three countries in the Caribbean: Antigua and Barbuda, Barbados and Jamaica. In Jamaica, the average ratio was extreme, at 68%. In the Bahamas, Grenada, Saint Kitts and Nevis, Saint Lucia and Saint Vincent and the Grenadines this indicator was between 20% and 40% (Bárcena, 2020[8]). This fiscal situation meant that the countries had very little room to compensate for any negative shocks such as disasters, which are recurrent in the Caribbean.

Figure 6.2. **Gross central government public debt in selected Caribbean economies and Latin-American average (% of GDP)**

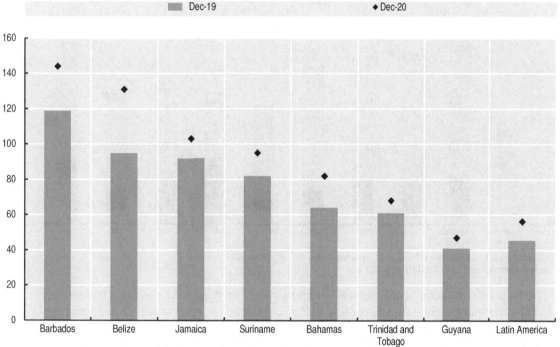

Source: (ECLAC, 2021[6]), *Fiscal Panorama of Latin America and the Caribbean 2021: Fiscal policy challenges for transformative recovery post-COVID-19.*
StatLink ▤▥ *https://doi.org/10.1787/888934287053*

Although with strong heterogeneity across the Caribbean economies, low tax revenues have also limited the fiscal space with which to face the pandemic and support the recovery. Tax-to-GDP ratios were relatively low in the sub-region, with an average of 24.9% of GDP in 2019[1]. This was slightly above the LAC regional average (22.9%) but considerably below the OECD economies (33.8%) (Figure 6.3) (OECD et al., 2021[9]). Since 1990, the average tax-to-GDP ratio of the Caribbean economies has increased by 5.6 points of GDP, a level below South America (9.2 p.p.) and Central America (5.9 p.p.). The increase in revenue collection was mainly driven by the introduction of VAT taxes in 1991 for Jamaica, 1997 for Barbados, 2006 for Belize (the General Sales Tax), 2007 for Guyana and Antigua and Barbuda, 2012 for Saint Lucia and 2015 for the Bahamas. Overall, in 2019, total tax revenues strongly varied among the sub region's economies, going from 16.6% of GDP in Bahamas to 33.1% of GDP in Barbados (OECD et al., 2021[9]).

In addition to the short- and medium-term impact of the COVID-19 crisis, Caribbean countries face longer-term vulnerabilities, including the adverse impacts of climate change, natural hazards and extreme weather events. This is of particular importance for the Caribbean, which is the second-most environmental hazard-prone region in the world (OECD, 2019[10]). Natural disasters are the main environmental challenge, along with concerns about climate change, loss of biodiversity, anthropogenic stressors on freshwater and land-based sources of pollution. The tourism industry, the main export sector of the economy, has also put pressure on natural ecosystems.

Figure 6.3. **Tax structure in selected Caribbean economies and LAC and OECD averages, 2019**

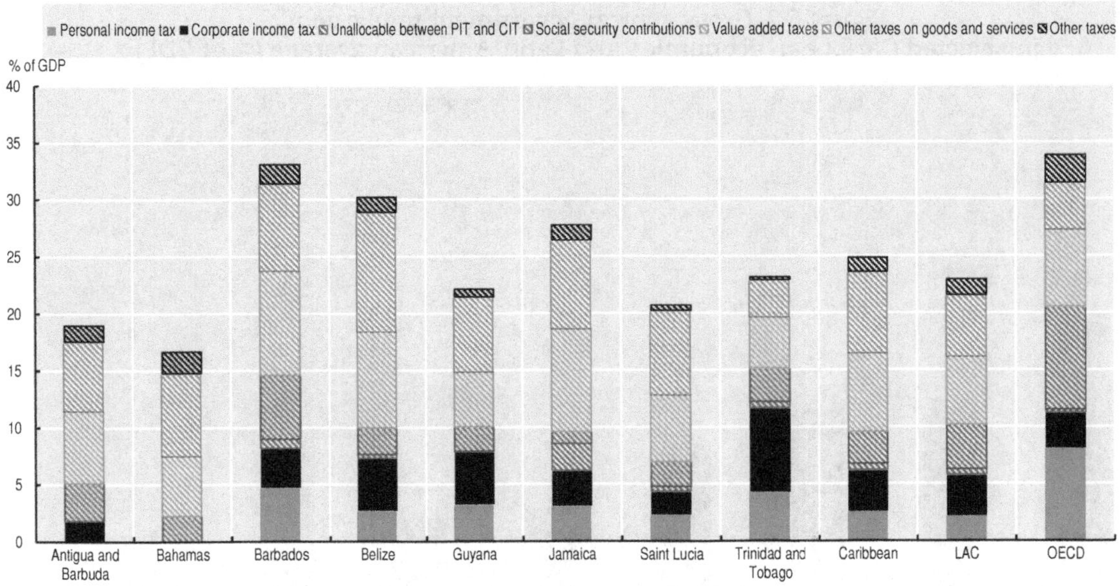

Source: (OECD et al., 2021[9]), Revenue Statistics in Latin America and the Caribbean 2021.
StatLink ▨▨▨ https://doi.org/10.1787/888934287072

The pandemic has possibly created greater awareness about the need to act collectively to face the – arguably – most pressing global challenge for the future: climate change. Seizing the opportunity to build a more environmentally sustainable recovery will be crucial. The complex environmental challenges will require co-ordination of economic, social and environmental policies and coherent governance frameworks. Some of these challenges are related to climate change adaptation, water resources and solid waste management, energy transition and sustainable transportation (OECD, 2020[11]) .

Policy response to the COVID-19 crisis and main areas of action for the recovery

Caribbean countries have put in place ambitious measures to respond to the immediate impact of the COVID-19 crisis and protect lives and livelihoods. Nonetheless, as the most urgent needs are addressed through specific measures, Caribbean countries will need to undergo structural reforms in key policy areas to build the pillars of a resilient, inclusive and sustainable recovery. This will involve, among others, progressive structural change, an expansion of social protection and progress towards welfare states (ECLAC, 2021[6]).

Maintain emergency transfers to most vulnerable populations and support to the productive sector

Measures to address the emergency and protect lives and livelihoods have been important in some Caribbean countries, and will need to be maintained to support the most vulnerable families, workers and firms.

Temporary monetary transfers should be combined with other measures, such as freezing basic utility payments or deferring debt payments. In the medium and long term, universal, comprehensive and sustainable social protection systems need to be constructed, framed by care societies that guarantee levels of well-being for the population, and which do not rely exclusively on women's unpaid work. Indeed, temporary supportive measures could be used to move towards a more permanent transformation of social protection systems. The universality, comprehensiveness, sufficiency and sustainability of social protection is more important than ever.

Within the framework of recovery strategies, it is crucial to consider options for strengthening pension systems. The emphasis should be placed on increasing coverage, the adequacy of the benefits, financial sustainability and social solidarity as cross-cutting criteria in their formulation.

In addition to monetary transfers and other support measures, some Caribbean countries have implemented emergency feeding programmes. The government of Antigua and Barbuda introduced the COVID-19 Emergency Food Assistance Programme, aimed specifically at older persons living alone, persons with disabilities, and unemployed persons with children. The government of Trinidad and Tobago boosted payments to current recipients of public assistance, including disability assistance grants. In addition, several countries opted to replace school meals programmes with different modalities: for example, a food card in Trinidad and Tobago, and a weekly food kit in Antigua (ECLAC, 2021[4]).

Continuing the support to productive sectors will be of the essence to avert large-scale bankruptcy among MSMEs, and promote pro-employment policies. Some countries in the Caribbean have implemented support programmes for the productive sector. For example, Jamaica has introduced the Business Employee Support and Transfer of Cash (BEST Cash) programme and the COVID-19 Tourism Grant for businesses in the tourism sector. Similarly, Grenada has introduced a payroll support scheme for the tourism sector. In Grenada, additional credit is being made available to hoteliers and small businesses (ECLAC, 2020[12]).

Barbados and Bahamas supplemented unemployment benefits that are part of their social security systems with temporary benefits for contributing persons and the self-employed. In Saint Kitts and Nevis, and Saint Vincent and the Grenadines, the new temporary unemployment benefits provided through the social security system are restricted to insured workers only (ECLAC, 2021[4]).

There have also been support programmes for housing payments for workers who have experienced loss of income owing to the pandemic and are at risk of repossession or eviction. Governments are working with financial institutions to prevent such occurrences. The government of Trinidad and Tobago, for example, is providing a temporary rental assistance grant for individuals and families affected by furlough schemes or termination of employment. Reducing utility bills or allowing deferred payment of them are other relatively easy ways of relieving pressure on household budgets that have been adopted by some countries of the Caribbean (ECLAC, 2020[12]).

Sustaining expansionary fiscal policies

The policy response of the countries of the Caribbean to COVID-19 has been constrained by limited fiscal space, caused by high indebtedness and debt service. Despite this restriction, they have increased spending and have granted credit and guaranteed support (ECLAC, 2020[1]; Bárcena, 2020[13]).

To underpin the recovery, it will be essential to support investment in key sectors, such as non-conventional renewable energy sources; urban electro mobility; universalisation of the digital transformation (OECD, 2020[14]); the pharmaceutical industry, especially with regard to vaccines; the bioeconomy; the care economy; the circular economy; and sustainable tourism. In all of these, there is room for productive and technology policies to create quality jobs and support innovation and export diversification, as well as climate change adaptation and mitigation, and regional co-operation efforts.

Given reduced fiscal space and high levels of indebtedness in Caribbean economies, sustaining an expansionary expenditure policy will require measures to access financing through globally co-ordinated debt management, reducing tax losses in the short term and strengthening tax revenues in the medium term. In the short term, it is essential to eliminate tax evasion, which represents a resource loss of USD 325 billion (6.1% of regional GDP), and to reduce tax expenditures, which account for forgone revenue equivalent to 3.7% of GDP. Similarly adequate debt management, proper fiscal frameworks, including fiscal rules, and a globally co-ordinated debt management under key guidelines will be essential to obtain and manage the needed resources (Chapter 1) (Nieto-Parra and Orozco, 2020[15]). Overall, for fiscal policy to be effective it must take into account the current complex context through well-defined sequencing of actions. It also needs to be backed by a broad consensus built through national dialogue and clear communication strategies (Mora, Nieto-Parra and Orozco, 2021[16]) (Chapter 1).

In the medium term, tax revenue must be progressively increased to make public spending sustainable. In the current complex context, the timing, speed and shape of these increases should be adapted to each country's situation. This requires improving the redistributive power of the tax system by increasing income taxes in a progressive way, extending the scope of property and wealth taxes, reviewing and updating royalties on the exploitation of non-renewable resources, and considering taxes on the digital economy and on goods and services that harm the environment or public health (Mora, Nieto-Parra and Orozco, 2021[16]).

The sustainability and orientation of fiscal policy demand new social and fiscal pacts (Chapter 4). These will be needed to create the consensus required to move forward, pending structural reforms to revive investment, employment, equality, social protection, the closure of gender gaps and climate action, among others (Cabutto, Nieto-Parra and Vázquez-Zamora, 2021[17])

Financing for development: empowering new initiatives

Debt relief initiatives require changes in the international debt architecture, placing particular emphasis on highly indebted economies, regardless of their income level. Traditionally, Caribbean economies, such as Haiti, Saint Vincent and the Grenadines and Dominica, have issued debt through bilateral creditors or multilateral banks (Nieto-Parra and Orozco, 2020[15]). An international sovereign debt restructuring mechanism is needed to deal with obligations to private creditors, as well as a multilateral credit rating agency. At the same time, the heterogeneity of debt profiles and vulnerability in the region require the design of a debt-reduction strategy that does not adopt a one-size-fits-all approach (Nieto-Parra and Orozco, 2020[15]) (Chapter 1). Caribbean economies will benefit from the recent Special Drawing Rights (SDR) issuance agreement, which is a historic allocation of SDRs equivalent to USD 650 billion (about SDR 456 billion) (Chapter 1). SDR allocations are distributed in proportion to countries' participation in the IMF's capital, which is also closely related to the size of their economies. Overall, Caribbean economies will benefit from about SDR 1 806 million supporting the countries' international reserves and making them more resilient financially and ensuring that, in case of urgent need, they can dip into their savings (for instance, for importing vaccines) (IMF, 2021[18]).

The reallocation of SDRs would be in three parts. The first would be to increase funding for the Poverty Reduction and Growth Trust (PRGT), which is already largely financed by SDR borrowing from developed countries. SDRs channelled to the PRGT would only benefit lower-income countries. The second would consist of a trust fund to finance efforts to combat climate change, digital transformation and health-related spending. The third part would support loans from multilateral development banks through the creation of another trust fund.

Latin America and the Caribbean would benefit from a new SDR allocation that would strengthen the external position of some of the smaller and more debt-burdened economies, thereby lowering their risk premium and freeing up resources for pandemic-relief financing.

The launch of multilateral funds, such as the Fund to Alleviate COVID-19 Economics (FACE) proposed by the Government of Costa Rica, can complement initiatives to recycle liquidity from developed to developing countries. Development banks can also help expand liquidity by increasing capitalisation and flexibility in their lending criteria.

Financing initiatives should be accompanied by greater use of innovative instruments such as hurricane clauses and state-contingent debt instruments, with a view to avoiding excessive indebtedness and increasing the capacity of countries to repay and service their debt. This is of high relevance in a sub-region with high exposure to the impact of climate change.

Strengthening health and education

Through the pandemic, Caribbean countries have increased health-care spending on testing for COVID-19, treatment of severe and critical cases, and enhanced public health surveillance. Regional co-operation and co-ordination among Caribbean countries and between them and the rest of LAC should continue to be promoted to strengthen and speed up vaccination processes.

Given the constraints in terms of the logistics of local vaccine distribution, the availability of critical inputs and the limited coverage of health systems, health-care investment should be increased, specifically in primary care, with sustainable schemes that strengthen the public health sector (ECLAC/PAHO, 2020[19]).

Educational institutions across the Caribbean were forced to close as early as mid-March 2020 as part of measures to curb the spread of COVID-19. Mobile devices were provided for students without Internet connections to access online platforms, and activity packages are being provided at the primary and secondary levels (ECLAC, 2020[12]).

A gradual and safe return to school in co-ordination with the health sector is a pressing need. Many countries in the Caribbean were forced to close schools fully to contain the pandemic. On average, schools closed for 20 weeks across the sub region, a figure below the 26 in all LAC but above the 15 weeks that schools were closed on average in OECD economies (Figure 6.4). Given the impact of the pandemic on the mental health of children and adolescents, due to both increased exposure to the Internet and to social isolation, the strategies for educational continuity and return should prioritise the socio-emotional well-being of students and teachers.

Investment in the care and well-being of children and adolescents is also urgently needed. The region cannot afford to lose a generation as a result of truncated educational trajectories and lack of access to basic conditions to guarantee their rights and well-being.

Figure 6.4. **Full school closures in Caribbean economies compared to LAC and OECD**

Number of weeks of full school closures due to COVID-19

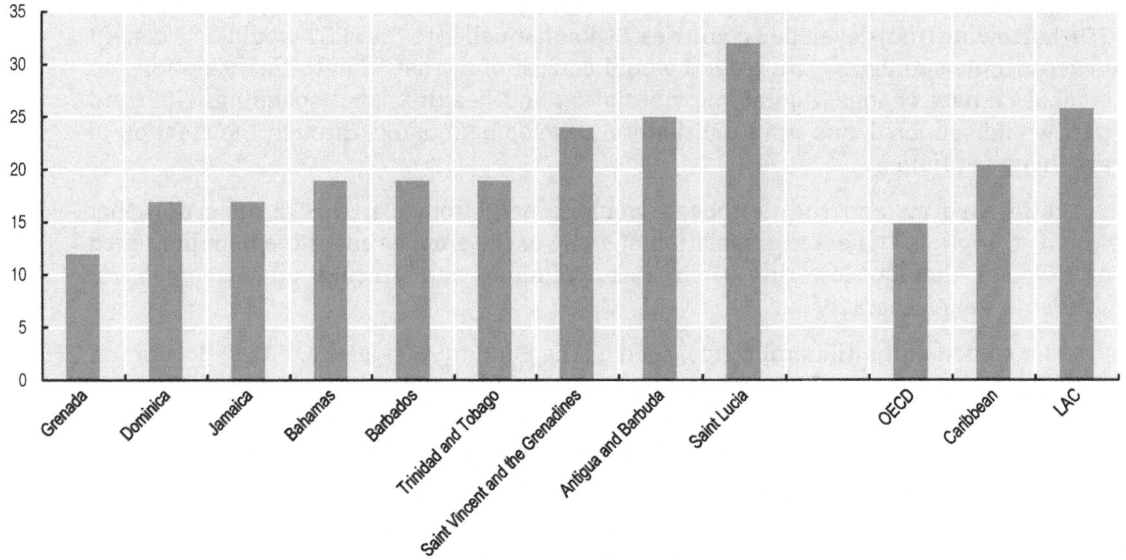

Note: OECD average includes the then 37 member countries. LAC average includes Brazil, Chile, Colombia, Costa Rica, Cuba, Dominican Republic, Ecuador, El Salvador, Guatemala, Haiti, Honduras, Mexico, Nicaragua, Panama, Peru, Uruguay and Venezuela. Updated until 1 May 2021.

Source: (UNESCO, 2020[20]), *Global Monitoring of School Closures caused by COVID-19*, https://en.unesco.org/covid19/education response#schoolclosures.

StatLink https://doi.org/10.1787/888934287091

Note

1. Simple average that includes eight Caribbean countries: Antigua and Barbuda, Bahamas, Barbados, Belize, Guyana, Jamaica, Saint Lucia and Trinidad and Tobago.

References

Bárcena, A (2020), *Regional dialogue to share experiences on fiscal responses to the crisis generated by the COVID-19 pandemic: The Caribbean perspective*, Economic Commission for Latin America and the Caribbean, Presentation by Alicia Bárcena, Executive Secretary of ECLAC, in the Virtual meeting of Ministers of Finance to discuss the economic impact of the COVID-19 pandemic in the Caribbean, https://www.cepal.org/en/presentations/regional-dialogue-share-experiences-fiscal-responses-crisis-generated-covid-19. [13]

Bárcena, A. (2020), *Mobilizing international solidarity, accelerating action and embarking on new pathways to realize the 2030 Agenda and the Samoa Pathway: Small Island Developing States*, Economic Commission for Latin America and the Caribbean, Presentation by ECLAC's Executive Secretary, Alicia Bárcena, in the High Level Political Forum 2020, https://www.cepal.org/en/presentations/mobilizing-international-solidarity-accelerating-action-and-embarking-new-pathways. [8]

Cabutto, C., S. Nieto-Parra and J. Vázquez-Zamora (2021), "A post-pandemic social contract for Latin America: the why, the what, the how", *Vox LACEA*, http://www.lacea.org/vox/?q=blog/social_contract_latam. [17]

ECLAC (2021), *Fiscal Panorama of Latin America and the Caribbean 2021: Fiscal policy challenges for transformative recovery post-COVID-19*, United Nations Publication, Santiago, https://www.cepal.org/en/publications/46809-fiscal-panorama-latin-america-and-caribbean-2021-fiscal-policy-challenges. [6]

ECLAC (2021), *Fiscal Panorama of Latin America and the Caribbean*, United Nations Publications, Santiago, https://repositorio.cepal.org/handle/11362/45731. [4]

ECLAC (2021), *The coronavirus disease (COVID-19) pandemic: An opportunity for a systemic approach to disaster risk for the Caribbean*, United Nations Publication, Santiago, https://www.cepal.org/en/

publications/46732-coronavirus-disease-covid-19-pandemic-opportunity-systemic-approach-disaster-risk. [3]

ECLAC (2021), *The recovery paradox in Latin America and the Caribbean Growth amid persisting structural problems: Inequality, poverty and low investment and productivity*, United Nations Publication, Santiago, https://www.cepal.org/en/publications/47059-recovery-paradox-latin-america-and-caribbean-growth-amid-persisting-structural. [5]

ECLAC (2020), *COVID-19 Special Report, No. 1. Latin America and the Caribbean in the face of the COVID-19 pandemic: economic and social effects*, United Nations Publication, Santiago, https://repositorio.cepal.org/bitstream/handle/11362/45351/6/S2000263_en.pdf. [2]

ECLAC (2020), *Fiscal Panorama of Latin America and the Caribbean 2020: Fiscal Policy Amid the Crisis Arising from the Coronavirus Disease (COVID-19) Pandemic*, United Nations Publication, Santiago, https://repositorio.cepal.org/handle/11362/45731. [1]

ECLAC (2020), *The Caribbean Outlook: Forging a People-centred Approach to Sustainable Development PostCOVID-19*, United Nations Publication, Santiago, https://www.cepal.org/fr/node/52477. [12]

ECLAC/PAHO (2020), *Health and the economy: a convergence needed to address COVID-19 and retake the path of sustainable development in Latin America and the Caribbean*, United Nations Publication, https://www.cepal.org/en/publications/45841-health-and-economy-convergence-needed-address-covid-19-and-retake-path. [19]

IMF (2021), *2021 General SDR Allocation*, International Monetary Fund, https://www.imf.org/en/Topics/special-drawing-right/2021-SDR-Allocation. [18]

Mora, S., S. Nieto-Parra and R. Orozco (2021), *Fiscal policy to drive the recovery in Latin America: the "when" and "how" are key*, Vox LACEA, https://vox.lacea.org/?q=blog/fiscal_policy_latam. [16]

Nieto-Parra, S. and R. Orozco (2020), *Public debt and COVID-19. Paying for the crisis in Latin America and the Caribbean*, Le Grand Continent, https://legrandcontinent.eu/fr/2020/07/22/public-debt-and-covid-19-paying-for-the-crisis-in-latin-america-and-the-caribbean/. [15]

OECD (2020), *Latin American Economic Outlook 2020: Digital Transformation for Building Back Better*, OECD Publishing, Paris, https://doi.org/10.1787/e6e864fb-en. [14]

OECD (2020), *Latin American Economic Outlook 2020: Digital Transformation for Building Back Better*, OECD Publishing, Paris, https://doi.org/10.1787/e6e864fb-en. [11]

OECD (2019), *Latin American Economic Outlook 2019: Development in Transition*, OECD Publishing, Paris, https://doi.org/10.1787/g2g9ff18-en. [10]

OECD et al. (2021), *Revenue Statistics in Latin America and the Caribbean 2021*, OECD Publishing, Paris, https://doi.org/10.1787/96ce5287-en-es. [9]

UNESCO (2020), *Global Monitoring of School Closures caused by COVID-19*, https://en.unesco.org/covid19/educationresponse#schoolclosures. [20]

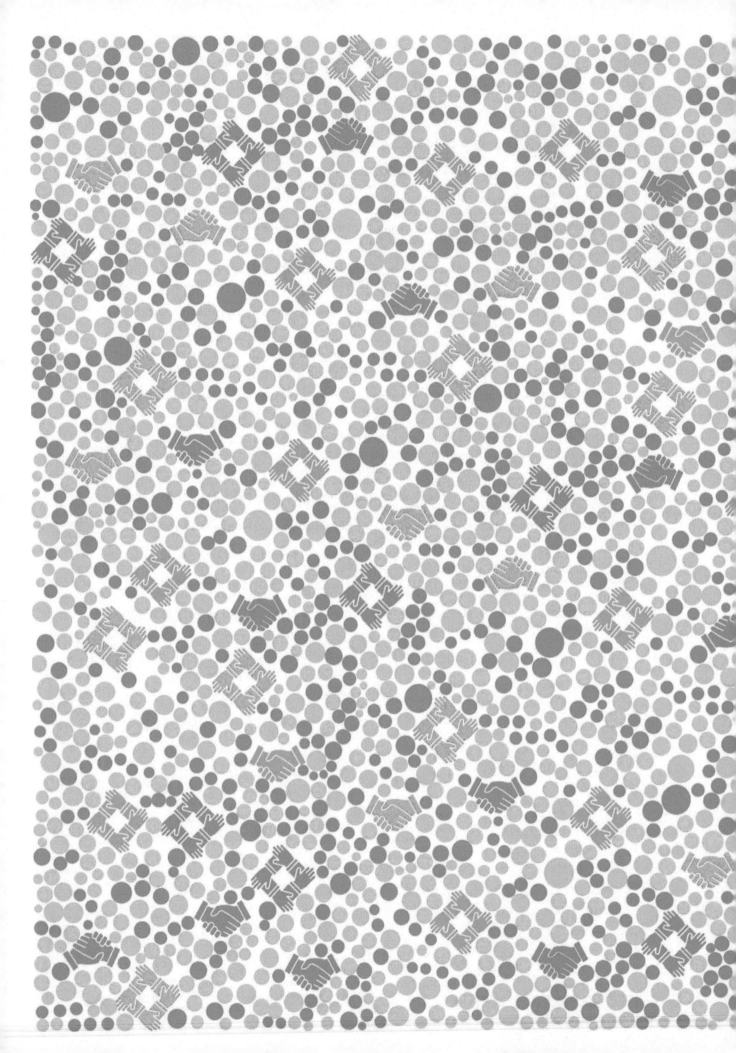

Country notes

- Argentina
- Brazil
- Chile
- Colombia
- Costa Rica
- Dominican Republic
- Ecuador
- El Salvador
- Guatemala
- Mexico
- Panama
- Paraguay
- Peru
- Uruguay

ARGENTINA

1. Socio-economic and perceived impacts of the coronavirus (COVID-19) pandemic

Argentina has been hard hit by the COVID-19 pandemic. In 2020, gross domestic product (GDP) contracted annually by 9.9%. Despite considerable policy efforts put in place, the COVID-19 crisis has decreased the income of the most disadvantaged people, increasing poverty by almost ten percentage points and extreme poverty by more than one percentage point, based on latest international comparable estimations. Between March 2020 and May 2021 schools were fully closed for 22 weeks, compared to 26 weeks in LAC and 15 weeks across Organisation for Economic Co-operation and Development (OECD) countries. Public expenditures on health increased by 0.5 percentage points in the last decade. Some 57.3% of people were satisfied with the public provision of health care in 2020, almost 2.5 percentage points less than in 2009. This figure is higher than the LAC average (48.2%) but lower than the OECD average (70.7%). People's perceptions of government have improved in the last decade. The share of people who think that the government is corrupt decreased by almost ten percentage points in the last decade, reaching 76.0% in 2020. This result is slightly higher than in LAC (72.4%) and above the OECD (58.8%).

2. National and international co-operation initiatives aimed to build forward better

Argentina has taken meaningful actions to support the most affected households, workers and enterprises throughout the crisis. Regarding households, Argentina adopted emergency cash transfers (*Ingreso Familiar de Emergencia*) to protect informal workers, the self-employed, domestic workers and the unemployed. Furthermore, Argentina granted additional cash transfers to families receiving the Universal Child Allowance, beneficiaries of the Universal Pregnancy Allowance, holders of Family Allowances and self-employed workers earning lower incomes. These measures incorporated a specific gender approach. Moreover, the coverage of existing income transfer programmes, such as: *Tarjeta Alimentar*, *Progresar* and *Potenciar Trabajo*, was extended. For workers, Argentina extended unemployment benefits for those who lost their jobs during the crisis, as well as emergency assistance programmes for workers in the food industry (*Programa de Asistencia de Emergencia al Sector Gastronómico*), tourism (*Programa Promover Turismo Federal y Sostanible*) and the health sector, granting exemptions on social security contributions. Last, to support the most affected enterprises, Argentina implemented the *Programa de Asistencia de Emergencia al Trabajo y la Producción*, which aimed to protect jobs and guarantee production during the COVID-19 crisis.

Going forward, Argentina has established the *Programa de Recuperación Productiva 2* to accelerate the economic recovery. It is intended to maintain employment by assigning an individual, fixed amount of money to be paid to workers belonging to the most affected sectors, particularly tourism and culture. Regarding education, the Federal Plan "Juana Manzo" was launched in August 2020, an e-learning platform available to all primary schools and secondary schools across the country.

Argentina's co-operation initiatives *within* and *beyond* the region are focused on immediate responses to the COVID-19 crisis and have medium- and long-term perspectives. *Within LAC*, Argentina engaged in non-financial co-operation schemes with Mexico to speed up the administrative processes and the production of the vaccine. With Chile, it supported small and medium-sized enterprises in the digitalisation process so they can access the public procurement market. Similarly, with the Southern Common Market, MERCOSUR, it created a network of biomedical research institutes to address health problems. Chile has also been active *beyond LAC*. Within the framework of the exchange of experiences on vaccination strategies with the United Kingdom, the Argentinian Ministry of Health is holding regular meetings with scientists in Oxford to learn about the progress of production strategies, new variants, reinforcements, and clinical trials in children and adolescents. With the European Union, they created the Economic and Social Council solidarity economy as an advisory forum to help formulate public policies backed by consensus that foster social cohesion and promote gender equality.

	Key indicators – Argentina[1]					
Socio-environmental	Argentina		LAC[2]		OECD[3]	
	2019	2020	2019	2020	N/A	N/A
Extreme poverty[4]	4.2	5.4	8.1	10.0	N/A	N/A
	2019	2020	2019	2020	N/A	N/A
Poverty[5]	27.2	37	26.8	30.9	N/A	N/A
	2009	2019	2009	2019	2009	2018
Gini index[6]	0.41	0.40	0.50	0.46	0.31	0.31
	Bottom 20%	Top 20%	Bottom 20%	Top 20%	Bottom 20%	Top 20%
Total population in informal households by quintile, 2018[7]	N/A	N/A	78.0	19.1	N/A	N/A
	2010	2017	2010	2017	2010	2017
Health expenditures[8]	8.6	9.1	6.5	6.8	8.1	8.8
	2010	2017	2010	2017	2010	2017
Out-of-pocket health expenditures[9]	19.7	15.0	35.6	34.1	20.2	20.6
			03/2020-05/2021			
Weeks of full school closure[10]	22		26		15	
			2018			
Effective online learning[11]	18.9		32.5		54.1	
			2018			
Effective online learning in disadvantaged schools[11]	5.1		21.5		48.8	
	2009	2019	2009	2019	2009	2019
Share of Internet users[12]	34.0	74.3	29.3	67.8	68.3	85.8
	-	2018	2015	2018	2015	2018
Number of students per computer[13]	-	2.1	2.4	1.6	1.8	1.1
	2010	2019	2010	2019	2010	2019
Exposure to PM 2.5[14]	14.1	13.8	18.1	18.0	15.7	13.9
			2000-16			
% change in intact forest landscape[15]	-2.9		-8.8		-6.3	
Competitiveness and innovation	Argentina		LAC[2]		OECD[3]	
	2009	2019	2009	2019	2009	2019
Labour productivity[16]	42.2	36.9	29.3	26.7	72.2	70.7
	2009	2019	2009	2019	2009	2019
High-tech exports[17]	9.1	5.2	8.7	8.3	19.5	17.9
	2009	2017	2009	2017	2009	2017
R&D expenditures[18]	0.6	0.5	0.4	0.4	2.4	2.5
	2009	2017	2009	2017	2009	2017
ICT patents[19]	69	43	726	521	173 440	141 358
Citizens' perceptions and institutions	Argentina		LAC[2]		OECD[3]	
	2009	2020	2009	2020	2009	2020
Citizens' perceptions of corruption in government[20]	85.8	76.0	72.0	72.4	67.5	58.8
	2009	2018	2009	2018	-	-
Citizens' perceptions of country governed in the interests of few[21]	92.8	84.9	64.8	82.0	-	-
	2009	2020	2009	2020	2009	2020
Satisfaction with health care[22]	59.8	57.3	56.9	48.2	69.2	70.7
	2009	2020	2009	2020	2009	2020
Satisfaction with water quality[23]	72.7	77.9	74.8	76.0	77.9	79.4
	2010	2016	2010	2016	N/A	N/A
% of people victim of criminality[24]	26.2	25.6	19.6	23.8	N/A	N/A
			2021			
Rank in the Press Freedom Index[25]	69		82		36	
			2009-18			
Change in political polarisation[26]	4.1		9.6		N/A	
			2019			
SIGI index[27]	N/A		25.6		16.3	
Fiscal position	Argentina		LAC[2]		OECD[3]	
	2009	2019	2009	2019	2009	2019
Total tax revenues[28]	28.9	28.6	20.6	22.9	31.6	33.8
	2009	2019	2009	2019	2009	2019
Share of VAT in total revenues[29]	24.2	24.9	25.3	27.7	19.8	20.7
	2009	2018	2009	2018	2009	2018
Social expenditures[30]	11.2	13.5	11.3	11.4	21.0	19.7

Sources, footnotes and technical details can be found at the end of the country notes.

BRAZIL

1. Socio-economic and perceived impacts of the coronavirus (COVID-19) pandemic

Brazil has been hard hit by the COVID-19 pandemic, but it experienced one of the smallest contractions of gross domestic product (GDP) in the region. In 2020, GDP contracted by 4.1% annually. In 2020, poverty and extreme poverty (16.3% and 1.4%, respectively) based on the latest international comparable estimations, although high, were lower than the average in the Latin America and the Caribbean (LAC) region (30.9% and 10.0%).

Between March 2020 and May 2021 schools were fully closed for 38 weeks, compared to 26 weeks in LAC and 15 weeks across Organisation for Economic Co-operation and Development (OECD) countries. Before the pandemic, effective online learning was present in 35.0% of schools, compared to 54.1% in the OECD. Public expenditures on health represented 8.7% of GDP, higher than the LAC average (6.8%) and similar to the OECD average (8.8%). However, according to Gallup data, just 34.4% of people were satisfied with the public provision of health care in 2020, seven percentage points less than in 2009. This figure is lower than in LAC (48.2%) and the OECD (70.7%). The share of people who think that the government is corrupt increased by more than five percentage points in the last decade, reaching 71.0% in 2020. This figure is lower than in LAC (72.4%) but higher than in the OECD (58.8%).

2. National and international co-operation initiatives aimed to build forward better

Brazil responded rapidly to the COVID-19 crisis. The deployment of measures to protect the most vulnerable households, workers and enterprises aided significantly in limiting the deterioration of the economy. In 2020, Brazil created one of the largest cash transfer programmes in the world (Emergency Aid), while greatly extending both the existing conditional cash transfer programmes (*Bolsa Familia Programme*) and home visitation for early childhood development (*Criança Feliz*). Additionally, Brazil implemented a food acquisition programme (*Programa de Adquisiçao de Alimentos*) to encourage and sustain the production of family farmers, and it supported vulnerable populations through social assistance. Concerning workers and firms, Brazil implemented the largest income preservation and job-retention scheme ever deployed in the country (Emergency Employment and Income Maintenance Benefit). It particularly targeted small and medium-sized enterprises and allowed for contracts to be suspended instead of terminated, while workers received the equivalent of unemployment benefit.

Going forward, Brazil will follow a structural reform agenda that aims to recover fiscal balance, increase productivity and prepare workers and firms to face the challenges of the post-pandemic economy. Digital platforms now allow citizens to examine their labour situation and obtain unemployment insurance. Last, Brazil proposed major reforms, such as the civil service reform, to reduce payroll costs and improve quality of public services, and the tax reform, to decrease the complexities of the current taxation systems.

Brazil's international co-operation projects give priority to enhancing the country's competitiveness, with a focus on reforms of the current tax system, encouraging market competition and further opening the economy to foreign trade. *Beyond LAC*, Brazil participates in international immunisation schemes, such as the Vaccine Accelerator Project, and engages in the COVID-19 Vaccines Access (COVAX) initiative. Additionally, Brazil chairs the Biofuturo Platform, an international initiative aiming to promote a sustainable bioeconomy, including defining general economic recovery programmes post-COVID-19. Moreover, Brazil's high-level co-operation strategies with the People's Republic of China, India, Spain, the United Kingdom and the United States have allowed the country to acquire meaningful donations to deal with COVID-19, as well as to boost its vaccine production. Last, within the framework of the last phase (2020-21) of the EUROsociAL+ co-operation programme with the European Union, the country received support for the creation of new orientation services amid the pandemic. This included a series of communication actions to support vulnerable population through the Accounting and Tax Support Nucleus.

	Key indicators – Brazil[1]					
Socio-environmental	**Brazil**		**LAC[2]**		**OECD[3]**	
	2019	2020	2019	2020	N/A	N/A
Extreme poverty[4]	5.5	1.4	8.1	10.0	N/A	N/A
	2019	2020	2019	2020	N/A	N/A
Poverty[5]	19.2	16.3	26.8	30.9	N/A	N/A
	2009	2019	2009	2019	2009	2018
Gini index[6]	0.53	0.54	0.50	0.46	0.31	0.31
	Bottom 20%	Top 20%	Bottom 20%	Top 20%	Bottom 20%	Top 20%
Total population in informal households by quintile, 2018[7]	70.5	10.7	78.0	19.1	N/A	N/A
	2010	2017	2010	2017	2010	2017
Health expenditures[8]	9.2	8.7	6.5	6.8	8.1	8.8
	2010	2017	2010	2017	2010	2017
Out-of-pocket health expenditures[9]	29.4	27.4	35.6	34.1	20.2	20.6
	03/2020-05/2021					
Weeks of full school closure[10]	38		26		15	
	2018					
Effective online learning[11]	35.0		32.5		54.1	
	2018					
Effective online learning in disadvantaged schools[11]	19.0		21.5		48.8	
	2009	2019	2009	2019	2009	2019
Share of Internet users[12]	39.2	73.9	29.3	67.8	68.3	85.8
	2015	2018	2015	2018	2015	2018
Number of students per computer[13]	3.7	6.0	2.4	1.6	1.8	1.1
	2010	2019	2010	2019	2010	2019
Exposure to PM 2.5[14]	14.1	11.7	18.1	18.0	15.7	13.9
	2000-16					
% change in intact forest landscape[15]	-8.0		-8.8		-6.3	
Competitiveness and innovation	**Brazil**		**LAC[2]**		**OECD[3]**	
	2009	2019	2009	2019	2009	2019
Labour productivity[16]	29.1	30.9	29.3	26.7	72.2	70.7
	2009	2019	2009	2019	2009	2019
High-tech exports[17]	14.5	13.3	8.7	8.3	19.5	17.9
	2009	2017	2009	2017	2009	2017
R&D expenditures[18]	1.1	1.3	0.4	0.4	2.4	2.5
	2009	2017	2009	2017	2009	2017
ICT patents[19]	346	223	726	521	173 440	141 358
Citizens' perceptions and institutions	**Brazil**		**LAC[2]**		**OECD[3]**	
	2009	2020	2009	2020	2009	2020
Citizens' perceptions of corruption in government[20]	65.7	71.0	72.0	72.4	67.5	58.8
	2009	2018	2009	2018	-	-
Citizens' perceptions of country governed in the interests of few[21]	55.2	92.3	65.0	83.8	-	-
	2009	2020	2009	2020	2009	2020
Satisfaction with health care[22]	41.5	34.4	56.9	48.2	69.2	70.7
	2009	2020	2009	2020	2009	2020
Satisfaction with water quality[23]	70.7	64.8	74.8	76.0	77.9	79.4
	2010	2016	2010	2016	N/A	N/A
% of people victim of criminality[24]	15.8	23.9	21.3	25.0	N/A	N/A
	2021					
Rank in the Press Freedom Index[25]	111		82		36	
	2009-18					
Change in political polarisation[26]	9.3		9.6		-	
	2019					
SIGI index[27]	21.2		25.6		16.3	
Fiscal position	**Brazil**		**LAC[2]**		**OECD[3]**	
	2009	2019	2009	2019	2009	2019
Total tax revenues[28]	32.0	33.1	20.6	22.9	31.6	33.8
	2009	2019	2009	2019	2009	2019
Share of VAT in total revenues[29]	20.8	21.2	25.3	27.7	19.8	20.7
	2009	2018	2009	2018	2009	2018
Social expenditures[30]	15.2	17.7	11.3	11.4	21.0	19.7

Sources, footnotes and technical details can be found at the end of the country notes.

CHILE

1. Socio-economic and perceived impacts of the coronavirus (COVID-19) pandemic

The crisis has been hard on Chile. Gross domestic product (GDP) contracted by 5.8% in 2020, compared to a year earlier. In 2020, poverty increased by 0.2 percentage points to reach 10.9% according to the latest international comparable estimations available, one of the lowest rates in the Latin America and the Caribbean (LAC) region (30.9%). Extreme poverty (1.6%) is also one of the lowest in LAC (average 10.0%). Between March 2020 and May 2021 schools were fully closed for 14 weeks, much lower than the LAC average (26 weeks) and close to the Organisation for Economic Co-operation and Development (OECD) average (15 weeks). The negative impact on education was partially offset by online learning, which was present in 38.7% of schools, higher than in LAC (32.5%) but significantly lower than in the OECD (54.1%). The healthcare system was put under pressure by the pandemic, but earlier investment by the government functioned as a cushion. Public expenditures on health have risen by two percentage points in the last decade to reach 8.9% of GDP, close to the OECD average (8.8%) and much higher than the LAC average (6.8%). However, people's perceptions of the quality of health services deteriorated. In 2020, only 34.2% of people declared being satisfied with health care, down by six percentage points in a decade. This figure is lower than in LAC (48.2%) and the OECD (70.7%). According to Gallup data on citizens' perception, in 2020, 84.9% of Chileans perceived the government as corrupt. This figure compares to 72.4% in LAC and 58.8% at the OECD level.

2. National and international co-operation initiatives aimed to build forward better

Since the start of the COVID-19 pandemic, Chile deployed a co-ordinated and far-reaching strategy to support the most vulnerable households, workers and enterprises. Chile effectively mobilised resources to expand and strengthen the social protection network for nearly 17.68 million Chileans. To support households, Chile allocated around USD 1.2 billion through the emergency cash transfer programme (*Ingreso Familiar de Emergencia*) for formal and informal households whose incomes were negatively affected by the crisis. Likewise, Chile implemented *Bono COVID-19*, a special transfer scheme aimed at supporting the most vulnerable families. Additionally, to protect middle-income households, Chile provided *Bono Clase Media*. To sustain workers, Chile established extraordinary transitory measures (*Ley de Protección del Empleo*) to protect income stability and jobs for formal workers. In addition, Chile implemented an employment subsidy as an economic reactivation measure to encourage hiring and retention of workers. To support micro, small and medium-sized enterprises, Chile instituted a fund for loans by providing guarantees (*FOGAPE*), established additional credit lines and provided tax refunds. Last, Chile encouraged programmes that provide technical assistance and promote digital and technical skills for MSMEs and enhance productivity for firms in this sector (*Digitaliza tu Pyme, Ruta Digital, Pymes en Linea, Pymes de Barrio, Elijo Pyme, Espacio del Emprendedor* and *Despega Mipe*).

Going forward, Chile designed the public investment plan for the period 2020-22, which aims to solve social and productive transformation demands and the water shortage threats. Special emphasis has been placed on projects that contribute to accelerating the transition to sustainable development and to mitigating and adapting to climate change. Moreover, Chile is taking a series of measures to support market competitiveness, including new transparency requirements and a new digital model regarding the means of payment.

As part of Chile's international co-operation framework *within LAC*, the Chile-Mexico Joint Cooperation Fund transferred over USD 1 million to the country for the acquisition of medical supplies to face the COVID-19 pandemic. *Beyond LAC*, Chile takes part in the Bilateral Fund for Development in Transition Chile-European Union, which allocated EUR 365 million to its newest project to provide support for the recovery of prioritised productive sectors of the macro-central-southern region of the country within the framework of COVID-19. The project aims to support the economic recovery of four regions of the country and to develop specific actions to boost employment. In addition, as a result of Chile's engagement with Japan's socio-economic development programme, the country became a beneficiary of a non-refundable USD 4.6 million financial donation to purchase medical equipment, which will be used in various health centres in the country.

	Key indicators – Chile[1]					
Socio-environmental	Chile		LAC[2]		OECD[3]	
	2017	2020	2019	2020	2019	2020
Extreme poverty[4]	1.4	1.6	8.1	10.0	N/A	N/A
	2017	2020	2019	2020	2019	2020
Poverty[5]	10.7	10.9	26.8	30.9	N/A	N/A
	2009	2017	2009	2019	2009	2018
Gini index[6]	0.48	0.45	0.50	0.46	0.31	0.31
	Bottom 20%	Top 20%	Bottom 20%	Top 20%	Bottom 20%	Top 20%
Total population in informal households by quintile, 2018[7]	34.9	9.4	78.8	19.3	N/A	N/A
	2010	2017	2010	2017	2010	2017
Health expenditures[8]	6.8	8.9	6.5	6.8	8.1	8.8
	2010	2017	2010	2017	2010	2017
Out-of-pocket health expenditures[9]	34.5	33.5	35.6	34.1	20.2	20.6
	03/2020-05/2021					
Weeks of full school closure[10]	14		26		15	
	2018					
Effective online learning[11]	38.7		32.5		54.1	
	2018					
Effective online learning in disadvantaged schools[11]	25.2		21.5		48.8	
	2009	2019	2009	2019	2009	2019
Share of Internet users[12]	41.6	82.3	29.3	67.8	68.3	85.8
	2015	2018	2015	2018	2015	2018
Number of students per computer[13]	1.7	1.1	2.4	1.6	1.8	1.1
	2010	2019	2010	2019	2010	2019
Exposure to PM 2.5[14]	21.9	23.7	18.1	18.0	15.7	13.9
	2000-16					
% change in intact forest landscape[15]	-1.4		-8.8		-6.3	
Competitiveness and innovation	Chile		LAC[2]		OECD[3]	
	2009	2019	2009	2019	2009	2019
Labour productivity[16]	53.1	56.2	29.3	26.7	72.2	70.7
	2009	2019	2009	2019	2009	2019
High-tech exports[17]	6.6	7.5	8.7	8.3	19.5	17.9
	2009	2017	2009	2017	2009	2017
R&D expenditures[18]	0.4	0.4	0.4	0.4	2.4	2.5
	2009	2017	2009	2017	2009	2017
ICT patents[19]	68	19	726	521	173 440	141 358
Citizens' perceptions and institutions	Chile		LAC[2]		OECD[3]	
	2009	2020	2009	2020	2009	2020
Citizens' perceptions of corruption in government[20]	65.8	84.9	72.0	72.4	67.5	58.8
	2009	2018	2009	2018	2009	2018
Citizens' perceptions of country governed in the interests of few[21]	61.0	77.4	64.8	82.0	N/A	N/A
	2009	2020	2009	2020	2009	2020
Satisfaction with health care[22]	40.8	34.2	56.9	48.2	69.2	70.7
	2009	2020	2009	2020	2009	2020
Satisfaction with water quality[23]	61.0	53.3	76.2	75.2	77.9	79.4
	2010	2016	2010	2016	2010	2016
% of people victim of criminality[24]	16.3	22.4	19.6	23.8	N/A	N/A
	2021					
Rank in the Press Freedom Index[25]	54		82		36	
	2009-18					
Change in political polarisation[26]	-2.5		9.6		N/A	
	2019					
SIGI index[27]	53.7		25.6		16.3	
Fiscal position	Chile		LAC[2]		OECD[3]	
	2009	2019	2009	2019	2009	2019
Total tax revenues[28]	17.3	20.7	20.6	22.9	31.6	33.8
	2009	2019	2009	2019	2009	2019
Share of VAT in total revenues[29]	42.1	39.9	25.3	27.7	19.8	20.7
	2009	2018	2009	2018	2009	2018
Social expenditures[30]	15.7	16.4	11.3	11.4	21.0	19.7

Sources, footnotes and technical details can be found at the end of the country notes.

COLOMBIA

1. Socio-economic and perceived impacts of the coronavirus (COVID-19) pandemic

Following years of socio-economic improvements in Colombia, the COVID-19 crisis has had a considerable impact in terms of economic performance and social conditions. Gross domestic product (GDP) growth declined by 6.8% annually in 2020. Based on the latest international comparable estimations, poverty increased by almost six percentage points in 2020, compared to a year earlier, to reach 37.5%, higher than the average in the Latin America and the Caribbean (LAC) region (30.9%). Extreme poverty in 2020 rose by four percentage points to reach 16.9% of the population, higher than the LAC average (10.0%). The crisis also affected the education system. Between March 2020 and May 2021, schools were fully closed for 23 weeks, less than in LAC (26 weeks) but higher than in Organisation for Economic Co-operation and Development (OECD) countries (15 weeks). This translated into hardship for students and families, as effective online learning was present in just 36.2% of schools. This figure is close to the LAC average (32.5%) but lower than the OECD average (54.1%). Colombia entered into the COVID-19 crisis with public expenditures on health (7.2% of GDP) higher than the LAC average (6.8%) but below the OECD average (8.8%). In 2020, 47.7% of people were satisfied with health services, down by more than seven percentage points in ten years. This figure is slightly lower than in LAC (48.2%) and considerably below the OECD average (70.7%). Regarding people's concerns with government's actions and according to international comparable data, in 2020, 78.7% of Colombians thought that the government was corrupt, slightly higher than in LAC (72.4%) and higher than the OECD average (58.8%).

2. National and international co-operation initiatives aimed to build forward better

Colombia undertook bold and timely measures to mitigate the impact of the COVID-19 crisis on both households and enterprises. Concerning households, measures implemented were mainly based on cash transfers, to smooth households' consumption throughout the crisis. First, Colombia expanded a VAT compensation scheme. It was designed as a permanent public policy in the form of a bimonthly repayment of a fixed amount to the poorest 1 million households. Second, Colombia established a national programme for non-conditional monetary transfers (*Ingreso Solidario*) directed towards 3 million poor and vulnerable households that were not beneficiaries of any other national programme. Regarding firms, as a job-retention strategy, the government created national programmes (*Programa de Apoyo al Empleo Formal* and *Programa de Apoyo a la Prima*) to aid the country's enterprises by subsidising a share of their social security obligations.

Going forward, in 2020, Colombia launched an economic recovery plan to revitalise industry and promote job creation. In 2021, the national government announced the "Economic and Social Recovery Policy" establishing an investment equivalent to 12.5% of Colombia's GDP distributed in 5 commitments on: job creation; clean and sustainable growth; vulnerable households; rural areas and peace and legality; and health care.

Colombia's international co-operation projects both *within* and *beyond* the region during the pandemic were flexible and had continuity, despite the sudden challenges due to the crisis. Projects *within* LAC were based on sharing best practices and experiences with Honduras and Peru. Those with Honduras involved electronic certification and legalisation of documents and the promotion of green businesses through financial mechanisms. Those with Peru included the promotion of youth political participation and the strengthening of capacities of production systems in protected border zones. *Beyond* LAC, Colombia engaged in co-operation projects with various actors, focusing on the crisis and the most pressing needs. The projects included: enhancing capacities and access to comprehensive healthcare systems in rural areas (Health for peace: Strengthening communities); a proposal for territorial development in the Department of Chocó by the Spanish Agency of International Cooperation and Development (AECID); the development of low-cost mechanical ventilator prototypes, with assistance from the Inter-American Development Bank (INNspiraMed); and developing capacities to prevent violence against youth (Colombia-teaches-Colombia [Col-Col]). Last, within the framework of the last phase (2020-21) of the EUROsociAL+ co-operation programme with the European Union, support was granted to cope with COVID-19-related issues, while: i) strengthening Family Police Stations to support victims of gender-based violence; ii) implementing employability strategies for young people; and iii) supporting the response to the Venezuelan migration crisis, particularly regarding gender.

	Key indicators – Colombia[1]					
Socio-environmental	**Colombia**		**LAC[2]**		**OECD[3]**	
	2019	2020	2019	2020	2019	2020
Extreme poverty[4]	12.8	16.9	8.1	10.0	N/A	N/A
	2019	2020	2019	2020	2019	2020
Poverty[5]	31.7	37.5	26.8	30.9	N/A	N/A
	2009	2019	2009	2019	2009	2018
Gini index[6]	0.56	0.53	0.50	0.46	0.31	0.31
	Bottom 20%	Top 20%	Bottom 20%	Top 20%	Bottom 20%	Top 20%
Total population in informal households by quintile, 2018[7]	91.9	21.6	78.0	19.1	N/A	N/A
	2010	2017	2010	2017	2010	2017
Health expenditures[8]	6.3	7.2	6.5	6.8	8.1	8.8
	2010	2017	2010	2017	2010	2017
Out-of-pocket health expenditures[9]	20.9	16.3	35.6	34.1	20.2	20.6
	03/2020-05/2021					
Weeks of full school closure[10]	23		26		15	
	2018					
Effective online learning[11]	36.2		32.5		54.1	
	2018					
Effective online learning in disadvantaged schools[11]	27.6		21.5		48.8	
	2009	2019	2009	2019	2009	2019
Share of Internet users[12]	30.0	65.0	29.3	67.8	68.3	85.8
	2015	2018	2015	2018	2015	2018
Number of students per computer[13]	1.6	1.1	2.4	1.6	1.8	1.1
	2010	2019	2010	2019	2010	2019
Exposure to PM 2.5[14]	25.7	22.5	18.1	18.0	15.7	13.9
	2000-16					
% change in intact forest landscape[15]	-1.6		-8.8		-6.3	
Competitiveness and innovation	**Colombia**		**LAC[2]**		**OECD[3]**	
	2009	2019	2009	2019	2009	2019
Labour productivity[16]	29.0	34.5	29.3	26.7	72.2	70.7
	2009	2019	2009	2019	2009	2019
High-tech exports[17]	5.6	9.1	8.7	8.3	19.5	17.9
	2009	2017	2009	2017	2009	2017
R&D expenditures[18]	0.2	0.2	0.4	0.4	2.4	2.5
	2009	2017	2009	2017	2009	2017
ICT patents[19]	24	13	726	521	173 440	141 358
Citizens' perceptions and institutions	**Colombia**		**LAC[2]**		**OECD[3]**	
	2009	2020	2009	2020	2009	2020
Citizens' perceptions of corruption in government[20]	77.7	78.7	72.0	72.4	67.5	58.8
	2009	2018	2009	2018	N/A	N/A
Citizens' perceptions of country governed in the interests of few[21]	62.4	83.4	64.8	82.0	N/A	N/A
	2009	2020	2009	2020	2009	2020
Satisfaction with health care[22]	55.0	47.7	56.9	48.2	69.2	70.7
	2009	2020	2009	2020	2009	2020
Satisfaction with water quality[23]	69.5	71.5	74.8	76.0	77.9	79.4
	2010	2016	2010	2016	N/A	N/A
% of people victim of criminality[24]	20.5	25.1	19.6	23.8	N/A	N/A
	2021					
Rank in the Press Freedom Index[25]	134		82		36	
	2009-18					
Change in political polarisation[26]	3.0		9.6		N/A	
	2019					
SIGI index[27]	15.0		25.6		16.3	
Fiscal position	**Colombia**		**LAC[2]**		**OECD[3]**	
	2009	2019	2009	2019	2009	2019
Total tax revenues[28]	18.8	19.7	20.6	22.9	31.6	33.8
	2009	2019	2009	2019	2009	2019
Share of VAT in total revenues[29]	27.5	29.6	25.3	27.7	19.8	20.7
	2009	2018	2009	2018	2009	2018
Social expenditures[30]	13.3	12.6	11.3	11.4	21.0	19.7

Sources, footnotes and technical details can be found at the end of the country notes.

COSTA RICA

1. Socio-economic and perceived impacts of the coronavirus (COVID-19) pandemic

Despite strong efforts to mitigate the impact of COVID-19, Costa Rica has been hard hit by the pandemic, particularly the tourism sector. The crisis is expected to reverse some of the country's previous socio-economic achievements. In 2020, the poverty rate increased by more than two percentage points compared to 2019 and extreme poverty by one percentage point, based on the latest international comparable estimations. The total population in informal households among the lowest quintile of income was 75.6%, slightly lower than in LAC (78.0%). Between March 2020 and May 2021, schools were fully closed for 39 weeks, compared to 26 weeks in LAC and 15 weeks across the Organisation for Economic Co-operation and Development (OECD). Moreover, effective online learning was present in only 20.0% of schools.

Costa Rica entered the pandemic with relatively higher public expenditures on health care (7.5% of GDP) compared to LAC (6.8%). According to Gallup data, 64.8% of people were satisfied with the public provision of health care in 2020, eight percentage points less than in 2009. This figure is higher than in LAC (48.2%) but lower than in the OECD (70.7%). Perceptions of a corrupt government increased by more than six percentage points in the last decade, reaching 85.1% in 2020. This result is higher than in LAC (72.4%) and the OECD (58.8%).

2. National and international co-operation initiatives aimed to build forward better

Costa Rica has made significant efforts to address the COVID-19 crisis and to help protect the most vulnerable households, workers and enterprises. Concerning households, food and home care were provided to aid the most vulnerable, including the most affected families and senior citizens. Concerning workers, Costa Rica implemented the direct cash transfer programme (*Bono Proteger*) to provide temporary economic relief to both formal and informal workers who saw their income affected by the crisis. Last, to help mitigate the impact of the crisis on firms, the government implemented a short-term job-retention scheme for companies that reported annualised income losses and extended tax moratoriums for enterprises, particularly in the tourism sector.

Going forward, Costa Rica's medium- and long-term goals are to boost economic growth and improve income distribution while maintaining its net-zero emissions by 2050 plan. With international support, Costa Rica launched a productive territorial strategy that outlines the path to have a decentralised, digitalised and decarbonised economy by 2050. This strategy includes key actions to accelerate the country's development pathway, create jobs and close existing social equality gaps.

Costa Rica's international co-operation projects *within* and *beyond* the region give priority to financial co-operation to address the pandemic's impact while advancing its long-term route for development. *Within* LAC, during the pandemic, Costa Rica engaged in co-operation schemes for financial assistance to respond to the crisis. Additionally, Costa Rica participates in Inter-American Development Bank platforms that aim for the transparency and accountability of public expenditures associated with the COVID-19 policy measures (*Rendir Cuentas/Mapa Inversiones + COVID-19*). The goal is for citizens to be able to access the details of public institutions' investments and efforts to respond to the pandemic. *Beyond LAC*, Costa Rica takes part in funds to lessen the impact of the crisis and finance the recovery. In particular, Costa Rica is one of the sponsor of the Fund to Alleviate COVID-19 Economics initiative, which on a solidarity basis, aims to provide funds from developed countries to finance the recovery in emerging and developing countries. Other initiatives aim to implement the country's long-term productive strategies and to achieve its goals (e.g. a fund created by the European Union and the IV phase of triangular co-operation with Spain). These co-operation initiatives are intended to keep Costa Rica accountable for the long-term recovery plan, besides promoting the implementation of projects to achieve the United Nations Sustainable Development Goals.

Key indicators – Costa Rica[1]					
Socio-environmental					
	Costa Rica		**LAC[2]**		**OECD[3]**

	Costa Rica		LAC[2]		OECD[3]	
	2019	2020	2019	2020	2019	2020
Extreme poverty[4]	3.4	4.4	8.1	10.0	N/A	N/A
	2019	2020	2019	2020	2019	2020
Poverty[5]	16.5	18.9	26.8	30.9	N/A	N/A
	2009	2019	2009	2019	2009	2018
Gini index[6]	0.51	0.49	0.50	0.46	0.31	0.31
	Bottom 20%	Top 20%	Bottom 20%	Top 20%	Bottom 20%	Top 20%
Total population in informal households by quintile , 2018[7]	75.6	6.1	78.0	19.1	N/A	N/A
	2010	2017	2010	2017	2010	2017
Health expenditures[8]	8.1	7.5	6.5	6.8	8.1	8.8
	2010	2017	2010	2017	2010	2017
Out-of-pocket health expenditures[9]	25.4	22.0	35.6	34.1	20.2	20.6
	03/2020-05/2021					
Weeks of full school closure[10]	39		26		15	
	2018					
Effective online learning[11]	20.0		32.5		54.1	
	2018					
Effective online learning in disadvantaged schools[11]	12.6		21.5		48.8	
	2009	2019	2009	2019	2009	2019
Share of Internet users[12]	34.3	81.2	29.3	67.8	68.3	85.8
	2015	2018	2015	2018	2015	2018
Number of students per computer[13]	2.8	1.3	2.4	1.6	1.8	1.1
	2010	2019	2010	2019	2010	2019
Exposure to PM 2.5[14]	18.2	17.4	18.1	18.0	15.7	13.9
	2000-16					
% change in intact forest landscape[15]	-3.1		-8.8		-6.3	

Competitiveness and innovation	Costa Rica		LAC[2]		OECD[3]	
	2009	2019	2009	2019	2009	2019
Labour productivity[16]	38.7	48.3	29. 3	26. 7	72. 2	70. 7
	2009	2019	2009	2019	2009	2019
High-tech exports[17]	44.3	17.6	8.7	8.3	19.5	17.9
	2009	2017	2009	2017	2009	2017
R&D expenditures[18]	0.5	0.4	0.4	0.4	2.4	2.5
	2009	2017	2009	2017	2009	2017
ICT patents[19]	3	3	726	521	173 440	141 358

Citizens' perceptions and institutions	Costa Rica		LAC[2]		OECD[3]	
	2009	2020	2009	2020	2009	2020
Citizens' perceptions of corruption in government[20]	78.9	85.1	72.0	72.4	67.5	58.8
	2009	2018	2009	2018	2009	2008
Citizens' perceptions of country governed in the interests of few[21]	62.4	83.4	64.8	82.0	N/A	N/A
	2009	2020	2009	2020	2009	2020
Satisfaction with health care[22]	72.9	64.8	56.9	48.2	69.2	70.7
	2009	2020	2009	2020	2009	2020
Satisfaction with water quality[23]	84.5	84.2	74.8	76.0	77.9	79.4
	2010	2016	2010	2016	2010	2016
% of people victim of criminality[24]	19.0	22.1	19.6	23.8	N/A	N/A
	2021					
Rank in the Press Freedom Index[25]	5		82		36	
	2009-18					
Change in political polarisation[26]	5.7		9.6		N/A	
	2019					
SIGI index[27]	27.9		25.6		16.3	

Fiscal position	Costa Rica		LAC[2]		OECD[3]	
	2009	2019	2009	2019	2009	2019
Total tax revenues[28]	22.1	23.6	20.6	22.9	31.6	33.8
	2009	2019	2009	2019	2009	2019
Share of VAT in total revenues[29]	21.3	18.5	25.3	27.7	19.8	20.7
	2009	2018	2009	2018	2009	2018
Social expenditures[30]	12.1	12.2	11.3	11.4	21.0	19.7

Sources, footnotes and technical details can be found at the end of the country notes.

DOMINICAN REPUBLIC

1. Socio-economic and perceived impacts of the coronavirus (COVID-19) pandemic

The COVID-19 pandemic has hit Dominican Republic's economy hard. In 2020, gross domestic product (GDP) contracted 6.7%, compared to a year earlier. Poverty remains a pressing issue. The poverty rate is high, although lower than in the Latin America and the Caribbean (LAC) region (30.9%), reaching 21.8% in 2020 based on the latest international comparable estimations, 1.5 percentage points higher than a year earlier. Extreme poverty was around 4.6%, 0.3 percentage points higher than in 2019, although lower than in LAC (10.0%). Between March 2020 and May 2021, schools were fully closed for 33 weeks, compared to the averages of 26 weeks in LAC and 15 weeks in the Organisation for Economic Co-operation and Development (OECD). The negative impacts of closures on children and families have been partially offset by access to effective online learning. Dominican Republic reports one of the highest online learning coverages in LAC (46.7% of schools), close to the OECD (54.1%). Dominican Republic entered the pandemic with a relatively low level of public expenditures on health care (6.1% of GDP), lower than in LAC (6.8%), even if it has increased by 0.5 percentage points in the last decade. People's perceptions of the quality of health care are relatively modest. In 2020, 52.2% of people declared being satisfied with health services, slightly higher than in LAC (48.2%) but lower than in the OECD (70.7%). One of the most remarkable improvements in recent years is connected to people's perception of corruption. In 2020, 57.7% of people thought that the government was corrupt, more than 20 percentage points less than a decade earlier at that time one of the highest figures in LAC (72.4%).

2. National and international co-operation initiatives aimed to build forward better

Dominican Republic implemented policies to deal with the crisis, to alleviate both salary losses and food insecurity. Concerning the protection of households, Dominican Republic used and expanded an existing social assistance scheme (*Tarjeta de Solidaridad*) to deliver cash transfers to the most vulnerable population. Additionally, Dominican Republic expanded and improved the quality of education and health care and pursued decent and adequate housing for the vulnerable population. Regarding firms, Dominican Republic took measures to strengthen the capacities of micro, small and medium-sized enterprises, the most affected by the crisis, sustaining their revenues and market access.

Going forward, Dominican Republic introduced the national multi-year public sector plan. To help the recovery, the government aims to improve living conditions, especially among the most vulnerable population affected by the pandemic. The initiatives include guaranteeing gender equality, fostering the productive capacities of agriculture-related industries, boosting the supply of high value added manufactured goods and promoting tourism, all in the framework of digital transformation and sustainable development.

Dominican Republic's international co-operation projects *within* and *beyond* the region are aligned with the priorities of the national agenda, including post-crisis recovery and sustainable development. *Within LAC*, Dominican Republic engaged in co-operation schemes with the Latin America Development Bank to reduce vulnerabilities exposed by the pandemic and to minimise the risks of the CARIFORUM States (strengthening the capacities of the emergency operations center to deal with COVID-19). Additionally, the country received donations from LAC countries, the Central American Bank for Economic Integration, the Ibero-American General Secretariat, the Inter-American Development Bank, Costa Rica and Peru to respond to the health crisis. *Beyond LAC*, Dominican Republic takes part in international co-operation schemes with other countries. Concerning structural needs, the projects focus on strengthening the institutional capacity of the Climate and Resilience Observatory, facilitating mutual understanding between Dominican Republic and Haiti and the formation of integrated health service networks. Within the framework of the third phase (2020-21) of the EUROsociAL+ co-operation programme with the European Union, support has been granted to both the Ministry of Labour and the Ministry of Economy, Planning and Development to design policies which aim to protect informal workers, with particular attention given to the impacts of the COVID-19 pandemic.

Key indicators – Dominican Republic[1]					
Socio-environmental	**Dominican Republic**		**LAC[2]**		**OECD[3]**	

	Dominican Republic		LAC[2]		OECD[3]	
	2019	2020	2019	2020	2019	2020
Extreme poverty[4]	4.3	4.6	8.1	10.0	N/A	N/A
	2019	2020	2019	2020	2019	2020
Poverty[5]	20.3	21.8	26.8	30.9	N/A	N/A
	2009	2019	2009	2019	2009	2018
Gini index[6]	0.49	0.43	0.50	0.46	0.31	0.31
	Bottom 20%	Top 20%	Bottom 20%	Top 20%	Bottom 20%	Top 20%
Total population in informal households by quintile, 2018[7]	N/A	N/A	78.0	19.1	N/A	N/A
	2010	2017	2010	2017	2010	2017
Health expenditures[8]	5.6	6.1	6.5	6.8	8.1	8.8
	2010	2017	2010	2017	2010	2017
Out-of-pocket health expenditures[9]	43.9	44.7	35.6	34.1	20.2	20.6
	03/2020-05/2021					
Weeks of full school closure[10]	33		26		15	
	2018					
Effective online learning[11]	46.7		32.5		54.1	
	2018					
Effective online learning in disadvantaged schools[11]	33.4		21.5		48.8	
	2009	2019	2009	2019	2009	2019
Share of Internet users[12]	27.7	75.8	29.3	67.8	68.3	85.8
	2015	2018	2015	2018	2015	2018
Number of students per computer[13]	3.2	1.4	2.4	1.6	1.8	1.1
	2010	2019	2010	2019	2010	2019
Exposure to PM 2.5[14]	17.1	18.1	18.1	18.0	15.7	13.9
	2000-16					
% change in intact forest landscape[15]	-29.0		-8.8		-6.3	

Competitiveness and innovation	Dominican Republic		LAC[2]		OECD[3]	
	2009	2019	2009	2019	2009	2019
Labour productivity[16]	32.3	40.9	29. 3	26. 7	72. 2	70. 7
	2009	2019	2009	2019	2009	2019
High-tech exports[17]	2.5	7.0	8.7	8.3	19.5	17.9
	2009	2017	2009	2017	2009	2017
R&D expenditures[18]	N/A	N/A	N/A	N/A	N/A	N/A
	2009	2017	2009	2017	2009	2017
ICT patents[19]	N/A	N/A	N/A	N/A	N/A	N/A

Citizens' perceptions and institutions	Dominican Republic		LAC[2]		OECD[3]	
	2009	2020	2009	2020	2009	2020
Citizens' perceptions of corruption in government[20]	78.0	57.7	72.0	72.4	67.5	58.8
	2009	2018	2009	2018	2009	2018
Citizens' perceptions of country governed in the interests of few[21]	89.8	85.1	64.8	82.0	N/A	N/A
	2009	2020	2009	2020	2009	2020
Satisfaction with health care[22]	55.3	52.2	56.9	48.2	69.2	70.7
	2009	2020	2009	2020	2009	2020
Satisfaction with water quality[23]	73.0	77.2	74.8	76.0	77.9	79.4
	2010	2016	2010	2016	2010	2016
% of people victim of criminality[24]	16.6	26.2	19.6	23.8	N/A	N/A
	2021					
Rank in the Press Freedom Index[25]	50		82		36	
	2009-18					
Change in political polarisation[26]	48.0		9.6		N/A	
	2019					
SIGI index[27]	18.2		25.6		16.3	

Fiscal position	Dominican Republic		LAC[2]		OECD[3]	
	2009	2019	2009	2019	2009	2019
Total tax revenues[28]	12.8	13.5	20.6	22.9	31.6	33.8
	2009	2019	2009	2019	2009	2019
Share of VAT in total revenues[29]	31.3	34.7	25.3	27.7	19.8	20.7
	2009	2018	2009	2018	2009	2018
Social expenditures[30]	6.7	8.0	11.3	11.4	21.0	19.7

Sources, footnotes and technical details can be found at the end of the country notes.

ECUADOR

1. Socio-economic and perceived impacts of the coronavirus (COVID-19) pandemic

Ecuador's economy has been hit hard by the COVID-19 pandemic. In 2020, gross domestic product (GDP) contracted by more than 7%, compared to a year earlier. In 2020, based on the latest international comparable estimations the poverty rate reached 33.5%, almost ten percentage points higher than in 2019. The extreme poverty rate was 12.8%, more than five percentage points higher than a year earlier. These rates are among the highest in the Latin America and the Caribbean (LAC) region, where average poverty and extreme poverty rates were 30.9% and 10.0%, respectively, in 2020. Between March 2020 and May 2021, schools were fully closed for 39 weeks, more than the averages in LAC (26 weeks) and the Organisation for Economic Co-operation and Development (OECD) (15 weeks). Given the overall low rate of Internet use (54.1%), school closures had a negative impact on both children's education and families due to expanded care responsibility. Ecuador entered the pandemic with increasing public expenditures on health. In the last decade, they increased by 1.2 percentage points of GDP and had reached 8.3% of GDP before the crisis. This figure is higher than in LAC (6.8%) but lower than in the OECD (8.8%). However, people's perceptions of the quality of health services are negative. In 2020, just 44.3% of people declared being satisfied with health care, compared to 48.2% in LAC and 70.7% in the OECD. In 2020, 86.0% of citizens thought that the government was corrupt. This proportion is high, both compared to LAC (72.4%) and the OECD (58.8%).

2. National policies and international co-operation initiatives aimed to build forward better

Ecuador's initial response to the COVID-19 crisis was very different from the majority of LAC countries. In May 2020, the government announced a comprehensive package aimed at cutting USD 4 billion from the national budget. The measures included reducing the workday for most workers, closing or merging 10 public entities, closing 11 embassies and restructuring Ecuador's public debt. A new Humanitarian Support Law went into effect in June. The law's primary new feature is to allow work hours and salaries to be reduced by up to 50% and 45%, respectively, for two years at a time. To help firms cope with the liquidity crisis, social security payments were postponed for 90 days, and taxes were deferred for the tourism and export sectors, as well as for micro, small and medium-sized enterprises (MSMEs), between April and June. An executive decree was issued that required about 1 200 companies that recorded a profit in the first half of 2020 to pay their income tax at least five months ahead of schedule. The country's tax authority estimated that it would collect USD 280 million through the measure, to be distributed to 125 000 MSMEs affected by the pandemic. To sustain households income, the government introduced a moratorium on utility cut-offs due to lack of payment. A programme that handed out USD 60 over two months to 950 000 families earning under USD 400 per month was expanded to reach 2 million people as part of the package.

Ecuador has put in place many international co-operation initiatives to cope with the COVID-19 crisis. In September 2020, an agreement was approved for a new programme with the International Monetary Fund under the modality of Extended Fund Facility. This programme foresees a total of USD 6.5 billion, of which USD 4 billion were disbursed in 2020. Its main objectives are to protect the living conditions of people, expanding social protection coverage, while guaranteeing macroeconomic stability, with the implementation of a tax reform package, and the ordering of public spending. Other multilateral organisations provide support to the country with various loans. Resources have been committed by the World Bank, the Inter-American Development Bank and the CAF-Development Bank of Latin America. The loan amount totalled USD 2.32 billion by the end of 2020. Within the framework of COVID-19, the last phase (2020-21) of the EUROsociAL+ co-operation programme with the European Union supported the judiciary council to develop measures guaranteeing access to services for victims of gender-based violence. Additionally, the European Union launched a pilot exercise of Team Europe country roundtables to discuss how better to join forces and provide coherent EU support to COVID-19 management and recovery in the country.

Key indicators – Ecuador[1]					
Socio-environmental					
	Ecuador		LAC[2]		OECD[3]	
	2019	2020	2019	2020	2019	2020
Extreme poverty[4]	7.6	12.8	8.1	10.0	N/A	N/A
	2019	2020	2019	2020	2019	2020
Poverty[5]	25.7	33.5	26.8	30.9	N/A	N/A
	2009	2019	2009	2019	2009	2018
Gini index[6]	0.48	0.46	0.50	0.46	0.31	0.31
	Bottom 20%	Top 20%	Bottom 20%	Top 20%	Bottom 20%	Top 20%
Total population in informal households by quintile, 2018[7]	N/A	N/A	78.0	19.1	N/A	N/A
	2010	2017	2010	2017	2010	2017
Health expenditures[8]	7.1	8.3	6.5	6.8	8.1	8.8
	2010	2017	2010	2017	2010	2017
Out-of-pocket health expenditures[9]	47.5	39.4	35.6	34.1	20.2	20.6
	03/2020-05/2021					
Weeks of full school closure[10]	39		26		15	
	2018					
Effective online learning[11]	N/A		32.5		54.1	
	2018					
Effective online learning in disadvantaged schools[11]	N/A		21.5		48.8	
	2009	2019	2009	2019	2009	2019
Share of Internet users[12]	24.6	54.1	29.3	67.8	68.3	85.8
	2009	2019	2009	2019	2009	2019
Number of students per computer[13]	N/A	N/A	2.4	1.6	1.8	1.1
	2010	2019	2010	2019	2010	2019
Exposure to PM 2.5[14]	22.1	20.6	18.1	18.0	15.7	13.9
	2000-16					
% change in intact forest landscape[15]	-5.7		-8.8		-6.3	
Competitiveness and innovation					
	Ecuador		LAC[2]		OECD[3]	
	2009	2019	2009	2019	2009	2019
Labour productivity[16]	25.4	26.1	29.3	26.7	72.2	70.7
	2009	2019	2009	2019	2009	2019
High-tech exports[17]	4.6	5.5	8.7	8.3	19.5	17.9
	2009	2017	2009	2017	2009	2017
R&D expenditures[18]	0.4	0.4	0.4	0.4	2.4	2.5
	2009	2017	2009	2017	2009	2017
ICT patents[19]	3	0	726	521	173 440	141 358
Citizens' perceptions and institutions					
	Ecuador		LAC[2]		OECD[3]	
	2009	2020	2009	2020	2009	2020
Citizens' perceptions of corruption in government[20]	80.3	86.0	72.0	72.4	67.5	58.8
	2009	2018	2009	2018		
Citizens' perceptions of country governed in the interests of few[21]	58.0	82.8	64.8	82.0	N.A	N/A
	2009	2020	2009	2020	2009	2020
Satisfaction with health care[22]	48.5	44.3	56.9	48.2	69.2	70.7
	2009	2020	2009	2020	2009	2020
Satisfaction with water quality[23]	63.7	78.6	74.8	76.0	77.9	79.4
	2010	2016	2010	2016		
% of people victim of criminality[24]	29.1	30.6	19.6	23.8	N/A	N/A
	2021					
Rank in the Press Freedom Index[25]	96		82		36	
	2009-18					
Change in political polarisation[26]	5.6		9.6		N/A	
	2019					
SIGI index[27]	28.9		25.6		16.3	
Fiscal position					
	Ecuador		LAC[2]		OECD[3]	
	2009	2019	2009	2019	2009	2019
Total tax revenues[28]	15.7	20.1	20.6	22.9	31.6	33.8
	2009	2019	2009	2019	2009	2019
Share of VAT in total revenues[29]	33.8	30.3	25.3	27.7	19.8	20.7
	2009	2018	2009	2018	2009	2018
Social expenditures[30]	8.1	9.0	11.3	11.4	21.0	19.7

Sources, footnotes and technical details can be found at the end of the country notes.

EL SALVADOR

1. Socio-economic and perceived impacts of the coronavirus (COVID-19) pandemic

The crisis hit El Salvador's economy hard. In 2020, gross domestic product (GDP) contracted by 7.9% annually. The population will not equally share the consequences. Based on the latest international comparable estimations, in 2020 the poverty rate reached 36.4%, among the highest in the Latin America and the Caribbean (LAC) region (30.9%). It has increased six percentage points from a year earlier, compared to an increase of four percentage points in LAC. The extreme poverty rate has reached 8%, an increase of 2.4 percentage points, compared to 10.0% and 1.9 percentage points, respectively, in LAC. Public expenditures on health before the crisis stood at 7.2% of GDP, slightly higher than in LAC (6.8%) but lower than Organisation for Economic Co-operation and Development (OECD) countries (8.8%). The perceived quality of health services was negatively affected. In 2020, 54.8% of people declared being satisfied with health care, compared to 48.2% in LAC. People's satisfaction was 11 percentage points lower than ten years before, a larger decrease than in LAC (8.7 percentage points). Between March 2020 and May 2021 schools were fully closed for 46 weeks, more than in LAC (26 weeks) and the OECD (15 weeks). In 2020, 41.4% of El Salvador citizens thought that the government was corrupt, a lower share than in LAC (72.4%) and the OECD (58.8%).

2. National and international co-operation initiatives aimed to build forward better

El Salvador has adopted several measures to lessen the impact of the COVID-19 crisis on the most vulnerable, workers and enterprises. Regarding households, since the start of the confinement measures, the government announced a subsidy of USD 300 for more than 1 million families, as well as the delivery of food packages to all households with greater emphasis on the most vulnerable. Additionally, El Salvador allowed for the temporary deferral of utilities, phone and internet bills payments, as well as freezing payments on mortgages, loans and credit cards. To protect the most affected workers and enterprises, El Salvador implemented a job-retention subsidy for micro, small and medium-sized enterprise (MSMEs) workers, a programme to grant loans to formal enterprises and a programme to help finance small business owners in the informal sector.

Going forward, El Salvador is committed to providing a new approach through technological modernisation and institutional transparency, to respond to structural problems worsened by the crisis. Accordingly, the government proposed the Economic and Social Welfare Plan 2019-2024, a flexible, evidence-based tool that will allow the country to overcome the crisis and work towards the United Nations 2030 Agenda. El Salvador granted 1.2 million computers to students, launched a plan to transform territorial development in rural areas and made financial inclusion and the digital transformation priorities. As for long-term plans, El Salvador aims to build forward better through the execution of policies to increase private and public investment and to boost formalisation and growth of MSMEs, focusing on innovation and adoption of new technologies.

El Salvador's international co-operation projects *within* and *beyond* the region focused on taking advantage of regional and international knowledge and resources to face the COVID-19 crisis. *Within LAC*, El Salvador's co-operation schemes included a partnership with Colombia to strengthen the capacity of the El Salvador's hospitals to attend to the pandemic and, through *Sistema de la Integración Centroamericana*, a donation to the Ministry of Health of the tools necessary for the detection of the virus. *Beyond LAC*, co-operation initiatives included the creation of the first university hospital in the country, with support from Luxembourg, and the construction of a speciality hospital dedicated to COVID-19 patients, with support from Morocco. To tackle the socio-economic challenges caused by the pandemic, El Salvador engaged in projects to prevent violence against women through a dedicated hotline (Spotlight Initiative) and created youth employability programmes through exchange of experiences and capacity building activities. Lastly, different Salvadorian women organisations, in close co-operation with the European Union, developed the programme "Strengthening agricultural cooperatives and peasant women's organisations for the enforceability of the Human Right to Food and food sovereignty in El Salvador" (2021-2023) with the objective of improving the resilience and sustainability of agro-productive development processes in vulnerable situations following the climate and health emergency in the country.

	Key indicators – El Salvador[1]					
Socio-environmental	El Salvador		LAC[2]		OECD[3]	
	2019	2020	2019	2020	2019	2020
Extreme poverty[4]	5.6	8	8.1	10.0	N/A	N/A
	2019	2020	2019	2020	2019	2020
Poverty[5]	30.4	36.4	26.8	30.9	N/A	N/A
	2009	2019	2009	2019	2009	2018
Gini index[6]	0.48	0.41	0.50	0.46	0.31	0.31
	Bottom 20%	Top 20%	Bottom 20%	Top 20%	Bottom 20%	Top 20%
Total population in informal households by quintile, 2018[7]	90.8	24.4	78.0	19.1	N/A	N/A
	2010	2017	2010	2017	2010	2017
Health expenditures[8]	8.2	7.2	6.5	6.8	8.1	8.8
	2010	2017	2010	2017	2010	2017
Out-of-pocket health expenditures[9]	33.6	29.2	35.6	34.1	20.2	20.6
	03/2020-05/2021					
Weeks of full school closure[10]	46		26		15	
	2018					
Effective online learning[11]	N/A		32.5		54.1	
	2018					
Effective online learning in disadvantaged[11] schools	N/A		21.5		48.8	
	2009	2019	2009	2019	2009	2019
Share of Internet users[12]	12.1	50.5	29.3	67.8	68.3	85.8
	2015	2018	2015	2018	2015	2018
Number of students per computer[13]	N/A	N/A	2.4	1.6	1.8	1.1
	2010	2019	2010	2019	2010	2019
Exposure to PM 2.5[14]	24.3	22.3	18.1	18.0	15.7	13.9
	2000-16					
% of change in intact forest landscape[15]	N/A		-8.8		-6.3	
Competitiveness and innovation	El Salvador		LAC[2]		OECD[3]	
	2009	2019	2009	2019	2009	2019
Labour Productivity[16]	N/A	N/A	29.3	26.7	72.2	70.7
	2009	2019	2009	2019	2009	2019
High-tech exports[17]	6.5	5.1	8.7	8.3	19.5	17.9
	2009	2017	2009	2017	2009	2017
R&D expenditures[18]	0.1	0.2	0.4	0.4	2.4	2.5
	2009	2017	2009	2017	2009	2017
ICT patents[19]	1	0	726	521	173 440	141 358
Citizens' perceptions and institutions	El Salvador		LAC[2]		OECD[3]	
	2009	2020	2009	2020	2009	2020
Citizens' perceptions of corruption in government[20]	66.0	41.4	72.0	72.4	67.5	58.8
	2009	2018	2009	2018	2009	2018
Citizens' perceptions of country governed in the interests of few[21]	46.1	89.0	64.8	82.0	N/A	N/A
	2009	2020	2009	2020	2009	2020
Satisfaction with health care[22]	65.8	54.8	56.9	48.2	69.2	70.7
	2009	2020	2009	2020	2009	2020
Satisfaction with water quality[23]	80.5	85.8	74.8	76.0	77.9	79.4
	2010	2016	2010	2016	2010	2016
% of people victim of criminality[24]	24.2	23.1	19.6	23.8	N/A	N/A
	2021					
Rank in the Press Freedom Index[25]	82		82		36	
	2009-18					
Change in political polarisation[26]	8.5		9.6		N/A	
	2019					
SIGI index[27]	22.9		25.6		16.3	
Fiscal position	El Salvador		LAC[2]		OECD[3]	
	2009	2019	2009	2019	2009	2019
Total tax revenues[28]	17.9	20.8	20.6	22.9	31.6	33.8
	2009	2019	2009	2019	2009	2019
Share of VAT in total revenues[29]	39.7	37.5	25.3	27.7	19.8	20.7
	2009	2018	2009	2018	2009	2018
Social expenditures[30]	9.2	9.0	11.3	11.4	21.0	19.7

Sources, footnotes and technical details can be found at the end of the country notes.

GUATEMALA

1. Socio-economic and perceived impacts of the coronavirus (COVID-19) pandemic

The crisis hit Guatemala's economy hard. In 2020, gross domestic product (GDP) contracted annually by 1.5%. The economic downturn has increased extreme poverty by more than three percentage points, reaching 18.7% in 2020, while the poverty rate remained relatively stable at 50.9%, based on latest international comparable estimations. Before the crisis, Guatemala's public expenditures on health stood at 5.8% of GDP, almost unchanged over a decade, compared to the averages of 6.8% in the Latin America and the Caribbean (LAC) region and 8.8% in Organisation for Economic Co-operation and Development (OECD) countries. In 2020, 56.0% of people in Guatemala declared being satisfied with health care, a proportion similar to LAC (48.2%) and much lower than the OECD (70.7%). The pandemic particularly affected education. Between March 2020 and May 2021, schools were fully closed for 33 weeks, compared to 26 weeks in LAC and 15 weeks in the OECD. Both children and families suffered a lot as a result, due to the disruption of education and the increased burden of childcare, especially considering that only 40.7% of the population had Internet access, in 2019.

2. National and international co-operation initiatives aimed to build forward better

The response of the government was aimed to support the most affected households, workers and enterprises throughout the crisis. In May 2020, the government introduced new programmes targeting workers, families and firms hit by the crisis. Among them, *Fondo de Protección del Empleo* provided a minimum payment of GTQ 75 (Guatemalan quetzal) per day for workers in the formal sector that decided to suspend contracts temporarily. An energy subsidy was introduced to help households cope with the contraction of income. Similarly, the income support measure *Bono Familia* is targeted through households' expenditures on energy. Families who consume less than 200 kWh may be candidates for this aid. The new social programme *Bono al Comercio Popular* was instituted to help the most vulnerable informal workers, enabling them to access a single bonus of GTQ 1 000. To tackle poverty, *Programa de Aporte Económico al Adulto Mayor*, a fund introduced in 2005, was reinforced. In August 2020, 100 000 people aged 65 or over living in poverty received a monthly subsidy of GTQ 400. Under the new provisions, older people are entitled to social assistance for life. More generally, in response to the COVID-19 pandemic, tax authorities in Guatemala also extended the deadline for filing certain tax returns. For example, the 2019 income tax return and the corresponding monthly value added tax return were postponed. In addition, the tax audit process, information requests and other procedures were suspended until 15 April 2020. For firms, the government instituted *Fondo de Crédito de Capital de Trabajo*, a fund that grants loans up to a maximum of GTQ 250 000 to companies affected by this crisis, specifically targeting small and medium-sized enterprises.

Guatemala's international co-operation projects *within* and *beyond* the region are aligned to address the short- and long-term challenges linked to the COVID-19 crisis. The Central American Council of Ministers for Social Integration instructed the Central American Social Integration Secretariat to develop an articulated response and prepare a Plan for Recovery: Social Reconstruction and Resilience of Central America and Guatemala. The plan includes strategic projects organised under three areas of intervention: i) social protection, ii) employability and employment; and iii) informal settlements and sustainable urban development. The projects seek to create the conditions for more resilient, socially just and environmentally sustainable societies. The plan is also an example international co-operation can work *beyond* the LAC region as it was carried out with support from international partners – the EUROsociAL co-operation programme within the European Union, in alliance with specialised United Nations agencies–.

Key indicators – Guatemala[1]					
Socio-environmental					
	Guatemala		**LAC[2]**		**OECD[3]**	

Socio-environmental	Guatemala		LAC[2]		OECD[3]	
	2019	2020	2019	2020	2019	2020
Extreme poverty[4]	15.4	18.7	8.1	10.0	N/A	N/A
	2019	2020	2019	2020	2019	2020
Poverty[5]	50.5	50.9	26.8	30.9	N/A	N/A
	2009	2014	2009	2019	2009	2018
Gini index[6]	0.56	0.53	0.50	0.46	0.31	0.31
	Bottom 20%	Top 20%	Bottom 20%	Top 20%	Bottom 20%	Top 20%
Total population in informal households by quintile, 2018[7]	N/A	N/A	78.0	19.1	N/A	N/A
	2010	2017	2010	2017	2010	2017
Health expenditures[8]	6.1	5.8	6.5	6.8	8.1	8.8
	2010	2017	2010	2017	2010	2017
Out-of-pocket health expenditures[9]	59.6	54.1	35.6	34.1	20.2	20.6
			03/2020-05/2021			
Weeks of full school closure[10]	33		26		15	
			2018			
Effective online learning[11]	N/A		32.5		54.1	
			2018			
Effective online learning in disadvantaged schools[11]	N/A		21.5		48.8	
	2009	2019	2009	2019	2009	2019
Share of Internet users[12]	9.3	44.4	29.3	67.8	68.3	85.8
	2015	2018	2015	2018	2015	2018
Number of students per computer[13]	N/A	N/A	2.4	1.6	1.8	1.1
	2010	2019	2010	2019	2010	2019
Exposure to PM 2.5[14]	29.0	27.8	18.1	18.0	15.7	13.9
			2000-16			
% change in intact forest landscape[15]	-16.0		-8.8		-6.3	

Competitiveness and innovation	Guatemala		LAC[2]		OECD[3]	
	2009	2019	2009	2019	2009	2019
Labour productivity[16]	21.8	22.2	29.3	26.7	72.2	70.7
	2009	2019	2009	2019	2009	2019
High-tech exports[17]	4.8	4.9	8.7	8.3	19.5	17.9
	2009	2017	2009	2017	2009	2017
R&D expenditures[18]	0.1	0.0	0.4	0.4	2.4	2.5
	2009	2016	2009	2017	2009	2017
ICT patents[19]	1.3	2.0	726	521	173 440	141 358

Citizens' perceptions and institutions	Guatemala		LAC[2]		OECD[3]	
	2009	2020	2009	2020	2009	2020
Citizens' perceptions of corruption in government[20]	88.1	77.9	72.0	72.4	67.5	58.8
	2009	2018	2009	2018	2009	2018
Citizens' perceptions of country governed in the interests of few[21]	75.3	76.6	64.8	82.0	N/A	N/A
	2009	2020	2009	2020	2009	2020
Satisfaction with health care[22]	66.0	56.0	56.9	48.2	69.2	70.7
	2009	2020	2009	2020	2009	2020
Satisfaction with water quality[23]	78.8	84.6	74.8	76.0	77.9	79.4
	2010	2016	2010	2016	2010	2016
% of people victim of criminality[24]	23.3	23.8	19.6	23.8	N/A	N/A
			2021			
Rank in the Press Freedom Index[25]	116		82		36	
			2009-18			
Change in political polarisation[26]	25.9		9.6		N/A	
			2019			
SIGI index[27]	28.6		25.6		16.3	

Fiscal position	Guatemala		LAC[2]		OECD[3]	
	2009	2019	2009	2019	2009	2019
Total tax revenues[28]	12.3	13.1	20.6	22.9	31.6	33.8
	2009	2019	2009	2019	2009	2019
Share of VAT in total revenues[29]	39.5	38.8	25.3	27.7	19.8	20.7
	2009	2018	2009	2018	2009	2018
Social expenditures[30]	8.1	7.0	11.3	11.4	21.0	19.7

Sources, footnotes and technical details can be found at the end of the country notes.

MEXICO

1. Socio-economic and perceived impacts of the coronavirus (COVID-19) pandemic

Mexico has been hard hit by the COVID-19 pandemic. In 2020, gross domestic product (GDP) contracted by slightly more than 8%. The COVID-19 crisis also worsened the income conditions of the most disadvantaged populations, increasing poverty by nine percentage points and extreme poverty by almost eight percentage points based on latest international comparable estimations. Income inequality was already high before the pandemic (around 0.48), as it was in the Latin America and the Caribbean (LAC) region (0.46), and had been stable in the last decade. Between March 2020 and May 2021, schools were fully closed for 53 weeks, compared to the averages of 26 weeks in LAC and 15 weeks in Organisation for Economic Co-operation and Development (OECD) countries. Effective online learning was present in only 33.8% of schools, close to LAC (32.5%) but much lower than the OECD (54.1%).

Public expenditures on health decreased by 0.5 percentage points in the last decade. Before the pandemic, in 2017, they stood at 5.5% of GDP, lower than in LAC (6.8%) and the OECD (8.8%). According to Gallup data, 50.5% of people were satisfied with the public provision of health care in 2020, almost 12 percentage points less than in 2009. This figure is slightly higher than the LAC average (48.2%) but lower than the OECD average (70.7%). In 2018, the latest available year, more than 90% of Mexicans thought that their country is governed in the interests of a few powerful people, one of the highest proportions in LAC (82%).

2. National and international co-operation initiatives aimed to build forward better

Before the COVID-19 crisis, Mexico was already focusing on well-being policies aimed at developing a universal model of social rights. Mexico's conditional cash transfer programmes particularly stand out. However, many poor families still do not benefit from social assistance. On 1 May 2020, the government undertook a constitutional reform that expanded social programmes to address the crisis consequences. COVID-19 relief measures for households mainly came in the form of cash transfers. These included the delivery of bimonthly pension support to the elderly (*Programa Pensión para el Bienestar de las Personas Adultas Mayores*) and people with permanent disabilities (*Programa Pensión para el Bienestar de las Personas con Discapacidad Permanente*). Concerning firms, low-cost loans and payment deferrals were made available to small and medium-sized enterprises in both the formal and informal sectors.

Going forward, Mexico aims to overcome the obstacles that currently inhibit social inclusion, advancing in tackling poverty and inequality. Mexico is committed to the execution of comprehensive interventions aimed at guaranteeing the social rights already established in the constitution. This structural transformation will also create opportunities for the development of human capital and productivity.

The COVID-19 pandemic was at the core of Mexico's international co-operation projects both *within* and *beyond* the region. The priority was given both to immediate needs, with a special focus on assisting LAC neighbour countries, and to measuring the socio-economic impact of the crisis to implement better policies in the medium and long term. *Within* LAC, Mexico's co-operation efforts were characterised by support and assistance to neighbours. They include the donation of medical ventilation devices to Central America and the Caribbean countries and, in collaboration with Argentina, the production and distribution of the Astra-Zeneca vaccine in the region, as well as co-operation to facilitate administration and approval of the Sputnik V vaccine. Mexico also participated in an initiative for adaptation and resilience to climate change in the Caribbean (Mexico-Caribbean Community-Food and Agriculture Organization), an initiative for strengthening food security (*Mesoamérica Sin Hambre*), and the implementation of a platform to reinforce the tourism sector through virtual training with the countries of the Pacific Alliance. *Beyond* LAC, within the framework of the EUROsociAL+ co-operation programme with the European Union, support has been provided to promote employment for vulnerable populations. EUROsociAL+ has also supported policies aimed to protect migrant children and adolescents in the context of the Mexico-Guatemala Binational Border Strategy.

	Key indicators – Mexico[1]					
Socio-environmental	**Mexico**		**LAC[2]**		**OECD[3]**	
	2019	2020	2019	2020	2019	2020
Extreme poverty[4]	10.6	18.3	8.1	10.0	N/A	N/A
	2019	2020	2019	2020	2019	2020
Poverty[5]	41.5	50.6	26.8	30.9	N/A	N/A
	2009	2019	2009	2019	2009	2018
Gini index[6]	0.51	0.47	0.50	0.46	0.31	0.31
	Bottom 20%	Top 20%	Bottom 20%	Top 20%	Bottom 20%	Top 20%
Total population in informal households by quintile, 2018[7]	70.9	17.4	78.0	19.1	N/A	N/A
	2010	2017	2010	2017	2010	2017
Health expenditures[8]	6.0	5.5	6.5	6.8	8.1	8.8
	2010	2017	2010	2017	2010	2017
Out-of-pocket health expenditures[9]	45.7	41.3	35.6	34.1	20.2	20.6
	03/2020-05/2021					
Weeks of full school closure[10]	53		26		15	
	2018					
Effective online learning[11]	33.8		32.5		54.1	
	2018					
Effective online learning in disadvantaged schools[11]	12.7		21.5		48.8	
	2009	2019	2009	2019	2009	2019
Share of Internet users[12]	26.3	70.1	29.3	67.8	68.3	85.8
	2015	2018	2015	2018	2015	2018
Number of students per computer[13]	2.2	2.4	2.4	1.6	1.8	1.1
	2010	2019	2010	2019	2010	2019
Exposure to PM 2.5[14]	21.5	20.1	18.1	18.0	15.7	13.9
	2000-16					
% change in intact forest landscape[15]	-4.6		-8.8		-6.3	
Competitiveness and innovation	**Mexico**		**LAC[2]**		**OECD[3]**	
	2009	2019	2009	2019	2009	2019
Labour productivity[16]	46.6	47.4	29.3	26.7	72.2	70.7
	2009	2019	2009	2019	2009	2019
High-tech exports[17]	22.7	20.4	8.7	8.3	19.5	17.9
	2009	2017	2009	2017	2009	2017
R&D expenditures[18]	0.5	0.3	0.4	0.4	2.4	2.5
	2009	2017	2009	2017	2009	2017
ICT patents[19]	132	199	726	521	173 440	141 358
Citizens' perceptions and institutions	**Mexico**		**LAC[2]**		**OECD[3]**	
	2009	2020	2009	2020	2009	2020
Citizens' perceptions of corruption in government[20]	73.2	77.2	72.0	72.4	67.5	58.8
	2009	2018	2009	2018	2009	2018
Citizens' perceptions of country governed in the interests of few[21]	78.3	90.5	64.8	82.0	N/A	N/A
	2009	2020	2009	2020	2009	2020
Satisfaction with health care[22]	62.1	50.5	56.9	48.2	69.2	70.7
	2009	2020	2009	2020	2009	2020
Satisfaction with water quality[23]	74.1	77.3	74.8	76.0	77.9	79.4
	2010	2016	2010	2016	2010	2016
% of people victim of criminality[24]	25.9	30.7	19.6	23.8	N/A	N/A
	2021					
Rank in the Press Freedom Index[25]	143		82		36	
	2009-18					
Change in political polarisation[26]	-1.0		9.6		N/A	
	2019					
SIGI index[27]	29.0		25.6		16.3	
Fiscal position	**Mexico**		**LAC[2]**		**OECD[3]**	
	2009	2019	2009	2019	2009	2019
Total tax revenues[28]	12.5	16.5	20.6	22.9	31.6	33.8
	2009	2019	2009	2019	2009	2019
Share of VAT in total revenues[29]	26.9	24.3	25.3	27.7	19.8	20.7
	2009	2018	2009	2018	2009	2018
Social expenditures[30]	9.4	8.7	11.3	11.4	21.0	19.7

Sources, footnotes and technical details can be found at the end of the country notes.

PANAMA

1. Socio-economic and perceived impacts of the coronavirus (COVID-19) pandemic

The crisis hit Panama's economy hard. In 2020, gross domestic product (GDP) contracted by almost 18% annually, due especially to the disruption in global trade and tourism. The poorest in society are the most affected. After years of improvement, in 2020, the poverty rate reached 17.8% based on latest international comparable estimations, an increase of more than three percentage points, compared to a year earlier. This figure is lower than in the Latin America and the Caribbean (LAC) region (30.9%). Extreme poverty was stable in 2020 at 6.4%, compared to a LAC average of 10.0%. Similarly to other LAC countries, the pandemic hit Panama's health sector hard. Before the crisis, Panama's public expenditures on health stood at 7.3% of GDP, slightly higher than the LAC average (6.8%). They have remained stable in the last decade, compared to an increase of 0.3 percentage points in LAC. Nonetheless, people's perceptions of the quality of health care deteriorated. In 2020, 50.8% of people declared being satisfied with health care, higher than the LAC average (48.2%) but considerably lower than the average across the Organisation for Economic Co-operation and Development (OECD) (70.7%). This proportion is almost 18 percentage points lower than ten years earlier. The pandemic had a harsh effect on education as well. Between March 2020 and May 2021, schools were fully closed for 55 weeks, one of the highest figures in LAC (26 weeks) and much higher than in the OECD (15 weeks). Effective online learning did not help much in cushioning the drawbacks for students, as it was available in only 23.9% of schools, compared to 32.5% in LAC and 54.1% in the OECD. Concerning perceptions of government transparency, 86.6% of Panamanians thought that the government was corrupt in 2020, considerably higher than in LAC (72.4%) and the OECD (58.8%).

2. National and international co-operation initiatives aimed to build forward better

Faced with the COVID-19 crisis, Panama's priority has been the protection of the most vulnerable households, workers and enterprises. The government's interventions were mostly focused on job-retention/ creation schemes to protect workers' livelihoods. Regarding households, Panama launched a cash transfer initiative (*Panamá Solidario*) to distribute funds and resources to those most affected by the pandemic. Regarding workers and enterprises, Panama established programmes dedicated to new credit lines, loans and guarantees for micro, small and medium-sized enterprises and the most affected economic sectors, such as agriculture and hospitality, including tourism, to promote their economic activity and job creation. Additionally, Panama started the *Plan Recuperando Mi Barrio* programme to generate temporary employment through investments in local infrastructure projects.

Going forward, Panama introduced an economic recovery plan that prioritises the preservation of jobs and the generation of new employment opportunities. In the long term, the government aims to tackle poverty and vulnerability, structural challenges that have been exacerbated by the crisis. Using quality public expenditure as a catalyst for economic recovery, Panama aims to address long-standing needs in public infrastructure. Some projects that stand out are those concerning education, transport and public service infrastructure. These quality investments are intended to create jobs, boost productivity and reinforce supply chains. Likewise, the attraction of foreign direct investment and the implementation of reforms to improve competitiveness and productivity remain central pillars of the recovery plan.

Panama's international co-operation projects *within* and *beyond* the region were focused on both immediate and medium-term challenges arising from the COVID-19 pandemic. Concerning co-operation *within LAC*, Panama collaborated with the Pan American Health Organisation in the distribution of more than 35 tons of supplies, medicines and protective equipment to fight against the pandemic in 26 LAC countries through the Regional Distribution Centre for Humanitarian Health Aid. Regarding co-operation *beyond LAC*, within the EUROsociAL+ co-operation programme with the European Union, assistance has been provided to ensure the bio-psycho-social well-being of the elderly population. In addition, Panama has co-operated with the United Nations on projects regarding education post-COVID-19, the proper disposal of COVID-19-related biohazards, and the development of a study codifying good practices in managing prison systems during the pandemic.

	Key indicators – Panama[1]					
Socio-environmental	Panama		LAC[2]		OECD[3]	
	2019	2020	2019	2020	2019	2020
Extreme poverty[4]	6.6	6.4	8.1	10.0	N/A	N/A
	2019	2020	2019	2020	2019	2020
Poverty[5]	14.6	17.8	26.8	30.9	N/A	N/A
	2009	2019	2009	2019	2009	2018
Gini index[6]	0.50	0.47	0.50	0.46	0.31	0.31
	Bottom 20%	Top 20%	Bottom 20%	Top 20%	Bottom 20%	Top 20%
Total population in informal households by quintile, 2018[7]	N/A	N/A	78.0	19.1	N/A	N/A
	2010	2017	2010	2017	2010	2017
Health expenditures[8]	7.2	7.3	6.5	6.8	8.1	8.8
	2010	2017	2010	2017	2010	2017
Out-of-pocket health expenditures[9]	28.4	33.3	35.6	34.1	20.2	20.6
	03/2020-05/2021					
Weeks of full school closure[10]	55		26		15	
	2018					
Effective online learning[11]	23.9		32.5		54.1	
	2018					
Effective online learning in disadvantaged schools[11]	11.2		21.5		48.8	
	2009	2019	2009	2019	2009	2019
Share of Internet users[12]	39.1	63.6	29.3	67.8	68.3	85.8
	-	2018	2015	2018	2015	2018
Number of students per computer[13]	-	1.6	2.4	1.6	1.8	1.1
	2010	2019	2010	2019	2010	2019
Exposure to PM 2.5[14]	15.5	13.2	18.1	18.0	15.7	13.9
	2000-16					
% change in intact forest landscape[15]	-20.1		-8.8		-6.3	
Competitiveness and innovation	Panama		LAC[2]		OECD[3]	
	2009	2019	2009	2019	2009	2019
Labour productivity[16]	N/A	N/A	N/A	N/A	N/A	N/A
	2009	2019	2009	2019	2009	2019
High-tech exports[17]	1.4	13.7	8.7	8.3	19.5	17.9
	2009	2017	2009	2017	2009	2017
R&D expenditures[18]	0.1	0.1	0.4	0.4	2.4	2.5
	2009	2017	2009	2017	2009	2017
ICT patents[19]	1	2	726	521	173 440	141 358
Citizens' perceptions and institutions	Panama		LAC[2]		OECD[3]	
	2009	2020	2009	2020	2009	2020
Citizens' perceptions of corruption in government[20]	87.8	86.6	72.0	72.4	67.5	58.8
	2009	2018	2009	2018	N/A	N/A
Citizens' perceptions of country governed in the interests of few[21]	44.8	84.9	64.8	82.0	N/A	N/A
	2009	2020	2009	2020	2009	2020
Satisfaction with health care[22]	68.1	50.8	56.9	48.2	69.2	70.7
	2009	2020	2009	2020	2009	2020
Satisfaction with water quality[23]	82.3	84.3	74.8	76.0	77.9	79.4
	2010	2016	2010	2016	N/A	N/A
% of people victim of criminality[24]	11.3	16.0	19.6	23.8	N/A	N/A
	2021					
Rank in the Press Freedom Index[25]	77		82		36	
	2009-18					
Change in political polarisation[26]	10.1		9.6		N/A	
	2019					
SIGI index[27]	N/A		N/A		N/A	
Fiscal position	Panama		LAC[2]		OECD[3]	
	2009	2019	2009	2019	2009	2019
Total tax revenues[28]	16.0	14.1	20.6	22.9	31.6	33.8
	2009	2019	2009	2019	2009	2019
Share of VAT in total revenues[29]	12.8	15.5	25.3	27.7	19.8	20.7
	2009	2018	2009	2018	2009	2018
Social expenditures[30]	9.2	8.8	11.3	11.4	21.0	19.7

Sources, footnotes and technical details can be found at the end of the country notes.

PARAGUAY

1. Socio-economic and perceived impacts of the coronavirus (COVID-19) pandemic

The economic impact of the crisis due to the COVID-19 pandemic on Paraguay's growth was modest – one of the smallest in the Latin America and the Caribbean (LAC) region – as gross domestic product (GDP) contracted annually by only 0.6%. In addition, poverty has been unchanged in the last few years. The modest shock has not much affected the poverty and extreme poverty rates (19.7% and 6.2%, respectively, in 2020 based on the latest international comparable estimations), which are lower than in LAC (30.9% and 10.0%, respectively). Just before the crisis, Paraguay's public expenditures on health stood at 6.7% of GDP, similar to LAC (6.8%) but much lower than Organisation for Economic Co-operation and Development (OECD) countries (8.8%). However, in the last decade, Paraguay made significant progress, as public expenditures on health grew by two percentage points of GDP, catching up with the region, which recorded a modest increase of 0.3 percentage points. In 2020, 38.4% of people declared being satisfied with the quality of health care, a proportion lower than in LAC (48.2%) and considerably lower than in the OECD (70.7%). The perceived quality has decreased by more than 15 percentage points in the last decade, compared to a decrease of almost ten percentage points in LAC and an increase of more than one percentage point in the OECD. Between March 2020 and May 2021, schools were fully closed for 32 weeks, compared to 26 weeks in LAC and 15 weeks in the OECD. In 2020, 87.2% of citizens thought that the government was corrupt, up by seven percentage points in a decade. Paraguayans share the concern with other Latin Americans, as 72.4% of people in the region have similar negative perceptions, much more than in the OECD (58.8%).

2. National and international co-operation initiatives aimed to build forward better

Paraguay introduced a significant set of measures to mitigate the negative impact of the COVID-19 crisis, targeted to alleviate the burden of the pandemic and contain the highly regressive impact on the most vulnerable households, workers and firms. Through Law N 6524/2020, Paraguay provided cash transfers for food and hygiene products to help families not covered by traditional social protection schemes. The new law entailed subsidised exemptions and payment deferrals for public services. Concerning workers, Paraguay introduced additional subsidies for those who lost their jobs during the pandemic, especially informal workers, and granted severance and suspension payments to formal employees. To help mitigate the impact of the crisis on firms, Paraguay performed transfers and guarantees so that national institutions could provide financing for small and medium-sized enterprises.

Going forward, *Plan de Recuperación Económica Ñapu'a Paraguay* is focused on three short-term goals: i) increasing social protection; ii) investment and employment; iii) financing of economic growth and medium-long term goals which consist of structural reforms aimed at the transformation of the State. Accordingly, the plan recognises that current institutions must be strengthened and the well-being of citizens placed at the centre of the economic development model. Proposals for the *Transformación del Estado* aim to move Paraguay towards a new social contract that reduces existing equality gaps and pursues a sustainable future.

Paraguay's international co-operation projects *within* and *beyond* the region have channelled collaboration with various partner countries and international organisations to overcome the challenges brought about by COVID-19. *Within LAC*, in the framework of the Southern Common Market (MERCOSUR) Structural Convergence Fund, a working network was built to provide health support and the development of acute diagnostic and serological tests. Paraguay also engaged with the Governments of Chile Colombia, Mexico, Uruguay, Argentina and Brazil in the exchange and strengthening of medical personnel among other cooperation initiatives. Additionally, the Latin American Development Bank (CAF) is supporting Paraguay in funding the *Ñapu'a Paraguay* plan for economic recovery. *Beyond LAC*, Paraguay's partners such as the European Union, the United States, Chinese Taipei, Qatar, UAE, India among other institutions, have redirected their co-operation efforts to projects that support key sectors of the economic and social recovery. These include the consolidation of social protection schemes, strengthening water and sanitation systems (e.g. providing water supply for towns in the Paraguayan Chaco), supporting small and medium-sized enterprises, quality education for all children, campaigns against gender-based violence, and the improvement of youth training opportunities.

Key indicators – Paraguay[1]					
Socio-environmental	**Paraguay**		**LAC[2]**		**OECD[3]**	

	Paraguay		LAC[2]		OECD[3]	
	2019	2020	2019	2020	2019	2020
Extreme poverty[4]	6.2	6.2	8.1	10.0	N/A	N/A
	2019	2020	2019	2020	2019	2020
Poverty[5]	19.4	19.7	26.8	30.9	N/A	N./A
	2009	2019	2009	2019	2009	2018
Gini index[6]	0.50	0.47	0.50	0.46	0.31	0.31
	Bottom 20%	Top 20%	Bottom 20%	Top 20%	Bottom 20%	Top 20%
Total population in informal households by quintile, 2018[7]	95.3	22.8	78.0	19.1	N/A	N/A
	2010	2017	2010	2017	2010	2017
Health expenditures[8]	4.6	6.7	6.5	6.8	8.1	8.8
	2010	2017	2010	2017	2010	2017
Out-of-pocket health expenditures[9]	45.9	44.2	35.6	34.1	20.2	20.6
	03/2020-05/2021					
Weeks of full school closure[10]	32		26		15	
	2018					
Effective online learning[11]	N/A		32.5		54.1	
	2018					
Effective online learning in disadvantaged schools[11]	N/A		21.5		48.8	
	2009	2019	2009	2019	2009	2019
Share of Internet users[12]	18.9	68.5	29.3	67.8	68.3	85.8
	2015	2018	2015	2018	2015	2018
Number of students per computer[13]	N/A	N/A	2.4	1.6	1.8	1.1
	2010	2019	2010	2019	2010	2019
Exposure to PM 2.5[14]	15.3	12.8	18.1	18.0	15.7	13.9
	2000-16					
% change in intact forest landscape[15]	-80.0		-8.8		-6.3	

Competitiveness and innovation	Paraguay		LAC[2]		OECD[3]	
	2009	2019	2009	2019	2009	2019
Labour productivity[16]	22.0	27.2	29.3	26.7	72.2	70.7
	2009	2019	2009	2019	2009	2019
High-tech exports[17]	12.0	7.2	8.7	8.3	19.5	17.9
	2009	2017	2009	2017	2009	2017
R&D expenditures[18]	0.1	0.1	0.4	0.4	2.4	2.5
	2009	2017	2009	2017	2009	2017
ICT patents[19]	N/A	N/A	726	521	173 440	141 358

Citizens' perceptions and institutions	Paraguay		LAC[2]		OECD[3]	
	2009	2020	2009	2020	2009	2020
Citizens' perceptions of corruption in government[20]	79.7	87.2	72.0	72.4	67.5	58.8
	2009	2018	2009	2018	2009	2018
Citizens' perceptions of country governed in the interests of few[21]	67.7	90.0	64.8	82.0	N/A	N/A
	2009	2020	2009	2020	2009	2020
Satisfaction with health care[22]	54.1	38.4	56.9	48.2	69.2	70.7
	2009	2020	2009	2020	2009	2020
Satisfaction with water quality[23]	88.0	79.6	74.8	76.0	77.9	79.4
	2010	2016	2010	2016	2010	2016
% of people victim of criminality[24]	18.3	23.7	19.6	23.8	N/A	N/A
	2021					
Rank in the Press Freedom Index[25]	100		82		36	
	2009-18					
Change in political polarisation[26]	8.3		9.6		N/A	
	2019					
SIGI index[27]	32.8		25.6		16.3	

Fiscal position	Paraguay		LAC[2]		OECD[3]	
	2009	2019	2009	2019	2009	2019
Total tax revenues[28]	11.5	13.9	20.6	22.9	31.6	33.8
	2009	2019	2009	2019	2009	2019
Share of VAT in total revenues[29]	34.6	35.7	25.3	27.7	19.8	20.7
	2009	2018	2009	2018	2009	2018
Social expenditures[30]	7.0	8.6	11.3	11.4	21.0	19.7

Sources, footnotes and technical details can be found at the end of the country notes.

PERU

1. Socio-economic and perceived impacts of the coronavirus (COVID-19) pandemic

The crisis due to the COVID-19 pandemic had a devastating impact on Peru's economy. In 2020, gross domestic product (GDP) fell by 11% annually. In 2020, poverty rates based on the latest international comparable estimations, increased by more than six percentage points, compared to a year earlier, reaching 21.9%; whereas, in the Latin America and the Caribbean (LAC) region, the increase was of less than five percentage points, reaching 30.9%. In years preceding the pandemic, public health expenditures stood at 4.9% of GDP, 0.2 percentage points higher than in 2010. This figure is lower than in LAC (6.8%) and Organisation for Economic Co-operation and Development (OECD) countries (8.8%), both of which experienced a similar slight increase. In 2020, 41.3% of Peruvians considered health care to be of good quality, a lower proportion than in LAC (48.2%) and the OECD (70.7%). Between March 2020 and May 2021, schools were fully closed for 26 weeks, the same as in LAC and higher than in the OECD (15 weeks). The disruption to education for children was particularly severe due to the lack of effective online learning, which was present in just 24.0% of schools, compared to 32.5% in LAC and 54.1% in the OECD.

2. National and international co-operation initiatives aimed to build forward better

To mitigate the economic and health impacts of COVID-19, Peru has implemented a wide range of support measures for the most vulnerable households, workers and enterprises. Concerning households, Peru implemented cash transfers for those living in poverty or extreme poverty and those located in geographical areas with the highest health risks (*Bono Familiar Universal* and *Bono Yo Me Quedo En Casa*). Likewise, Peru enacted a subsidy with a particular target on rural households that were excluded from traditional social assistance programmes during the pandemic (*Bono Rural*). In addition, Peru implemented the *Trabaja Perú* programme in 2020, targeting people living in poverty or extreme poverty through the generation of temporary jobs for investment projects and immediate intervention activities. To protect workers, Peru encouraged job preservation and hiring by granting a subsidy to private employers affected during the pandemic. Moreover, Peru authorised workers to withdraw pension funds without penalty and implemented a subsidy for self-employed workers (*Bono Independiente*).

Concerning the recovery, Peru's medium- and long-term plans are based on the preservation of productive sustainability. *Arranca Perú* is a programme for economic resilience and job creation. It consists of subsidies for new jobs and support for business financing (e.g. *Reactiva Perú, Fondo de Apoyo Empresarial a las MYPE* and *Programa de Apoyo Empresarial a las MYPES*), which comprises loan portfolio guarantee programmes, promotion of public procurement for MYPE and various tax measures (e.g. investment promotion and tax relief). Peru will also implement the Strategic Plan for National Development to achieve the structural national objectives. The plan aims to tackle livelihoods, productivity, comprehensive social security and dialogue for the country's integral development.

Peru's international co-operation projects *within* and *beyond* the region respond to national development priorities while facing the adverse effects of COVID-19. *Within LAC*, Peru has engaged in various co-operation schemes to respond to the pandemic. These include rural migration (in co-operation with the Inter-American Development Bank), regional co-operation for climate management of agricultural ecosystems (with the Food and Agriculture Organization) and earthquake-resistant adobe construction techniques (with Argentina). *Beyond LAC*, Peru participated in diverse international partnerships to accelerate the response to COVID-19 (e.g. participation in Access to COVID-19 Tools Accelerator, COVID-19 Vaccines Access [COVAX], COVID-19 Technology Access Pool, Support Group for Global Infectious Disease Response, and the international Ministerial Coordination Group on COVID-19). Additionally, Peru engaged in specific co-operation schemes to develop plans for the mitigation of the pandemic in indigenous communities and rural centres in the Amazon with Germany and Switzerland. Lastly, within the framework of the last phase (2020-21) of the EUROsociAL+ co-operation programme with the European Union, support has been provided to the most vulnerable population affected by the pandemic by strengthening the Protection Network for the Elderly and Disabled.

Key indicators – Peru[1]					
Socio-environmental	Peru		LAC[2]		OECD[3]	

	Peru		LAC[2]		OECD[3]	
Socio-environmental	2019	2020	2019	2020	2019	2020
Extreme poverty[4]	3	3.5	8.1	10.0	N/A	N/A
	2019	2020	2019	2020	2019	2020
Poverty[5]	15.4	21.9	26.8	30.9	N/A	N/A
	2009	2019	2009	2019	2009	2018
Gini index[6]	0.48	0.43	0.50	0.46	0.31	0.31
	Bottom 20%	Top 20%	Bottom 20%	Top 20%	Bottom 20%	Top 20%
Total population in informal households by quintile, 2018[7]	89.2	18.2	78.0	19.1	N/A	N/A
	2010	2017	2010	2017	2010	2017
Health expenditures[8]	4.7	4.9	6.5	6.8	8.1	8.8
	2010	2017	2010	2017	2010	2017
Out-of-pocket health expenditures[9]	35.9	28.9	35.6	34.1	20.2	20.6
	03/2020-05/2021					
Weeks of full school closure[10]	26		26		15	
	2018					
Effective online learning[11]	24.0		32.5		54.1	
	2018					
Effective online learning in disadvantaged schools[11]	12.3		21.5		48.8	
	2009	2019	2009	2019	2009	2019
Share of Internet users[12]	31.4	60.0	29.3	67.8	68.3	85.8
	2015	2018	2015	2018	2015	2018
Number of students per computer[13]	2.2	1.4	2.4	1.6	1.8	1.1
	2010	2019	2010	2019	2010	2019
Exposure to PM 2.5[14]	30.4	31.1	18.1	18.0	15.7	13.9
	2000-16					
% change in intact forest landscape[15]	-7.8		-8.8		-6.3	

Competitiveness and innovation	Peru		LAC[2]		OECD[3]	
	2009	2019	2009	2019	2009	2019
Labour productivity[16]	18.1	24.5	29.3	26.7	72.2	70.7
	2009	2019	2009	2019	2009	2019
High-tech exports[17]	0.1	0.1	8.7	8.3	19.5	17.9
	2009	2017	2009	2017	2009	2017
R&D expenditures[18]	0.1	0.1	0.4	0.4	2.4	2.5
	2009	2017	2009	2017	2009	2017
ICT patents[19]	6	7	726	521	173 440	141 358

Citizens' perceptions and institutions	Peru		LAC[2]		OECD[3]	
	2009	2020	2009	2020	2009	2020
Citizens' perceptions of corruption in government[20]	91.9	88.7	72.0	72.4	67.5	58.8
	2009	2018	2009	2018	2009	2018
Citizens' perceptions of country governed in the interests of few[21]	84.6	87.5	64.8	82.0	N/A	N/A
	2009	2020	2009	2020	2009	2020
Satisfaction with health care[22]	41.1	41.3	56.9	48.2	69.2	70.7
	2009	2020	2009	2020	2009	2020
Satisfaction with water quality[23]	62.7	63.5	74.8	76.0	77.9	79.4
	2010	2016	2010	2016	2010	2016
% of people victim of criminality[24]	31.1	33.0	19.6	23.8	N/A	N/A
	2021					
Rank in the Press Freedom Index[25]	91		82		36	
	2009-18					
Change in political polarisation[26]	6.8		9.6		N/A	
	2019					
SIGI index[27]	24.5		25.6		16.3	

Fiscal position	Peru		LAC[2]		OECD[3]	
	2009	2019	2009	2019	2009	2019
Total tax revenues[28]	16.9	16.6	20.6	22.9	31.6	33.8
	2009	2019	2009	2019	2009	2019
Share of VAT in total revenues[29]	38.4	38.5	25.3	27.7	19.8	20.7
	2009	2018	2009	2018	2009	2018
Social expenditures[30]	10.2	11.1	11.3	11.4	21.0	19.7

Sources, footnotes and technical details can be found at the end of the country notes.

URUGUAY

1. Socio-economic and perceived impacts of the coronavirus (COVID-19) pandemic

The economic crisis due to the COVID-19 pandemic has negatively affected Uruguay's economy. In 2020, gross domestic product (GDP) fell by 5.9% annually. The impact of the crisis has affected, above all, the most vulnerable groups. In 2020, the poverty rate based on latest international comparable estimations has reached 5.1%, increasing by two percentage points, compared to a year earlier, although it continues to be one of the lowest rates in Latin America and the Caribbean (LAC) and considerably below the regional average (30.9%). The quality of health services helped cushion the crisis. In 2020, 75.1% of people in Uruguay declared being satisfied with the quality of health care, just two percentage points lower than ten years earlier. This proportion is much higher than in LAC (48.2%) and even higher than the Organisation for Economic Co-operation and Development (OECD) average (70.7%). Uruguay stands out as the country with the highest public expenditures on health care in LAC: 9.3% of GDP, compared to 6.8% average in LAC and 8.8% in the OECD. Although the pandemic affected the education system as well, Uruguay was among the LAC countries that managed to minimise disruption in education for students. Between March 2020 and May 2021, schools were fully closed for 14 weeks, much less than the LAC average (26 weeks) and below the OECD average (15 weeks). Moreover, during the weeks of closure, online learning helped mitigate the negative impact on students. In Uruguay, 47.4% of schools had access to effective online learning, more than two times higher than the LAC average (32.5%), although slightly below the OECD average (54.1%).

2. National and international co-operation initiatives aimed to build forward better

Uruguay has undertaken broad mitigation efforts to tackle the health crisis and reduce the impact of COVID-19 on the most vulnerable households, workers and enterprises. The COVID-19 Solidarity Fund was instrumental to implement these measures. When the pandemic hit the region, Uruguay reinforced and extended an existing successful cash transfer programme (*Asignación Familiar Plan de Equidad*) to support the most vulnerable households. Uruguay implemented an electronic wallet application (*TuApp*) that allows users to receive government coupons for food redemption and to make diverse payments. Additionally, the government introduced a special unemployment benefits scheme for all workers affected by the pandemic and has extended its duration. Furthermore, Uruguay granted tax extensions and benefits, particularly regarding pension contributions, and added a monthly monetary incentive for businesses to reintegrate or hire employees. To help mitigate the impact on firms, Uruguay implemented a series of transfers, credit possibilities and other benefits, particularly for micro, small and medium-sized enterprises (MSMEs).

Going forward, Uruguay's medium- and long-term plans focus on the importance of firms' resilience and job creation and the sustainability of social policies. The main drivers are investments to promote employment, new legal frameworks for investments and social housing, tax innovations for MSMEs, and a social security reform. Moreover, Uruguay is designing a foreign trade policy to improve the presence of national products abroad.

Uruguay's international co-operation projects *within* and *beyond* the region focus on long-term structural needs and on responding to the pressing challenges due to the crisis. *Within* LAC, Uruguay engaged in a co-operation project with Mexico that aimed to strengthen the capacities of health teams in the prevention and containment of the pandemic. With Colombia, both countries launched an initiative to share strategies and good practices for overcoming poverty throughout the crisis. Furthermore, with the private sector and the IDB, the "Renewable Energy Innovation Fund" was created, aiming to decarbonise the industry and transport sectors and ensure universal access to renewable sources. *Beyond* LAC, Uruguay participated in co-operation projects focused on gender and intergenerational perspectives in response to COVID-19 socio-economic impacts with the United Nations. Regarding job creation and consolidation of an entrepreneurial ecosystem, triangular co-operation was promoted with Germany and Paraguay. In addition, Uruguay currently takes part in a bilateral partnership with the European Union that aims to strengthen their strategic dialogue, adapting triangular co-operation initiatives to respond to the effects of the pandemic and promoting the Development in Transition approach and the United Nations 2030 Agenda.

	Key indicators – Uruguay[1]					
Socio-environmental	Uruguay		LAC[2]		OECD[3]	
	2019	2020	2019	2020	2019	2020
Extreme poverty[4]	0.1	0.3	8.1	10.0	N/A	N/A
	2019	2020	2019	2020	2019	2020
Poverty[5]	3.0	5.1	26.8	30.9	N/A	N/A
	2009	2019	2009	2019	2009	2018
Gini index[6]	0.45	0.39	0.50	0.46	0.31	0.31
	Bottom 20%	Top 20%	Bottom 20%	Top 20%	Bottom 20%	Top 20%
Total population in informal households by quintile, 2018[7]	48.0%	2.2%	78.0	19.1	N/A	N/A
	2010	2017	2010	2017	2010	2017
Health expenditures[8]	8.6	9.3	6.5	6.8	8.1	8.8
	2010	2017	2010	2017	2010	2017
Out-of-pocket health expenditures[9]	20.5	17.5	35.6	34.1	20.2	20.6
			03/2020-05/2021			
Weeks of full school closure[10]	14		26		15	
			2018			
Effective online learning[11]	47.4		32.5		54.1	
			2018			
Effective online learning in disadvantaged schools[11]	55.7		21.5		48.8	
	2009	2019	2009	2019	2009	2019
Share of Internet users[12]	41.8	83.3	29.3	67.8	68.3	85.8
	2015	2018	2015	2018	2015	2018
Number of students per computer[13]	2.7	2.3	2.4	1.6	1.8	1.1
	2010	2019	2010	2019	2010	2019
Exposure to PM 2.5[14]	9.5	9.6	18.1	18.0	15.7	13.9
			2000-16			
% change in intact forest landscape[15]	N/A		-8.8		-6.3	
Competitiveness and innovation	Uruguay		LAC[2]		OECD[3]	
	2009	2019	2009	2019	2009	2019
Labour productivity[16]	36.4	48.2	29.3	26.7	72.2	70.7
	2009	2019	2009	2019	2009	2019
High-tech exports[17]	6.4	8.3	8.7	8.3	19.5	17.9
	2009	2017	2009	2017	2009	2017
R&D expenditures[18]	0.4	0.5	0.4	0.4	2.4	2.5
	2009	2017	2009	2017	2009	2017
ICT patents[19]	9	3	726	521	173 440	141 358
Citizens' perceptions and institutions	Uruguay		LAC[2]		OECD[3]	
	2009	2020	2009	2020	2009	2020
Citizens' perceptions of corruption in government[20]	38.7	48.2	72.0	72.4	67.5	58.8
	2009	2018	2009	2018		
Citizens' perceptions of country governed in the interests of few[21]	32.9	70.4	64.8	82.0	-	-
	2009	2020	2009	2020	2009	2020
Satisfaction with health care[22]	77.2	75.1	56.9	48.2	69.2	70.7
	2009	2020	2009	2020	2009	2020
Satisfaction with water quality[23]	89.2	83.9	74.8	76.0	77.9	79.4
	2010	2016	2010	2016	N/A	N/A
% of people victim of criminality[24]	21.0	23.5	19.6	23.8	N/A	N/A
			2021			
Rank in the Press Freedom Index[25]	18		82		36	
			2009-18			
Change in political polarisation[26]	2.3		9.6		N/A	
			2019			
SIGI index[27]	22.2		25.6		16.3	
Fiscal position	Uruguay		LAC[2]		OECD[3]	
	2009	2019	2009	2019	2009	2019
Total tax revenues[28]	26.0	29.0	20.6	22.9	31.6	33.8
	2009	2019	2009	2019	2009	2019
Share of VAT in total revenues[29]	33.4	25.4	25.3	27.7	19.8	20.7
	2009	2018	2009	2018	2009	2018
Social expenditures[30]	12.7	17.2	11.3	11.4	21.0	19.7

Sources, footnotes and technical details can be found at the end of the country notes.

Technical notes

1. As best as possible, the table follows the key areas identified in *Latin American Economic Outlook 2021*: i) socio-environmental aspects; ii) economic competitiveness and innovation; iii) citizens' perceptions and institutions; and iv) fiscal position.

2. Latin America and the Caribbean (LAC) average is a simple average of the largest set of LAC countries for which data are available in the latest year.

3. Organisation for Economic Co-operation and Development (OECD) average is a simple average that includes all OECD member countries as of May 2021.

4. Data refer to the definition of extreme poverty as specified by the United Nations Economic Commission for Latin America and the Caribbean (ECLAC, 2021[1]), *Social Panorama of Latin America 2020*. www.cepal. org/sites/default/files/publication/files/46688/S2100149_en.pdf. Data for 2020 refer to an estimate based on 2019 data, as specified in Annex I.A2 of (ECLAC, 2021). Projections are based on 2017 data for Chile, 2014 for Guatemala and 2018 for Mexico. Applying the same criteria as in previous LEO editions, data selection prioritizes comparability across LAC countries and shows the latest comparable data available at the report's publication date.

5. Data refer to the definition of poverty as specified by (ECLAC, 2021[1]), *Social Panorama of Latin America 2020*, www.cepal.org/sites/default/files/publication/files/46688/S2100149_en.pdf. Data for 2020 refer to an estimate based on 2019 data, as specified in Annex I.A2 of ECLAC (2021). Projections are based on 2017 data for Chile, 2014 for Guatemala and 2018 for Mexico. Applying the same criteria as in previous LEO editions, data selection prioritizes comparability across LAC countries and shows the latest comparable data available at the report's publication date.

6. Data for LAC from ECLAC, CEPALSTAT | Databases and Statistical Publications, https://cepalstat-prod. cepal.org/cepalstat/tabulador/ConsultaIntegrada.asp?idIndicador=3289&idioma=i. Data for Chile refer to 2017, instead of 2019, data for Guatemala refers to 2014.

7. Data for the OECD from OECD Income Distribution Database, www.oecd.org/social/income-distribution-database.htm.

8. Indicator provides the distribution of the total population living in informal households by quintile. An informal household has all of its workers in informal work. Quintiles are based on monthly total household consumption or income. The source of this indicator is the OECD Key Indicators of Informality based on Individuals and their Households database, https://stats.oecd.org/Index.aspx?DataSetCode=KIIBIH_B5.

9. Health expenditures as % of gross domestic product (GDP). Data from OECD (2020), *Health at a Glance: Latin America and the Caribbean*. Share of current expenditure on health. Data are from OECD (2020), *Health at a Glance: Latin America and the Caribbean*.

10. Data from UNESCO, https://en.unesco.org/covid19/educationresponse#schoolclosures.

11. Data from OECD et al. (2020), *Latin American Economic Outlook 2020*, www.oecd.org/publications/latin-american-economic-outlook-20725140.htm.

12. Data from International Telecommunication Union (2020), www.itu.int/en/ITU-D/Statistics/Pages/stat/default.aspx.

13. Data from OECD et al. (2020), *Latin American Economic Outlook 2020*, www.oecd.org/publications/latin-american-economic-outlook-20725140.htm.

14. $\mu g/m^3$. Data refer to population exposure to more than 10 micrograms/m^3 and are expressed as annual averages. Data from OECD, https://data.oecd.org/air/air-pollution-exposure.htm.

15. Data from OECD, https://stats.oecd.org/Index.aspx?DataSetCode=INTACT_FOREST_LANDSCAPES.

16. Output per employed person as % of United States 2019 output per person employed. Data from the Conference Board, https://conference-board.org/data/economydatabase/total-economy-database-productivity

17. High-technology exports as % of manufactured exports. Data from The World Bank, https://data.worldbank.org/indicator/TX.VAL.TECH.MF.ZS.

18. Research and development expenditure as % of GDP. Data from The World Bank, https://data.worldbank.org/indicator/GB.XPD.RSDV.GD.ZS.

19. IP5 Patent families. Data from OECD, https://stats.oecd.org/Index.aspx?DataSetCode=PATS_IPC.

20. Percentage of people who think that the government is corrupt. "Is corruption widespread throughout the government in (this country), or not?" Data from Gallup 2021.

21. Percentage of people who think that the country is governed in the interests of few. "En términos generales ¿diría usted que (país) está gobernado por unos cuantos grupos poderosos en su propio beneficio, o que está gobernado para el bien de todo el pueblo?" Data from Latinobarómetro, 2020.

22. Percentage of people who think that the health care is of good quality. "In your city of area where you live, are you satisfied or dissatisfied with the availability of quality health care?" Data from Gallup 2021.

23. Percentage of people who think that the water is of good quality. "In your city or area where you live, are you satisfied or dissatisfied with the quality of water?" Data from Gallup 2021.

24. Percentage of people who are victim of criminality, "have you been a victim of any type of crime in the past 12 months?" Data from Latin American Public Opinion Project, www.vanderbilt.edu/lapop/data-access.php.

25. Data from RFS, Reporters without Borders, https://rsf.org/en/ranking_table.

26. Percentage of people who declare being left or right on a 1-10 scale (1=left, 10 = right). "In politics, it is normal to refer to left and right. On a scale where 0 is the left and 10 is the right, where would you place yourself?" Data from Latinobarómetro, 2020.

27. Data from OECD, www.genderindex.org/ranking/.

28. Revenues as % of GDP. Data from OECD et al. (2021), *Revenue Statistics in Latin America and the Caribbean (2021)*.

29. Value added taxes as % of total revenues. Data from OECD et al. (2021), *Revenue Statistics in Latin America and the Caribbean (2021)*.

30. Social protection expenditures as % of GDP. Data from OECD and ECLAC.

References

Conference Board (2015), *The Conference Board's Alternative China GDP*, http://www.conference-board.org//retrievefile.cfm?filename=FAQ-for-China-GDP_9nov1511.pdf&type=subsite.

ECLAC (2020), *Social Panorama of Latin America*, United Nations Publication, http://www.cepal.org/sites/default/files/publication/files/46688/S2100149_en.pdf.

Eurosocial (2021), *The roadmap for EU Cooperation on social cohesion*, https://eurosocial.eu/en/.

Gallup (2021), *Gallup World Poll* (database), www.gallup.com/analytics/232838/world-poll.aspx.

ITU (2020), *World Telecommunication/ICT Indicators Database 2020*, https://www.itu.int/en/ITU-D/Statistics/Pages/stat/default.aspx.

Latinobarómetro (2020), *Vanderbilt* (database), Latin American Public Opinion Project, http://www.vanderbilt.edu/lapop/data-access.php.

OECD (2021), *OECD.Stat* (database), Social and Economical Indicators, https://stats.oecd.org/Index.aspx.

OECD et al. (2020), *Latin American Economic Outlook 2020: Digital Transformation for Building Back Better*, OECD Publishing, https://doi.org/10.1787/e6e864fb-en.

OECD/The World Bank (2020), *Health at a Glance: Latin America and the Caribbean 2020*, OECD Publishing, https://doi.org/10.1787/6089164f-en.

Reporters without Borders (2021), *World Press Freedom Index* (database), https://rsf.org/en/ranking_table.

SIGI (2019), *OECD.Stat* (database), Social Institutions & Gender Index (SIGI), http://www.genderindex.org/ranking/.

UNESCO (2020), *COVID-19 impact on education school closure*, https://en.unesco.org/covid19/educationresponse#schoolclosures.

World Bank (2020), "Research and development expenditure (% of GDP)", https://data.worldbank.org/indicator/GB.XPD.RSDV.GD.ZS.

World Bank (2019), "High-technology exports", https://data.worldbank.org/indicator/TX.VAL.TECH.MF.ZS.

Made in the USA
Coppell, TX
29 November 2022